# People with Profound and Multiple Learning Disabilities

## A Collaborative Approach to Meeting Complex Needs

Edited by
**Penny Lacey and Carol Ouvry**

# People with Profound and Multiple Learning Disabilities

## A Collaborative Approach to Meeting Complex Needs

Edited by

Penny Lacey and Carol Ouvry

**David Fulton Publishers**

London

David Fulton Publishers Ltd
Ormond House, 26–27 Boswell Street, London WC1N 3JD

First published in great Britain by David Fulton Publishers

Note: The right of Penny Lacey and Carol Ouvry to be identified as the editors of this work has been asserted by them in accordance with the Copyright, Designs and Patents Act 1988.

*British Library Cataloguing in Publication Data*
A catalogue record for this book is available from the British Library

ISBN 1–85346–488–0

Typeset by FSH Print & Production Ltd.
Printed in Great Britain by The Cromwell Press Ltd.

# Contents

# Contributor Profiles

**Mark Barber** is a teacher who has worked for over 15 years with pupils who experience profound intellectual disability and multiple physical and sensory disabilities. He is currently involved in research into failure to learn among pupils with PMLD. He teaches at Melland High School.

**Celine Barry** has been teaching pupils with special needs in schools for severe learning difficulties for ten years, and has a special interest in advocacy and students with profound and multiple learning difficulties.

**Alice Bradley** is Training and Development Adviser for Leonard Cheshire International and has had many years experience of work in developing countries. She was formerly principal lecturer in Special Needs at University of Wales Institute, Cardiff.

**Helen Bradley** taught children with severe learning disabilities for five years. She then trained as an Educational Psychologist working with adults and children with learning disabilities as a clinical psychologist. Her special interest is communication.

**Norman Brown** is joint programme coordinator of the University of Birmingham distance education course on Multisensory Impairments. He also works for Sense (The National Deafblind and Rubella Association) as their specialist on congenital deafblindness. He has lectured and taught on courses concerning deafblindness in this country and abroad for a number of years.

**Richard Byers** currently works part-time as lecturer in SEN at the University of Cambridge, School of Education and at the Centre for the Study of Special Education, Westminster College, Oxford. He is a Regional Tutor in learning difficulties for the University of Birmingham and also works as an independent consultant on curriculum development.

**Judith Cavet** is a principal lecturer at Staffordshire University. She was employed for many years as a social worker, before becoming a researcher at Manchester University and subsequently at King's College, London. Her research studies, which focus upon user and carer perspectives, include a two year European Project investigating the leisure alternatives available to people with profound and multiple disability.

**Caroline Downs** is a teacher, researcher and staff development trainer and consultant. She has worked in a variety of education and health settings with children and adults with learning difficulties and with staff and parent groups. She has recently worked with Ann Craft with whom she carried out research and co-authored a series of staff training manuals on sexuality and people with profound and multiple disabilities.

**Juliet Goldbart** teaches and researches in the areas of cognitive and communicative development with particular reference to people with learning disabilities in the Department of Psychology and Speech Pathology at Manchester Metropolitan University. She is involved in the evaluation of a parent involvement project for children with cerebral palsy in Calcutta.

**John and Liz Goldsmith** have worked together for many years to develop equipment, teaching materials and measuring techniques to be used in the management of posture.

Liz is a physiotherapist who has been closely involved in encouraging carers in their work with the practical care of people with multiple disabilities. She was involved in a research project, funded by Action Research, which resulted in the publication of a system of measurement of body symmetry. She has been involved in the development of the RNIB Certificate in Multiple Disability and is a tutor on the course.

Over the past 15 years John has designed and manufactured a range of furniture and equipment for people with postural problems. Recently John and Liz have started working with pressure relieving foams to further increase the comfort of new ranges of equipment for people in need of postural management.

**Dave Hewett** has been involved in special needs work since 1976 and was Headteacher at Harperbury Hospital School. He is now an independent consultant and trainer to staff since 1990 and has authored and co-authored a number of publications on communication and challenging behaviour. The topic for his PhD thesis was communication.

**Christine Hutchinson** is a Community Nurse in Learning Disabilities in the North West and a Regional Tutor with the University of Birmingham. She supports people of all ages and is involved in multi-agency training. She has recently been involved in the Curriculum Development of Learning Disability Nurse Training at a local University. She sits on the Practitioner Panel of the Professional Conduct Committee at the United Kingdom Central Council for Nursing, Midwifery and Health Visiting and is involved in the work of the Royal College of Nursing.

**Penny Lacey** is a lecturer in the School of Education at the University of Birmingham. She specialises in profound and multiple learning disabilities, running courses, conducting research and writing in this area. The topic for her PhD thesis was Multidisciplinary Teamwork, for which she carried out a case study of a school for pupils with multiple disabilities. Previously, she worked in schools for pupils with severe and profound and multiple learning difficulties where her responsibilities included Creative Arts. In her training capacity, she runs music, dance and drama workshops for staff, particularly for those who are not arts specialists.

**Loretto Lambe** has worked in the field of learning disabilities for the past 20 years. She has worked primarily with people with profound and multiple learning disabilities and their families. She is editor and co-author of *Leisure for People with Profound and Multiple Learning Disabilities: A Resource Training Pack.* She is at present Projects Director of PAMIS, (Profound and Multiple Impairment Service), a registered charity delivering a training and information service to families with PMLD and is also a freelance researcher based at the University of Dundee.

**Claire Marvin** has taught children for nearly 30 years in the UK and abroad. Her interest in profound and multiple learning difficulties emerged after moving to Special Education over ten years ago. She now teaches part-time and lectures in education (learning difficulties) at the University of Birmingham. She is a contributor to Distance Education Courses, several books and staff training. Her present interest is in the uses and effectiveness of multisensory environments for students with profound and multiple learning disabilities.

**Roy McConkey** is Professor of Learning Disability at the University of Ulster, Northern Ireland; a post jointly funded with the Eastern Health and Social Services

Board. A psychologist by training, he has previously worked at the University of Manchester, St Michael's House, Dublin and with the Brothers of Charity in the Scottish Borders. He is consultant to UNESCO, Cheshire Foundation International, British Council, Save the Children Fund (UK) and the Guyana CBR Programme and has undertaken assignments in many countries.

**Mike McLinden** is a lecturer in Special Education (Visual Impairment) at the University of Birmingham. He has particular responsibility for aspects of courses in visual impairment relating to Multiple Disabilities . He has worked with a range of children and young people with special educational needs, his most recent teaching experience being at a residential school for children with a visual impairment. Prior to taking up his current position, Mike worked as a Research Fellow at the University of Birmingham on the 'Moon as a Route to Literacy' Project .

**Jenny Miller** is currently Head of Occupational Therapy Service for people with learning disabilities, Dundee Healthcare Trust. She has been working within this field of Occupational Therapy for the past 13 years. She is actively involved in fieldwork education for Occupational therapy students and lectures at one of the Universities. Jenny is involved with the local PAMIS (Profound and Multiple Impairment Service) group which has run workshops and has an active parent and professional consultative group.

**Carol Ouvry** originally trained as an occupational therapist, but retrained as a teacher in the 1970s, working in schools for pupils with severe learning difficulties. Throughout her teaching career she has had a particular interest in all aspects of work with children with profound and multiple learning difficulties and has pursued this interest through studying, writing and training. She edited, and is currently coordinator of a distance education course on Interdisciplinary work with people with PMLD at the University of Birmingham, and is also an associate tutor at Westminster College, Oxford. She has written and contributed to a number of publications and is editor of PMLD-Link.

**Jill Porter** has worked in the area of special education for a number of years, both as teacher and lecturer. She has recently directed a DfEE/ Sense research project looking at the strategies teachers use to access the curriculum for pupils who are deafblind and has also been involved in an RNIB project aimed at improving provision for pupils with multiple disability and visual impairment. She is currently a lecturer at the University of Birmingham where her role has particular reference to learning disabilities and challenging behaviour.

**Helen Sanderson** works as a Quality and Service Development Officer in Manchester. She was seconded part-time to the Joseph Rowntree Foundation funded project on person centred planning from 1995-1997. Helen has a background in occupational therapy, a masters in quality assurance in health and social care and is completing her PhD in person centred planning with people with profound and multiple disabilities. She is an Essential Lifestyle Planning mentor trainer and works as a consultant for the National Development Team and Scottish Human Services. She has contributed course material for the Open University, Birmingham University, and Manchester University.

**Robina Shah** is a psychologist with a specific interest in ethnicity and learning disabilities. She is currently based at the Manchester Council for Community Relations, and is engaged at the Hester Adrian Research Centre, Manchester in research into stress and coping skills in south Asian families with a child with a disability. She has just completed a training pack and good practice guide on telling parents about their child's disability.

**Jennifer Taylor** has worked with children with severe and profound learning disabilities since 1970 and spent two years in FE developing provision, much of it inclusive, for adults with learning difficulties. She has had a close involvement with educational technology from the first introduction of computers into schools, and worked at SEMERC (Special Education Micro Electronic Resource Centre) for five years in training and software development. She is a member of NCET's (National Council for Educational Technology) SLD group. She is now a freelance developer of software and materials, OFSTED inspector, works on projects for NCET in the field of special needs and often includes work with adults.

**Christina Tilstone** taught in the area of severe and profound and multiple learning difficulties for over 30 years. She was a major supporter of the transfer in 1971 from Health to Education of pupils with SLD and became a lecturer at Westhill College on the four year BEd for teachers of pupils with SLD. She is now Senior Lecturer at the University of Birmingham and responsible for the Distance Education Course in Learning Difficulties. She has published widely and is editor of the British Journal of Special Education.

# Meeting Complex Needs Through Collaborative Multidisciplinary Teamwork

*Penny Lacey*

This book is designed to be useful to practitioners working with children and adults with profound and multiple learning disabilities (PMLD). It was born out of a need for a practically-based text book for participants on a course devoted to the study of PMLD but became a project to provide discussion of interest to anyone wishing to reflect on their work in this field. The chapter authors were chosen for their expertise in PMLD and they were asked to write about some of the more difficult or contentious aspects of their topic, bearing in mind that the book should not become outdated too quickly. They were also asked, as far as was possible, to try to write from the point of view of people with PMLD. The result is nineteen chapters exploring different aspects of the lives of people with PMLD, written by a variety of professionals involved, including representatives from Health, Education, Social Care and the Voluntary sector.

In this first chapter, there are three sections. The first is concerned with facts and figures about PMLD to make clear the population that is the subject of the book and to highlight some of the complexity of the difficulties they have to face. The second, and longest, relates to the carers and professionals who work with people with PMLD and the importance of collaborative multidisciplinary teamwork when attempting to meet complex needs. The third section contains preparation for the rest of the book, alerting readers to the broad content in each of the three parts.

## People with profound and multiple learning disabilities

There are a variety of different terms used to describe the disabilities of the people who are at the centre of this book. The one selected for use here, profound and multiple learning disabilities (PMLD) indicates two of the most important facets of the difficulties faced by these people; that is, they have more than one disability and that one of these is profound intellectual impairment. Often the multiplicity of disabilities include sensory or physical impairment but others may be involved, such as autism or mental illness. Behaviour which may be very challenging and or self-injurious may also be present.

If IQ was measurable, the World Health Organisation suggest that people with PMLD would lie in the below 20 range, indicating that they are in a very early stage of development (WHO 1992). This can be equated to Piaget's sensory-motor stage through which 'typically developing' children will pass in the first year of life (Piaget 1952). Another definition suggests that people with PMLD will be functioning at equal to or less than one fifth of their chronological ages, so that someone of ten years old who is functioning at the age of two years or less would be said to have profound intellectual impairment (Sebba 1988).

So far, these definitions have given a negative picture of people with PMLD which is, of course, only part of what is important to know. No-one can deny the difficulties and disabilities faced by those with PMLD, but carers and professional staff can provide many examples of the abilities of individuals.

> Carl has a broad smile with which he greets people. He glances at them several times when he wants them to stay and talk to him and makes little noises in 'conversation'. He drinks well when his carers help him slowly, allowing each sip to settle and he likes mashed food that is presented with each taste separate. Carl will choose between two favourite objects by looking intently at the one he wants his carers to help him with and will remain interested for several minutes as long as the object remains within his gaze. He will get agitated and even cry when members of his family appear and again when they depart. He smiles and looks about with interest when he goes out, especially if there are lots of people prepared to stop and talk to him.

When it is revealed that Carl is nineteen years old, so the extent of his difficulties can be appreciated but also so can his real achievements and abilities. He is able to communicate, make his needs known and demonstrate his feelings. He is enormously dependent upon others for support but with their help, he can achieve a good quality of life.

The most recent survey of children with severe learning difficulties including those with PMLD was carried out by Male (1996) and this revealed a growing number of children entering special schools who have either profound and multiple learning difficulties, life threatening conditions and / or challenging behaviour. More and more very premature babies are surviving, some of whom are multiply disabled and generally medical science is preserving lives which, in the past, would have been lost at birth or in childhood. This means that the number of people growing into adulthood with seriously disabling conditions is constantly increasing. In addition, people who might have spent their whole lives hidden away in long-stay institutions are now visible in schools and community homes. Their needs can no longer be ignored.

People with learning disabilities have been emerging from hospitals since the 1970s but the last groups to be discharged have been those with the most profound disabilities and those with the most challenging behaviour. Thus the history of their education and care is very short indeed. Child and adult services have been struggling, firstly to understand the nature of their needs and secondly to find ways of meeting them. Teachers are wrestling with a school curriculum which was not designed for children at a very early stage of development and staff in adult services are endeavouring to find meaningful ways in which older people with PMLD can access what their community has to offer. Research to support practitioners is still in its infancy and much practice is carried out on a trial and error basis. However, there are anecdotes indicating that giving opportunities for learning to people with PMLD have revealed the ability of many to reach hitherto undreamed of achievements. Given the means with which to indicate simple choices has shown that many people thought to have no communication ability at all can and do have preferences (Glenn and O'Brien 1994). Placing some people in upright positions instead of semi-recumbent has revealed their ability to focus and take an interest in their surroundings (MOVE undated). Encouraging the development of meaningful relationships with a small number of people has shown that they do recognise individuals and enjoy being with some more than others (Ware 1996).

Professionals and carers have learned so much in the last generation about the most profoundly disabled members of society. There is now a small but growing body of literature setting down people's experience with this group. However, their needs are complex and, according to Male's (1996) survey, changing. The last ten years have seen an enormous increase in the numbers of children arriving in school who are tube fed or need access to oxygen several times a day. They may have degenerative conditions and demand as much care as education. Whatever their individual needs, they are likely to be complex as a multiplicity of impairments are compounding in effect (McInnes and Treffry 1982).

# Multidisciplinary collaboration

The complexity of needs presented by people with PMLD makes it impossible for one person or discipline to meet them all. The combination of health, social care and learning needs means that it is inevitable that several agencies will be involved throughout their lives, though which agencies and when, will vary according to the age of the person with PMLD and his or her location in the country. For example, therapists are often more available in childhood than in adulthood but in some regions they are in very short supply at any age. In infancy, there may be a bewildering number of 'experts' offering advice and services to families. Sometimes the information is conflicting or certainly unconnected as individual agencies work in isolation from each other, at best merely providing written reports for others to read, at worst unaware of each other's existence. When the age of nineteen is reached, most of the services change, often with little communication between them at the transition stage. Then in some community homes, adults with PMLD experience little professional support and a constantly shifting population of untrained multi-role carers who are, understandably, more concerned with everyday chores than meeting the complex needs of their clients.

The picture drawn above is a 'worst-case' scenario, but it is possible to find similar examples in most areas of the country. In a general sense, members of the human services have been aware of the unsatisfactory way in which they work together since the middle of this century (Davie 1993). There has been a constant call for more effective multidisciplinary teamwork and many initiatives designed to support it, for example joint funding in the 1980s where Health and Social Services were rewarded for running shared projects funded from both bodies (Wistow and Hardy 1991). The All-Wales Strategy for running learning disability services was built on the premise that agencies would work together and they were funded accordingly. Results from a survey of community mental handicap teams in Wales, conducted by McGrath (1991) indicate that the incentives to work together have been at least partially successful. Success can be seen where there is: a broad framework of policies and principles with explicit agreements; representatives of different agencies with delegated authority to make decisions; effective channels of communication between the teams of fieldworkers and county policy-makers; and skilled, committed managers.

Despite projects such as the All Wales Strategy, agencies have still not fully achieved collaboration. What is so difficult about multidisciplinary collaboration and what strategies seem to support it best? Before attempting to answer these questions, it is necessary to find a suitable definition of multidisciplinary collaboration and explain why this term was chosen for this book over the plethora available.

## Terms

Leathard (1994) identified 52 terms referring to agencies and professionals working together in what she calls a 'terminological quagmire'. It is certainly a bewildering array from which it is very easy to produce muddled thinking, especially over the term 'multidisciplinary teamwork'. Some writers use the term 'multidisciplinary' to denote any example of more than one discipline or agency working together, however badly or effectively they work. Others want to define it more precisely and describe it as the least satisfactory way in which members of different disciplines work together. For example, Orelove and Sobsey (1991) describe multidisciplinary work as little more than agencies working alongside each other. They go on, then, to describe 'interdisciplinary' work, where members of agencies meet together and exchange information and finally, 'Transdisciplinary' work, where members of agencies work jointly, sharing aims, information, tasks and responsibility.

'Transdisciplinary' is an American term not widely used in the UK and, although the definition covers the aspects of working together promoted throughout this book, it was decided not to use it. The UK term which most fits agencies sharing and working jointly is 'collaboration'. This is not be confused with 'liaison' (where agencies just know of each other's existence), 'cooperation' (where agencies exchange reports) or 'coordination' (where agencies agree who does what) (Lacey 1995). 'Collaboration' is a commitment to meet together, plan and work jointly, often selecting one team member to coordinate services and have the direct contact with the person with PMLD. At its most developed, 'collaboration' includes families and carers and people with PMLD themselves, all sharing in the daily life and the necessary decision-making.

'Collaboration', then, is the preferred term in this book. However, as this refers to a way of working which members of the same discipline should aspire to as well as members of different disciplines and agencies, it was necessary to find a term which embraced that difference. The final decision was to combine 'collaboration' with 'multidisciplinary', using the latter, in this case, as a generic term, rather than in the sense meant by Orelove and Sobsey (1996). Thus, 'multidisciplinary collaboration' means members of different disciplines and agencies (including families, carers and the person with PMLD), working jointly towards providing the highest quality of life possible for that person.

The final term that will be used is 'teamwork'. This is coupled with 'collaborative' to denote its joint nature, as there are several different kinds of teamwork possible. It is also helpful to distinguish between a 'team' and a 'network' as that can clarify who is in a team and who actually belongs to a wider 'network' of people and services. Amongst other writers, Adair (1987) suggests that a team should not exceed 6–8 members before it must be broken into smaller units as it is very difficult to maintain the intensity of communication and sharing with more than this number. Often there will be considerably more than eight people involved in providing services for an individual with PMLD, especially if that person has complex medical needs. However, it is actually not possible for them to work together collaboratively all of the time, although it is essential that those who have daily and even weekly contact with the person with PMLD should strive to do so. Those who have a more intermittent role may only work collaboratively with this inner team of people at their point of contact. The rest of the time, they will be names on a network list. In this manner, the team is kept to a manageable size, helping to promote collaboration that is practicable.

## Challenges to multidisciplinary collaborative teamwork

From the previous section, some of the challenges to effective collaboration are evident. Misunderstandings over what 'collaboration' and 'teamwork' actually mean is just one, the sheer numbers of people involved is another. Others relate to differences in the disciplines and agencies themselves. It is not surprising, for example, that people from different agencies find it hard to work together when their methods, their lines of management, their salaries, their conditions of employment, their hours, their training, their geographical responsibilities are all at variance with each other. Davie (1993) describes the difficulties besetting professionals from different agencies who desire to work together in terms of 'internecine relationships' and 'empire' building and of power struggles between the different departments. His language is strong but many people will have experience of its reality, especially in relation to 'confidentiality'.

Different attitudes to confidentiality can prove an intractable challenge to collaborative teamwork. Social services, in particular, have very strict rules governing confidentiality and although it is possible to understand the origins of these rules, it is hard to justify when professionals are trying to work in a collaborative team. The Warnock Report (DES 1978) uses the term 'extended confidentiality' and the Home Office *et al.* (1991) on the topic of child protection, suggest that 'confidentiality may not be maintained if the withholding of information will prejudice the welfare of the child'. From their research into identifying models of inter-agency working, Maychell and Bradley (1991) report that some of their respondents suspected that information of a non-confidential nature was withheld in the interest of maintaining power and control over others.

Another area of difficulty analysed by writers is that relating to the roles that individuals have within teams. It is recommended that roles should be very clearly defined so that there is no doubt concerning the experience, expertise and guiding values of each person (Clough and Lindsay 1991, Home Office *et al.*, 1991, HMI 1991). This does not necessarily mean that each person's role has to be completely separate from everyone else. There are times when roles should actually be overlapping so that people with PMLD receive the same input from each person who works with them (Orelove and Sobsey 1991; Rainforth, *et al.* 1992) For example, if everyone who works with a particular person with physical disabilities knows how to position her so that she can be comfortable and well-supported, she will be able to join in all activities to the optimum degree. This implies the willingness on the part of individuals to share expertise with each other in a form of 'role release', that is that they are prepared to 'release' part of their roles to others, trusting them to carry out those roles in their places. This is very demanding and implies that professionals feel secure in their roles and have confidence in their own abilities (Hart 1991).

To share information and pass over one's own expertise, suggests that it is important for professionals from different disciplines to share a language and an understanding of each other's point of view. A study by Miller (1996), shows that, after an opportunity to exchange understandings on a training course, speech and language therapists and teachers felt that they could communicate more effectively; plan and work together more closely; and generally experience a better professional working relationship. She does, however, suggest that some participants felt threatened by sharing knowledge.

Thus at both service and individual level, there are still many challenges to multidisciplinary collaborative teamwork, despite years of attempts to overcome them. A few have been highlighted in this section, but as yet, there has been no mention of the difficulty most often cited by those attempting to work together; that is having sufficient time (Lacey 1997). This topic will be dealt with in the next section which is about some of strategies that can be employed to aid collaboration. Time is deliberately placed there to suggest that it is not immutable: there are possibilities for reorganising it.

## Strategies for aiding collaboration

On being asked about their experiences of multidisciplinary collaboration, almost all respondents, in a study of one particular school for pupils with multiple disabilities, cited insufficient time for talking to team members (Lacey 1997). This was the topic which gave rise to the most emotive language of the interviews conducted within the study, most of the words and phrases indicating that people felt they were not in control of their own time. One of the problems was related to the different use of time between teachers and therapists. Teachers are strictly timetabled into lessons with little or no free moments, while therapists run an appointments system which cuts across the timetable and can be more flexible. Difficulties arise when trying to run these together which lead to few compatible moments for meeting to plan and share work.

Finding such times are vital, as it is impossible to be a team without time to talk. Collaboration is dependent upon good communication and sharing and this cannot be achieved through written reports and snatched conversations in the corridor or over the telephone. Management support for reorganising time is essential and this must come from all involved agencies. Some services operate only on four and a half days a week, keeping half a day for meetings, planning, assessments and other activities where collaboration with colleagues is important. Other services cluster their time, so they spend several days in one place before moving on. This enables peripatetic staff to meet with school, college or centre staff and for both sets of people to work alongside each other, passing on skills and ideas. Services that work in this way are usually available at particular times for telephone support during the periods they are elsewhere.

There are other ways of reallocating time; for example, a school took one of their compulsory training days and converted it into twilight planning sessions throughout the year. In this way, hourly paid staff were able to stay extra time after school in return for a day off. Smaller amounts of time can be traded in this way, by sending hourly paid staff home fifteen minutes early four evenings a week in return for an hour of planning on the fifth. However it is achieved, time must be viewed as flexible and changeable if sufficient is to be allocated to supporting collaborative teamwork.

Allotting time for talking and working together does not guarantee that this time will be used effectively. Collaborative teams often need strategies for helping them to run meetings well, or make best use of their work time together and often one of the best strategies is to agree on a leader. Although the importance of good leaders to teams is well documented (Adair; 1987 Hastings et al. 1987), it is not unusual for multidisciplinary teams to be leaderless. Representatives from different disciplines often find themselves working together with little preparation and without a leader to help them through the time-consuming stages of team development. They are expected to collaborate without effort, without support, and most importantly, without a leader.

Leaders of collaborative teams are not traditional hierarchical bosses, but people who take on the coordination of the work, providing or organising a chairperson at meetings, keeping the momentum of the team going, ensuring monitoring and evaluation is carried out and generally supporting the work of individuals. Specific jobs are likely to be divided amongst members and whatever the leader does is likely to be agreed by others. Delegation is not appropriate but sharing out the work is common. The role of leader can be rotating and can certainly change depending upon the emphasis of a particular meeting or period of the person with PMLD. For example, following an orthopaedic operation, a physiotherapist is likely to offer leadership to the team during the time of recovery and adjustment.

There appear to be several reasons for reluctance to agree on leaders for multidisciplinary teams. One seems to be that leadership is normally associated with line management and when several disciplines are brought together, there is no immediately identifiable person in charge: a basic misunderstanding of team leadership. Another seems to relate to lack of team and team leadership training: people just do not know how to help a team work effectively. Yet another is about the lack of time and importance given to team development: agencies do not take teams and team leaders sufficiently seriously.

When it works well, a multidisciplinary team with an energetic leader can be a powerful strategy for encouraging effective collaboration. Consider this example:

> Martin has profound intellectual impairment, visual impairment and self-injurious behaviour. He lives in his own home (with another person with PMLD) supported by a team consisting of his parents, support workers, a nurse, a social worker and a college lecturer. The team can call upon a network of agencies who provide the services Martin needs. For example, the housing department of the local authority were very closely involved when the house was set up but are now only occasionally asked for advice. The whole team (including Martin) meet once a month for planning but there are many other times when individual team members can exchange information and work alongside each other. Consistency of approach and a good supply of attractive activities are contributing to a good quality of life for Martin.

> One of the support workers has taken on the role of team leader as he spends the greatest amount of time with Martin. He is a confident person, well able to chair meetings, make sure records are kept up to date and represent the team when accompanying Martin to his GP or the psychiatrist. He also arranges three-monthly evaluations of the way in which the team is functioning, monitoring the results of previous agreements. For one meeting, the support worker invited the manager of the local sports centre with whom the team negotiated convenient times for Martin to use the children's soft play room as this is a favoured activity.

Martin's support worker is not a qualified professional but he was thought to be the best person to lead the team. Status does not necessarily dictate who should be team leaders as it is often important for the person most involved on a daily basis to take on that role. In schools, this is likely to be the classteacher or nursery nurse but in adult life, this is much more likely to be an unqualified support worker. Whether or not that person has professional training, she or he will undoubtedly need training to fulfil the leadership role. Chairing effective meetings is a skill that can be learned as is conducting an audit or keeping succinct records.

## *Importance of investment*

Training in team leadership is just one aspect of the amount of time, resources and funding that are necessary for collaboration to be effective. It cannot happen without some form of investment. Exhorting agencies and staff to work together, as has been the case over the last 30-40 years, has not been sufficient. What is needed is consistent investment, particularly in time, to move forward in the future. When teams are helped to find time to talk and work together, members can begin to understand each other's points of view and then harness those into improved problem solving with and for the person with PMLD. It is often said that 'several heads are better than one' and that 'the whole is better than the sum of the parts'. In a well-run team, this synergy can be exciting as people spark ideas off each other.

Investment in time to talk and carry out joint work is not often allocated in the human services. Most services are built on crisis management rather than on investment for pay-off at a later date. Shortages of funds and staffing contribute to a climate of 'make do and mend' which is not sympathetic to reaping rewards at a later date. The business world is familiar with investment and there are many examples of the moves towards teamwork in manufacturing or service industries (Tjosvold 1991; Morgan and Murgatroyd 1994) and although the development of teams has not been without its difficulties, there are reports of success and enthusiasm for that kind of structure (Liswood 1990).

Returning to a small collaborative multidisciplinary team working with a child or adult with PMLD, investment might amount to opportunities for daily or weekly contact, regular planning meetings (weekly or fortnightly), joint assessments, shared work, mutual and joint training and three-monthly evaluations. For those who are involved with the person with PMLD on less than a weekly basis, there might be opportunities for them to join the team or a member of the team regularly to enable exchange of information and skills which can then be employed until the next visit. Records of all of this work could be shared amongst everyone involved. Those records could belong to the person with PMLD and everyone could contribute. If records are designed not only with the person's needs in mind, but also in relation to the demands of each agency, it should be possible for there to be just one set of records, open to all in the team and photocopiable for returning to agency managers.

Teams of staff and carers who are able to work in this way are more likely to be in a position to meet the complex needs that are presented by children and adults who have PMLD. One person or one agency just cannot have the depth of knowledge and skills to address them all. Working in isolation from each other produces a fragmentary life for the person who has hearing aids from one professional who never discusses comfortable positioning for using them with another. It also produces isolation for staff and carers as everyone struggles to solve problems for which they have only part of an answer. Working together collaboratively may take longer at the outset, as team members get to know each other, but it can be very effective and satisfying for all involved in the long run.

# This book

The chapters of this book are written by researchers and practitioners who are all committed to the principle of collaborative multidisciplinary teamwork. Some write extensively about it, giving examples of collaboration in action, whilst others merely mention it. Some are explicit in their support, others implicit. The range of topics selected for inclusion in the book is wide in an attempt to explore as many aspects of the complexities of PMLD as possible. There are, of course, many other topics that could have been covered but it is hoped that this will become a useful textbook for all those who work with or care for people with PMLD.

The book is divided into four sections following this introduction, beginning with things personal and concluding with aspects of the wider world. The first section contains four chapters on health, physical, sensory and personal needs and current ways of meeting them. The second section is entitled 'Social' and relates to making relationships and developing communication. 'Learning' focuses on different angles of 'life-long learning', both from the point of view of the person with PMLD and in relation to current trends in education and social care. The last section, 'Community', begins with families and moves through advocacy towards community integration, cultural issues and leisure. The final chapter shifts right out beyond our own shores to the provision of services for the most profoundly disabled people in the developing world.

It is hoped that the nineteen chapters in this book will provide a broad ranging resource for practitioners who work with children and/or adults with PMLD in education, health, social care and voluntary settings and for those studying on advanced courses. Writers were asked to present up-to-date thinking in their specialisms and present readers with challenges to provoke reflection on their own thinking and practice. It was conceived as a book for reference, although it is hoped that readers will be interested in aspects of working with people with PMLD that are not directly within their own spheres. The greater understanding all members of multidisciplinary collaborative teams have of each other's specialisms, the greater the likelihood there is of children and adults with PMLD experiencing a good quality of life, characterised by met needs, fulfilling relationships and stretching activities which lead to life-long development and enjoyment.

# Part One:
## Personal

# Chapter 1

# Positive Health: A Collective Responsibility

*Christine Hutchinson*

## Introduction

Is there anything worse than feeling ill, under the weather, or a little off colour? Yes... feeling all this and those around not recognising this and supporting you in the way you prefer, either by pampering, getting you what you need or leaving you alone.

This chapter is aimed at highlighting some of the many issues connected with the vast field of health and learning disabilities. The majority of the literature relates to the wider field of learning disabilities rather than directly to profound and multiple learning disabilities (PMLD). However it is still of relevance to this more specialist area of practice. The chapter is not intended to be a guide for diagnosis or treatment.

The term health, as used here, is taken to include the broader picture as defined by the World Health Organisation (1946) as 'a state of complete physical, mental and social well-being', not just the absence of disease or infirmity.

The underpinning principles within this area of practice, as with all aspects of working with those who have a learning disability, are that people with a learning disability are individual citizens with rights and personal needs. They are trying, and should be supported in their attempts, to live as ordinary a life as possible. It is important to recognise that those with learning disabilities or PMLD have exactly the same range of health needs as any person may have regardless of the level of learning disability.

Many people make regular checks of themselves. The information is compared with the people's own expectation of how their own bodies should be and should feel. It is when there is something out of the ordinary that further action is taken either to monitor the situation, treat the ailment themselves or seek medical attention. This action is often based on a number of aspects, such as how much pain it is causing, how much it is affecting daily functioning, how it makes one feel. Those things which cause the most problems or distress are usually those upon which medical attention is sought.

What will be explored within this chapter is how people with a profound learning disability, having made these assessments of themselves, communicate this to their carers in order to obtain the most satisfactory resolution to the problem and provide consent for any necessary procedures. The same principles which will be outlined also apply to their ability in coming to understand the diagnosis and treatment.

Some of the more common health issues are briefly described and the responsibility for meeting these needs explored. The main emphasis within this chapter is that services and carers need to be proactive in meeting the health needs of people with PMLD, they need to have a level of knowledge and there needs to be regular health surveillance and screening with actions being taken as early as possible.

# Policies

Due to concern about the state of health of the British population, efforts have been made on a national basis for a number of years now to re-educate society and promote positive health practices. The Department of Health (DoH) launched its plan to address some of the priority needs through The Health of the Nation (DoH 1992). This document sought to approach what were seen as the five main areas of health which posed a significant problem within society:

- coronary heart disease and stroke
- cancer
- mental illness
- accidents
- HIV/AIDS and sexual health.

These key areas are those on which the Department of Health felt services should 'work together', the focus being on the promotion of good health and prevention of disease (DoH 1992).

Their strategy for people with learning disabilities was not published for a further three years with its aim to 'ensure that those with a learning disability are included in the action taken for the whole population' (DoH 1995 p.4). This document sought to provide a clear proactive agenda and emphasise that the needs and experiences of those with a learning disability are the same as those of the rest of the population (Holmes and Parrish 1996).

What the Department of Health's 1992 document assumes, is that the basic health care needs of the population are being met. The need to be free of pain and to have all health issues addressed is one which is extended to everyone. However, what has been clearly overlooked is the fact that those with learning disabilities, especially those with PMLD, and some other groups of individuals, do not have even these basic needs met.

# Recognising the problem

There has been a great deal of research into the area of health needs of those with learning disabilities over the last decade; studies highlighting the unmet needs of hospital and community populations. Cole (1986), in his study of the needs of 53 individuals, found that 35 needed medical attention, 4 as a matter of urgency. Wilson and Haire (1990) found that of the 65 people they examined only 8 did not have an appreciable problem. Essex (1991) found that over one third of those in his study had a previously undiagnosed hearing or vision problem. Ganesh et al. (1994), who have provided the only recent study of health needs of those with a profound learning disability, found that 93.8% were underweight, 15.6% were severely underweight, all were at a high risk of pressure sores, 68.4% had epilepsy and 21% had a high level of health care need. Meehan et al. (1995) provided findings where 92% of those examined in their study had a previously undetected but treatable condition.

The most recent study is that of Turner and Moss (1996), funded by the Department of Health. They use the *Health of the Nation* key areas and compare information about these with the information available on the mortality and morbidity of people with learning disabilities. They found that cardiovascular health is a major concern to all those with learning disabilities, including PMLD; however, those with profound learning disabilities are at less risk of cancer than those with mild, moderate or severe learning disability. The prevalence of mental illness is at least as high as in the general population. The most common cause of death is respiratory disease with infections continuing to play a disproportionate role in the deaths of those with learning disabilities. There were no specific findings related to people with learning disabilities with respect to accidents or sexual health. They also provided information which supported the findings of other studies regarding unmet needs in the areas of vision and hearing.

From all of this research it is clear that the needs of those with learning disabilities are seriously overlooked. It highlights how important it is for carers to listen to people with PMLD and watch for changes in their behaviour. This is the only way they have of telling others that something is wrong. An additional strategy would be regular health checks, and this will be explored in the next section. There needs to be some action taken as a matter of urgency to correct the service deficits in detecting and treating illness. So why should we give any great emphasis to the *Health of the Nation* document?

# Health surveillance

The *Health of the Nation* document provides a starting point. If it is ignored then the needs of people with learning disabilities will always be lagging behind in terms of national action. What is needed is additional resources to reduce the gap. One very useful way of starting to address this is through health surveillance and screening, the use of a structure which regularly checks the status of a person's health. Some children receive this through their school medical, school nurse services and health visitor interventions. Quite often it is when people move into adult services, where everything is in its own department and requires a separate referral, that areas of need become neglected.

The study conducted by Wilson and Haire (1990) found that the rate of GP consultations of people with learning disabilities was at a reduced rate (an average of 2.7 visits per year) compared with figures for the general population (3 per year for men and 5 per year for women) published in 1985 by the *General Household Survey*. This is further supported by Holmes and Parrish (1996) who state that 'people with learning disabilities are known to have higher rates of illness, yet access services less frequently than the general population' (p. 1184).

Why is it that people with learning disabilities and PMLD do not attend their GP as often? More concerning is why do those who do attend GP surgeries regularly, and do receive checks still have health needs which are not addressed? One reason may be the belief that 'it's all part of their learning disability'. Many signs which carers observe which could be an indicator of ill health, such as changes in mood, behaviour or appetite, are frequently dismissed as being part of unusual or inconsistent behaviour which is frequent in someone with a label of learning disability and particularly those with PMLD. It is in these cases that evidence needs to be provided to confirm that the aspects of the person's behaviour which are being presented are not the norm for that person, that there are changes and are therefore an indicator of something.

Many colleagues and peers believe that they are meeting the health needs of those they serve, and may feel that much of the evidence in these studies is not true of their own district, but they may not have considered what percentage of the local population of those with a learning disability are in fact offered a service. The studies outlined above were conducted with people who are supported, mainly in day centres but also in hospitals and specialist support groups, and yet there is a high level of health need identified. Clearly this support does not always guarantee that need will be met. Some professionals and carers are haphazard and reactive, awaiting observable signs of illness or distress before taking action. Leifer (1996) suggests that people with learning disabilities are less likely to complain until something is seriously wrong. How long then will those with PMLD have been suffering before it comes to the attention of those supporting them? This causes some concern if the matter is then left untreated for some time.

Holmes and Parrish (1996) feel that there are additional health needs for those with learning disabilities to those outlined in the *Health of the Nation* document pertaining to the general population. Some of these are detailed in the *Strategy for People with Learning Disabilities* (DoH 1995). They suggest that these should be highlighted and addressed through activities of health promotion and surveillance. Health promotion and surveillance are essentially proactive, especially if repeated in a systematic way on a regular basis (Jeffery and Higgs 1995). Accurate recordings would show the slightest deviation from previous surveillance findings, or patterns may be highlighted. In order for it to be most effective it would be best carried out on a regular basis by a carer who has a great deal of contact with the person, someone who knows him or her well, can communicate best with him or her and can recognise changes from the norm for the individual. It would be completed with a nurse or medic who would be able to interpret the recordings to highlight any issues which would require further investigation. Not only would some of the information be likely to dismiss the 'it's all part of the learning disability' syndrome but it may also detect early signs of abuse so that the most appropriate action can be taken. For this type of regular surveillance to be successful, carers must be vigilant and their observations discussed with others who support the person concerned.

There is evidence to suggest that people with PMLD may be denied access to regular screening services available to the general population. A colleague recently told me of her experiences of supporting a woman she works with at an appointment with the GP. This woman has profound learning disabilities and some physical disabilities. She had been suffering from some discomfort in her vaginal area and urine testing had not shown anything significant in terms of urine infections. My colleague was asking for a cervical smear to be considered. The woman was 29 years old and had never had one done so not only was it seen to be of benefit in checking there was nothing wrong, it was also her right to have the screening which is offered to all women in this country. The GP refused on the basis that the woman was not sexually active. How many other people would be asked if they were sexually active before the GP agreed to a smear? MacRae (1997) in her study of 24 women with learning disabilities found that only 10 had ever had this procedure completed. This is just one example which shows the clear discrimination which people with learning disabilities face. They need support from their carers to advocate for them and challenge the system and professionals within that system, not only for themselves but for all those with learning disabilities.

# Communicating the symptoms

One of the main challenges in supporting people with profound learning disabilities is in establishing an effective and reliable communication system. It is impossible to overemphasise just how important this area is, especially when there may be additional barriers to communicating with those with profound disabilities. At times getting someone to communicate what they would like to drink can be a major hurdle, taking a considerable amount of effort from both parties to achieve. The communication of symptoms of illness will take even more effort and time. If a person's communication lands on 'deaf ears' then that channel of communication will close down.

Often we rely on the signs of illness or discomfort, changes in a person's behaviour, mood or general demeanour. This nonverbal communication is vitally important and it is imperative that it is interpreted as accurately as possible. Where possible, the interpretation should be relayed back to the person for confirmation, and action should then be taken based on that interpretation. The same principles apply when giving information to the person regarding consultation with the doctor or nurse, or about any investigations, treatment or other information relating to the issue. It is only when this is achieved, with the clarification of understanding, that consent can be better informed.

Detailed and accurate written communication and recording is needed, with careful and sensitive sharing of this with other people involved in supporting the person. Frequently signs of ill health appear in a progressive manner, or in clusters, and it is only when the whole picture is presented that a diagnosis can be made. For example, one may start with a headache, begin to feel hot or cold, move on to feeling as if there is swelling in the head and around the eyes, then feel a tickle in the throat, and within the space of one or two days one has a cold or 'flu. This build up would not be noticeable to anyone other than the person suffering, until they started coughing or wiping their nose frequently. Systematic records can help to remind people of different things that have been noticed and this is particularly important where there are a number of carers, any one of whom may be supporting the client when they go to see their GP. It may even be useful to have a separate sheet within a person's notes or a diary where such information can be easily accessed. Two published recording packages have been designed specifically for use with people who have a learning disability (Kitt *et al.* 1997; Matthews 1996). These records, as with others, should be factual and nonjudgmental. Recording opinions on how someone's mood appears can be useful, but it is important to state that it is an opinion and to try to offer some justification for the comment in terms of the observations upon which that conclusion is based.

Confidentiality is clearly an issue and, where possible, the person's permission should be sought before any information is shared. However, inter-agency working is essential in meeting the needs of those people we support and the sharing of confidential information is a necessary part of that collaboration. A balance has to be struck between breaching a person's privacy and providing essential information to others for them to be able to carry out their job or task. There are no easy, step by step rules about this. Personal and professional judgement is essential.

# Whose needs?

Doctors' time during appointments is often precious to them and because of this pressure a consultation can seem very rushed. As a result it is often the carer's or professional's views and information which is acted upon rather than that of the person concerned. In fact, there can be times when the person is neither spoken to nor listened to. In these situations one often wonders whose needs are really being addressed. One woman who the author visited, often woke during the night and would walk around the hostel in which she lived. There were staff on duty who stayed awake during the night and could come to her aid if needed. In spite of this, the staff team sought to have her placed on medication to help her to sleep because the ironing, which the night staff were supposed to do, was often not finished because of the need to attend to this woman. In these circumstances the answer to the question 'Whose need?' is obvious; the medication prescribed to her by the GP was not so much for her benefit as for that of the staff.

Another example is that of a nineteen year old young man with profound learning and physical disabilities, who had difficulties with continence and was often constipated. He was given enemas three times per week in addition to other medications for different health needs. On exploring his history with his mother it became evident that he had his first period of constipation when he was about two years old. The GP prescribed enemas and he has been receiving this invasive procedure ever since. At the time of the first consultation there may have been valid reasons for this form of treatment. However, his mother was sure that no alternative ways of dealing with her son's constipation had been explored. She had made her own attempts at altering his diet without success but knew nothing of the benefits of massage combined with diet, or of less invasive medications which are available. Unfortunately for this man his mother was not willing to try to change his treatment after seventeen years, expressing her concern that it would be too time consuming and might not work.

Conflict between the professionals and the direct carer are not uncommon and can create a situation which proves to be very difficult. Sometimes conflict is between two professionals with the same result. Professionals and carers may not always be right, but the guiding principle must be to do what is best for the person concerned, and take account of what he or she would want or prefer.

# Consent issues

Consent is a right of every individual. It is unlawful for any health practitioner to do anything to someone else without his or her consent or, in the case of children, the consent of a person with parental responsibility. This seems very clear until the law is examined in terms of those who are labelled as 'incompetent'. There is a dearth of literature in the area of learning disabilities regarding consent. The law, which is rather inadequate, is all there is to provide a guide. (Ashton 1994; Holman 1997; Arscott 1997).

The Medical Defence Union (MDU 1996) set out two types of consent, implied and expressed. Implied consent is where the individual acts in a manner which allows the procedure to take place, such as offering their arm for a blood sample or undressing for a physical examination. Expressed consent can be given orally or in writing and is a specific statement of agreement to the procedure being carried out which allows the practitioner to proceed. Expressed consent is nearly always obtained when an operation or other major procedure is being considered.

Assessing the person's ability to consent is the area which can cause the most difficulties. Often people with learning disabilities will allow doctors, dentists and nurses to treat them with little resistance, but whether their consent has been obtained in these situations, either expressed or implied, is debatable. Surely for consent to be given a person should have knowledge and understanding of the procedure, the risks involved and any alternative options. How often is all this talked through with people with PMLD, their understanding checked and then a decision shared? Ashton (1994) suggests that even if a person has been found incapable of consenting to one thing, this does not exclude him or her from being competent to consent to something else.

A child's situation appears to be quite clear, the person with parental responsibility makes the decisions and provides consent for treatment. However, a number of cases which have reached the High Courts suggest that children may consent for themselves if they have sufficient understanding of all the risks, although the withholding of consent by children may be overridden by someone with parental responsibility, if this is in their best interests (Ashton 1994).

Ultimately it is the responsibility of the doctor to decide what is in the best interests of a person who is not able to consent, and it is the duty of all doctors under common law to provide necessary treatment and proper care. It is not the responsibility of the carer or any other person involved. They cannot give consent on behalf of an adult with a learning disability. This does not merely cover emergency situations but also routine medical treatment. However the MDU (1996) recommends that any decision making process, including the decision of whether someone is competent to consent or not, should involve others as a matter of good practice and this is where carers or professionals may be asked to share their opinion.

Holman (1997) recommends that the 'best interests' guidelines be followed. The Law Commission in 1995 (cited by Holman 1997) produced a checklist to guide individuals in determining whether their decisions are the person's best interests. The four factors to be considered are:

- the ascertainable past and present wishes and feelings of the person concerned, and the factors that the person would consider if able to do so;
- the need to allow and encourage the person to participate, or to improve his ability to participate as fully as possible in anything done for, and any decision affecting him;
- the views of other people who it may be appropriate and practicable to consult about the person's wishes and feelings, and what would be in his/her best interests;
- whether the purpose for which any action or decision is required can be as effectively achieved in a manner less restrictive of the person's freedom of action.

(Holman 1997; Medical Defence Union 1996; Ashton 1994).

# Common health issues

Within this section it is intended to look at six of the most common health problems encountered when working with people with profound learning disabilities. It is not intended to go into any details about the medical condition but more to raise some of the issues which need to be explored, or the information which carers should seek out when considering the everyday management and implications for a person with PMLD. The format adopted is that of listing some questions which will hopefully provoke thought and reflection. They should help in the development of individualised management plans for the individuals being supported.

# Epilepsy

Baker (1993) feels that epilepsy is one of the most important areas in the provision of adequate and comprehensive care, and states that a third of all those with learning disabilities will eventually develop epilepsy. Ganesh *et al.* (1994) found the ratio to be much greater for the people with profound learning disabilities who took part in their study, with a percentage of 68.4. This finding would fit with the assumption that the prevalence of epilepsy increases with the increase in severity of the person's learning disability (Clarke 1990). There are a number of publications which provide very detailed and eloquent accounts of the prevalence, causation, manifestation and treatment of epilepsy, for example, British Epilepsy Association (undated), Orelove and Sobsey (1991), Clarke (1990) and Shanley and Starrs (1993).

Listed below are a number of questions about which anyone who is supporting an individual who has epilepsy should have some information, knowledge and answers.

- What is epilepsy? How is it caused? How was this particular person's epilepsy caused?
- What different forms of seizure does the person experience? How do each of these manifest themselves? Is there a pattern to the frequency of the person's seizures?
- What triggers a seizure for the person? Does the person get a warning that a seizure is about to occur?
- How should the different types of seizure be dealt with? What type of first aid should be offered? In what way and for how long does the person prefer or need to recover?
- How would the need for medical attention be determined? Are suppositories required for status epilepticus or prolonged seizures? Who is competent to give this treatment if necessary? Is there a protocol in place for guidance?
- Is the person's epilepsy controlled? How is it treated or controlled? What side effects does this treatment bring? In what ways and how often is it reviewed? How does the information you have about this person's epilepsy get fed into the review process?
- Is the person's epilepsy considered when making risk assessments? Does this unnecessarily limit the person's freedom?

The answer to these questions will provide the information needed for an individualised management guide for anyone with epilepsy. It is essential that anyone supporting a person who has epilepsy is aware of all of these issues if they are to provide a good quality, well equipped and sensitive service to the individual.

# Continence

This area of personal care is one which causes many carers the most concern. This is probably because of the societal taboos on discussing the subject and the expectation that everyone by school age has continence under control. It may be assumed that people with learning disability are incontinent because of general developmental delay in achieving control. However, lack of continence is often due to some factor such as infection, weak sphincter muscles or emotional upset, and as such it is treatable. Although in some cases the lack of continence cannot be cured, nevertheless it can be well managed, to the extent that no one other than the carer need know. Halliday (1990) calls this effective management social continence, and aiming for social continence is a realistic option for the majority of people with profound disabilities. Management includes such aspects as regular times for going to the toilet, planning the changing of pads, the use of other appliances or, very infrequently, surgery. Well managed continence can lead to more physical comfort for the person and less risk of skin problems and infections; it also makes it less of an issue for carers, converting a generally negative issue into a positive aspect of life; it leads to improvement in the attitude of others to the person with PMLD; and, hopefully will help to increase his or her self-esteem. This is a realistic goal.

There are a number of common misconceptions about managing continence, and consistency and an effective regime are all-important. Many people feel that they can ease a person's urinary incontinence by reducing their fluid intake. This is not the case and this action can, in fact, make the person more susceptible to urine infections. The other common course of action is to take the person to the toilet more frequently. The average person goes to the toilet once every 2-3 hours, and to go every half hour or hour would in fact impinge on the natural urinary cycle and may be counterproductive unless it is a short stage in a training programme to help a person to obtain control of their bladder.

A woman who was referred to a service was holistically assessed and, among other things, was discovered to have what the learning disability nurse thought was a mixture of stress and urge incontinence. The district nurse who made the continence assessment also diagnosed stress/urge incontinence, but rather than providing the usual treatment of pelvic floor exercises or electrotherapy with some medication, she arranged for pads to be delivered weekly. It was only when this was challenged through the continence adviser that the woman was given electrotherapy (as she could not comprehend pelvic floor exercises) combined with medication. The continence problem was resolved. Had this challenge not been made a woman would have been wearing pads, unnecessarily, for the rest of her life.

The following questions should be considered when working with someone who has a lack of continence.

- Has the person been assessed by a continence adviser, community learning disability nurse or GP? Some forms of incontinence are treatable and in the general population the majority of cases are cured. Accurate assessment and diagnosis is essential and crucial to successful treatment.
- What type of continence problem does the person have? What would be the treatment or management regime if the person did not have a learning disability? Has this treatment or regime been recommended – if not why not? The reason that the person has a learning disability is not sufficient in most cases. Achieving continence is something which we train ourselves to do and does not require a high level of intellectual functioning.
- What training has been given to carers regarding the continence cycle and how this is affected within the individual? Often having some understanding of the biological process of continence is a tremendous help in understanding what the issue is and how to go about rectifying it.
- Is there anything about the person's diet or medication which is likely to cause or aggravate the lack of continence? Some of the common things are caffeine, alcohol and major tranquillisers. There are many more medications and common foods which can also cause a problem.
- Have your thoughts about this issue been discussed and explored?

## *Promoting rest*

Sleep is seen as a time when the body recovers from its previous exercise or activity. Disturbances in sleep pattern, whether sleeping too much or too little, are often caused by external factors and it is now recognised that a disturbed sleep pattern can affect a person's physical and emotional well-being (Bradley and Darbyshire 1993). It is not uncommon for people with PMLD to have a disturbed sleep pattern which can have a detrimental effect on their everyday lives as well as on the health and well being of their carers which will also, indirectly, affect their own quality of life.

Aspects to consider are:

- What is the usual sleep pattern for this person? We all have different patterns and so cannot judge what the person needs based upon our own needs.
- Is there an established routine to indicate sleeping and waking times? Often the introduction of a wind down period can assist those who find it difficult to settle. A programme of activity may help for those who sleep too much.
- Is there anything physical which is causing a problem? For example, being uncomfortable, having difficulty changing position (see Goldsmith and Goldsmith in this volume), sensory impairments which may cause insecurity or an inability to distinguish day from night, being hungry or thirsty, lying on wet bedding or pads, being ill or in pain or taking medication which affects the sleep pattern.
- Is there anything which might be worrying the person? Might the person be upset, experiencing loss or be lonely?
- Are there any night-time activities which may be disturbing the person's sleep? For instance, the activities of carers at night in changing pads or bedding can be disturbing and is usually unnecessary. More suitable continence aids for night-time use should be sought. If the person is in a staffed environment then staff activities should be as non disturbing as possible.
- Is the person's position causing discomfort, pain or further physical contractures? An occupational therapist and physiotherapist can advise on positioning and supports for the person for use during the night.
- If the person is on night sedation, is it effective? Is it really necessary? Many of the medications which are used for night sedation are not very effective and can even disrupt a person's sleep pattern even more. They should only be used where absolutely necessary and over short periods with regular reviews.

## *Infections*

Turner and Moss (1996) found that infections account for more deaths of people with learning disabilities than in the general population, with respiratory infections accounting for half of the deaths of people within institutions. People with profound learning disabilities are even more at risk. Fryers (1984) suggests that this is due to the likelihood of an inadequate level of self care and the additional medical problems which render them susceptible to respiratory infection.

In prevention and treatment of infections the following should be considered:

- What are the signs of infection? Early detection is desirable in treating infections and therefore carers must be sure that they are aware of the signs of infections and are observant for them.
- What is the person's most usual position? Positioning is an important aspect of

reducing chest infections. Prolonged periods of time on the floor or lying on their back can increase the person's susceptibility by increasing the likelihood of them inhaling saliva, vomit or regurgitated food and reduce the natural process of the lungs in clearing mucus through the body's systems. When lying down for extended periods, pools of mucus develop in the lungs, encourage growth of bacteria and so promote infections.

- What are the person's eating and swallowing abilities? Is there a need for a speech therapy assessment around eating issues? Does the person obtain food from unhygienic places such as bins or the floor?
- Is the person prone to ear infections, urine infections, gastric infections? What is being done to investigate and prevent the recurrence of these?
- Are the practices adopted during personal care of a sufficiently safe standard to prevent the passing of infections such as hepatitis from, or to, the person? What equipment, resources or support needs to be in place to support these practices? Is this available? The use of gloves is not pleasant but is necessary when dealing with bodily fluids and secretions to reduce the risk of the passing of such infections. If gloves are used as a matter of course with all people who need assistance with personal care then there will be no discrimination toward anyone.

## Mental illness

It is now recognised that there is a higher incidence of mental illness in people with learning disabilities than in the general population (Baker 1993; Quinn and Mathieson 1993). However, due to major problems in diagnosing mental illness in those with learning disabilities, the prevalence rates found in existing studies are thought to be underestimates. Baker (1993) feels that in order to diagnose those with severe and profound learning disabilities, the information and observations of carers is invaluable. Quite often a change in a person's mood or mental state is displayed through a change in their behaviour. This can sometimes be seen as challenging and attempts are made to eradicate, reduce or replace unwanted behaviour. This behaviour, however, may be a sign of something else, it may be due to some distressing event, thought, or image which could be part of a mental illness. Life events are stressors to everyone and checklists and scales have been widely publicised where people can score their stress level. Life events are stressors to those with learning disabilities also, and a high level of stress can be a precipitating factor in mental illness.

The following questions will help to ensure that mental illness is recognised and treated appropriately:

- What awareness have you about the signs of mental illness?
- Do the people you support have access to a psychiatrist who specialises in learning disabilities?
- Is the person prescribed any psychotropic medication? What is this medication for? When and how is it reviewed?
- Is the person showing signs of withdrawing from their environment, more than usual?
- Does the person appear to be responding to some vision or sound which is not there in reality?
- Does the person have any behaviours which prevent them from participating in everyday activities? Are these behaviours considered to be obsessive or compulsive?

11

- Does the person have a low self-esteem? It is often thought that low self-esteem is part and parcel of having PMLD; however, this is not necessarily the case.
- Has the person made attempts to seriously injure themselves, or even commit suicide?

## Diet

Holmes and Parrish (1996) state that obesity is a common problem amongst people with learning disabilities. However, Ganesh *et al.* (1994) found that being underweight was a greater problem for those with profound learning disabilities. Mealtimes often form the family gathering and provide a social context in which to enjoy that which is essential to life. For many people, and people with PMLD are no exception, food may be one of the greatest pleasures in life. A significant number of people with PMLD receive their food through a nasogastric tube, or have a gastrostomy. In these circumstances a fundamental source of pleasure and satisfaction is denied to them.

Diet is an important part of everyone's survival and as such should be taken seriously. Often diet is the only aspect of life which people with learning disabilities can control in terms of whether they will, or will not, eat.

When helping a person with PMLD to eat and drink you should consider:

- What type of experience are mealtimes for the person? Are they rushed, relaxed, or a non event?
- Does the person have the necessary support, including furniture, to be able to sit with others for their meals? Is an occupational therapy assessment required and suitable seating and utensils provided?
- How much does the person usually eat and drink? Is the diet sufficiently balanced to ensure that the daily amount of vitamins and minerals are obtained? Is there enough roughage to encourage bowel movements? Does the person need any supplements? How much variety is there in what the person eats and where they eat?
- How often is the person weighed? Is this recorded? Is the weight expected realistic? What action is taken if the person is underweight?
- Does the person require special feeding techniques? What training has been given or is needed about these techniques?

# Whose role is it?

The best people to monitor the health of a person with PMLD are those who provide the daily care to the individual, those who know him or her well and can easily identify even the most subtle changes. It has been said that generic services have a negative attitude towards those with learning disabilities (Selvin and Sines 1996; Thornton 1996; Selvin 1995) which is compounded by their lack of knowledge. Selvin (1995) found that there were more positive attitudes in those nurses who had been given experience within learning disability services during their training. Hopefully, as this is a requirement of all nurse training now, the response towards those with learning disabilities who need nursing support will improve over the longer term. Perhaps other professions should review their educational curriculum to ensure that an experience in learning disability becomes mandatory. However, there are a large number of nurses, and possibly other professionals, trained 'traditionally' with no planned learning experience in the field of learning disabilities, who still have many years to work. Education of these members of staff by carers and learning disability services is essential if the treatment of people with learning disability is to improve in the short term also.

The structure, function and role of the learning disability team will vary from area to area. The learning disability nurse is a resource which is sometimes unknown, underused or overworked. They have received specialist training in learning disabilities and also have some medical knowledge. They are well placed to bridge the gap between the client and medical services and provide many other aspects of support to the person and their carers. As Cox (1993) states they are 'tailor made for the job'.

Recent documents from the Department of Health have provided the speciality with some guidance on what is expected from learning disability nurses (DoH undated, Kay *et al.* 1995, 1996), the priority being the health needs of those they serve. There have also been documents aimed at primary health care services (Dorrell 1996). These services, mainly through district nurses and health visitors, are often the first contact which a person will have with the National Health Service other than their GP. These professionals need to be highly skilled in detecting other needs which people may have, referring the person on (with permission) to other appropriate services. For this process to run smoothly primary care staff and learning disability staff need to communicate effectively, appreciating each other's roles. There are probably many people with a learning disability living in the community who do not receive specialist services. They may not want to, and this decision, if informed, should be respected; but what if they do want some support?

The philosophy of Normalisation and Social Role Valorisation (Wolfensberger 1972) has underpinned services for many years now, and this philosophy encourages staff to recognise that people do have special needs which require specialist services. However, there are still those who believe that the meeting of health needs is the role of generic services and not for learning disability nurses to become involved in. This approach is clearly not working. It is disappointing to think that philosophical beliefs could be preventing health needs from being met.

Health promotion as defined by the World Health Organisation (1986) is the 'process of enabling people to increase control over, and to improve, their health'. This is the key to making positive changes in a proactive way which is the responsibility of all those who provide support to people, and it fits snugly with services' philosophies of empowerment. Health promotion is about empowering people to control their own health and identify their own health needs through accurate knowledge and informed choice. Beattie (1994) sees health promotion as a place for innovation in multidisciplinary collaboration.

Little effort has been put into health promotion for those with learning disabilities with many reporting the lack of accessible materials to assist in people's learning (MacRae 1997; Rodgers and Russell 1995). Traditionally what have been seen as valued social activities, such as smoking and drinking, are also seen to produce risks to health. Education regarding alternative valued roles and activities is essential so that people with learning disabilities can still use facilities such as pubs, but in a more healthy way. As with the general population, dictating the behaviour and actions which people must take to improve their health is futile. An explanation of why people should change behaviour, routines and habits is much more productive and one which requires constant reinforcement by everyone. One of the many challenges facing those who work with people with PMLD is how to involve them in their own healthcare in a proactive way. The process must begin in the early years and continue throughout life.

# Conclusions

Meeting the health care needs of those with learning disabilities is not merely the role of the medical profession. It is the responsibility of everyone the person comes into contact with. Collaboration is crucial and is a key element which appears in many documents applicable to health services, local authorities and the education service. For collaboration to work people have to rid themselves of professional superiority and really work together, working jointly and effectively in the person's best interests. This theme has already been broached in the introduction to this volume which discusses the importance of collaborative working with people with PMLD.

The prevalence of complex health care needs is higher among those with profound and multiple learning disabilities (Lehr and Noonan 1989). This is due to the combination of better obstetric care and more effective treatments throughout life. More people with profound learning disabilities are surviving through gestation and birth, and they are also living longer. The issues outlined here will not go away, action has to be taken and resources will be needed to concentrate on this area. Rodgers and Russell (1995) eloquently state 'In the long term, what is needed to meet the health needs of people with learning difficulties... is adequate support and social justice '. The lack of expansion and sometimes reduction of learning disability services has to stop, as does the prejudice and discrimination which many people with learning disabilities face.

Chapter 2

# Physical Management

*John and Liz Goldsmith*

## Introduction

The physical care of people with profound and multiple disabilities can be seen as either a very simple or a very complex task. It is possible to maintain basic life needs with a minimum of intervention, but to enable an individual to lead a healthy, happy and meaningful life is a complicated challenge which affects not only the individual but all those who care for them (Tizard 1960, 1978).

In the past it was traditional for such people to live within substantial institutions, segregated from society at large and even segregated within the institution so that people with the most complex needs were cared for together in wards catering for twenty to thirty people. In this setting it was only possible to offer basic care and even this was a physically and emotionally exhausting task for carers. Social isolation was a common feature of this style of care. Oswin (1978) carried out observational studies which revealed that children living on a long stay ward received an average of five minutes 'mothering attention' in a ten hour period. Under this regime the opportunities for movement offered to the individual were also very limited, and Oswin documents with compassion how people deteriorated so that they became more and more immobile with consequent distortion of body shape and associated health problems. Within the segregated culture of institutions it was a commonly held view that the secondary consequences of emotional and motor deprivation were an inevitable result of the initial disabling condition. The pattern of deterioration became self perpetuating and concepts of the possibility of maintenance of body shape or even some development of movement came to be regarded as a naive viewpoint.

Within this culture of low expectations and relaxed pessimism the therapists experienced limited demand for their skills. Consequently the infrastructure to offer people with complex needs the opportunities to learn to move combined with a programme of postural care are only now in the early stages of development. Recognition of the need to change as documented in the Kings Fund Project Paper (1981) brought about the closure of institutions, and the introduction of community care has transferred responsibility to parents and carers in much smaller living units. In these circumstances humane attitudes are able to flourish with the result that therapists and educationalists are pleased to find that they are receiving increasingly militant demands for a more successful outcome in terms of physical care.

This is a fast changing and exciting aspect of medical care and it is to be hoped that therapists are able to respond to these demands, develop radical new methods of working and forge alliances to deliver the very best of physical management. A change of emphasis is needed from brief episodes of therapy, to be justified by short term improvements, towards a life long commitment by therapy services to work with carers and ensure that the individual receives postural care combined with opportunities to learn to move. This style of therapy creates the conditions in which the individual can develop where possible, but gives comfort and support during periods of deterioration. Therapeutic management becomes a way of life, dominated by the carer and other hands-on practitioners, influencing the majority of the individual's time; rather than an ineffective ritual, dominated by the therapist, in the few hours that are spent within a school, clinic or day care centre.

In this chapter there will be a consideration of the future, influenced by pioneering work being carried out by The Children's Rehabilitation Services in Mansfield, Nottinghamshire (Peters 1997). The following related aspects of physical care will be covered:

- identification of the individual in need of postural care;
- service delivery of postural care;
- encouraging normal sleep patterns;
- development and maintenance of function.

# Identification of the individual in need of postural care

Fulford and Brown (1976) identified the need to control the posture of individuals with severe movement problems in order to protect body shape. The human body is a soft structure. When the individual is able to move in a conventional, symmetrical manner the person will tend to grow and remain straight. However, when a person has severe difficulty in moving and the body stays in a limited number of destructive asymmetric postures the force of gravity flattens it and the body fixes into asymmetric shapes (Goldsmith and Goldsmith 1996a and b).

**Figure 2.1** Children with asymmetric postures

The following photographs are of Sarah and they show how her body adapted over the years, to suit her habitual position (ENB. 1985, Goldsmith and Goldsmith 1996a and b).

## 8 MONTHS OLD

At 8 months old Sarah was not able to sit unsupported.

## 18 MONTHS OLD

When Sarah was 18 months old she used to sit in a baby chair, because the chair fitted her she was able to sit in a conventional sitting position.

## 3 YEARS OLD

By the time Sarah was 3 years old she was beginning to grow quite tall and had outgrown her baby chair.

## 4 1/2 YEARS OLD

At $4^{1}/_{2}$ yrs old Sarah began to be placed in the corner of the settee. She began to adopt a destructive asymmetric posture with her legs falling to the right. Sarah's mother noticed that her legs lay in the same way when she lay in bed. At this time, Sarah's parents were told that her left hip had dislocated.

## 11 YEARS OLD

Although she received physiotherapy and symmetrical positioning at school, Sarah continued to sit in the corner of the settee at home, and to be unsupported in bed at night. Sarah's shape changed so that her pelvis rotated backwards on the left and her spine and chest became asymmetric.

## 13 YEARS OLD

By the time Sarah was in her teens her body shape had flattened and twisted. It began to be very difficult for her to sit.

**Figure 2.2** Sarah's story

In order to identify the individual at risk of developing these problems it is important to look at their physical characteristics. Various methods of assessing ability and body shape have been devised: Chailey Scales of Lying and Sitting Ability (Pountney *et al.* 1990; Mulcahy *et al.* 1988); Physical Ability Scales (Hallett *et al.* 1987); and Goldsmith Index of Body Symmetry (Goldsmith *et al.* 1992).

## Body asymmetry predictors

The following table sets out four easily identifiable predictors, which may be useful to parents and others involved in care, to help find out whether there is a need for support to protect body shape. If the answer is 'yes' to any of these questions it would be advisable to seek advice from a therapist·as to whether postural management would benefit the individual.

| Body Asymmetry Indicators | Yes | No |
|---|---|---|
| Predictor 1: Does the body tend to stay in a limited number of positions? | ■ | ☐ |
| Predictor 2: Do the knees seem to be drawn to one side, or outwards, or inwards? | ■ | ☐ |
| Predictor 3: Does the head seem to turn mainly to one side? | ■ | ☐ |
| Predictor 4: Is the body shape already asymmetric? | ■ | ☐ |

**Table 2.1** Body asymmetry indicators

## Service delivery of postural care

If it is found that the individual is in need of symmetrical support to protect body shape, it is important for carers to seek advice from a therapist and to begin to plan a programmme to provide this physical care as a way of life. In time, good postural care becomes second nature to the individual and all those who care for and work with them. Organisation and training during the early stages require intensive input but, given the fact that many people with complex needs are totally physically dependent, the work involved in providing good postural care is not significantly greater than routines providing poor postural care and the long term benefits are immense. The elements required to provide this care are:

• counselling, training and support for the carer;
• provision of equipment as and when required;
• cooperation from all those who care for the individual.

## Counselling, training and support for the carer

The majority of time for an individual with PMLD is spent with the carer. As illustrated in Sarah's story, there are 8,760 hours in the year with approximately 7,620 hours spent at home (figure 2.3). The ineffectiveness of school or day care based therapy when dealing with severe disabling conditions comes as no surprise when these calculations are made. The carer therefore has to be seen as the key to provision of postural management. Serious efforts must be made to understand the situation from their point of view, developing their skills and knowledge so that they are able to monitor and adapt the regime daily in the same role as the parent of a diabetic child.

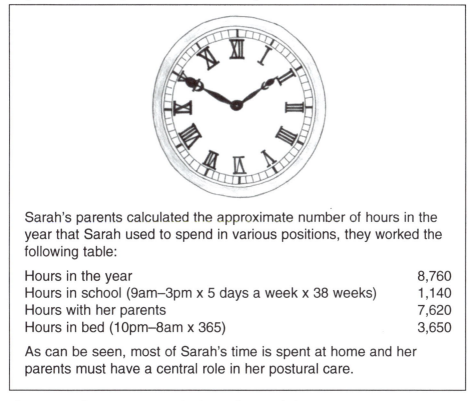

Sarah's parents calculated the approximate number of hours in the year that Sarah used to spend in various positions, they worked the following table:

| | |
|---|---:|
| Hours in the year | 8,760 |
| Hours in school (9am–3pm x 5 days a week x 38 weeks) | 1,140 |
| Hours with her parents | 7,620 |
| Hours in bed (10pm–8am x 365) | 3,650 |

As can be seen, most of Sarah's time is spent at home and her parents must have a central role in her postural care.

**Figure 2.3** The position in which Sarah spends her time

Professional carers find that the extreme dependency of the individual with PMLD predisposes to a close relationship and they often experience fierce protectiveness towards the person. Carers are in a position to know individuals much better than transitory professionals and therefore their opinion should always be sought and acted upon. However, professional carers should realise the seriousness of this responsibility and make sure that the decisions they take are in the best interests of individuals, in the light of up to date knowledge and that the longterm consequences of their actions are taken into account.

The parent's role is pivotal. They are often the main advocate, with varying degrees of success, for as long as they are able to carry out the role. Thus it is worth considering the process by which parents come to terms with the realisation that their child has profound and multiple disabilities. From the experience of high hopes felt at the birth of a child, parents have gradually to relinquish many expectations. The child will not provide them with the comfort of support in their old age, will not marry and give them grandchildren, may not be able to talk, walk, see, hear or sleep properly and in fact may not even grow into a conventional human shape. This is a hard and long emotional journey and most professionals involved will be familiar with the consequences of the strain placed on many families. A useful analysis of this process is contained in the stages of adaptation to disability as described by Hornby (1994) with observation and reporting of initial reactions of shock, denial and anger, a chronic state of sadness and loss, detachment and hopefully a reorganisation of the state of mind allowing adaptation to the situation. Hornby (1994) comments on the differences between individuals and the contrast between some families who seem able to accept the individual and their problems within a short period of time and others who never seem to progress through the stages of denial and anger.

If the parent is to be recruited as an efficient force to provide longterm postural care a supportive infrastructure must be developed. Initially this should provide a sensitive process by which they are told specifically that their child is at risk of developing an unconventional body shape. This needs to be treated as an important issue in its own right, separate from the general diagnosis. The following guidelines may be useful to ensure that this task is carried out as kindly as possible (Hornby 1994).

- Important health issues are generally discussed with a doctor.
- A planned interview should take place, both parents should be at the interview, and in the case of a single parent support should be arranged.
- It may be advantageous to include the therapist who is to coordinate care.
- The interview should be held in private and everyone involved should be sitting down.
- The parents should be given the opportunity to ask questions.
- A written summary of the issues should be supplied to be taken away by the parents.
- A follow up appointment should be made so that parents have a chance to think about the implications of what has been said and formulate further queries.

After the initial interview and discussion about the physical risks there should be:

- Longterm access to emotional care.
- A structured training programme with appropriate learning materials.
- Provision for ongoing practical help, support and encouragement.
- Assurance to parents that therapeutic input is to provide comfort and protect body shape. That by doing this we create the conditions for whatever improvements are possible but that intervention is not conditional on their son or daughter succeeding or improving and that they will continue to be supported, longterm, particularly during periods of deterioration.

## Provision of equipment as and when required

Everyone involved in this care must become sensitive to the differences between symmetrical postures and the destructive asymmetric postures that lead to painful changes in body shape. Periods of activity should be encouraged but during periods when the individual is unable to move around, for instance in the evening or during the night, equipment to provide symmetrical body support should be available, in good condition and adjusted exactly to the individual's needs. Substantial resources are already directed towards this provision including orthotics, wheelchairs, static seating and night time positioning equipment. Orthopaedic surgery also features in the efforts to maintain body shape and function. At present however, these provisions are not integrated resulting in an expensive but haphazard, and all too often unsuccessful, aspect of care. Therapists see thousands of pounds being spent on orthopaedic surgery only for the individual to go back to lack of provision of equipment and the destructive postures which contributed to the problem in the first place.

Typically, equipment is provided from a variety of sources with division of responsibility between health, education and social services. Failing these, personal funds are used and charities are frequently approached. Parents, therapists and carers battle continuously for provision of funding and the individual has to fit into the agenda of different providers rather than their needs being seen as paramount. In the future, being at risk of developing an asymmetric body shape must be seen as a medical condition in its own right which is susceptible to treatment. If progress is to be made, responsibility for coordination of this treatment must be invested in a single agency, however funded. Connections must be forged between adult and child services so that care does not stop when the child leaves school.

The model of care commonly provided by diabetic clinics may be useful for us to study so that we can learn from a well established programme which relies on parents as the main provider of care and gives a longterm commitment in response to a longterm deteriorating condition. Children with diabetes and their families receive training, equipment and support from a central source. It is not difficult to imagine the deterioration in care that would arise if a child's distressed parents had to take responsibility for discovering the best treatment, designing the care package, co-ordinating care and fighting for funds through education departments for the insulin that was to be used during school time, social services departments for the medicines to be used at home and charities for top-up funds. Termination of treatment because the child leaves school would be unthinkable.

There are many similarities between the condition of diabetes and development of asymmetric body shape in that both are lifelong conditions, susceptible to treatment and requiring skilled daily monitoring and intervention. However, the immediate negative consequences of the neglect of treatment in diabetes probably provides a natural impetus to develop services and explains their relatively advanced state.

## Cooperation from all those who care for the individual

Typically, people with PMLD are cared for by many different agencies. The family network is usually active, and schools, day opportunity services, respite care agencies and hospital admissions all contribute to day to day care. In order for a programme of postural support to be effective, all these agencies must be aware of and contribute to the regime. Coordination of this provides the therapist and main carer with a substantial challenge. The need for structured training, truthful and open communication and encouragement is vital as this has to be a team effort.

The following chart (Figure 2.4) enables the team to identify what is happening to the individual in terms of postural care both during the day and night and to plan and inform others of the support programme. The examples shown on the chart give an illustration of an excellent programme in that the individual is supported symmetrically during the majority of the twenty four hours and there are many changes of position. If the chart were to be applied to Sarah, whose story is used earlier in this chapter, the shaded squares would represent times during which Sarah's body was supported symmetrically. As she spent the majority of her time in destructive asymmetric postures, most of the chart would be left blank and the eventual result of severe structural asymmetry would have been easy to predict.

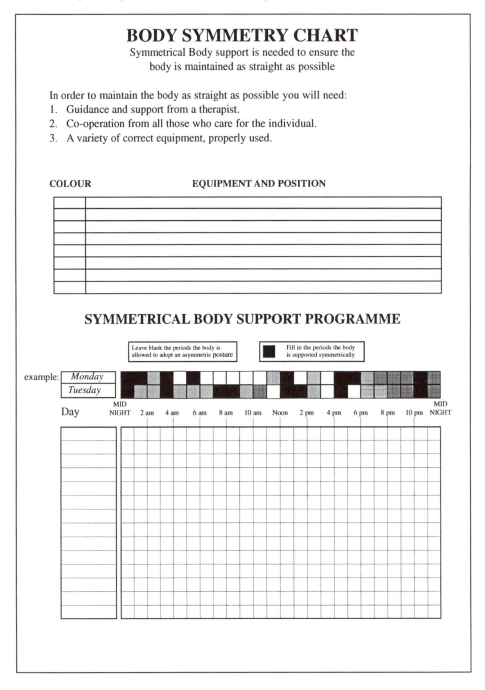

**Figure 2.4** Symmetrical body support (Goldsmith and Goldsmith 1996a and b)

# Encouraging normal sleep patterns

It has been recognised that people with multiple neurological disabilities associated with distortion of body shape often have disturbed sleep which does not respond easily to treatment. Polysomnographic evidence reveals increased obstructive apnoea, in which breathing is interrupted; decreased ability to change body position; and epileptiform discharges in the sleep of people with severe cerebral palsy (Kotagel *et al.* 1994). Circadian rhythms may also be disturbed so that the natural rhythm of sleeping at night and waking during the hours of daylight may not apply (Okawa *et al.* 1986). The behavioural approach, sedation and analgesics may be tried but are often found to be ineffective with this group (Jan *et al.* 1994). In these circumstances educationalists are presented with an exhausted individual, suffering from chronic pain and making up for lack of sleep by tending to catnap throughout the twenty four hour period. Implications for the family are even more significant with high stress levels reported as they struggle to cope with inadequate sleep on top of all the usual commitments and pressures of everyday life.

It has been found that melatonin may be helpful in the management of individuals whose main problem is interruption of circadian rhythms (Jan *et al.* 1994). Consideration of postural support is suggested as another factor which may be useful for those who are unable to control their lying posture adequately with consequent pain and damage to skeletal structure (Turrill (1992). The importance of positioning at night is recognised by therapists, as more damage to the body system is likely to arise from uncontrolled lying than uncontrolled sitting (Pope 1997). In these cases newly available equipment prescribed by therapists to protect body shape has been found in many cases to have the side effect of increasing comfort and helping individuals to sleep.

The following pictures of a little girl show how she is unable to move from a destructive asymmetric position when left unsupported but can lie relatively straight with support (Goldsmith and Goldsmith 1996a and b). Her mother, a physiotherapist, has been providing her with postural care day and night and has maintained good lung function, the ability to adopt a variety of supported sleeping positions and the ability to correct her body shape despite severe neurological problems. This personal experience has had a significant influence on the therapy service provided in their area in Mansfield, Nottinghamshire, where postural care is provided for all children at risk along with a formal training program for parents.

# Development and maintenance of function

There have been many different treatment approaches devised over the past fifty years. The uniqueness of each new approach has been stressed and, despite sometimes contradictory theoretical underpinning, success is claimed by the devotees of each approach. A common theme is apparent in many of the approaches based on physiotherapeutic principles, quality in the performance of movement becoming an important aim with more normal movement and posture as the eventual goal (Partridge 1996). Short-term goals provide impetus for those concentrating on the functional approach with more able individuals being able to build on success to achieve lasting benefits.

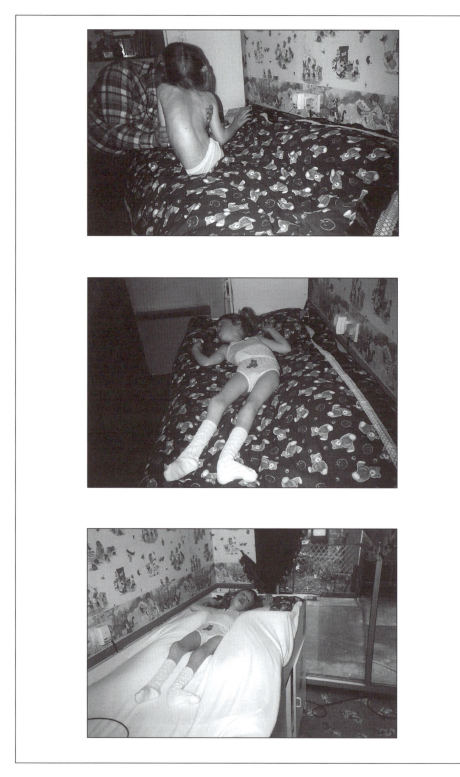

**Figure 2.5** Asymmetric sleeping positions (Goldsmith and Goldsmith 1996b)

# Locally based services

Many of the insights and skills provided by these practitioners are gathered from different approaches and incorporated into methods of handling and treatment by therapists providing physical management for people with profound problems as a locally based service to create the conditions for improvement.

# Specialist therapeutic approaches

There are specialist clinics and centres which offer a more intensive approach and adhere more rigidly to a particular philosophy. It is fundamental to many of these specialised therapeutic approaches that individuals treated enhance the reputation of the philosophy by improving in some way. If the individual is not able to fulfil this obligation the relationship is usually a short-term one. It is difficult for the person with profound and multiple disabilities to fit into a success orientated culture. As they grow older, bigger and more difficult to handle, losing the attractiveness of childhood, in spite of the fact that their needs may become more acute there is often a parting of the ways during which time both sides may experience a degree of disillusionment.

## Specific approaches

The stated aims of a selection of specific approaches are as follows:

*Conductive Education*

This approach was based on the work of Andras Peto and the Institute for Conductive Education in Budapest (Coton and Kinsman 1983). He set up a new method of teaching using a professional, a conductor, trained to deal with all the problems of the relatively able child. In Hungary the educational provision for multiply disabled children was minimal and therefore an intensive regime designed to train disabled children to walk and enable them to access conventional schooling was particularly sought after. The functional approach utilises group work, a 'task series' is worked out for each child and incorporated into a group goal. Learning is considered to be facilitated by chanting a 'rhythmical intention' so that individuals are required to chant a description of their movements as they perform tasks. The rigorous approach, combined with the necessity to make a pilgrimage, has an irresistible appeal to parents from other countries, even if their children have difficulties which are too complex to be helped by such a regime.

*Neurodevelopmental approach as advocated by Bobath*

Dr and Mrs Bobath commenced their work in the 1940s exploring the 'problems of coordination in relation to the normal postural reactions or central postural control mechanism'. Mrs Bobath's skills of astute observation and sensitive handling led her to an understanding of how to change spasticity, previously considered unalterable. These principles are widely accepted and utilised by therapists using a neuro-developmental approach. The Western Cerebral Palsy Centre was established as a charity in 1957. In 1985 it was renamed The Bobath Centre. The aim of the Bobath approach is, 'through specialised techniques of handling to give children with cerebral palsy the experience of a greater variety of coordinated movement patterns.' (Bobath Centre 1996) More recently there has been recognition 'that the approach needed to be more functional to enable carry over into daily life.' (Mayston 1992)

*British Institute for Brain Injured Children*
This Institute based in Bridgwater, Somerset was founded in 1972 and seeks to provide parents with an intensive programme which is carried out at home, often enlisting friends and neighbours to help with passive movements called 'patterning'. Claims such as 'we believe that the effects of even severe brain injury can be largely eradicated in children' are made in the literature. (British Institute for Brain Injured Children, undated). It is understandable that these unsubstantiated claims have a dramatic effect on susceptible parents and it is a matter of concern that the delicate body structures of young children are manipulated in an intensive programme by people who have little comprehension of the longterm implications of their actions.

*The Brainwave Charity*
This Centre, also based in Bridgwater but founded in 1982, would appear to have a similar philosophy to the British Institute for Brain Injured Children but recommends that therapy needs to be carried out for no more than 15 hours a week and claims to be a less intensive approach than some other comparable treatments. The unqualified claim made in the literature is 'young children who suffer various forms of brain damage often recover from their injuries' (The Brainwave Charity, undated).

*MOVE*
The MOVE Curriculum (Mobility Opportunities Via Education) was developed in the USA (MOVE International, undated). It is a 'teaching program used by teachers, therapists and carers to help learners with severe disabilities to sit, stand and walk'. The curriculum is supported by videos and clinics. This curriculum offers the advantage of structured prescription of movement activities which could help in the coordination of treatment if carefully applied. At present it is unfortunate that sales literature and techniques employed by the organisation follow the general trend with an emphasis on short-term goals and a disregard of the principles of postural care.

## Specialised physiotherapy techniques
There are many techniques to handle, mobilise and strengthen which are traditionally used within the formal clinical physiotherapy setting. An historical overview of these techniques is available as collated by Partridge (1996).

## Comparative benefits
Comparative studies of different treatment approaches have shortcomings in that it is difficult to define the approach, to control variables and collate longterm results, so that practice is not yet evidence based (Partridge 1996). Many studies report improvements, not surprisingly, when effort and skill is expended in encouraging movement. There is no doubt that there is a brisk demand for hands-on physiotherapy and that people who are able to access this service may be seen to improve at the time. It is easy to understand the beguiling nature of approaches which promise short-term improvements, particularly to those parents still struggling with the early stages of grief, shock, anger and denial in response to their child's initial diagnosis. They may go through a period during which they are immune to warnings about unsubstantiated claims and as we have little evidence to support or refute the longterm results of any regime it is important for locally based therapists to support families as they search for answers, at the same time making every effort to instil the habits required to provide postural care to protect body shape. Many therapists would agree with Scrutton (1984 ) in his view that:

The skilled handling of cerebral palsy infants can be impressive to watch and the immediate effects obvious and dramatic. Such treatments, accompanied by confidently stated longterm aims are persuasive and hard to contest. However, experience has led me to consider that however good the immediate effect, the carry-over into out of treatment life is often small (particularly after the first year of life) and the longterm outcome is by no means so impressive. Clinical experience points to the conclusion that the effective parts of treatment are those which become part of the child's life.

# General guidelines

For those responsible for the ongoing care of individuals with PMLD the often contradictory theories and advice with regard to encouraging movement can be daunting.

Given the significance of the frightening responsibility which is often placed on day to day carers, consideration of the following topics may be useful when trying to decide if a particular activity is beneficial or not:

- health status of the individual;
- degree of difficulty of the activity;
- age of the individual;
- proposed benefits of the activity.

### Health status of the individual

Consideration of the general condition of individuals should be given priority. A person needs to be healthy, well rested, well fed, emotionally secure and free from acute pain in order to take part in activity programmes with enthusiasm. Work on all these areas should be regarded as basic groundwork before additional demands are made of the individual.

### Degree of difficulty of the activity

Movements should be relatively easy for individuals to carry out and they should look relatively normal while engaged in the activity. All too often individuals are asked to perform activities which are far too difficult for them, resulting in an abnormal posture with consequent damage to body structures, the spine being particularly vulnerable. A common example of this is when children who have difficulty with head control are given insufficient head support in the mistaken hope that this will somehow help them to gain ability. Damage done to soft tissues of the oesophagus and trachea by stretching often results in difficulties with swallowing and breathing, along with interruption of sleep due to obstructive apnoea syndromes (Kotagel et al. 1994), which lasts for the rest of their lives.

### Age of the individual

The age of the individual should be taken into consideration when decisions are made about appropriate activities. When a child is young it is imperative to create the conditions which capture and encourage any natural developmental drive within that child in order to extend joint range, voluntary control and function. However, it is also natural for an individual to reduce the intensity of their physical activities as they grow older. People with complex, multiple physical problems combined with difficulty with formal communication require a particularly sensitive approach.

## Proposed benefits of the activity

The most important aims when encouraging movement are to increase independence, protect body shape and improve general health and morale. Careful consideration should be undertaken as to whether activities benefit individuals in these terms or whether the activities are being devised to gratify either the requirements of an arbitrarily imposed curriculum or the short-term emotional needs of carers or onlookers.

Table 2.2 shows a quick checklist which should be used to gauge the advisability of any proposed activities.

| ACTIVITY LIST |
|---|
| **Is the individual:** |

| | | |
|---|---|---|
| well enough? | rested enough? | willing enough? |
| comfortable enough? | old enough? | young enough? |

**Is the activity:**

| | |
|---|---|
| easy enough? | promoting a normal, symmetrical body shape? |

**Table 2.2** Activity Checklist

Although there is no objective right answer to any of these questions, if a carefully considered, sympathetic reply is 'yes' to all these questions it is likely that the person will benefit from the proposed activity. If the answer is 'no' to any of the questions, alternative, more suitable activities should be considered and any personnel involved should be prepared to explain and defend their opinion as individuals have to live with the damage done by inappropriate activities for the rest of their lives.

# Conclusion

Therapeutic physical management should comprise a two pronged attack with postural care to protect body structures being regarded as fundamental, on top of which is built development and maintenance of function. A collaborative multidisciplinary approach must form the essence of any attempt to help those with multiple and complex problems. Hands-on carers should occupy the central role with professionals listening more than talking, offering support, friendship and encouragement, teaching, discussing and giving advice, planning, providing equipment and coordinating intervention. These services should be integrated by a single agency and be locally based so that individuals can receive the care they need in the context of a family group which is able to function as normally as possible.

# Chapter 3

# Sensory Needs

*Norman Brown, Mike McLinden and Jill Porter*

## Introduction

Within the wide and complex range of needs covered by the term profound and multiple learning difficulties (PMLD) the significance of sensory needs can easily be overlooked.

Sensory needs can be described at a number of levels. At one level they are the needs arising directly from a difference, loss or reduction in sensory function; for example, a visual or hearing impairment. There are, additionally, needs which arise more indirectly from sensory impairment. Thus the reassurance through touch an individual with reduced vision and hearing may seek from others when attempting independent mobility in a new environment can in itself create quite distinct needs. Awareness of this range of sensory needs will require consideration of appropriate settings and resources to meet the needs, and will help inform *how, what, where* and with *whom* an individual is able to learn.

The aim of this chapter is to increase staff awareness of the importance of meeting sensory needs and to introduce a number of guiding principles in considering sensory function, structuring the learning environment and working collaboratively with parents, professionals and the learner, in order to address the needs of learners within the population. For a more detailed discussion the reader is encouraged to seek out additional resources and to turn to specialist colleagues.

## Sensory function

Information received through the senses can be considered as the basis for an individual's learning about and acquiring a conceptual understanding of the properties of the physical world (Warren 1994). The concept of sensory function can be used to describe how an individual uses this information to carry out activities in everyday situations. Sensory function is a deceptively complex notion, however, and will be influenced by a wide variety of factors. Prior to considering these factors it will be useful briefly to review the role of the senses in receiving and processing sensory input.

## The role of the senses

It is through our senses that we have contact with, and come to know about, the physical world (Warren 1994). In this process, we often think of five classes of sensations, those of touch, vision, taste, smell and hearing, each of which is directly related to the functions of specific sense organs, skin, eyes, mouth, nose and ears. However, this rather simplistic description does not match the complex process by which the body actually receives and processes the range of sensory input and interprets it as sensory information. For example, seven major types of sensory input to the brain have been identified: visual, tactile, vestibular, proprioceptive, auditory, olfactory, and gustatory (Rosen 1997). Additionally, sensory input to the homeostatic system can also be considered. This particular input relates to maintenance of internal equilibrium within the body and provides, for example, information which prevents overheating or chilling of the body temperature (Bartley 1980), but it also plays a more subtle role in enabling us to retain our equilibrium when faced with stress and anxiety, or even lack of sensation.

For the purposes of this discussion, a broad distinction can be made between two main types of sensory input:

- External sensory input received from environmental features, such as light reflected from an object which provides information relating to shape, size, colour, etc.
- Internal sensory input received from within the body system, such as proprioceptive input which provides information about the body's position in space.

External sensory input can be further divided into that received from a distance, for example sounds and light, and that received at close proximity, for example through tactile stimulation of the skin. When considering sensory function, a useful, although somewhat simplistic, distinction is commonly made therefore between the 'distance' senses of hearing, vision and smell, and the 'close' senses of touch and taste.

## Early development of sensory function

For individuals with no sensory impairment, the two dominant modalities for perception of sensory input external to the body are vision and hearing (Bartley 1980). Developing infants however can be observed responding more readily to sensory experiences that are close to their body space, suggesting that their 'close' senses, that is touch and taste along with smell, are more developed at this early stage than their distance senses. Bower (1977, 1979) proposed that there was little differentiation between the senses at birth and outlined a theory based on a 'primitive unity' of senses. Within this theory it was suggested that with limited distinction between information received through different sensory modalities, visual, auditory and tactual information was not treated as being separate. The very young infant was not aware therefore whether he or she was seeing something or hearing something in response to particular sensory stimulation (Barraga 1986).

As the infant develops there is clear evidence of differentiation of sensory input, and studies of infants during their first year of life highlight significant developments in the ability of the infant to use hearing and vision as separate modalities. By four to five months vision may be used as the initial modality of exploration, replacing to a large extent oral contact (Rochat 1989), and with significant control over hand activity (Warren 1982).

Understanding the various factors that influence sensory function at a particular stage in development can be important in helping to interpret how an individual may be using his or her senses in functional contexts. These factors can be broadly grouped as either 'internal' or 'external' to the learner (Aitken and Buultjens 1992). Internal factors relate to personal aspects of the learner and will be influenced by a variety of factors including level of development, general health, motivation, level of arousal, previous experience. External factors or settings relate to various settings or environments in which a learner is found. These factors include lighting, body position, background noise, etc. As we will discuss more fully later, observation of individual sensory function during an activity will need to consider carefully how these personal aspects relate to particular settings. This interpretation can be aided by providing those who work with learners in the population with opportunities to explore the use of their own sensory repertoire.

As an example, imagine you are asleep in a dark room and are awakened by an unfamiliar sound outside your bedroom window. You assume that the noise was made by a cat knocking over a garden ornament. How easy in this situation is it to interpret, what the sound is, where it is coming from, how the sound was made, and then use this information to inform your next course of action, either to ignore the sound and go back to sleep, or else to act on it?

Now compare this scenario with one experienced when your hearing has been distorted but your vision remains unaffected. You may be relaxing in a bath with the water covering your ears and your eyes closed. You hear a muffled crashing sound and open your eyes just in time to see your cat running out of the room. An empty cup lies broken on the floor. Although the sound that alerted you was distorted, and you missed the beginning of this action sequence, you are not unduly worried. You are able to use the visual information available to you to work out exactly what happened and reassure yourself. In this situation you decide there is no immediate need to act, you close your eyes and continue with your relaxing bath!

This very simple example serves to illustrate not only the different quality of distance information that we rely on in our own everyday functioning, but also our own role in alerting to, receiving and organising this information and then selecting an adaptive response based on this information. Additionally it highlights an equally important and perhaps often neglected role of distance information, namely its impact on our own feeling of security and well being in a particular environment. Of significance in this example therefore might be not just the noises and sights which alerted you, but the constant reassurance beforehand from the normality of input that there was nothing to worry about. This last consideration is of enormous importance when considering learners with PMLD who have sensory impairments.

A key factor in each of these situations of course is access to accurate sensory information which can be used to inform your next course of action, i.e. determine an adaptive response. When this information is reduced however, in either *quantity* or *quality*, the world can become altogether a less secure place. In the first situation you would have been alerted by auditory input. Despite your initial adaptive response to the sound, that is opening your eyes, it was too dark to utilise visual information. To acquire this additional sensory input would have meant taking further action, such as shining a torch outside.

Before reading on it might be useful to reflect briefly on possible parallel situations which learners with significant sensory impairments may experience in the course of their everyday activities. Are there any situations for example when a learner may hear an unfamiliar sound at a distance, such as somebody walking into a room, but as a result of a visual impairment or inability to turn is unable to supplement this information with accurate visual information? What additional sensory information might this learner require access to in order for him or her to begin making sense of what was heard? How might this additional sensory information be presented, using both the distance and close senses, to the learner in a way that is appropriate to his or her level of sensory functioning? And what might be expected of the learner if no additional information is forthcoming?

In many tasks of course it will be difficult to make a clear distinction between sensory input received through our distance and close receptors, and usually in carrying out everyday activities we do not need to pay attention to how this information is integrated.

It has already been noted that from an early age, vision serves to coordinate or integrate the mass of sensory information and as such is considered as a unifying sense. Accurate visual information allows us to make sense of events in the world, link cause and effect and anticipate what is about to happen next. When we are faced with a situation where accurate visual information is not readily available however, it is still possible for us to structure the situation, and make use of particular 'compensatory' strategies.

Consider the experience of Jacky, a young woman with profound and multiple disabilities, when presented with an ice-lolly. Jacky has multi-sensory impairment which severely limits the quantity and quality of information available through her vision and hearing. In addition she has limited motor control of her arms and is totally dependent on others for feeding. Jacky is more reliant therefore on information from the environment received through her close senses. The following case study describes how a learning sequence was structured to maximise sensory information presented to her at close proximity to provide her with opportunities to begin to anticipate what is about to be presented to her.

> Prior to presenting her with an ice-lolly Jacky's support worker spends some time exploring with her its range of sensory qualities. The ice-lolly, still in its wrapper, is placed in the palm of each hand for tactual exploration. It is gently rolled over the palm and the back of the hand. The lolly is placed close to Jacky's lips to provide her with opportunities to feel the cold air around the wrapper. It is unwrapped very close to her lips so that she is provided with an opportunity to feel the cooler air around the lolly as the wrapper is taken off. The tip of the lolly is first placed near to her lips and then gently brought onto her lips. As Jacky begins to make sucking movements the ice-lolly is placed into her mouth.

We are aware from our own experiences, of the unique way sensory input is received and interpreted, providing us with a very personal perspective of an event. When working with individuals with significant learning difficulties gaining access to introspective information can be limited. We can go a little way towards understanding their perspective through simulation activities, but we can never really understand exactly how they interpret the world. For Jacky's teacher, determining Jacky's sensory function will be more dependent on interpretation of behavioural responses to particular sensory stimuli, such as smiling when the cold ice-lolly is rubbed on the back of her hand. Jacky's responses to sensory stimuli may be so limited by her disability, however, that an unfamiliar observer might misinterpret or miss them altogether. Attention to detail and the knowledge that comes from familiarity is vital when working with learners such as Jacky. Video recordings can be used to focus on the tiny reactions or expressions of a learner that might be missed in 'real time' and allows others to assist in understanding how a learner is interpreting his or her world in a particular situation.

# Being understood

Realising that a learner has such limited or distorted information to process, regardless of processing ability, immediately focuses attention on communication. In concentrating upon making our communication meaningful and looking for evidence that it is understood, we may forget that our main responsibility is to ensure that the learner is understood, and that he or she realises it. Attention is increasingly being given to fostering and engaging in activities with learners which are similar to the early exchanges between mother and baby, and which build up enjoyable, often music-like dialogues or duets, giving understanding of turn-taking and reciprocity that underlies communication. Such an approach is especially useful where such learning will not take place incidentally and where the temptation is always to be directive.

The necessary concentration on the learner in order to encourage and extend these exchanges is also likely to make us aware that the learner has in fact a number of expressive actions of which we may have been unaware, and that before we can be understood we have to be understanding. Attempts to impose our chosen means of communicating may succeed only in teaching responses to particular stimuli. True conversations come from shared meanings and modes, or put another way, we need to 'make sense of how an individual is making sense of world' before we can help expand that knowledge.

# Significance of the environment

When distance senses are impaired, the more immediate environment increases in significance. Its effects are increased because the wider context cannot be so easily apprehended, altered or allowed for by personal initiative or understanding. The constant struggle by those involved with learners who have sensory impairments is to make the environment meaningful, which usually entails simplifying or adapting it in some way. It may be argued that the natural environment is unpredictable and therefore we should not teach in an adapted environment. However, it is easy to overlook both the established conventions by which we organise and signpost the world, and also how we have come to interpret it. For example, we assume that we shall probably be able to make sense of any new building we enter, and might become angry and distressed if we cannot gain information from anything inside. If an interior designer disguised the access to the toilets or refused to allow any signs of their whereabouts, we should take it as unnatural and an offence.

The learner with impairment of the distance senses is denied this way of learning or has it severely restricted. The environment, therefore, for anyone who cannot learn incidentally, by independent experience, by observation or by overhearing the experience and opinions of others, is much more than physical surroundings; it encompasses the physical environment of objects and places but also includes the social environment of people and events.

We therefore have to think in terms of what is sure and reliable, and what can therefore become understandable and eventually manageable. In terms of the physical environment, much has been learned about how to create visual distinction and clarity by using colour contrast, borders and edging, by paying attention to lighting, positioning, troublesome reflection and glare. (A useful overview can be found in Best 1992.) Much less attention is generally paid to creating acoustically meaningful surroundings with sound absorbing surfaces, and the muffling or removal of incidental sound sources such as chair legs, banging doors, or idle chatter. Many learners in fact learn to ignore sounds because they cannot make sense of them all. (A useful overview can be found in Rikhye *et al.*, 1989.)

With respect to other senses, attention is sometimes paid by deliberately addressing them, as in using massage, aromatic oils and scents, novel tastes and exercises, but little attention is generally paid to the information being drawn from the 'close' senses on a regular basis. Smells can be very evocative and it should be no surprise for a learner to be fearful of entering a building in which you have planned for 'good things' to happen, if that building smells like the hospital where the learner had painful experiences. Before we can refine a particular learner's environment, we need to learn what is significant for that learner — how the environment already communicates to that learner. The choice of disinfectant in this instance may be more significant than the teacher's programme!

Particular difficulties arise where the physical environment for a learner with sensory impairments has to be shared with others who do not have those impairments. The challenge for many teachers is to bring to the learner as much expertise, consistency and appropriateness of environment and curriculum as can be brought to a setting designed for other needs. Adaptations made to improve the visual and acoustic environment can benefit all, including individuals without sensory impairment. It is the necessary change within those environments and the numbers of people within those environments which present the challenge. As the scenario outlined earlier in the chapter highlighted, the situation of a learner with impaired distance senses can be full of anxieties. It is hard for example, to be sure of where everything is if some things are moved, to relax if people keep appearing and disappearing without warning or reason, to feel secure if you do not know what is going on around you. A multi-purpose room or even a normal lively classroom will not be an optimal learning environment for someone with impairment of the distance senses, except to learn that the world is chaotic, unreliable and a potential threat. In such a situation, exploration can become a very risky business and it may seem safer to retreat within yourself and stay there or to put up a barrier of intense or stereotypic activity.

Since we as educators cannot always manage the physical environment for maximum benefit we must take pains to bring to the attention of our learners those parts of it upon which they can rely, the parts of the room or items of furniture that do not move, the landmarks and pointers along their journeys that are permanent, the places where they are safe, the things that are theirs. We must make sure that certain areas at certain times are set up for their maximum benefit, distraction-free and playing to their strengths, and in which we can give them our undivided attention.

Overwhelmingly, for most learners with PMLD and sensory impairments, the most important part of the environment will be the people in contact with them at a particular time. If that is us, then we must ensure that we are safe, consistent, responsive, communi- cative, motivating and fun to be with, or at least part of a 'pleasurable' experience.

We shall need to rely upon personal contact, so we must be aware of the power of touch; that 'normally' personal touch is rarely used on another person without permission, that the learner may be able to find out more about us from the way we touch than can be gained through vision or hearing, that invasion of another person's close personal space can be very threatening, that touch should never be given suddenly or unannounced unless safety demands it.

Such close contact can be enormously reassuring and motivating and we will want to ensure that every time the learner realises who it is making contact, he or she is relieved, excited or at least secure enough to be open to learning. In the chaotic world of puzzlement and powerlessness created by PMLD and sensory impairment, we as trusted individuals can help the learner to make sense of his or her world, pointing out significance, mediating sensations, understanding expressions, protecting from overload and enabling achievement.

We can also develop other skills and awareness. In order to work effectively, we will need to pay close attention to detail, looking for, responding to and trying to make sense of any expression from the learner, intended or not. We must pay great attention to the learner's emotional as well as physical state, we must allow time for the processing of what we are presenting and must await and look for the response. We must respect the learner's space and be prepared to pause or allow a break in what we are so eager to achieve. In fact, one of the most helpful signs or words we can teach the learner is one for 'wait/pause' or 'give me a break', so that the learner can use it to control the pace and tempo of our interaction.

We can begin by thinking about how we introduce ourselves, not only when we first meet but after every disappearance, however briefly, to fetch something or attend to someone else. Think of the care taken to introduce an ice-lolly to Jacky and compare this with the way a person is introduced or introduces him or herself to a learner with PMLD. Although the person may be recognised by his or her smell, voice or other distinctive attribute, it can be invaluable to have a personal and more consistent symbol, often a distinctive bracelet, as an identification symbol. More details of this kind of approach can be found in studies of multi-sensory impairment (e.g. Nafstad 1989; Visser 1988).

# The need for a collaborative approach

As we have seen, the learner with additional sensory impairment provides the teacher with a complex picture from which to unravel particular strengths and needs. There is a danger that a learner's lack of response is taken as a sign of their profound learning difficulty rather than raising questions about his or her ability to see and hear. Inconsistent responding may be interpreted that the learner is 'off colour', whereas in fact, the variations in his or her behaviour may reflect the differences in the way materials are presented or people interact. It is likely therefore that staff will need to build up a picture over time of the learner's abilities and disabilities and to do this they will need to call on the experiences and skills of others. As Best (1997) has stated 'Each professional involved with the child must think of themselves as part of the team supporting that child. No person will have all the answers to all the challenges presented by a child: they should feel dependent on colleagues.' (p.377)

An important task for staff is to locate all the sources of expertise who can help contribute a piece of the jigsaw. We can make a distinction between those who have regular contact with the person with PMLD and those who might be involved 'as needed' (Sobsey and Wolf-Schein 1996). For children, these may include:

- audiologist;
- optometrist or orthoptist;

- a specialist advisory teacher for pupils with a visual or hearing impairment, or those with a multisensory impairment;
- regional (or national) branch of voluntary associations for people with a sensory or multisensory impairment;
- nearest special school or service for pupils with a sensory impairment.

In some instances these professionals will not be experienced with learners with PMLD but they will still have important knowledge about the use and development of the senses, sources of aids and equipment. It may be inappropriate to consult these professionals as the 'expert' who will be able to provide all the answers. However, providing opportunities for joint problem solving, their knowledge, together with the teacher's own experience, can lead to new insights into the learner's needs.

The picture, however, would remain fragmented without the knowledge and understanding of caregivers, family members and paraprofessionals. Indeed, all those who come into regular contact with the learner have vital pieces of information about the ways in which he or she responds in different situations. Contexts will differ in relation to their physical properties, the ways in which sound, light, temperature and tactile clues are provided. Additionally, the people will have different social roles and therefore different relationships and styles of interaction, thereby responding to and providing different cues to the learner. Together, insights can be gained into learners' understanding of the world, their responses to sensory input, their interests, ways of communicating and the 'topics' on which they like to communicate. If we take the example of bus guides, they may be significant people in a learner's life, having regular contact, forming an important link between home and school or centre. They may have observed how the learner responds to changes in light, to contact with peers, the point at which anticipation is shown that home is near, how the learner demonstrates recognition of the family, the point at which those responses are shown. This information may provide vital clues for staff to explore further.

Whilst a whole host of people may have valuable information, unless this is systematically investigated, details of the learner's responses may be undiscovered. An important first step is to recognise and value the contribution of others and to think of ways in which this positive regard can be conveyed to them. However frequently (or infrequently) they are seen, it is important to establish a dialogue. An important element of this is to recognise both the need to listen and to understand (Lacey and Lomas 1993). Information needs to be both given and received using a form of language that both parties find accessible, in a medium in which they are comfortable. Whilst 'conversations' may be spur of the moment, it is important for staff to be clear about what each party would like to know, otherwise important opportunities may be lost, perhaps for ever. This does not, however, necessarily mean giving a list of questions to be answered (both parent and professional may find this rather daunting). Volunteering information, for example a learner's interests and reactions that have been noted in the classroom, can be the start to a useful dialogue about that learner's responses in a number of different situations.

# Assessment

If teachers are to maximise learning opportunities, it is vital that they and other staff know the conditions in which each learner responds best to sensory stimuli. An essential element is therefore the assessment process. A recent project with children with both hearing and visual impairments revealed that many teachers feel uncertain about their pupils' use of these senses (Porte, *et al.* 1997). This is understandable given the uncertainty of many of the measures used and the difficulty of interpreting the results (McCraken 1994).

Assessment measures have been largely developed for use with infants following a normal pattern of development and therefore demand time, considerable patience and more than a little ingenuity before there can be any confidence in the results for people with learning disabilities, including sensory impairment. For example, a learner with a visual difficulty may not turn towards a source of sound, not because the sound has not been heard but because there is little incentive to do so (Murdoch 1994). Typically also, a learner's responses may be delayed. Murdoch (1994) describes how a case study child blinked in response to sound but smiled some five to ten seconds later. Even assessment methods based on measuring electrical responses in the brain to stimulation which require no active response from the learner provide results which are easy to misinterpret (McCraken 1994). Those based on operant methods, such as rewarding the learner for responding to auditory or visual stimulation may be inappropriate given the learner's profound learning difficulty and, in many cases, additional motor difficulties. A useful review of assessment procedures can be found in Coninx and Moore (1997) in relation to assessing hearing and in Erin (1996) for visual assessment of children with multiple disability.

Clinical information will help to establish a starting place; however, more meaningful measures can result from a functional assessment of the way the learner uses vision in everyday life (Buultjens 1997). In this way staff can determine how the person with PMLD responds to meaningful or preferred stimuli, including naturally occurring reinforcers such as sound or appearance of a favourite person or object. Three key questions are:

- What equipment/activities/people does the learner show an interest in?
- What senses do they stimulate?
- Under what conditions, or in what context does the learner respond?

A functional assessment involves the collection of information in relation to both 'input' and 'output'. We need therefore to keep a record of the characteristics of the sensory *input* and the *nature of the response* ( i.e. the output). In relation to sound we need to be aware of whether learners responded to loud or quiet, high or low pitched sounds (i.e. the frequency), the direction from which they were presented and whether there was background noise or not. In relation to vision we need to be aware of the complexity of the visual information, the brightness or intensity of the sensory input, the size, distance and direction in which the stimulus was presented to the learner, the lighting conditions and the presence of other cues, such as sound or smell which might have helped the learner orientate him or herself towards it.

An important distinction has been made about the type of response a learner makes. The response to particular sensory information not only reveals his or her 'reception' of this information, the fact that his or her senses have detected it, but also his or her cognitive understanding of what the information provides. Buultjens (1997), for example, lists five categories of response with reference to vision:

- Awareness (something has changed or happened)
- Attending
- Localising

- Recognising
- Understanding

These five levels underpin the useful guide to assessment *Vision for Doing* (Aitken and Buultjens 1992). We can, however, apply these categories to the way learners use other senses. The learner at an awareness level could show a simple 'startle' response; he or she might blink or show a different breathing pattern. Attention may be revealed by the learner 'stilling' to listen, decreasing or increasing vocalising etc. Localisation occurs when the learner can identify where the stimulus came from. Here posture and motor control is particularly important as it will determine whether learners are able to turn their eyes or heads, or move their limbs towards a source of stimulation. Recognition may be revealed by selective responding to particular stimuli, for sound, for example, a particular voice or music. Understanding may be revealed by the ability to relate particular stimuli to particular events and thus show anticipatory behaviour, for example, lunchtime sounds or smells may be responded to by swallowing. What may need careful analysis is the particular sensory stimulus being responded to, whether, for instance it is sound, smell, vibration or the particular combination of them all.

If we further consider these levels we can see that it is likely that the learner will respond to the familiar at higher levels than to unfamiliar or novel sensory input. With regard to responses, we also need to make a note of the speed of responding and the delay in starting to respond. Additionally we might wish to make a note of other factors, for example the learner's general level of wellbeing, or arousal, and other aspects such as changes resulting from new or different sleep patterns, changes in medication which might impact on perception and attention. What can be seen is that any form of assessment needs to be part of an ongoing process which incorporates information from a range of sources. Considering the many subtle but significant influences that may be in play at any one time, it is such assessment that can give us anything like a reliable judgement of a learner's potential.

# Conclusion

Learners with sensory impairments will have the same needs as all learners but will be unable to receive as much undistorted information as thoses whose senses are intact. Studies of young typically developing infants point to the shift from reliance on the 'close senses' of taste and touch to distance senses of sight and hearing. They also learn to distinguish between input through different modalities. Throughout the chapter we have drawn attention to the concept of sensory function — how the learner uses sensory information in their everyday life. Interpretation of a learner's response is the responsibility of all professionals involved with the learner, as each has unique opportunities to make observations that will help them to understand the learner's experiences. An important task for staff is to ensure that both the physical and social environment is structured in a way that will build on these experiences and promote an understanding of the world, one that is safe, consistent, interactive, fun and responsive to the learner. The question often is not *what* should I do with a learner, but rather *how* can I do it, and *who* shall I do it with? It is hoped that in this chapter we have given you some ideas to explore and some avenues for further study.

# Chapter 4

# Personal Needs and Independence

*Jenny Miller*

One of my most vivid working memories is the expression on the face of Joe, a forty six year old man with multiple disabilities, feeding himself for the very first time in his life. I realise now that it was not just the emotional experience of having facilitated this first time experience for Joe that made it so memorable, but the fact that it reflected all the facets that contribute to client-centred and collaborative multidisciplinary practice.

Joe had been fortunate enough to be able to communicate his needs and desires effectively with the help of a communication system. I had worked alongside the speech and language therapist, the physiotherapist and the seating engineers, and together with Joe we positioned him, provided splinting to enable him to use adapted eating utensils and carried out training to enable him to eat independently.

The desire to be independent at mealtimes was obviously a strong motivating factor for Joe, the look of triumph exhibited on his face that day highlighted this. Most of us wish to have some control over our personal independence, why should this be different for a person with profound and multiple learning disabilities (PMLD)?

As human beings we all have an innate desire to occupy our time. The occupations which we choose are all very personal and what may be important to one person is not necessarily important to another. These occupations can be broadly divided into *self-care*, (e.g. personal care) *productivity*, (e.g. paid/unpaid work, household management or school) and *leisure*. A range of physical, mental and social skills is needed in order to engage in these areas. The environment in which the individual lives, works and plays must provide support to enable her or him to acquire and maintain these skills and to support the desired occupations (Canadian Association of Occupational Therapists 1991).

In his *Model of Human Occupation*, Keilhofner (1995) defines human occupation as 'the action or doing through which humans occupy their world'. He, too, describes three general areas of occupation: doing culturally meaningful *work, play* or *daily living tasks* in the stream of time and in the contexts of one's physical and social world. This model provides a framework within which appropriate physical, social and psychological approaches can be used.

The importance of finding the volitional force behind any individual is the key to motivation and development of skills. Keilhofner (1995) defines volition as 'being what one holds as important, how effective one is in acting in the world and what one finds as satisfying and enjoyable.' Discovering this force within a person with PMLD can be extremely difficult and is likely to require the collaboration of all those who are a part of that person's life in order find out what is enjoyable and motivating to him or her. It requires the people involved to have an open mind and not to place their own values on others.

If people are asked what parts of their life they would most miss if they suddenly acquired a disability, they would give a wide variety of responses. However, they are likely to reflect the areas mentioned above: self-care, where the loss of being able to eat, wash or use the toilet independently would be greatly missed; productivity, not being able to go out to work or have a role as family provider or carer; and leisure, not being able to read a book, listen to music, go out for a drink with friends or to drive the car.

These responses are the foundation of a person-centred approach and they should always be borne in mind when planning for people with PMLD. If they are ignored a person's potential may never be realised, as activities or occupations which are not motivating or desired by the individual are likely to result in very limited response, or no response at all. Alternatively, the person with PMLD may use up so much time or energy in one activity that there is little left for any other area of their life.

For example, Campbell (1994) describes how a woman with a physical disability has been given so much assistance and equipment to make her independent in her daily living skills that she is 'incarcerated' in her own home. These activities take up her whole day and do not allow her to go out and socialise, an activity which had been of extreme value and importance to her.

On a similar note, it was a brave special needs teacher, whose own child had PMLD, who dared to contradict the professionals by not following the eating programme at home. She felt that by the time she and the family were in from school or work, time was so precious that she and her son had to prioritise the most important activities for them. These priorities were not self-feeding but enjoying a range of leisure pursuits.

Developing effective ways of communicating and participating in a whole range of activities and occupations are essential to enable the person with PMLD to take informed decisions and to make them known to others. In the following sections of the chapter these themes of communication and occupation will be discussed in the context of personal activities of daily living, and practical methods of supporting this aspect of personal independence will be explored.

# Personal activities of daily living

Activities of daily living refer to self-care and related tasks of daily life necessary for a person to maintain him or herself in the everyday environment. The development of any degree of independence within this aspect of life is very much dependent upon the functional skills of the individual. Peck and Hong (1988) suggest that these skills fall into three levels: basic, intermediate and advanced. Basic living skills are those which are necessary to use the body to make needs known and to learn, and it is on this level that this chapter will focus. Physical skills (including hand function) and mobility, sensory understanding and communication are the basis of personal daily living skills. A number of these themes are discussed in depth in other chapters in this volume, and will not be elaborated upon here. (See Bradley, H. on Communication; Brown, McLinden and Porter on Sensory Needs; Goldsmith and Goldsmith on Physical Management.)

Involving the person with PMLD in personal activities of daily living may mean assisting the individual to gain complete independence with the provision of equipment and/or training; or it may enable control of a small component of the activity, for example choosing the fragrance of bubble bath that will be used. It is about accessing the appropriate equipment, advice or training in order to allow a person with PMLD to have as much control as possible over their personal activities of daily living. But it is also about developing a means to ascertain whether or not that individual wants to spend the time and effort in developing independent skills.

## Physical skills and mobility

Good physical management is essential for active participation in all areas of daily living. Two aspects are particularly important to consider: firstly, positioning which is an essential prerequisite for optimum functional ability; secondly, independent mobility, which opens up a whole range of opportunities to a person with PMLD. It allows him or her to pursue interests, wishes and desires and just as importantly, it gives that person the opportunity to opt out by removing themselves from a situation.

### Positioning

Naturally positioning will vary according to the activity being performed although a sitting position is usually best for most activities of daily living. However, other positions such as lying or standing in a standing frame may be more suitable for some individuals or occupations. Goldsmith and Goldsmith in this volume stress the importance of good positioning and adequate support both to maintain body shape, and to enable the person to concentrate effort on the activities which are important for him or her.

The positioning of the person helping the individual with PMLD is also important as incorrect positioning may encourage unwanted reflexes or patterns of movement. Generally, the most appropriate positions for the helper are either face to face, which promotes symmetry and eye contact or behind the individual, which allows for physical facilitation of movement patterns and also removes distractions.

Finding the best position will involve close collaboration between the professionals who have technical knowledge about physical management and equipment (the physiotherapist, occupational therapist, speech and language therapist and the seating engineers); the person with PMLD, in order to ensure that the position is comfortable and desired; and the people who support the person in his or her everyday life (carers, teachers, occupational centre staff, volunteers, for example). Close collaboration between all these people will ensure that positioning is appropriate for each individual in his or her occupation and activities throughout the day.

### Mobility

There are devices on the market which can increase the individual's physical independence and can also provide those with visual disabilities the opportunity to experience independent mobility. A thorough assessment of mobility needs and training will need to be carried out by the team. This will include an evaluation of the mobility requirements of the person and the type of control required in order to operate a mobility aid. The needs of the person with PMLD and their carer is of paramount importance, for example the needs within a work or everyday environment may be quite different from the needs within the home or leisure situation.

Provision of specialist equipment for positioning and mobility, along with adaptations and specific programmes will assist physical function, prevent contractures, minimise abnormal reflexes and reactions, and facilitate independence.

A single chapter does not allow discussion of all areas of daily living in detail. In the next section, two different areas are used to illustrate the main aspects to be taken into consideration in developing a plan for helping an individual with PMLD to gain greater independence. The two areas selected are activities which take place daily in all everyday settings. Family and practitioners at home and in daytime services are therefore likely to be involved in both activities.

Discussion of each activity will show the importance of that particular area in everyday personal life and also identify:

- the specific difficulties which may be encountered in each area;
- the techniques and strategies which can help towards independence;
- the equipment which can be used to alleviate difficulties and promote independence;
- ways of involving the person with PMLD in the activity.

## Eating and drinking

One of the most sociable activities is that of eating and drinking and for most people mealtimes are pleasurable and enjoyable experiences. However, for people who are unable to feed themselves it can be a distressing and miserable experience, often leading to isolation and, if not treated sensitively, to humiliation.

For many people with PMLD the complex problems associated with eating and drinking will require the involvement of a multidisciplinary team. The professionals involved will include speech and language therapists, occupational therapists and physiotherapists, and may also include dieticians, surgeons, consultants or paediatricians and clinical psychologists. But the most crucial members of the team are those who are involved in the eating and drinking process on a daily basis – the person with PMLD and his or her carers, teachers and mealtime helpers.

The development of functional skills may range from being able to take food from a spoon to being able to eat independently, and will very much depend on the person's acquired physical, sensory and communicative skills, as well as the nature of his or her disability. It will also depend on the significance of this area of daily living to this individual and whether or not he or she is motivated to develop these skills. Hewett, in this volume, points out that for some people with PMLD mealtimes may be a precious time when they enjoy a close relationship with their helper. Both may see this as an important part of the helper's role and to change this pattern because it is seen to be a development area for the person with PMLD may not necessarily be appropriate. For Joe, mentioned at the beginning of the chapter, it was appropriate as he had been able to express that desire, but it is important to ascertain the wishes of people with PMLD even if they have limited communication skills.

### Specific difficulties

A person with PMLD may experience any of the difficulties listed below, in various combinations. Any one of them will make eating or drinking more difficult, and may turn what should be a pleasurable experience into a struggle, or something to be endured. Common difficulties include:

- primitive reflexes such as bite or gag reflex;
- tongue thrust;
- swallowing difficulties;
- affected facial muscles;
- poor lip and/or tongue control;

- excessive drooling;
- sensory impairment;
- reinforced and learnt behaviours and roles;
- communication difficulties;
- limited physical ability, in particular limited upper limb function.

## Techniques and strategies

Clearly, mealtimes will be more enjoyable if these problems are alleviated, and appropriate methods will be suggested by a member of the interdisciplinary team following assessment. These may include:

- inhibiting *bite* and *gag reflexes* by the development of effective chewing and swallowing. The speech and language therapist will work with both the person with PMLD and those involved at meal and snack times. Bone or plastic coated spoons are advisable during eating if these reflexes are present.
- the use of thickened liquids such as thick milk shakes or custard in an attempt to stimulate the *swallow reflex*. Fluids are difficult to control orally as they do not stimulate this reflex and often leak from the mouth.
- controlling *tongue thrust* by applying gentle pressure on the front of the tongue with the spoon or cup. This encourages the tongue downwards and backwards and the food or drink can then be released. A cup with a spout may help with drinking.
- a programme of specific facial desensitising or proprioceptive neuromuscular facilitation (PNF) prior to eating which will assist those who have *affected facial muscles*. These techniques stimulate the narrow blood vessels underneath the surface of the skin in order to relax or tense the muscles depending on the outcome required. If the person with PMLD has flaccid (floppy) facial muscle tone, rapid stimulation will be used, whereas for spastic (stiff) muscle tone slow, firm movements are used. Special techniques using brushing or icing are also used and the speech and language therapist will advise and implement such programmes if and when necessary.
- encouraging *lip and tongue control* by using a small spoon in the early stages to encourage the individual to take the food from the spoon using the upper lip. Chewing can be encouraged by placing small pieces of food on alternate sides of the mouth and stimulating the chew reflex by physical stimulation and jaw control. This involves the application of pressure in a circular movement to the cheek muscles in order to stimulate lateral chewing. The correct positioning of the helper's hand on the lower jaw provides support and control (McCurtin 1997).

The texture of the food is important in the eating process. Frequently the food provided for people with eating difficulties has a smooth, runny texture. This does not encourage or stimulate chewing and some of the sloppy food often oozes down the individual's chin which is both unpleasant and undignified for the person concerned. Thickeners such as wholemeal bread added to a liquidised main meal will completely change the texture, and once this is tolerated a more solid diet can be introduced where and when appropriate. The dietician can give advice about the type of diet and may work alongside the speech and language therapist and the people involved at mealtimes – the cooks, the helpers and the person with PMLD.

Ascertaining preferences for specific foods will be an integral part of any plan of action and may then be used to provide the motivation to try different textures and eating habits. Different textures of food can be explored at times other than mealtimes when the atmosphere may be more relaxed. The popular makes of crisps and snacks often prove very useful in introducing new sensations and textures of food and can help to develop new skills. Finger feeding can be more motivating than using cutlery, and snacks are an ideal time for encouraging this.

Finger feeding can also be used as a first step towards independent eating for people who are already on a solid diet, progressing on to the use of a spoon. However, we should be aware that for some people eating without cutlery is the normal practice, and the skilful use of the hands may be a more important goal than the use of cutlery, although this skill will also be important in the context of daily life in the community.

## Equipment

A wide range of adapted cutlery and equipment is available for people who have physical disabilities affecting the upper limbs. These include:

- angled spoons, cutlery with padded or adapted handles or with hand attachments to enable them to be held and used more easily;
- plates with raised edges to allow food to be scooped;
- non-slip mats or suction based plates;
- stay-warm dishes for those who require time to eat;
- non-return valved straws, ordinary straws or lids which allow a decreased flow of liquid to help with drinking;
- adapted handles or devices to stabilise the cup to enable some individuals to take the cup to their mouth independently.

The range is extensive and with appropriate advice and training from an occupational therapist, can go a long way to facilitate independent eating.

Joe, introduced earlier, required a splint to position his hand functionally in order to be able to hold the spoon as he had no active wrist extension. He was also supplied with an angled spoon which was attached to the splint and a sloping bowl which enabled him to perform the manoeuvre of loading the spoon. The bowl was placed on a non-slip mat so that the position was stable and by careful positioning of his shoulders and elbow he was able to coordinate all the movements required to enable him to eat independently. He was also supplied with a large cup and a straw with a non-return valve which prevented the fluid from draining back once sucked up. The cup was placed in a holder that stabilised it and made it accessible for him.

Many of the items of equipment supplied for assistance with eating and drinking are far more aesthetically pleasing than in the past and can now be used in public places without drawing unwelcome attention. This may be an important issue for both the person with PMLD and their carers.

## Involving the person with PMLD

We have already seen that motivation is an important factor in helping a person with PMLD towards independence. People with extreme physical disabilities and/or sensory impairments who are unable to eat without assistance, can be involved in mealtimes in other ways. Allowing them a choice of foods and understanding their needs during mealtimes is an important starting point in the quest for some form of independence.

A number of questions should be asked when helping a person with their meal. How do I know the person I am helping to eat:

- is enjoying the food?
- likes or dislikes the texture, flavour, temperature?

- wants a drink in between mouthfuls?
- wants to stop for a rest?
- has had enough or wants more?
- would like some additional flavouring?

These questions relate to how well we understand the individual's way of communicating, and are fundamental if we are to transfer control of eating to the person with PMLD. They also give us clues about the way we should help a person with PMLD to eat.

A consistent approach is vital so that the individual knows what to expect and when. A routine is important – eating at the same time, with the same utensils, and the same cues. Cues may involve any, or all, of the senses and allow the individual to feel more in control of the process (McCurtin 1997). They may be verbal, 'here comes the sausage, open your mouth'; auditory, such as tapping the spoon on the plate; through smell, giving enough time for the person to savour the aroma of the food or drink; or through touch.

Meal times should be enjoyable and should not be rushed. It is important to allow enough time for the person with PMLD to eat their meals and to be given appropriate attention so that their preferences in terms of different foods and the temperature of the food can be discovered and taken into account.

However, mealtimes are not always the most desirable time for developing eating skills. They can be stressful or over stimulating for many people with PMLD, even though they enjoy their food. This may result in abnormal reflexes and disrupted patterns of movement and it may be more beneficial to practise eating skills in a quieter and more controlled environment. This can also benefit the carer as it allows time to develop interventions in a situation where the person is not as hungry, and may therefore be more willing to spend time in trying new skills. However, this may also work in reverse if the person's motivation to eat is not strong. In this environement a person's specific likes and dislikes can be explored, new experiences of tastes and textures can be tried and more variety can be introduced.

Involvement in preparation of food and drinks can be a particularly useful activity as it helps to promote sensory awareness, and enables a person to practise skills relating to eating and drinking within an enjoyable activity. It can also be used as a time to ascertain preferences. It is an activity that can be readily adapted to allow individuals to develop independent skills. For example, the provision of a simple switching system will allow a person with PMLD to operate a food processor to make a milk shake or the milk pudding for dessert. The development of a role for that individual and involvement in preparation of the food before a meal can stimulate the senses and motivate the individual to practise eating skills.

Other activities such as 'pretend' play activities with dolls, using utensils to feed the doll may be useful in familiarising children with the equipment to be used and the routines of eating.

There are an increasing number of people with PMLD who are now being referred for gastrostomies which feed directly into the stomach so that food does not have to be taken orally. These are used with people who have severe eating difficulties and are unable to eat or drink adequate amounts of food or liquids by mouth. Lack of nutrition can set up a vicious circle, as the person involved will experience lack of energy, motivation and ability to participate in activities including those of eating and drinking. Research has shown a significant improvement in the involvement of individuals in activity, in their mood and in motivation once gastric feeding has been introduced (Canadian Paediatric Society 1994).

There are obvious drawbacks to this form of intervention including the deprivation of the sensory experiences that eating and drinking provide and the complete lack of control over the process. However, it may be possible to include some eating experiences to compensate but this will, of course, depend on the specific difficulties of each individual. The social aspect of mealtimes should also be preserved so that the people concerned can still take part in the interactions.

# Dressing

The way in which we dress says much about us as people. The style of clothing often reflects our age, occupation and even the mood we are in that day. This aspect of self expression should not be ignored for people with PMLD and opportunities to involve individuals in their own choice of clothes should be explored wherever possible.

## Techniques, strategies and equipment

The process of dressing and undressing is complex and involves physical, cognitive and perceptual skills. Peck and Hong (1988) suggest that independent dressing will only be achievable if a series of linked sequences are mastered. They describe these sequences as:

- functional sequencing: patterns of movement required to put on or remove clothing;
- serial order sequencing: identification of garments and sequencing of dressing/undressing;
- coordination sequencing: the ability to choose matching and co-ordinating clothing;
- appropriateness sequencing: choosing appropriate clothing for age, activity or weather conditions, and to be aware when clothing should not be worn, for example, when it is dirty.

If these sequences are to act as a framework for developing independence, each one needs to be analysed for opportunities for involvement.

A person with PMLD may have such profound physical disabilities that the functional sequencing may be completely impossible, but nevertheless involvement in choice of clothing and communicating the sequence of dressing may be feasible, and this will allow the individual to play a part in the whole process.

Activities that encourage the body movements used in dressing and recognition of body parts are useful. Music and movement activities, dressing up or dressing a doll up can be used with children. Drama and dance can incorporate these activities in an appropriate way for adults. Swimming provides the opportunity to practise dressing and undressing in an appropriate situation.

To make dressing accessible to people with PMLD the type of clothing should be carefully considered. Clothing which is loose in fitting and with limited fastenings is recommended. The use of elasticated openings or 'velcro' can be invaluable when it comes to encouraging dressing and undressing skills. The ease with which lower clothing can be removed will affect independence in toileting, and independence in dressing has implications in other areas of daily living, such as bathing, going outside, swimming, or any other activities which require special forms of clothing.

Clothing made from natural fibres will reduce the amount of static electricity in clothing. As natural fibres allow the skin to breathe, they reduce the risk of skin irritations which can be caused by sweating.

There are many types of aids which can be used to allow more independence in dressing. The local Ability Centre can provide advice on these or give information about companies that specialise in them.

With imagination, protective clothing can be incorporated into outfits without appearing too obtrusive, for example, western style neck scarves instead of bibs, required because of excessive drooling.

## Involvement of the person with PMLD

The use of particular clothing to communicate an activity can be a useful signal, for example wearing an old, warm jumper when attending gardening sessions. Once established, this process can be reversed, and if the person with PMLD is aware of the activities that they are taking part in they can choose appropriate clothing, or indicate choice of activity through their choice of clothing. Consistency is, of course, essential in teaching this skill.

Involving people with PMLD in shopping for their own clothes is important, and a good way of finding out about their preferences. It does however require a reliable means of communication to make sure that the right interpretation is being made. Downs, in this volume, shows how difficult it can be for practitioners and carers to be confident that they have made the right interpretations of communication, even if they know the person well.

Preference may need to be coupled with gentle assistance in what is appropriate to the age and status of the individual and catalogue shopping can be very useful in helping individuals to develop preferences and become involved in choosing their own clothes.

# Conclusion

In each of the areas of personal activities of daily living the recognition of an individual's personal desires and motivation is essential in order to support and enable independence. The key to this is in the ability to understand the communication of the person with PMLD.

Keilhofner (1995) acknowledges the difficulties in assessing the volition or motivation in individuals who have communication and cognitive limitations. Volition and motivation are ever changing forces which will need to be constantly re-evaluated (CAOT 1991). Keilhofner suggests the use of the *Volitional Questionnaire* in an attempt to recognise that while such individuals have difficulty expressing their interests verbally, they are often able to communicate them through actions. This assessment instrument focuses on the conditions and the types of supports and environments in which the person expresses volition. Observations are both sensitive to the individual and the environment and need to take place over a period of time so that reliable data can be gathered.

Motivation to become as independent as possible in daily living tasks is not just an issue for the person with PMLD, it has implications for the person or people caring for that individual. Enabling independence is often very time consuming and expensive. It can completely disrupt family life and add additional strain to family relationships. But involvement of the carers in the acquisition of personal living skills is vital. Knowledge of the situation, the personal preferences of the individual with PMLD and relationships within the family are invaluable if a successful programme is to be instigated.

Working with carers to establish patterns of independence and an understanding of the importance of allowing control to be given to the person with PMLD are the first steps. Providing training, equipment, access to financial grants and continuing support and encouragement will be the next and following steps.

The cost of equipment, adaptations to the environment, carers' and practitioners' time as well as the energy and personal time put in by the person with PMLD must all go into the equation of 'to enable or not to enable'. In the climate of cost benefit analysis this issue will not go away and will require the person with PMLD to have a voice to keep their needs in the financial equation. This makes the assessment of personal needs and preference of even greater importance. Priorities made must be realistic not just for the person with PMLD but also for the carer and/or family. This raises the complex issues of advocacy which are discussed in detail by Tilstone and Barry in this volume.

A constant theme throughout the chapter has been the importance of communication in the process of enabling independence. Communication is a two way process. It is about developing ways to enable a person with PMLD to communicate their needs, wants and aspirations and also about how the facilitator or carer communicates with that person. Helen Bradley explores the issues of establishing effective and reliable communication in her chapter in this volume.

Enabling independence is also about the state of mind of the carer who must seek out methods of transferring control, facilitating independence and then reinforcing the action or behaviour by positive verbal feedback and/or carrying out requested action.

Developing ways of involving the person with PMLD in their personal care is not straightforward. There are often no easy answers and much of the work is done on a trial and error basis. The collaboration of a whole host of individuals is often the only way of reaching a reasonable solution. The complex difficulties experienced by people with PMLD mean that it is not a question of coming up with a solution immediately but of 'knowing a man who can'. This is the spirit of collaborative work which is so essential if these complex problems are to be addressed.

# Part Two:
# Social

# Chapter 5

# Assessing and Developing Successful Communication

*Helen Bradley*

Opportunities for successful, enjoyable and spontaneous communication are often taken entirely for granted. It is only when one is trapped in a situation where communication falters or fails altogether that one gets a glimpse of the highly stressful world of people with communication delays and disorders. Communication is the rock upon which all social activities rest and if the communication fails, other things go awry as well – relationships, learning, behaving appropriately in line with other people's expectations, to name but a few.

In this chapter the best ways of facilitating successful communication in people who have profound and multiple learning disabilities will be considered. In order to do this the following areas will be explored:

- attempts to define the many aspects of communication, with a special emphasis on early functional communication;
- a working model of communication in its earliest stages;
- approaches to assessing and intervening in various aspects of communication. The various uses of meetings and interviews, observational approaches and development scales and schedules will be discussed.

Examples of multidisciplinary collaboration working will be provided throughout.

## Communication: some definitions and key terms

In the 1960s and 70s researchers were very preoccupied with language and its development, and for a while the building blocks of early social interaction from which the words and sentences emerged were relatively neglected. Definitions of language and communication based on work from that era stressed intentionality. For example, Kiernan *et al.* (1986) state that 'communication involves responses which the child or adult makes intentionally in order to affect the behaviour of another person with the expectation that the other person will receive the message'. This insistence on intentionality effectively removed very young babies and many people with profound and multiple learning disabilities (PMLD) and those communicating with them from the communication equation. This narrow focus also doomed many individuals to be labelled as 'non-communicating', very probably a self-fulfilling prophesy. Yet a brief observation of interactions between people with PMLD and their parents, carers and friends would have revealed a whole spectrum of successful and exciting relationships, all based on communication and shared understanding of each other.

As researchers (e.g. Snow 1984) began to look at communication from birth onwards, a whole new world of communication strategy and design began to unfold and this research was of great relevance to people with PMLD because it revealed that successful communication can occur where there is no intentionality on the part of one of the partners. This gave rise to new definitions of communication which encompassed neatly the communication skills and abilities of people with PMLD. An example of a wider definition is provided by Siegal and Causey *et al.* (1987) who state that communication can be viewed as 'the successful transmission of a message from one person to another'.

Intentionality is not a prerequisite for communication in this definition. Pre-intentional communicative behaviour has been defined in its own right, for example, 'The individual's motor acts on people and objects are assigned communicative significance by others' (McLean and Snyder-McLean 1987). For the purposes of people with PMLD, a truly useful definition of communication needs to encompass both *intentional* and *pre-intentional* aspects.

Early attempts to assess and intervene in developing language and communication skills often involved rather artificial situations and skills such as signing nouns in response to pictures. This kind of skill, even if acquired, was of little use in everyday situations and bore little resemblance to everyday conversation where speech and body language are used socially to control attention, share information, comment on events, express emotions, share jokes and ask for meaningful things to happen, to name but a few functions.

Disillusionment with mechanical teaching of speech and signs led to an emphasis on 'functional communication'. Functional communication sadly remains a rather ill-defined term, but is generally understood to be about communication being used as a tool to control personally meaningful experiences, events and activities. Roland and Scheweigert (1993) stress three important aspects of functional communication:

- it occurs in everyday, real life, and natural situations;
- it results in real consequences i.e. the act affects the environment which changes in accordance with the intent of the communication;
- it includes (but is not limited to) spontaneous communication. Communication skills are not fully functional if the communicator is incapable of using them except when prompted to do so.

Sadly, complete spontaneity in communication poses many difficulties for people with multiple disabilities (Light *et al.* 1985).

Placing an emphasis on functional communication is compatible with different theoretical perspectives on early language development. Using ideas from cognitive development (see Bloom 1973), a functional approach would look closely at assessing and developing conversational turns that focus on first meanings. For example, acknowledging existence or non-existence of objects, or more or less of something.

Sociolinguistic theorists (see Mclean and Snyder-Mclean 1978) emphasise the importance of the relationship between the communicative partners and joint action routines which allow both partners to have increasingly sophisticated 'turns' in the conversation. An emphasis on pragmatics (see Reichle and Sigafloos 1991) highlights the importance of a person having a reason to communicate, for example, to request attention, ask for repetition or cessation of an activity. Both sociolinguistic and pragmatic theories are useful in explaining how the communication skills demonstrated may vary widely from one situation to another. One context and partner may be able to elicit skills not seen in other places or situations.

The present emphasis by researchers and practitioners on functional communication has led to attempts to find topics of conversation that are meaningful to conversational partners. For example, Marian enjoys a visual joke so her carer puts something down and then asks Marian where she has put it. This allows Marian quite deliberately to eye point to the wrong place and enjoy the wild goose chase that ensues.

Functional communication is more than just asking for tangibles, it is also about asking for more or less attention, an opportunity to express emotions, signal healthcare needs, etc. It is important to have a knowledge of the wide range of functions of communication because an assumption that a communication simply seeks tangible reward can lead to misinterpretation (see Grove and Park 1993).

In order to structure communication in a way that allows a person with profound and multiple learning disabilities to understand what is happening and hopefully express a view about it (either positive or negative) it is now widely accepted that a total communication approach is likely to be necessary. In this approach meaning is conveyed by a variety of different methods which are likely to include speech plus special touches or body clues, natural gestures, real objects (also called objects of reference) and more formal signs.

Alternative and augmentative communication (AAC) are two terms that have relevance to total communication. Alternative communication consists of alternatives to speech, for example, using objects, signs, symbols, or pictures to convey meaning. Augmentative communication uses similar means to provide support to speech which is still the medium for conveying meaning. Both alternative and augmentative communication may involve low technology such as objects or pictures, or high technology such as speech synthesisers. (For more detailed discussion of the use of technology in communication see Taylor in this volume.)

# A model of communicative development

It is important for anyone with an interest in communication at the earliest stages to have access to some sort of working model of how communication develops and how different communicative domains (social skills, cognitive skills, motivational factors) interrelate. An excellent discussion of this topic is provided by Goldbart (1994). Bradley, H. (1994) provides a very simplified model designed to guide the assessment and intervention process by highlighting key stages and the implications in terms of broad communicative needs (Figure 5.1).

# Planning assessment and intervention

Assessment and intervention are, in practice, so tightly interwoven in the field of early communication that to separate them seems artificial. This section will therefore be a consideration various forms of assessment and the types of interventions that should naturally follow from them. The success or failure of the intervention will provide additional assessment information.

| Communication Skills | Communicative Needs |
|---|---|
| 1. The person responds to her internal feelings – such as hunger, etc. She does not try to communicate or change the situation. | To have a close relationship with key carers.<br><br>To have clear routines.<br><br>To have a quick response to distress or happiness. |
| 2. The person tries to alter a situation e.g. to push away an empty cup, to push someone away. They still do not intend to communicate. | To have behaviour treated as if it is intended to communicate e.g. when a cup is pushed away, carers interpret this as 'I've finished'.<br><br>To have opportunities to act on the environment e.g. the cup is not automatically removed when empty, the person is encouraged to push it away when she is finished.<br><br>To have clear clues about what is about to happen next. |
| 3. The person makes the discovery that she can alter other people's behaviour e.g. pulling a friend or carer over for a cuddle, waving a cup when thirsty, making a certain sound e.g. 'eeee' when wanting attention. | To have lots of opportunities to try to influence carers, make choices, etc.<br><br>For carers to respond quickly and consistently e.g. the cup is filled when the disabled person waves it around.<br><br>For the carers to accept the informal attempt at communication, but to model a more advanced form e.g. to fill the cup up and help the person make a sign for 'drink'.<br><br>To have clear communication about what is going to happen next. |
| 4. The person uses formal communication e.g. speech, signs, words, symbols, etc. | For all carers to understand and respond to the system and to use it themselves.<br><br>For systematic encouragement to extend the formal communication. |

(Bradley, H. 1994)

**Figure 5.1** A model of communicative development

Bradley, H. (1994) identifies some of the many challenges people with profound and multiple disabilities may face in becoming effective communicators:

- they may have visual disabilities ranging from blindness to some useful vision;
- they may have hearing impairments;
- they may not have reached a developmental level where speech is processed and understood;
- they may have physical disabilities which affect speech production or the coordination required for gesture or signing;
- they may have difficulties in accepting touch;
- they may communicate in very idiosyncratic ways which are difficult for carers to recognise and interpret.

Any assessment or intervention approach needs to take into account that people with multiple disabilities do not have two or three separate disabling conditions. The effects on communication are interactive so, for example, it is quite usual to use vision to comprehend sound. A person who cannot see or cannot move to look at the source of a sound, may not respond to that sound if they do not realise its significance.

Communication assessments and interventions need to be very carefully tailored to meet individual needs and patterns of ability and disability. They also need to take into account the daily routines of the person with PMLD as a person may respond very differently in familiar and unfamiliar situations. Carers and professionals involved with people with PMLD also face a number of challenges in developing communication assessments and interventions:

- communication may be very brief and may be overlooked;
- communication may be very idiosyncratic and difficult to interpret;
- it can be difficult to tell which behaviours are random and which might potentially have communicative value;
- early communications may be very negative and rejecting of people and activities;
- carers may find some people with PMLD have a set response of either accepting or rejecting most objects or activities so it is difficult to offer meaningful choices;
- standardised checklists on communicative skills may be of little use for someone with PMLD;
- time to use assessments may be very limited by the amount of time taken in everyday caretaking routines. If a special time is set aside to assess, the person with PMLD may not necessarily be receptive or showing their full range of skills at that point (i.e. assessment has to take place throughout the day);
- working in teams has many advantages, but it means there are real difficulties in developing strategies for sharing information and using consistent intervention strategies amongst different staff members;
- detailed record keeping is essential.

Without any doubt, the greatest resource available in planning an assessment is the vast array of essential information that is already known about the client's communicative abilities and strategies. This knowledge exists in the form of observations that carers have consciously or unconsciously made about their client during the course of their interactions. A good assessment will use this information, add to it, and reinterpret it to form the basis of intervention strategies which facilitate and expand existing skills and hopefully teach some new ones.

It is likely that a full assessment will involve the following types of information gathering.

- meetings and interviews with people who know the person well;
- direct observation in a range of situations;
- some use of schedules of skills drawn either from the normal developmental continuum or from research on communication skills and strategies in people with PMLD.

Ideally, assessment leads directly to intervention so examples of interventions suggested by different assessment techniques will be given throughout.

## Using meetings and interviews

Time spent in a meeting of any type is very valuable and needs to be utilised to the full. It is essential to prepare carefully for the meeting by having a list of areas where information needs to be gathered.

The Assessing Communication Together (ACT) materials (Bradley 1991) are to encourage people who know the person with PMLD to meet and share information systematically. Such people are likely to include family members, teachers, carers, the speech and language therapist, the occupational therapist and the physiotherapist, and the psychologist. There are five sections.

### Section 1: Background information

This consists of collecting information on vision, hearing, physical abilities, relationships, touch and existing receptive and expressive communication skills. The implications of this information for the communication programme are agreed. Areas where further information is required (for example about a person's functional vision) are identified.

### Section 2: Social needs

This section explores the social needs of the person with multiple disabilities and areas examined include personal identity, personal possessions, social greetings and social control. For each area of social communication existing communication routines are noted and, where necessary, a new consistent strategy agreed. The following example illustrates this process.

*How does Philip ask for attention or affection?*
Philip vocalises and starts to throw objects – this particularly happens when he is left alone in a room. Once someone arrives, he tries to involve them in a game of throwing.

**If necessary, agree the method to be used.**
As soon as Philip starts to vocalize, go over and say and sign 'hello' hand over hand. Try and give him at least five minutes attention and if possible involve him in a turntaking activity.

*How does Philip ask people to leave him alone?*
Philip hits out at people – sometimes very hard.

**If necessary, agree the method to be used.**
Get Philip's hand and make an adapted 'finish' sign when he is about to hit, then leave him alone for about five minutes. Then reoffer the activity.

## Section 3: Activities and routines

The most useful assessments and interventions are firmly centred around a person's lifestyle and interests. This section is designed to allow carers to take an objective look at their client's lifestyles and the things which are most important for them to understand and express. In particular, the choices that a person needs to make and their ability to control important events are examined. Routines and methods to help the person to anticipate and participate are examined. For example:

*How does Andrew ask for a drink?*
He may cry – he bites his jumper.

*How do carers offer a drink?*
We just give him a drink by helping him hold the cup.

**If necessary, agree the method to be used.**
If possible, as soon as Andrew cries and bites his jumper, go and get a drink for him. Touch his lips with his fingers and say 'Andrew, do you want a drink?' Help him to hold the cup for a moment, then help him to take it to his lips. If he frowns or spits it out he may be hungry so offer food instead. Use this method for all offers of drinks.

## Section 4: Core signals and signs

There are certain areas of communication that are essential for day to day living. ACT suggests some areas where it is important to have an agreed form of communication, for example, Yes/OK, No, Well done, Wait, Finished. Others may be added according to the client's and carer's routine and needs.

| | |
|---|---|
| 1. Which parts of the communication programme could be implemented right away? | *Let's start with the signs for hello, goodbye, more, finished, food, drink, no and walk, plus name objects for Helen and Trisha.* |
| Who will write up and monitor the programme? | *Helen.* |
| 2. List any problems which may undermine the programme. Also list any ideas to problem solve. | |
| Problems | Positive suggestions |
| Everyone needs to sign so some staff training and support needs to be organised. | *Helen will make up a list of the signs with pictures and illustrations. We could use the next two staff meetings to practise them. We could spend some time practising the signs under blindfold.* |

**Figure 5.2** Implementing the programme

## Section 5: Implementing the programme

An ACT assessment should highlight a number of ideas and possibilities for intervention. However, the extent to which the interventions can be introduced will be governed by existing circumstances. As consistency is vital to the success of the intervention, it is usually preferable to start in a small way with interventions that everyone feels happy and confident about managing. Figure 5.2 is an example of the steps to be taken in implementing the programme.

The ACT assessment materials are specifically designed to encourage consistency amongst different professionals through the process of joint recording and planning. Detailed record keeping strategies and forms are suggested throughout.

An ACT assessment leads directly into intervention because at each stage implications for intervention are discussed. ACT materials are particularly useful where carers feel that the person with PMLD is using challenging behaviour as a form of communication. ACT II Assessing Challenges Together (Bradley, in preparation) further explores the link between challenging behaviour and communication through workshop and assessment materials.

Collaborative multidisciplinary meetings and interviews like ACT frequently identify areas where further information about a person needs to be collected and are therefore a useful starting point for planning observations.

## Using observational techniques

Observational techniques have many advantages as they allow the collecting of information gradually, in situations that are relevant to the client and carers. Responses in different situations can also be evaluated and compared. Observation can also prevent the focus becoming solely on the skills of the person with PMLD because the impact of other essentials like the skills of the conversational partner and the suitability of the context can also be taken into account.

Some specific observational techniques will be discussed here under the following headings:

- Likes and dislikes
- Tactile defensivenes
- Interactional style
- Observing everyday routines
- Conversational strategies
- Analogue assessment to check out hypotheses about the communicative function of different behaviours.

## Likes and dislikes

Earliest functional communications about activities or objects are likely to be of a 'great — give me more' or 'yuk — take it away' variety and being able to express choice successfully is a huge motivation to communicate.

For some people a careful consideration of their needs and behaviours plus some basic observation can form the basis of lists of people, activities or objects which appear to be liked, disliked or neutral (this process is covered by sections of ACT). Opportunities for choice can then be built into an intervention. However, for other people it can be very hard to decipher which behaviours signify 'accept' and which 'reject'. This can be particularly hard when someone has a very limited repertoire of behaviours or where there are many possibly involuntary movements clouding the picture and for such a person collaborative multidisciplinary work involving occupational and physiotherapists is essential.

The Affective Communication Assessment (ACA) (Coupe and Goldbart 1988) is an observational schedule specifically designed for the study and categorisation of pre-intentional and early intentional want/don't want behaviours. Various sensory experiences are offered to the person and their responses are carefully recorded. From this recording, patterns of behaviour which indicate like/dislike may emerge, and subtle distinctions may be noticed which are easily overlooked without a means of systematic observation. For example, John holds his body very stiffly, turns his head and goes 'er er er' when he dislikes something. He makes a similar sound when he wants something but the sound is softer and his body is more relaxed. Carers make a point of offering both liked and disliked activities and allowing John to express a preference.

Jones (1989) provides a useful reinforcer assessment which is also based on careful observation of behaviours in response to sensory stimulations. Again, particular patterns of body movement, vocalisation, etc. may emerge and detailed recording sheets are provided.

## Tactile defensiveness

Some people with PMLD are severely restricted in their ability to respond to everyday communications because they have difficulties in accepting touch (tactile defensive-ness). For people with this type of difficulty it is most useful to observe which types of touch are best tolerated and to use this information as a baseline for a systematic intervention designed to increase tolerance of touch. Evans and Theiss-Tait (1986) provide useful descriptions of this type of approach. Bradley (1991) provides an example (Figure 5.3) of a format for assessing tolerance of touch based on the McInnes and Treffrey (1982) sequence of responses to interaction.

Any type of touch may be entered on the left hand column and its effects recorded easily. The same record sheet may be used to record progress over time. Further information on this approach to assessment can be found in the Rebecca Goodman Centre's Communication Curriculum (1987).

For some people with PMLD very minimal touch experiences may need to be assessed, for example, the effect of blowing gently on the person's hand, or the effect of stamping on the floor so the touch travels in the form of vibration. Some people with tactile defensiveness may need this sort of preliminary cue before they are ready to be touched at all.

An assessment of touch should lead to an intervention that is followed by all staff. When programmes designed to promote touch are in place, clear communication between all carers is essential because someone who does not understand or follow the programme may undo all the progress that has been made.

## Interactional style

It is a truism that everyone naturally seems to hit it off better with some people than with others and it seems sensible to suggest a continuum of 'getting on' that ranges from almost being able to read someone's mind at one end to a complete breakdown in communication at the other. What we are considering here is the subtle ability to communicate effectively and acceptably at a number of levels both verbally and non-verbally.

This ability is of value when communicating with someone with PMLD and is worth studying in its own right with a view to defining an interactional style that brings out the best in the client. This interactional style will be different with different clients and has been particularly studied in reference to working with people with challenging behaviour (Burchess 1990). Hewett, in this volume, discusses observation of interaction and how to make it more appropriate to the clients' needs.

| type of touch | body part | very resistant | accepts passively | enjoys | signals for more | initiates |
|---|---|---|---|---|---|---|
| Stroking | Right hand | ✓ | ✗ | ✗ | ✗ | ✗ |
|  | Left hand | ✓ | ✗ | ✗ | ✗ | ✗ |
| Stroking | Head | ✓ | ✗ | ✗ | ✗ | ✗ |
| Stroking | Right leg | ✗ | ✓ | ✗ | ✗ | ✗ |
|  | Left leg | ✗ | ✓ | ✗ | ✗ | ✗ |
| Stroking | Stomach | ✗ | ✓ | ✓ | ✓ | ✓ |
| Stroking | Back | ✗ | ✓ | ✓ | ✗ | ✗ |
| Pouring warm water slowly on to: | Right hand | ✗ | ✓ | ✓ | ✗ | ✗ |
|  | Left hand | ✗ | ✓ | ✓ | ✗ | ✗ |
| Pouring warm water slowly on to: | Right arm | ✓ | ✓ | ✗ | ✗ | ✗ |
|  | Left arm | ✓ | ✓ | ✗ | ✗ | ✗ |
| Pouring warm water slowly on to: | Right foot | ✗ | ✓ | ✗ | ✗ | ✗ |
|  | Left foot | ✗ | ✓ | ✓ | ✓ | ✗ |
|  |  |  |  |  |  | (Bradley 1991) |

**Figure 5.3** A format for assessing tolerance of touch

## Observing everyday routines

McInnes and Treffrey (1982) describe the importance of carers creating a 'reactive environment' by responding quickly and appropriately to any communicative attempts. It is important for carers to analyse and structure the day so that as many everyday events as possible are used to promote communication.

A useful technique is to write down the key events which make up the day of the person with PMLD, for example, mealtime, toileting, going on the minibus, hand and face washing, hydrotherapy.

The next stage is to pick one of these events and to analyse it to see that opportunities exist for encouraging communication and what types of communication the person with PMLD offers. It is possible to devise a simple format so that this information can function both as a baseline and a record of progress.

The following table is the first part of an assessment of developmental skills during lunchtime activities expanded and adapted by the author from work by Langley (1986).

| Communicative Behaviours | Record | Comments |
|---|---|---|
| If mobile move towards table in response to:<br>  physical prompt<br>  object clue<br>  gesture<br>  sign<br>  speech<br>  other – please specify.... | | |
| Responds appropriately to own:<br>  bib/apron<br>  cup<br>  spoon<br>  plate<br>  other – please specify.... | | |
| If mobile collects own:<br>  bib/apron<br>  cup<br>  spoon<br>  plate<br>  other – please specify.... | | |
| Responds to signs or words for the following:<br>  bib/apron<br>  cup<br>  spoon<br>  plate<br>  other – please specify.... | Sign  Word | |
| When asked if ready to eat by<br>(a) sign [ ]<br>(b) speech [ ]<br>responds with:<br>  body movements (increase,<br>                decrease or other)<br>  facial expression<br>  vocalisation<br>  sign<br>  speech<br>  other – please specify.... | | |
| Opens mouth when touched with:<br>  cup<br>  spoon<br>  other – please specify... | | |
| Opens mouth when approached with:<br>  cup<br>  spoon<br>  other – please specify.... | | |
| Requests help with eating by:<br>  screaming/crying<br>  reaching<br>  tugging<br>  pulling | | |

| | | |
|---|---|---|
| vocalising<br>gesture<br>signing<br>speech<br>other – please specify.... | | |
| Indicates food preferences by:<br>　turning head away<br>　turning head towards<br>　closing mouth to refuse food<br>　opening mouth to accept food<br>　pushing food away<br>　reaching for food<br>　shaking head<br>　spitting out<br>　signing<br>　speech<br>　other – please specify.... | | |
| Shows when he has finished by:<br>　refusing food<br>　taking off bib<br>　pushing utensils away<br>　signing<br>　speech<br>　other – please specify.... | | |
| Shows wants more by:<br>　leaning forward<br>　reaching forward<br>　vocalising<br>　touching adult's hand<br>　holding up empty plate/cup<br>　gesture<br>　signing<br>　speech<br>　other – please specify.... | | |
| | | (Bradley, H. adapted from Langley 1986) |

**Figure 5.4** Observation of communicative behaviour at lunchtime

Langley (1986) provides more information on this approach and also shows how everyday events may be used as a guide to a variety of areas of development. The advantage of this is that it makes use of familiar events and leads to direct intervention by the carers who should easily be able to spot opportunities to encourage the development of communication. A shared checklist also encourages consistency amongst carers if they all follow the same sequence and use the same methods of promoting communication.

Analysing a key event in this way also alerts carers to any previously missed communicative opportunities, e.g. in the case of toileting routine. For example, rather than being taken to the toilet without any advance warning, a new routine in which someone is forewarned or asked if he or she needs the toilet, would make it possible for that person to show anticipation, or to indicate need.

Another useful application of this technique is in checking that the communication in familiar events are clear and not subject to confusion. For example, John has limited vision and hearing and a hip problem, but can walk for short distances with a guide. He understands everyday objects, and he goes swimming regularly. He is sitting on his bed and Jane says 'Hello John, it's time to go swimming'. She collects John's bag and trunks and helps him down the stairs, but then remembers that she has no towel for him. She sits him down in the kitchen while she goes upstairs for a towel. When she returns, John bangs the kitchen table angrily and refuses to move. (adapted from Bradley 1991).

Many aspects of this routine were confusing and many opportunities for effective communication were missed. For instance, John did not know who he was with, where he was going or why. Conflicting clues and a poor routine may have led him to expect a drink, or something to eat. A careful observation can lead to an intervention that clarifies a routine by using consistent clues, maybe in the forms of touch, smell or sound clues, gestures, and objects of reference.

An analysis of routines may also highlight those activities that the person with PMLD most enjoys or dislikes. Both enjoyment and dislike are useful motivations to communication. Where it is still not clear to carers which activities are liked or disliked, the Affective Communication Assessment (Coupe *et al.* 1985) or the reinforcer analysis in the Kidderminster Curriculum for Children and Adults with Profound, Multiple Learning Disabilities (Jones 1989) are useful tools. Cragg and Garvey (1991) provide an extensive checklist of daily living activities which can be used to enhance the range of opportunities offered to an adult, and can be used to promote choices for adults who can use pictures as a method of communication.

## Conversational strategies

The observational assessment of early interactions (Goldbart 1994;, Goldbart and Rigby 1989) is an elegant tool for assessing the way in which people with PMLD initiate, maintain and terminate conversational interactions.

Different conditions are observed, for example, someone may turn away in the middle of a conversation to see what the person with PMLD does to bring them back into the interaction. That person may, for example, vocalise, or make a particular body movement and this is noted on the assessment.

This sort of observation is an excellent tool for making interactions more successful by recognising the strategies the person with PMLD is using, or by highlighting areas where a strategy needs to be taught or modified. Information may be checked systematically using analogue assessments.

## Analogue assessments

Analogue assessments are a means of testing out a hypothesis about the function of a behaviour. For example, at certain times of the day Evan shouts and screams and bangs his wheelchair. Diaries suggest this happens when a pleasant activity is interrupted, for example, he is being fed and his carer leaves him for a minute, or the tape of music he is listening to comes to an end.

To test whether the hypothesis 'Evan is asking for more' is correct, analogue situations may be specifically engineered to collect information more speedily under controlled situations, rather than gathering evidence in situations as they occur naturally. For example, five separate recordings are made on different days of Evan's response when a carer switches off the music tape that he is listening to, and five separate recordings are made where a carer who is feeding Evan is called away for a moment.

If the hypothesis was correct these interactions should consistently elicit loud vocalisation and wheelchair banging. If this happens, carers could then interpret this behaviour as, 'I want more' and devise a number of communicative opportunities throughout the day for Evan to tap his wheelchair (gently!) for more. Fast reaction by staff could prevent this signal escalating into a challenging behaviour.

For a more detailed discussion of analogues, including ethical considerations, see Emerson, Barrett and Cummings (undated).

## Using schedules to assess communication

The huge variety of patterns of ability and disability which make up the profiles of people with PMLD means that no one schedule of communicative behaviour is likely to meet everybody's needs. However, schedules can be a useful supplement to assessment and may also be useful in suggesting the type of skills that require further observation or intervention.

Three published schedules of communication development warrant a special mention because they are focused particularly upon people with very early communication skills and/or profound and multiple learning disabilities. They are all applicable to people requiring alternative or augmentative communication strategies.

### The Callier Azuza H Form (Stillman and Battle 1985)

Callier Azuza H Form are scales for the assessment of communicative abilities of deaf, blind and multi-handicapped children.

The scales concentrate on very early communications up until the point of first formal signs. These are coded by observers who know the child well, observing over a period of two weeks.

The Callier Azuza provides a very detailed record of early communications and because it is so detailed provides ideas about what to teach next.

### The Preverbal Communication Schedule (PVCS)
### (Kiernan and Reid 1987)

The PVCS consists of twenty seven sets of questions on areas of development such as use of vision and hearing, vocalisation, use of hands and fingers, informal communications such as pictures or gestures, and formal communication using signs, symbols and or speech. The resulting profile helps assessors to decide on appropriate communication methods and motivations.

The PVCS is not as detailed as the Callier Azuza but is quite widely used and provides useful information.

### The Kidderminster Curriculum (Jones 1989)

The Kidderminster Curriculum is a very detailed assessment designed for people with profound and multiple disabilities and it has very useful sections on motivation and communication.

## Multidisciplinary interventions

Moving from assessment to intervention depends on good communication between different professionals and carers. The detailed intimate knowledge of family members and friends can usefully be combined with the skills of a range of professionals and professional carers to create a supportive environment which continually challenges the person with PMLD to use their communicative skills functionally. There follows an example of a communication intervention derived through multidisciplinary collaboration. It concerns Joe who is 30 years old and has just moved from hospital to the purpose built house in the community which he shares with four other new residents.

*Visual Assessment* shows Joe has light and dark perception in his right eye.

*Auditory Assessment* shows Joe has profound hearing loss.

*Mobility Assessment* shows Joe can walk but is very unsteady. He walks better when guided from the right. For walks over 10 minutes long he needs the option to use his wheelchair.

*Occupational Therapy Assessment* shows Joe has a good range of movement in his right hand but his left is very weak. An occupational therapy sensory assessment shows Joe responds best to equipment that provides bright lights, particularly things he can hold up and tap against his head near his right eye such as a light rod. He does this gently and it is not a danger. He does not like his hands touched suddenly, and needs a warning that someone is there, for example, a light touch on the arm. He prefers to have wrists rather than arms touched. He will hold objects briefly but often throws them.

*Communication Assessment.* Observations and interviews of carers by the speech and language therapist and the psychologist shows Joe uses some pre-intentional gestures such as putting his hands out when trying to find more, hitting out at people or himself if he wants an activity to stop. He also screams if he is unhappy or in pain. He uses some objects functionally e.g. cups and his sponge in the bath. Carers report a long list of favourite foods and drinks and a hatred for cold things like ice cream. He loves the foot spa and a warm bath or swimming in the hydrotherapy pool. He also enjoys the trampoline.

## Intervention

Joe needs to be alerted to people's presence by a verbal 'hello' and brief squeeze on his right wrist.

He needs some body clues to alert him to what activity is on offer. These should be made with speech, as speech makes interaction flow more naturally. Body clues need to be used consistently by all carers.

1. 'Hello' — a squeeze on the arm
2. Janet, Joe's key worker, will get him to briefly touch her copper bracelet when she says hello. She will also use a special 'pat on the wrist' body clue to help Joe to distinguish her from other carers.
3. 'Stand up, Joe' should be communicated by carers gently pushing up his right wrist, from beneath, before helping him to stand.
4. 'Sit down, Joe' should be communicated by carers gently pushing down his right wrist before helping him to sit.
5. Joe should be given opportunities to ask for *more*. Carers should pause in a favoured activity and wait for a response. If Joe tries to bounce or puts his hands out, start bouncing again. If Joe has finished his food and starts screaming and hitting himself carers should take his hand and prompt a reach gesture, then quickly give more food or drink. Joe can be helped to use the 'more' gesture in a number of situations.
6. Carers should let Joe know it is bath time by helping him feel his bath sponge and then making gentle washing gestures on his arms and his back. Carers should do this before they ask him to get up to come for a bath.

7. If carers are with Joe and he starts hitting and screaming he probably wants to be left alone. They should help him do a push away gesture with his right arm and then if possible give him a few moments alone.
8. Joe needs a range of interesting 'light makers' such as the rod and computer programmes like 'Just look'. Carers should let him know they are on offer by gently tapping his head above his right eye and letting him feel the objects (computer games are also an ideal incentive for Joe to put his hand out to ask for 'more lights').

A detailed functional communication programme such as Joe's, which is designed to be used across all aspects of his life, is absolutely dependent on multidisciplinary collaboration, detailed record keeping and communication between carers and professionals. In order to run smoothly, it will require substantial levels of consistency, commitment and skill from everyday carers and this has huge implications for supporting and training everyday carers. A programme such as Joe's is also very vulnerable to staff changes if time is not put aside to train new staff and support them as they get to know Joe. Any new staff coming into contact with Joe (e.g. new respite cover) will also need help and support. It is most important that carers are given information that stresses the value of total communication, as there is evidence that families and carers of people with learning disabilities may be reluctant to use alternatives to speech (Jones and Cregan 1986). Any alternative or augmentative communication programme, especially one requiring pre-intentional and non-formal gestures and clues, needs constant reviews to make sure everyone is communicating consistently. Staff training in communication is an essential element so that the significance of very small attempts at communication can be realised. Where high or low technology is required, there are known to be problems involving equipment being kept available and in particular being used spontaneously (Light *et al.* 1985), so carers need to be alert to these potential difficulties.

In conclusion, this chapter has examined various definitions of communication, a model of communicative development and a variety of approaches to assessment and intervention. The importance of functional communication and consistency of intervention has been stressed throughout. Multidisciplinary collaboration is seen as an essential part of achieving a full assessment and intervention plan.

# Chapter 6

# Making Relationships

*Carol Ouvry*

## Introduction

Social relationships are one of the most important aspects of most people's lives. There are, of course, many different kinds of relationship, each of which affirms and supports people in different ways, and individuals have different social needs which are met by different kinds of social life, 'But for almost everyone, with or without a disability, the relationships with the people with whom they live, together with other social relationships, are a major contribution to the quality of their lives' (Firth and Rapley 1990, p.16). However, it is only relatively recently that the quality of relationships of people with profound learning disability has been considered and their need for a range of relationships acknowledged.

In schools, the focus of practice has been on developing an appropriate curriculum for development and learning and, since the introduction of the National Curriculum, on entitlement for all pupils to participate in 'a curriculum for all'. With the move from institutions into the community over the last two decades, the focus in adult services has been upon where people live, and the support services which they need in their practical, everyday life. However, as Firth and Rapley (1990) point out, less attention has been given to social relationships although 'It is social relationships and the activities associated with them which are central to community life' (p.17).

More recently, attention on quality of life issues has highlighted the importance of relationships and the limitations experienced by many people with learning disability. This has resulted in much greater attention being given to the process of bonding and forming close relationships for people with PMLD. The work of Nind and Hewett (1994) in developing the Intensive Interaction approach based upon research into the very early stages of caregiver-infant relationships is widely known. The focus on the rights of people with disabilities to live ordinary lives has given rise to work in the area of sexuality, some of which specifically relates to people with PMLD (see Scott 1994; Downs and Craft 1997a; Downs in this volume).

Both these forms of relationship are close, intimate and usually focus on a single person, or at least a small number of people who are particularly special. But what of the wide variety of relationships which most of us ordinarily form during childhood, adolescence and throughout adulthood as we become more independent and roles change within the family and the community? These relationships are less often thought about for people with PMLD.

The amount of literature in relation to people with PMLD is small, and most research focuses on people with mild or moderate learning difficulties, generally those who can communicate verbally. From his study of social networks of people with learning difficulties Whittington (1993) concludes that 'people with learning difficulties have fewer social contacts and that the relationships they do have often differ in negative ways from those enjoyed by peers without learning difficulties' (p. 7). Although clearly the social networks and experience of each individual will vary (Seed 1988b) it is likely that, in general, people with PMLD have similarly restricted social lives.

In this chapter I shall examine different types of relationship throughout the lifespan and discuss some of the issues for people with PMLD in making satisfying relationships. How important are relationships? How are they formed and maintained? How does profound and multiple disabilty affect this process? What can we do to help people to make and sustain satisfying relationships of all kinds? There are no easy answers, but there are steps that carers and practitioners can take to increase the opportunities and provide support for people with PMLD to make satisfying relationships.

# The importance of relationships

The significance of social relationships will be different for every individual. Some people are very gregarious and only happy when they are socially involved with a large number of people, others prefer to have relationships with a smaller number of people. Clearly each person differs in what they look for in their personal relationships and the kind of relationships in which they are most comfortable, and it is important to recognise that people with PMLD will also differ in their preferred pattern of relationships. However, it is equally important to realise that a person's responses in social situations may not necessarily be a reliable indication of their preferences. This may be because of past experiences, and the possibility that previous attempts at interaction may have been unrecognised, dismissed or ignored. Downs, in this volume, discusses the difficulties that carers and practitioners can encounter in interpreting the personal needs and preferences of people with PMLD.

Firth and Rapley (1990) suggest that relationships fulfil our social, emotional and practical needs by providing:

- companionship, which can create opportunities for new and different experiences;
- security and intimacy, a high degree of closeness which can develop within some relationships;
- practical help, advice and guidance in everyday matters as well as at times of crisis;
- a sense of self-identity and self-esteem, which is formed from the responses of others.

Bayley (1997) adds nurturance, the ability to give, to this list and considers it an important part of the interdependence which is part of all relationships.

All these functions of relationships are important, but will vary in significance according to the age and social needs of each individual at any given time. They are also important to people with PMLD, but their ability to make relationships which satisfy all these needs may be limited by their everyday circumstances, or by the difficulties posed by the nature of their disabilities.

# Different types of relationship

The spectrum of relationships ranges from the most intimate, through friendships of different degrees of closeness and acquaintances which are cordial rather than close, to occasional or transitory contacts. The nature of each kind of relationship changes throughout a person's life as independence increases, and their roles within the family and in the community change.

In an approach which aims to open up a variety of relationships to people with learning disability, Wilson and Newton (1996) identify four types of relationship:

- the 'circle of intimacy' which includes those who are closest to us, and who provide anchors for other aspects of our lives;
- the 'circle of friendship' which is not quite as close, but provides good friends and allies;
- the 'circle of participation' which includes associates and acquaintances, and people we see regularly in social or work settings;
- the 'circle of exchange' which comprises those people who are paid to be in our lives, such as teachers or doctors.

These 'circles of friends' focus our attention on the roles that are played by the parties within each relationship circle. They comment that, for people with a disability, the circle of friendship and the circle of participation are 'relatively empty and the only people involved in the person's life are family and people who are paid to be there' (Wilson and Newton 1996, p.17). Bayley (1997) describes this as a 'relationship vacuum' and suggests that the result may be that other types of relationship are invested with meaning inappropriately, for example, people whose job it is to be part of a person's life are regarded as friends.

Bee (1995) identifies two main types of relationship: vertical relationships, those with someone with more power and knowledge; and horizontal relationships, those with same age peers and equals in terms of power. As social roles change over the lifespan, the nature of relationships will change, moving gradually from mainly vertical in infancy to predominantly horizontal in full adulthood, and perhaps on to a stage when vertical relationships increase in old age or illness.

It is likely that someone with PMLD will experience relationships which are predominantly vertical throughout his or her life, but it is important to consider to what extent this is an inevitable consequence of the dependence associated with profound and multiple disability, or due to lack of opportunity or support for interdependence and more equal relationships.

## *Attachment and intimate relationships*

The earliest relationship is the infant-caregiver bond which starts to form at birth through the routines and interactions which are carried out by the caregiver while caring for and playing with the infant. Both parties use a number of specific behaviours during this bonding process which include gaze, smiling, babbling and talking, and reciprocated touching and embracing. These behaviours in the infant have the effect of attracting others, and the baby and caregiver develop 'a highly specific system of communication' (Smith *et al.* 1997, p.12) with which to regulate each other's behaviour. This early intimate relationship enables the caregiver to satisfy the needs of the infant and it provides both with positive emotional experiences of affection and delight in each other. These experiences lay the foundations for a variety of relationships to develop through childhood, adolescence and adulthood.

There are a number of ways in which it can be difficult for a child with PMLD to develop this close relationship. Physical or sensory impairments can limit or disrupt the behaviours which attract others, or the responses they give to others who approach them. They may smile less, be unable to engage in mutual gaze, have limited or uncontrolled movements. Some 'respond in ways which are unusual ... or their responses are delayed to such an extent that the parent is then unclear about the way in which to respond. Such behaviours can inhibit reciprocity' (Smith *et al.* p.11).

Although there are some conflicting opinions about the importance of cognitive development in the ability to make attachments, recognition of familiar people and the development of object permanence are seen as necessary for attachment to a particular person and the protest which separation from that person brings (Smith *et al.* 1997). This will necessarily have implications for those people with PMLD who may not have reached this stage of development, but this should not discourage carers and practitioners from providing opportunities for people with PMLD to form close relationships.

Clearly, these early relationships are 'vertical' in that the balance of power between the infant and caregiver is unequal, but nevertheless there is a strong element of partnership in the interactions. Early relationships need the superior interaction skills of the caregiver to ensure that the smooth sequences of interaction are sustained, and the relationship is consolidated.

A secure attachment early in life provides a 'safe base' and the confidence to explore the surroundings. It opens up opportunities for the child to learn about his or her world, and to develop ways of operating which bring interesting and rewarding results. Early intimate relationships may change in nature during childhood and the transition to adolescence and adulthood as the roles played by each partner may change, but these early relationships are, perhaps, the most enduring of all. The experience of close personal relationships in infancy paves the way for a variety of future relationships of differing degrees of intimacy.

Although the first attachment is developed in infancy, close and intimate relationships are important throughout life. Bayley (1997) emphasises the importance of attachment and 'belonging' for adults and notes that it is around these relationships with spouse, partner, child or close friend that people organise their lives. These relationships are more likely to be of the 'horizontal' variety with the partners being more or less equal as in close friendships, and sexual relationships.

Some people with PMLD have reached adulthood without having experienced satisfactory early close relationships. This may be because of lack of opportunity: there are still adults who spent their infancy in large institutions with little individual attention beyond the provision of the necessities of life, of which at that time, emotional needs were not considered to be one. It may, however, be because the person has always been difficult to make contact with: he or she may be unaware, uninterested or averse to social contact. Some people may have personal characteristics or behaviours which do not make them pleasant to be with. Skilful encouragement and help are often needed to help people with PMLD 'to understand the benefit to be gained from human contact' (Lacey 1996). Nind and Hewett (1994), in developing Intensive Interaction, were concerned to rectify longterm deficits in the emotional and social lives of the people with whom they were working and to help them to accept and enjoy companionship.

## Friendship

The notion of friendship can encompass a very wide range of relationships, and everyone has their own particular idea of what friendship entails. Friendship may be a close relationship with one special person with whom to share the intimate details of one's life, or it may represent less intense but still warm and supportive relationships within a wider circle. People tend to be friendly with people who they see regularly in contexts of shared interests and activities, and closer friendships can emerge within these situations.

Most definitions of friendship involve shared interests and values, mutuality and support (Nunkoosing and John 1997) and caring about the wellbeing of another person. Whatever form they take, friendships are important to children and adults alike and they provide for different needs and create different opportunities at different ages and stages of life.

Roffey *et al.* (1994) suggest that children have two social worlds: the adult world which is caring, provides protection and instruction and is based in inequality, dependence and powerlessness (relationships within this world will necessarily be 'vertical'); and a world of peers which provides companionship, reality, measures of equality and opportunities to develop relationship rules, social skills and behaviours. This is a world where horizontal relationships can flourish. Early intimate relationships are not discarded, rather, they become a backdrop to the friendships which are often the most prominent form of relationship in childhood, and which play an important part in supporting the increasing independence of the child in developing towards adulthood.

There is a discernible pattern in the social relationships underpinning friendships in childhood and adolescence. Very young children generally take very little interest in their peers, and the earliest social relationships are more in the nature of playmates than friendships. A friend is regarded as someone who is available and willing to play, or someone who does things for you or gives you things. It is unusual for strong preferences for particular playmates to be formed. At this stage, the relationship provides a context for developing social skills, and learning how to get on with others on an equal footing.

During childhood an understanding of others develops, and the reciprocal nature of friendship is understood. Preferences for certain friends emerge as the personal qualities of the friend become more important. Towards the end of this period the friendships become more stable and enduring.

In the preadolescent period, friendships are based on similarities and shared views. Gender split in friendship groups is evident and there is a tendency for boys to be involved in large and active groups, girls in smaller and more intimate groups.

During adolescence stronger ties are formed, with an emphasis on trust, loyalty and commitment. Strong peer pressures are in operation. Friendship groups provide the context in which sexual identity is incorporated into self identity. Friendships become 'more intimate and supportive than at earlier developmental stages' (Smith *et al.* 1997) and pairing will take place with a variety of different friends.

Adults are likely to have the whole range of friendships which provide emotional support, companionship, and practical help and support. Most people have a small number of particular friends with whom they share their inner lives and these friends may or may not include a sexual partner. Most people also have a wider circle of people who they consider to be good friends whose welfare matters to them and to whom they can go in need. They will also have a network of acquaintances, people they see regularly in the course of their everyday life at home and in the community.

## Acquaintances

Acquaintances are also an important part of people's everyday lives. They help people to feel that they are accepted and belong in their local community. Many acquaintances are people who provide a service such as the postman, people who work in shops where we are regular customers, or the hairdresser. They may be people whose lives cross our own on a regular basis; they catch the same bus, walk the dog past our home, or pass by regularly in their car. We recognise them, and they us. We greet them when we see them, comment on the weather; perhaps we know them well enough to ask about their family or how their holiday went.

Practitioners also play an important part of the social network of people with PMLD. Lacey (1996) points out that 'children with PMLD have contact with many people — teachers, nursery nurses, therapists, medics, bus escorts, dinner supervisors, family and classmates. Many of these people will appear and disappear with little time to build up meaningful relationships' (p.73). This is also likely to be true for many adults with PMLD who may have a wide number of acquaintances providing support either in their home or in day services, people who provide transport, members of staff in the day centre or adult education class, therapists or mealtime helpers, for instance. Indeed, some services actively discourage the formation of close relationships between workers and service users on the basis that this will avoid any possibility of distress in the future, when a particular worker is no longer involved with that person.

Acquaintances are also made in the context of shared work, interests and activities. These acquaintances are people who have chosen to do the same things and go to the same places, and probably have more in common with each other than people whose work, or daily routines merely cross. They may become friends in time, as they get to know each other and to value each other's personal qualities.

Some people make friends very easily — they have the personal qualities and temperament which attracts other people, and they are able to establish close relationships with people they choose. Making friends is not so easy for everyone, and for people with PMLD it is likely to be more difficult than for most. Not only are they likely to have a smaller network of contacts and therefore fewer opportunities to make relationships, but the complex interpersonal skills required to initiate and sustain friendships will make it more difficult for them to make use of such opportunities as they do have.

# Making relationships

Making relationships depends upon both personal factors and opportunity.

## Personal factors

Both personality and interpersonal skills will affect the ease with which a person forms relationships. Interpersonal skills develop and change over time and continue to develop during adulthood as ways of interacting are adapted and extended to fit the different social situations experienced.

Communication is one of the most important skills involved in making relationships. Without some means of communication, it is virtually impossible to form a relationship with another person. In the past, it was common to hear practitioners refer to many people with PMLD as 'non-communicating' (Evans and Ware 1987) but it is now generally acknowledged that however disabled, either physically or intellectually, everyone is able to communicate in some way Goldbart 1995; Bradley, H. in this volume).

Goldbart (1995) describes an 'inclusive model of communication', in which all actions are regarded as communicative. This model ranges from the simplest forms of communication to the most sophisticated (Goldbart 1995). Nevertheless, difficulties in communication can be a major barrier to making relationships. Lacey (1996) points out that because people with PMLD may have difficulty in expressing their emotions, carers and practitioners can find it diffcult to recognise these emotions, or may even assume that they do not exist. Either way, their responses will not encourage the development of clearer expression of feelings.

Difficulties can also be created by the length of time a person with PMLD may need to react, with the result that when the reaction comes, it is not recognised as a response.

Communication and intellectual development are inextricably linked at the early stages. Lacey (1996) stresses the importance of an infant's social world to both cognitive development and communication. Intentional communication, with all that this brings in terms of indicating choice and interacting with other people, is clearly an important factor, and intentionality depends upon a degree of understanding of the surroundings and effective actions.

It has been suggested that the level of intellectual development may be an important factor in the kinds of relationships that a person can make. Firth and Rapley (1990) note that a number of researchers have linked the stages in intellectual development to the changing nature of relationships in childhood. The implication is that people with profound learning disabilities who appear to be at an early stage of development, will not be able to make any but the earliest forms of relationship. However, the parallel between the functioning of a baby of a few months and a person with PMLD at the very early stage of development cannot be exact. Not only will their experience of life be much longer, depending on the age of the person, but their experiences will inevitably be different from those of a normally developing baby.

Firth and Rapley suggest that 'Developments in relationships may be more usefully seen as a result of growth in individuals' personality, confidence, social skills and security, than as a consequence of intellectual development' (p.55). They also point out that people's preferences for others are influenced by the way those people relate to them and assert that '...there is no evidence to suggest that severity of intellectual disability is linked in any simple way with the capability to maintain relationsips which others would describe as friendships' (p.58). Oakes (1997) considers that the ability to make relationships of all kinds depends upon 'personality, experience and opportunity, not intellectual ability' (p.258).

## Opportunity

An important part of the equation in making relationships is having opportunities to meet people in circumstances which are conducive to social interaction. Bayley (1997) gives many examples of the failure to initiate or sustain relationships because of the absence of structures to support them.

The context of childhood is an ever widening world. To begin with it consists almost entirely of the home, perhaps with occasional visits to family, friends or to the local clinic, doctor, hospital or community group. A constant feature is the presence of parents or a well known caregiver. As children get older their world expands to include playgroup or school, and more community facilities such as the park, the swimming pool, shops or special classes or activities. With growing independence, these are likely to be experienced in the company of friends or professionals such as their teacher as well as with family members. Ultimately, in adulthood, the variety of possible environments and the choice of company is even greater. This choice opens up many opportunities for making different types of relationships.

However, this pattern may not be the same for people with PMLD. The dependence on others which is the reality for children and adults with PMLD means that opportunities for widening their experiences are likely to be restricted to those which are more normal for young children and social contact is likely to be mediated by carers or practitioners, rather than being spontaneously initiated. The opportunities for extending their circle of friends and for having 'horizontal' as well as 'vertical' relationships are limited.

Much of the research into relationships, and in particular friendships, is concerned with the integration of people with learning disability into the local community. The emphasis is often upon friendships with non-disabled people as opposed to friendships with peers who have a disability. Perske and Perske (1988) give a number of examples where friendships between children or adults with PMLD and non-disabled peers have been formed and provide both with fulfilling relationships.

The value attributed by others to such friendships is very high but, by implication, friendships between two people who both have a disability may be seen to be of less value. There are examples of friendships which are ignored and shattered by people being moved away from their friends within an institution. Bayley (1997) tells of Christopher Johnson whose positive relationship with another user of his day centre was abruptly ended when the friend was moved to another centre. No-one had considered the impact of this move on Christopher's life or the steps that could be taken to maintain the relationship.

It is a common assumption that people with PMLD do not interact with each other, but Ware (1994) found that, in situations where social interaction was made possible, they made contact through touching and vocalising. Firth and Rapley (1990) suggest that

> People with PLDs may not be able to develop friendships which involve understanding each other's needs for dependence and interdependence. But they may be able to develop friendships with a high degree of intimacy and reciprocity in terms of non-verbal behaviour. The elements of choice, reciprocity, persistence, and commitment (as judged by attention and concentration) may all be present (p. 58).

It is therefore important for carers and practitioners to make sure that opportunities for interaction with peers are created as often as possible, and any signs of preference for particular members of their group fostered by making sure that people sit near those they like, that they are included in the same activities or groups, and that they are positioned so that they can interact with each other most easily.

# Helping people to make relationships

If we acknowledge that people with PMLD need a full range of relationships to provide for all their emotional and social needs, and if we also acknowledge that people with PMLD can make relationships of all kinds, how can carers and practitioners help people with PMLD to have relationships which fulfil these broad needs?

Relationships do not just happen. Bayley (1997) argues that structures are all-important to support relationships. These structures are the contexts of the daily lives of people with learning disability and he identifies the following:

- Residence/home: where people live, and also where they lived in the past.
- Work/education/occupation: what people do during normal working hours. Do they have meaningful occupation at these times, and if so where? Some people with PMLD do not have any day provision and spend their time at home with very little to do.
- Leisure/social/spiritual: what people do outside 'working hours'. He distinguishes these pursuits from the leisure activities which are often part of the daytime provision.
- Supportive services and people: these include statutory services, family and others such as neighbours or family friends.

The importance of these structures is in providing the setting and opportunities for developing relationships and, just as importantly, providing support to ensure that once formed, these relationships will survive. Different kinds of relationships tend to develop in each setting, although once a relationship is formed it can change. For example, the occupation setting is initially likely to foster acquaintance but this can develop into friendship and even into a close friendship or partnership. The more people who are involved and the wider the range of contacts, the more possibilities are created for developing relationships of all kinds.

But structures alone will not ensure that people with PMLD have a full range of relationships. Making and keeping relationships require the right circumstances and support. Firth and Rapley (1990) make some suggestions of ways of getting to know other people:

- spending a good deal of time together;
- doing physical activities in a group or team;
- joining a common cause;
- working with someone to help others;
- watching or taking part in events with strong emotional content.

All of these are possible for people with PMLD within the settings described above. Support will be needed to foster the relationships and to ensure that they endure for as long as the people concerned want them to. This might involve:

- Help and guidance: teaching appropriate behaviours, being a role model, introducing people, nurturing friendships, suggesting meeting again or inviting someone home, solving practical problems.
- Practical support: providing transport so that people can attend clubs, then visit each other's homes as friendships develop. Help may be needed to make telephone calls or send a postcard to keep in touch when contact is irregular.
- Particular schemes: Circles of Friends or Circles of Support involve a group of people who meet on a regular basis to help a person with a disability to overcome obstacles, to gain new opportunities or to 'plan, dream and act on that person's behalf'. (see Neville 1996; Wilson and Newton 1996; McConkey in this volume.) Befriending schemes provide companionship and enable people to get involved in activities which interest them (Walsh 1986; Bayley 1997).
- Advocacy: a powerful force in opening up opportunities for people with PMLD (see Tilstone and Barry in this volume for a detailed discussion of the issues).

- Special approaches: such as Intensive Interaction developed to enable people with PMLD who had not experienced the bonding and attachment of early infancy to experience intimate and caring relationships.

# Conclusion

Firth and Rapley (1990) point out that 'It is not possible to provide friendship, or to make friends, for other people'. But it is possible to create circumstances and give support which will make it easier and more likely that people with PMLD can establish a variety of relationships which will fulfil their social, emotional and practical needs.

This chapter has drawn upon the work of many researchers and practitioners to highlight some of these issues, and to give suggestions for ways in which to provide those circumstances and support.

# Chapter 7

# Sexuality: Challenges and Dilemmas

*Caroline Downs*

## Introduction

A three year project based in the Department of Learning Disabilities at the University of Nottingham brought practitioners together from a variety of professional contexts across the country to explore strategies and approaches relating to the sexuality of children and adults with profound and multiple learning difficulties.[1] The project was designed as a piece of action research of the 'professionalising type' (Hart and Bond 1995) in which it is intended that:

- problems emerge from professional experience and practice;
- improvement in practice is defined by professionals on behalf of students/service users;
- advocacy is undertaken on behalf of students/service users.

The processes and work undertaken are described in detail elsewhere (Downs and Craft 1996a, 1996b) and the outcomes and recommendations of this project form the basis of a pack entitled Sex in Context (Downs and Craft 1997a, 1997b, 1997c). In this chapter I want to focus on some of the issues and concerns which confronted professionals from the different disciplines who participated in the project, and to discuss some of the processes which they found to be particularly helpful in addressing these.

## Challenges

When staff in workshops from a variety of settings in different parts of the country were invited to ideas storm difficult aspects of their work, all groups produced long, and remarkably similar, lists. When the items were analysed it became clear that the majority of the concerns expressed, which apparently had a practical origin, actually seemed to result from the difficult and uncomfortable feelings staff experienced, evoked by different aspects of their work. We identified three core feeling statements, which seemed to encompass all other expressed sources of difficulty; even these three are related and seem to overlap to some extent.

These three core challenges were identified as:

- engaging in what is normally a very private matter;
- being responsible and accountable for the assessment of students'/service users' needs;
- encountering and confronting personal and deep seated belief systems.

For some people, even acknowledging they had feelings in relation to their work was a challenge in itself, particularly for those staff who believed that emotions were incompatible with 'professionalism'. However, having overcome this hurdle, there was a general and shared sense of relief, firstly that it was legitimate to have feelings at all and secondly that the feelings they had were acceptable and indeed often shared by some of their colleagues. Believing oneself to be alone in having certain difficulties is generally acknowledged to be a major stressor at work (Kyriacou and Sutcliffe 1978;Fletcher and Payne 1982). Taking the opportunity to discover that others also experience strong feelings and difficulties, whether similar or different, often appeared to remove that source of stress.

A generalised feeling of being of 'low status' at work emerged. Some people reported having grumbled about this frequently with colleagues, and had felt better for having 'got it off their chests'. However, few people had taken it further and tried to unpick this: to explore, for example, the impact of feeling that they were not valued on their self esteem and on their relationships with each other and their students and service users. In some settings this exploration and the voicing of concerns led to some general organisational remedies to the problem, including increased 'integration' or 'inclusion' into mainstream groups. In one Centre role exchanges took place between staff, which increased the understanding of other members of staff of issues which related specifically to people with profound and multiple learning disabilities.

However, it was found that simply focusing on Personal and Social Development[2] which increased the profile of personal care and wellbeing as an integral part of students' and service users' education, elevated the status of those providing this care. Attributing high status to intimate care was seen as the key.

# Exploring the challenges

## Engaging in what is normally a very private matter

An urgent need for clear policies and guidelines in this area quickly became apparent. Most establishments now have policies in the area of sexuality. Child protection legislation and procedures have been in place for some time and Section 241 of the *Education Act 1993* requires all maintained schools to have a written statement of their policy on sex education. Within adult services there is no such legal requirement to have a policy but increasingly social service departments and other agencies have produced policies relating to sexuality and sex education. The Department of Health and Social Services Inspectorate for England and Wales recently recognised and emphasised the importance of agency policies and funded a publication entitled *It Could Never Happen Here!* which offers a model protection policy for adult services to adopt or adapt (Churchill *et al.* 1996).

Even where clear policies in this area do exist however, they are seldom found by hands-on staff to give sufficient guidance in relation to people with profound and multi-ple learning disabilities, for whom unambiguous statements are required regarding touch, intimate care, enabling and supporting sexual expression, masturbation and sexual health screening in the absence of informed consent. Downs and Craft (1997a) seek to remedy this omission by providing models and exercises to aid staff teams to devise guidelines which are specific to the needs of the individuals with whom they work, whether adults or children. Some of these involve trying to put oneself in the position of a person receiving the care, however with an emphasis on a reflective, rather than a subjective, approach.

Even when presented in the context of focused activities, staff often still feel challenged, as these necessitate talking openly about issues which are otherwise seldom discussed and about which many people feel embarrassed or have strong, sometimes conflicting, beliefs and feelings. The common practice of hiding behind catch-all words and phrases and assuming that everyone feels and believes similarly is relatively comfortable; spelling out in guidelines what we mean by 'appropriate' behaviour or precisely how the service will respond to a person masturbating in public quickly removes that refuge and complacency.

Being involved in sexuality work compels staff to confront many feelings and it is important that those working in the field have taken time to address and explore these issues prior to embarking on work in this area. When sexuality matters are approached in relation to someone with high dependency needs, particularly in relation to someone who is sexually mature, this results in what Ann Craft used to refer to as a 'challenging conjunction' (Downs and Craft 1996b).

Colleagues, particularly from adult settings, have talked about having to adopt a 'mindset' or 'way of distancing' themselves to make some experiences more manageable. One workshop participant said: 'It's not easy to admit this, but if I'm honest, I think I cope (providing intimate care to adults) by temporarily denying their human-ness'. Referring to people as 'wheelchairs' or 'non-verbals' or 'children' irrespective of age, is a well known and well documented strategy for coping with otherwise dissonant or intolerable feelings in relation to the lives of people with learning disabilties (Ryan and Thomas 1987).

A common strategy which we noticed that staff in the project adopted, apparently to ease this discomfort, was that of minimising or playing down the degree of disability or the limitations resulting from the disability. Several members of staff involved in our project, for example, commented on the political unsoundness of the term 'profound and multiple impairment'. Parents and carers and some staff we worked with on the other hand embraced the term, the intention of which was to acknowledge the extreme difficulties experienced by the people for whom the project was designed, and by those living and working with them. Underplaying the effects of a disability is evidenced by statements often made by staff to parents, in response to the latters' expression of sadness or concern. Often well-meaning responses, motivated by embarrassment or discomfort, such as 'Oh, all 15 year olds do that!' result in staff protecting themselves at the expense of parents. Comments of this nature can lead parents and carers to question their own, generally correct, view of the situation, presuming, or hoping, that the professional knows best. Alternatively such a comment may be interpreted as a reluctance on the part of the member of staff to listen, as a lack of interest or care, or a recognition by the parent that the professional cannot bear to face the realities of the situation. Some parents and carers working with us in the project reported feeling a sense of obligation to 'protect' professionals from the truth with the result that they felt that they have to take sole responsibility for the problems and issues arising. Some parents and carers withdrew all former trust from that particular member of staff or from all professionals.

## Being responsible and accountable for the identification of students' or service users' needs

A great deal of anxiety was expressed by staff in relation to their confidence and competence to understand the behaviour and communications of students or service users. While recognising that assessing the needs of the people with whom they work is a part of the teaching and learning process in which they are engaged daily, many staff working with the project reported feeling almost paralysed at the prospect of misinterpreting a student's or service user's communication in relation to touch or sexual expression. Many staff recognised wide discrepancies between their assessments of different individuals' needs and told stories about assumptions they had made, which they later discovered to be misinterpretations of communications.

One project participant told the story of a student in her group who suddenly started requesting drinks, by pointing to a cup, with a frequency which alerted the staff team to the possibility of diabetes. Close monitoring was undertaken of the frequency with which he demanded drinks; urine samples tested negative, but 'Tom' continued to ask for drinks repeatedly until one day he stopped as suddenly as he had started. The fact that this coincided with the replacement of children's illustrated cups by more 'adult'

**Figure 7.1** The Care Review                    (Downs and Craft 1997c)

ones passed unnoticed until one day two weeks later a member of staff spotted, in Tom's overnight bag, his personal Thomas the Tank Engine plate and cutlery set which he was taking to the respite care unit. A telephone call to his mother confirmed that he had recently developed a strong interest in Thomas the Tank Engine and would point to anything carrying the illustration; only then was the cup which Tom had repeatedly pointed to remembered. While staff consoled themselves that this misinterpretation of Tom's communication was relatively insignificant, inasmuch as Tom had not experienced too much irritation or frustration (although people did feel guilty that he had been unsupported in his attempt to communicate), it was sufficient to sap staff's confidence to get it right, particularly in relation to what they saw as more significant communications. Case conferences in which staff involved in a student's life had been unable to agree upon his or her needs were also reported to be common (see Figure 7.1).

A frequent lack of agreement between communication partners as to the meaning or intention of a given piece of communication is an area of extreme concern. Brown and Lehr (1989) for example, describe a study in which familiar adults were asked to interpret the communications of children with profound and multiple learning disabilities. Over half of the attempts to communicate were either missed or misinterpreted, according to the interpretation given by the child's principal carer (generally the mother). Similar findings have been noted in other studies (e.g. Hogg *et al.* 1995; Latchford 1989; Withers 1991). The frequency with which communications may be misinterpreted has been more widely recognised as a cause for concern since Facilitated Communication was introduced as a method for working with people with very limited expressive communication.

Facilitated Communication has been defined as 'a strategy for improving motor skills to enable someone to point to or touch objects, pictures or letters for communication purposes' (Attwood 1993, cited in Bedko, *et al.* 1996). The method generally involves the facilitator giving physical support, for example, hand-on-hand/wrist to an individual to enable them to point to a symbol, picture, object or to spell out words. Although it is acknowledged that for some students and service users this method may be very helpful, there has also been much concern about the authorship or ownership of the messages generated. In experimental situations designed to test authorship, in which an individual and the communication partner are given different questions, the answer given is invariably a response to the question posed to the communication partner who, it is generally recognised, unconsciously projects his or her own wishes, needs and motives on to the service user.

A recognition of the subjectivity of interpreting behaviour is not conducive to staff feeling confident they have understood accurately, particularly in areas they regard as highly significant or controversial in a student's or service user's life. This lack of confidence is accentuated for staff when they are working in partnership with parents and carers. The increased 'consumer power' of parents can be daunting for many staff, especially if they feel they must not demonstrate any uncertainty if they are to retain parents' respect and trust (Scott 1996). This is further exacerbated in the area of sexuality where parents are themselves having to address changing roles within the family, adulthood juxtaposed with extreme dependence and a range of difficult feelings, often including fear, worry and shock.

Under these circumstances, if parents and carers are to be encouraged to consent or assent to their son or daughter taking part in any aspects of a Personal and Social Development programme (see Figure 7.2), aspects of which depart from the familiarity and safety of customary care and conventional activities, staff need more than ever to feel certain and to convey their conviction in relation to their assessments of need.

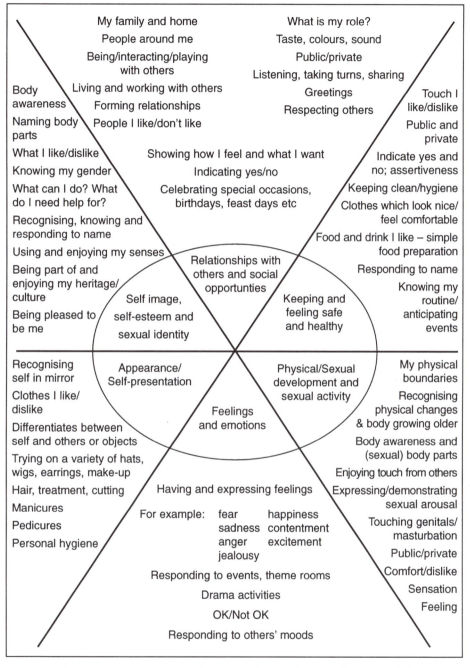

**Figure 7.2** A summary of topics included in the Personal and Social Development Programme

The 'selling feature' of relationships and sex education for parents and carers is generally the increased safety which increased knowledge and assertiveness allows, being relieved of having to explain the 'embarrassing bits' and the clearing up of any misapprehensions sons and daughters may have gained from peers or the media. For people with profound and multiple impairment these aspects become less compelling.

The last two issues are often seen as irrelevant and, while learning to differentiate between good and bad touch and being able to indicate 'yes' and 'no' are vital aspects of their education, parents recognise that these accomplishments of themselves do not by any means guarantee safety; people with severe communication and learning difficulties are more reliant than anyone on the integrity of those supporting them.

Within the project it was therefore regarded as high priority that staff who are working with people whose communication is unconventional should develop skills, strategies and confidence to interpret communications and assess students' and service users' needs as accurately and decisively as possible. Many staff were shocked to learn that not responding to behaviour, for fear of misinterpretation, is not the 'safe option' they had assumed it to be. Carson (1992) points to the law of negligence demanding a certain standard of care and level of intervention, even where this involves intimate physical contact. He argues that this is the case particularly where, in the absence of such intervention, the service user's opportunities for enjoyment or socialising may be diminished. An example of this would be inappropriate masturbation preventing a person's participation in social events.

We decided to concentrate on two areas to clarify and objectify observation and assessment of need.

The first was to ensure that, where possible, the individual's condition or syndrome and any implications it may have are known in order to increase the competence and confidence of staff to interpret facial expression, gesture, movement and so on. Staff with whom we worked recognised that, on occasion, meaning or intent — or both — may be ascribed to, for example, a cry or rapid breathing when, in actuality, it is out of the person's control and may have been epileptiform in nature or some other manifestation of the person's condition.

Secondly, to give staff the opportunity to bring into awareness their own feelings and motives in relation both to the people with whom they work and to the work they do, in order to decrease the extent to which these, when unacknowledged, become projected on to others thereby distorting their observations.

We believed that concentrating on increased awareness of feelings and motives is justified as, without this, perceptions of what is actually going on are inevitably influenced outside of awareness, which can result in the confusion about authorship of the communication. Ensuring that all staff feel confident about their own individual feelings and the effects of these, serves to decrease the effect of the so-called 'acquiescent response set'. This occurs when an individual, unsure of the 'right' answer, will have their confidence eroded by other people's beliefs which differ from their own and will come to agree with the majority. If the only factor we can rely upon to feel more confident of the accuracy of our interpretations is agreement between different people as to the meaning or intention of the communication, then it is clearly crucial that this is not undermined by uncertainty derived from persuasion.[3]

It is a well known and well documented phenomenon that service users come to look like their key workers (Kitson and Supple 1997). Normalisation, while undoubtedly having improved practice and services offered to people with learning disabilities, may also have increased our assumptions that individual's likes and dislikes are the same as our own, however much tastes may be seen to differ between colleagues. The result may be that not only clothes, but also furniture and decor and leisure pursuits reflect the tastes and interests of staff rather than of the people they support. Unfortunately, for some time, this approach seemed also to generate complacency that a good service was being provided; it is only relatively recently that we have started to question whether we are perhaps meeting our own needs, rather than addressing those of the people with and for whom we work.

As the staff we were working with became more aware of their individual feelings, beliefs and motives, they reported noticing that these did indeed affect their ways of perceiving events. In our project, in order to move away from practice built on assumption, staff found it helpful to work through a series of exercises designed to help them to become more at ease discussing and working with sexuality, to look at their feelings, motives and projections and to recognise and share their perceptions. These formed the background to a simple checklist for staff to go through to help them to scrutinise and confirm their interpretations, thereby increasing confidence and competence to 'get it right'.

In the checklist, staff are invited to respond 'yes' or 'no' to a series of questions, all of which they will already have addressed while working through prior staff development exercises, for example:

- Do you in general experience any strong feelings towards this person?
- Are you aware of having any strong feelings towards this specific communication?
- If you put yourself in the person's shoes, is this what you would be communicating?
- Do you think you can put to one side any feelings, needs, motives or beliefs relating to the person or the situation which you may have?
- Have you recorded the communication?
- Is your description of the communication factual? clear? detailed?
- Have other people observed similar communication?
- Is there any support for your communication?
  and so on.

Self Advocacy for students and service users developing some autonomy in the context of relationships and sexuality presents staff with additional challenges over and above the consideration of whether communication has been interpreted accurately and the ever present power dynamic between the person with a learning disability and the helper. (For further discussion of this subject see Tilstone and Barry in this volume.) The tensions and dilemmas which arise when making decisions and delivering a service in what one presumes to be the best interests of a person even when he or she appears to be indicating dislike or 'No', are present on numerous occasions with issues relating to touch, health checks and so on. Guidelines in this area are vital and it is useful if, in devising them, these tensions and the effects of individual staff members' priorities and motives, are acknowledged (see Downs and Craft 1997a).

## Encountering and confronting personal and deepseated beliefs

Becoming more aware, through discussion, of the range of different beliefs and feelings towards sexuality issues seems initially to make staff less rather than more confident to define the scope of sexual expression for children or adults, whose needs and life experiences are so very different from their own.

The success of sexuality work undertaken with people with learning disabilities tends to focus on the extent to which people have been helped to attain the outlets for sexual expression generally approved or endorsed in this country. Brown suggests that 'marriage, as the least contentious outlet for sexual activity (has) joined open employment or literacy as illusory goals for many mentally handicapped (sic) people in their struggle to normalcy' (Brown 1982, p.46).

Some people with learning disabilities, to their credit, do choose and achieve

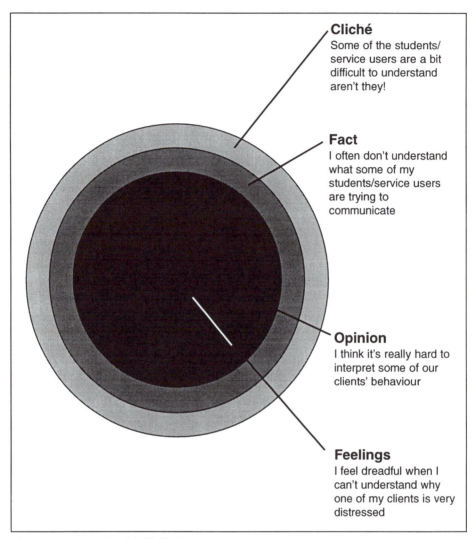

**Figure 7.3** Levels of self-disclosure

marriage (Craft and Craft 1979). However, this is not an option which is open to the majority and, when working with people with very severe or profound learning disabilities, it is particularly important that staff try to remain open to alternative ways of expressing sexuality. This demands a degree of self-awareness and openness to difference in order to put to one side our own feelings and beliefs and to resist the influence of media images of sexuality and sexual expression. As many disabled writers demonstrate, the wider the gulf between the idealised sexual norm and the individual, the less will any sexual characteristics be ascribed to them by society (Fulton 1994; Polio 1994).

Some of the shortcomings of normalisation are discussed above and, in terms of sexuality, staff groups we worked with recognised that valuing for their students and service users what they valued for themselves could, ironically, result in seeing as aberrant any 'different' forms of sexual expression, and indeed possibly any sexualised behaviour on the part of the people with whom they worked.

The opportunity to explore and share feelings[4] in relation to sexuality and the individuals with whom staff groups worked, boosted their confidence, firstly, about having feelings at all in relation to their work and secondly, about the feelings they had. Some project participants kept journals or logs to help them to notice and record their feelings and to gain insights into service users' and students' lives. Different levels at which the sharing of feelings with colleagues occurred were identified (see Figure 7.3). This generally depended both on self-awareness and on the degree of trust felt; an increase in either or both resulted in a move towards honest sharing of uncensored feelings.

Within the project, staff involved in some workshops had the opportunity to practise self disclosing in this way, either in a facilitated group or in pairs and trios, until disclosing information and feelings no longer felt false or forced. Relating with colleagues in this way was generally felt to be beneficial for peoples' wellbeing and satisfaction at work; it increased the levels of trust and respect they felt for other staff and improved their relationships with students and service users.

In two work settings staff tried to measure and compare the contentment of the people with PMLD with whom they worked before and after they had started working in this way. They looked at students' or service users' levels of engagement in activities, levels of distress and crying, the amount of self-injurious behaviour and incidents of aggression towards other people and objects. In both settings an increase in levels of engagement and a decrease in all other events was noticed, and staff felt sure that this resulted from their increased trust in each other and their feeling safe to talk openly and honestly in their staff teams.

As noted above, motives and feelings can get in the way of or distort perceptions of others' communications. This is true of all interchanges as communicators negotiate meaning, but becomes increasingly the case when interacting with a person whose communication is unconventional, where the listener has to rely to a far greater extent on inference. Self-disclosing never becomes risk free; however, the risks diminish as people know and accept more and more about each other and there is less 'face' to be lost. Some project participants reported feeling more confident to speak out on behalf of a student or service user as they became less concerned that others might find them 'odd' or 'wrong'.

## Hierarchy of acceptability of feelings

Once staff involved in the project had become confident to disclose their feelings, they started to identify some which they found were riskier to share with colleagues than others. In an exercise designed to enable staff to identify what aspects of their students' and service users' behaviour or other aspects of their work they found difficult, people were invited to list these, to identify the feelings they experienced in relation to them and to grade the level of difficulty on a scale of 1–5. They were asked to try to be as honest as they were able to be, with the knowledge that their lists were for their own private use and they would be invited to share only what they wished to.

Of the many staff across the country who took part in this exercise, most felt that there existed an unspoken rule regarding feelings which the majority would view as acceptable and those which would be seen as unacceptable and therefore were, to begin with, inadmissible. For example, most people felt quite comfortable declaring 'negative feelings' (anger, sadness, pain) towards one student hurting another or not being able to meet a service user's needs because of a lack of resources.

Feelings generally regarded as less appropriate, and therefore riskier to discuss, were those which highlighted a professional or personal failing or shortcoming, for example, acknowledging someone's lack of progress or finding difficult or distasteful an integral part of their work. Many people felt guilty or embarrassed because they disliked dealing with a service user's sexual arousal; responding to frequent, and particularly unsatisfactory, masturbation; problems related to menstruation. A few people said, tentatively to begin with, that they felt very guilty owning their difficulty with dribbling and the smell of saliva. Learning of the prevalence of this difficulty was an immense relief. Several writers (e.g. Ware 1994) point to the disproportionate lack of interaction between staff and people who dribble.

Predictably, the most difficult feelings to acknowledge were those which reflect a deepseated need to be needed or a fear of rejection. Some of these statements were, at face value, thought to belong to the category above and comprise distaste for an aspect of a service user's behaviour, for example feeling really bad if, when trying to feed someone, they regurgitate the food. However, particularly where a feeling was graded as being extremely difficult to cope with, this invariably indicated a feeling of rejection. Staff felt strongly that recognising this and being able to cope with not being needed was necessary if they were to be able to encourage self advocacy in their students and service users.

# Conclusion

Fairbairn (1996) has suggested that difficulties which staff experience when working around sexuality with people with learning disabilities are moral dilemmas. Once these have been resolved, he maintains, practice becomes clear and responding and teaching in this area is no more problematic than teaching mathematics or geography. Staff involved in our project agreed with this sentiment and found that the more they explored the issues, the more complex they became. They examined moral issues and their personal beliefs; they also examined their feelings, needs and motives in relation to their work. As a result of this increased awareness of moral issues and increased self understanding, they felt more confident to assess and meet their students' and service users' needs in relation to Sexuality and Personal and Social Development.

# Notes

1. The project entitled Safeguards, Strategies and Approaches Relating to the Sexuality of Children, Adolescents and Adults with Profound and Multiple Impairments was directed by Ann Craft and coordinated by Caroline Downs. It was funded by the Joseph Rowntree Foundation.
2. We use the term Personal and Social Development (PSD) to refer to the area of activity and work referred to variously as Personal, Social (and Health) Education; Sexuality Education; Relationships and Sex Education; and so on.
3. It is useful to differentiate between the reliability and the validity of our interpretations. A high level of agreement between several self-aware individuals as to the meaning or intent of some behaviour testifies to increased reliability of interpretation. The validity or accuracy of the interpretation of the communicative intent is not confirmed: it is theoretically possible that the entire staff team agree on one interpretation and that they are all wrong. See Grove, Porter and Bunning (forthcoming) for an exploration of reliability and validity issues in relation to

validating the communications of people with severe and profound learning difficulties.

4. Gerda Hanko talks about the dangers of 'untutored' feelings, i.e. those which are not understood and are therefore out of control and liable to engender `knee jerk' reactions to situations (Hanko 1995). Similarly Ann Craft pointed to the importance of individual awareness of feelings and beliefs so that students and service users are not at the mercy of the individual sexual attitudes of different care givers (Craft 1987).

Chapter 8

# Challenging Behaviour is Normal

*Dave Hewett*

## Introduction

As the title of this chapter indicates, I see the challenging behaviours produced by people with very severe learning difficulties as an appropriate (in personal terms) response to the forces which are affecting them in their lives. We usually greatly desire to help the person to behave differently, but I would suggest that this stance of understanding, of viewing the behaviours that the person produces as a natural, normal response, is the best starting point in terms of the attitudes we carry with us in our everyday work.

That challenging behaviour is normal is the main theme of this chapter. The first section of the chapter introduces the concept of challenging behaviour being attributable, for each individual, to a variety of interacting factors. This theory will be illustrated by considering the assumed factors applying to a service user, and discussing some of the more prominent and regularly occurring factors likely to affect many people with very severe and profound and multiple learning disabilities. This leads to a discussion and critique of the ways in which our services and the daily practices of staff may be responding to challenging behaviour viewed from this standpoint.

The third part of the chapter presents a theoretical model for the living and working atmosphere in which we place children and adults who present challenging behaviours, together with some principles and some challenges concerning the implementation of this model in practice. Though I use residential work as an example of service delivery, I hope the reader will accept that I am making points about multi-disciplinary work in schools, day centres and residential establishments equally. Throughout, the term 'service user' is used to embrace the people of all ages, including school-age children, with whom we work.

## Understanding why our service users may have behaviours which are challenging

The complexity of the various interacting sources or factors in the challenging behaviours of any individual with learning disabilities is increasingly being recognised and documented (Felce and Emerson 1996). This is reflected, in my estimation, in

## Personal Factors

Genetics e.g.
- genetic conditions which are thought to influence behaviour directly

Constitutional or Physiological e.g.
- hormonal state
- hunger/food/water
- allergies
- brain damage
- drug regimes
- illnesses
- epilepsy
- mental health problems
- mobility/physical abilities

Relationships
- difficulty experiencing understandable relationships

Personality & Character e.g.
- limited emotional development – emotions still 'raw'
- extremes of extroversion or introversion
- neuroticism
- impulsiveness
- limited knowledge about enjoying life, having fun, finding each passing moment pleasurable
- changeable moods
- arousal pattern
- coping styles (ability to cope with own emotions)
- unstable early upbringing experiences

Sense of Self e.g.
- self-esteem – unable to see self as valuable – as 'good to be with'
- self-view e.g. 'this is how I am' – seeing self as a difficult or violent person
- degree of self-knowledge/insight
- feelings of powerlessness

Damage
- e.g. sexual or physical, or emotional/phsychological abuse
- first-hand experience of e.g. violence

Difficulty with Communication e.g.
- not able to use or understand language
- difficulty with verbal expression
- difficulty with understanding others, e.g. perceptual problems

Basic Needs & Abilities e.g.
- still not socialised into the way of behaving shared by other people due to communication/relationship difficulties
- unfulfilled sexual needs
- still at early developmental stage
- still has basic security and social needs

## Environmental Factors

Quality of Physical Environment e.g.
- lighting
- acoustics
- noise levels
- space available
- humidity
- heating
- colours

Quality of the social environment e.g.
- general social complexity
- environment not complex enough
- unstimulating
- environment has challenging behaviour normally occuring

Placed in Position of Powerlessness e.g.
- being goal-blocked
- unreasonable punishment
- extensive use of punishment
- lack of access to decision making
- lack of access to choice over own actions
- staff stress on compliance and conformity
- staff reliance on confrontation and win/lose scenarios
- behaviour constantly scrutinised with frequent interventions from staff
- staff focus on behaviour more than feelings

Unpredictable Occurrences e.g.
- being startled/cornered
- lack of understanding about what is happening in the environment
- other people's outbursts

Other people's high expectations e.g.
- 'good' behaviour always
- behave your chronological age always
- staff set unachievable objectives

All Communication Difficulties e.g.
- lack of access to communications at own level of ability
- lack of access to communications with staff
- staff lack expertise in communication activities
- communication difficulties between staff – staff not 'getting their act together', not working consistently with shared understandings

etc.

**Figure 8.1** Possible factors in the production of challenging behaviours

working practices of staff everywhere, a point endorsed by Mansell (1994), but with the qualification that an 'important part of this understanding is that mainstream learning disability services everywhere have to improve their competence' (p.3).

One of the improvements which, it seems, should remain a priority is that the techniques or approaches, or interventions adopted by staff in meeting their service users' challenging behaviours, do more than simply focus on the behaviour of the person. In schools, day centres and residential establishments there should also be major consideration, for each individual, of the person's feelings and attitudes, and of what 'quality of life' is like from that person's point of view.

Figure 8.1 shows an outline of examples of typical factors which may be playing a part in the production of challenging behaviours for many people with learning disabilities. I view it as a 'working model' for staff understanding. It is not particularly scientific in that every item has not been corroborated beyond all doubt. However, many of the items have an obvious relationship with scientifically demonstrated theories about the human condition in general, or with recent and current thinking concerning work in the field of learning disabilities. It is difficult to give an original attribution for this model, though I do not claim it. I first encountered something like it in Arnett (1989) in connection with purely violent behaviour, and it has been reworked gradually since (Hewett 1995; Harris and Hewett 1996). Its main advantage is the graphic way it sets out many of the possible and often complex things which are likely to be contributing to the behaviour of the service users. Another advantage is concerned with a central issue. Surely we can all look at Figure 8.1 and see something of ourselves there, many of the things which might be contributing to our own episodes of difficult behaviour or at least, difficult feelings.

In this example, the personal factors which seem to be generally prominent in the lives of people with the most severe and profound and multiple learning disabilities have been given additional emphasis. These are the kinds of personal factors which I frequently find myself discussing with staff in thinking about work with their service users. Although the factors and the combination of factors are likely to be different for each individual, and the behaviours arising from the interaction of the factors are also different, those particularly highlighted here arise frequently for many individuals. These factors have particular relevance to the lives of people with severe or profound learning disabilities, focusing on problems which are likely to be general for their life experiences: communication, relationships, feelings and emotional understandings, and their continuing basic needs and abilities which may be comparable with early stages of human development.

In the rest of this chapter, it is the personal factors and service responses to them which will be the particular focus, though at this stage it is worth looking at the list of environmental factors and thinking about these things in terms of curriculum or service delivery, the atmosphere of our schools and other establishments, and our working practices.

Figure 8.2 shows the personal factors assumed to be affecting one person with profound and multiple learning disabilities. This list was put together during course groupwork by staff who work with Jane. Jane has been chosen as an example because her behaviour difficulties are severe and her learning needs fundamental. The extreme nature of her difficulties help to make the points here, but the points may also apply to people whose behaviour and learning difficulties are not so severe.

The first point arising from looking at Jane's list is a simple, even obvious one, already mentioned. But this is one of the most significant issues affecting our working attitudes and practices and it seems that many of us still struggle on a daily basis to

## Personal Factors

Constitutional/physiological
- mobility difficulties – has limited ability to walk, though she bum-shuffles fast (don't know how aggravating this is for her), very good with arm/hand coordination
- she is so dependent on us for everything
- we suspect serious regularly occurring PMT – past records indicate this, too
- very focused on food, gorges whenever possible, steals other clients' food
- has brain damage (well, assumed, we can't see it) but unclear that this directly affects her behaviour
- continuous runny nose (must be really aggravating), suspected headaches, stomach aches, pain from occasional self-injury?
- mental health – we always worry that she experiences bad depressions, but can't get this addressed (we are not 'qualified' to decide)

Relationships
- we agonise – she does not relate to anyone very well, seems rejecting of relationships, seems to be alone and hard – she's lovely sometimes though, lets you 'in' now and again
- she likes tickle, and tumble sometimes (we are careful though – it is difficult to relax when you are near her)
- has so little ability to communicate, this will obviously affect her ability to form relationships – oh, see 'communication'

Personality and Character
- difficult to be precise about her emotional development but it seems to be very basic, she behaves exactly the way she seems to be feeling at that moment, must be difficult to have emotional development without relationships
- she's kind of extrovert in that she has no inhibition on her bevaviour
- impulsive – well, yes
- she certainly can have fun, she has days when she laughs, she likes to be tickled sometimes, but mostly she looks sad and angry
- her moods seem to change very quickly, little emotional stability
- arousal pattern – she gets triggered into being horrible very quickly – food, people, coming too near, etc.
- coping styles – she doesn't seem to have them – she behaves the way she feels at the moment, she doesn't seem able to have self-discipline
- we don't know much about her early life but we do know she was separated from her family early on and she was on the 'at risk' register

Sense of Self
- self-esteem – we don't think Jane likes herself at all, especially when she's hitting herself
- it must be difficult for Jane to see herself as someone who could behave better and enjoy life more, her behaviour has been so established for so long (we don't all agree on this)
- she must have big feelings of powerlessness, particularly over food and being kept in the room when she wants to go out – she has so little opportunity to decide what will happen, everything she wants to do seems to be things we have to stop
- damage – we suspect!

Communication
- no verbal language or representation abilities, makes a range of noises, doesn't look at other people much, relates only a little, likes some physical contact for fun though we are careful when close – doesn't relate well with us or her peers

Basic needs and abilities
- well no, Jane is not well socialised, it is so difficult to relate with her – she doesn't eat well (that is getting better), she has lots of 'habits'
- sexual needs – she does quite a bit of sexual self-stimulation
- developmental stage – we don't know what that is but she doesn't communicate or relate well, she is obsessed with food, she has difficulty with emotions
- security/social – Jane seems very anxious a lot of the time, specially if we approach her wrong, she doesn't like change and reacts badly to it, she doesn't seem to like being in the room with us and the others, she likes to be alone a lot of the time

**Figure 8.2** Possible factors contributing to Jane's challenging behaviours

maintain the positive attitudes arising from sober consideration of this issue. Effectively, Jane deserves to have challenging behaviours. Being difficult to be with is an understandable response to her life circumstances, particularly to what she has going on inside her. Jane's challenging behaviour is understandable to the point of being legitimate. Of course, her behaviours may well be extremely antisocial, negatively affecting the lives of people around her. We should view these behaviours as, perhaps, unacceptable and use this attitude for part of the motivation to help her. However, in helping her this attitude – that her behaviour is understandable – should be prominent and visible in all of our practices. This is often not the case, particularly with staff groups whose practices are based first and foremost on remediating visible behaviours and, in accordance with some classic British child rearing styles, viewing good behaviour at all costs as the objective. I believe that many of the more negative attitudes and staff practices I observe are related to our traditions in child rearing. O'Hagan (1993) sets out arguments that mild to severe emotional and psychological abuse is implicit in the highly controlling child rearing practices of the early twentieth century, still influential today. In such practices, or the 'moral hygienist' movement, the focus is on the visible behaviours of the child, with the child's feelings secondary or not considered.

In fact, there is nothing particularly wrong with a relationship between child rearing practices and our work with people with learning disabilities who have challenging behaviours. It is almost inevitable that staff base their everyday practice in part upon their experiences of life in general. I will argue however, that in so doing, we should think carefully about more positive models of child-rearing than ones that simply control and focus on behaviour. I suggest that the concept of 'Helping the Person Learn How to Behave' which I will set out later, and the attitudes and practices which can derive from it, is just such a positive model.

It is intensely important for helping Jane that such positive models are adopted. The staff working with her have the very real perception that Jane feels awful and that focusing on her 'emotional antecedents' (Novaco 1997) must form part of the picture of helping her. Hopefully, carrying out the exercise helps the staff to feel even more empowered and determined to do things with and around Jane that would address her personal factors. They may do things which are intended to have an effect on Jane's sense of self-esteem, her emotional stability, to help her to view herself a little more positively, to relate better, particularly to staff and to benefit from a greater sense of security and self-worth derived from developing relationships. Naturally, given Jane's experiences and knowledge so far, this is going to be hard work. It will need commitment and determination to be positive in action-planning and seeing the plan through in a methodical fashion. The staff will also need positive attitudes about Jane and their work with her which are visible to Jane. In addition, they need to maintain positive attitudes about what they are undertaking. A degree of realism about the nature of the difficulties the person is experiencing and that there is no 'quick fix' is a helpful attitude. One of the purposes of the exercise that the staff carried out together is to foster this realism. They will also need to consider the reality that Jane's behaviour should be viewed as normal and that they are 'accepting that it is legitimately part of one's job to work with such a person' (Zarkowska and Clements 1988, p.175). This positive attitude is central to good work with people with challenging behaviours and to the creation of a healthy team which carries it out.

# Emotions, relationships, communication – implications for services

So far then, the general issues that I am attempting to illustrate by thinking about Jane are concerned with our work on emotions and relationships. Hegarty and Gale (1996) see this issue as central, that challenging behaviours may even be a 'symptom of emotional stress and psychological isolation' (p.31). Jane seems to have all sorts of needs around her emotional development. In particular, she needs simply to carry out some further emotional development which may so far not have been available to her due to the degree of her learning disability and her ability to communicate and relate to other people. I have the very positive impression, that all around the country in schools and adult services, these matters are increasingly being addressed by staff. They are thinking and talking about these matters more openly and there are visible aspects of their approaches and practices which are geared towards these needs in their service users. They are also less abashed, less 'English' (Gibson 1983), about discussing deeply things such as 'feelings', 'self-esteem' and 'relationship', viewing these matters as inevitable, even welcomed aspects of their work with people who can nonetheless sometimes be horribly difficult to be with.

Sinason (1992) points to a lack of available and helpful literature concerned with providing emotional experiences for people with learning disabilities, although recently there seems to be a greater focus on this topic appearing in the literature. Gardner and Smyly (1997) write:

> Our assumption was that to work proactively with people who show challenging behaviour we needed to look more closely at the relationships within which such behaviour occurs. More specifically, we felt from our experience that the absence of good quality positive valuing relationships, where clients are given time to explore emotional aspects of their lives, can lead to an increase in 'challenging behaviour'. The nature of the relationship between people who provide services and those who receive them is a vital part of the lives of people with learning disabilities. (p. 26)

Gardner and Smyly are more pessimistic than I am with regard to the present situation of staff practice, however. They cite work by Clegg *et al.* (1991) which found low rates of staff contact with service users, despite improvements in staffing ratios. This study found also that social contact is rarely mutual, with interactions too frequently being concerned with staff delivering one-way directives.

Creating and maintaining nurturing relationships with people with profound and multiple or severe and complex learning disabilities can be far from easy. For Jane, two of the barriers to these experiences will inevitably be her lack of experience of them although she is thirty-six years old, and her lack of ability, desire and experience around communicating and giving attention to other people. We are still at a relatively early stage in the development of approaches to, say, the development of communication abilities for such service users. Gardner and Smyly describe their workshop approach to the development of what can be termed 'active listening' skills for staff. There is an implicit recognition within their work that everyone working in the field needs help and advice with the often very technical nature of doing things such as communicating and developing relationships with people who find these human attainments classically difficult.

There are other barriers though. Some of the values and attitudes apparently fundamental to our services may also create barriers to these aspects of our work. One of the values which should concern us is one of which we should also be rightly proud. This value is about the dedication that services generally have to doing developmental work with individuals. In schools, of course, it is a legal obligation, but in all services there is mostly a powerful, intrinsic expectation that all people with learning disabilities can and will learn more, gain new knowledge and skills. This is one of the most wonderful aspects of our services. However, we need to keep thinking about its implications for all people with learning disabilities, and to be careful about the manner in which this value is enacted to the individual service user. It may generate an atomosphere of relentless demand that they fulfil tasks or take part in task and goal-orientated activities. This atmosphere may be one of their major life experiences and characterises most interactions and relationships with staff.

The result of this may be that we run the risk of devaluing, even damaging the feelings of our service users with our understandable drive for their attainments. We must be careful that the message from us is not something like 'yes, yes, you are a really good person if you achieve this; well done, good person, now I have something else for you to learn and you will be an even better person if you achieve that'. It is so important that people with learning disabilities, as well as all the task-orientated achievements we have in mind for them, also receive plenty of attention with no strings attached. The message of such activities would be 'well, here I am, I'm with you for the next few minutes or so, but I haven't particularly got in mind anything I want to do with you — I'm happy to do nothing, but with you'.

This is a social experience which most of the rest of us receive regularly with a wide range of friends and acquaintances. Actually, it is surely the main social experience we all receive. Anything task-orientated which we do with other people occurs all the better because we so frequently rehearse simply being with other people in situations where there is no target to be attained. However, we are all in better emotional shape to achieve, due to the enhanced self-esteem we receive because other people seem to like spending time with each one of us — with no clear purpose other than spending that time.

Staff working with people who have the more severe learning disabilities need to make sure that whatever else they do, they see it as part of their duty to sit and do nothing in particular with their service users. Gardner and Smyly (1977) term this aspect of practice 'coffee drinking behaviour'. It is particularly important in residential work where the first priority is to provide a 'home' — a place which is agreeable, comfortable, relaxed, nurturing, where there is emotional support and understandable relationships. The provision of 'home' in residential work is the absolute priority, and 'coffee drinking behaviour' is not at odds with any of the other things we are trying to get service users to achieve. On the contrary, it is the essential basis for the person being in good shape to achieve all of those things, including making progress with challenging behaviours.

> staff often feel self-conscious and concerned that they are not doing proper work if they are seen to be just sitting and being with clients in an informal way. In contrast, leisure activities and domestic tasks, 'doing things', are valued as task-oriented learning opportunities. (p.27)

This point is underlined by French (1993) who is critical about services and staff interpreting 'independence' as getting the service user to do as much as possible for her or himself on her or his own. She makes the point that for people with disabilities, the single-minded drive toward this sort of 'independence' may often have two undesirable side-effects. Firstly, the service user may be stressed repeatedly by the daily efforts of the staff toward the attainment of such targets as, for instance, unassisted eating. Secondly, having achieved an 'independence skill', the service user may then have lost an opportunity to have at least some sort of interaction with a member of staff. French is not advocating that we give up teaching such skills, but certainly we examine the worth of independence training in a manner individualised to each service user, taking into account such things as the emotional and social environment they may need, and whether 'independence' has priority over this.

In some services, staff may feel that to be seen to be doing their job, they must be seen to be busy, doing 'busy work'. A shift in thinking and attitudes is required if the working situation is to be altered in order to allow a proper focus on emotional, relationship and communication activities. There is a management issue here about the signals which are sent to staff everywhere concerning what constitutes valid work. Of course, managers also need to make sure that doing nothing in particular with service users is actually more than opting out.

These pressures can be intense for staff in schools. The learning culture is such an absolute expectation and the emphasis placed on things such as implementation of the National Curriculum has been severe. Teachers and teaching assistants can feel under great stress to deliver identifiable, measurable attainments — and quickly. This stress can affect the social environment experienced by children with PMLD. It can affect it because the staff may feel they must work in an intensively task-orientated way to achieve visible attainments. It can affect it also because highly stressed staff may themselves not be in good emotional condition to be relaxed interactors with pupils who are still learning the basics of communication.

This part of the discussion now provides a link to helping people to learn more about communicating and, by implication, to relate more effectively to the people around them. For Jane, as for so many people with PMLD, communication abilities, or the comparative lack of communication ability, is likely to be a prime factor in the way that they behave. If you are focusing on doing something about a person's challenging behaviour, the person's communication ability is the first area to start doing work. Developments in communication ability are likely to have correspondingly beneficial knock-on effects on their behaviour, almost without doing anything else about their behaviour (Nind and Hewett 1994), though these other things should be done too. We may also view the fundamentals of communication as some of the fundamentals of relating generally. For instance, the more that a person is able simply to tolerate another person's presence and then take on gradually more complex interactions, the more likely it is that the relationship, and the emotional well-being that goes with it, will develop.

Figure 8.3 outlines some points about why communication ability may be such an important factor in challenging behaviour. Even those of us who have been working with people with PMLD for a long time may still find it difficult to visualise the problems that may exist in the lives of people who are unable to indulge fully in that wonderful human ability of highly sophisticated communication. People who cannot communicate as fully as the rest of us will probably seem different, often difficult. Thus work on communication for each individual service user should be correspondingly prominent in all our services. Unfortunately, this is not always the case, and there are several reasons for this.

One contributory reason is simply the present state of affairs concerning our knowledge and technique. We are still at an early stage of knowing how to help people to learn more about communication, particularly people with profound and multiple learning disability. The nature of our own abilities as staff is, in itself, a contributory factor in Jane's challenging behaviours, and probably always has been. We may well also be able to perceive it as a contributory factor in her learning disability, or even a central aspect of it.

---

- Communication problems are likely to be profoundly frustrating.
- Communication problems are likely to be even more frustrating when you are aware that you have them.
- Communication problems, especially severe ones, can get in the way of effective relating with other people unless the other people have the ability to communicate in a way that is meaningful. Not relating with other people effectively is likely to be a personal factor in its own right.
- Human beings are genetically 'programmed' to have the potential to communicate in a rich and fulfilling way, and have a great deal of energy available for this purpose. The energy may well be available to a person who nonetheless has considerable communication difficulties.
- The development of communication structures, organises, moderates and controls behaviour.
- Without communication abilities, you are more likely to behave the way you feel.
- Communication abilities help a person to deal with their emotions, to have a more balanced and ordered emotional life.
- Communication abilities enable more reason, insight and rationality.
- Difficulties with communication and relating mean it is more difficult for the person to be socialised into the manner of behaving shared by most other people.
- To communicate is to exercise considerable personal power. People are less likely to behave in ways that are challenging if they are exercising agreeable amounts of personal power.
- Difficulties with communication may make it more difficult to 'defuse' a person with good challenging incident management techniques.

---

**Figure 8.3** Possible factors contributing to Jane's challenging behaviours

The approaches to helping people to know more about communicating and relating such as Intensive Interaction (Nind and Hewett 1994), the work of Caldwell (1996), Augmented Mothering (Ephraim 1986), Communication Through Movement (Burford 1986, 1989), are a start — but only a start. There are now also helpful texts providing more general advice on bringing the use of interactive techniques and responsiveness to many types of activity (e.g. Collis and Lacey 1996; Ware 1996).

In Intensive Interaction activities, the teaching activities themselves have an atmosphere of 'tasklessness'; each activity is distinguished by the absence of a pre-determined outcome, target or behavioural objective. They are essentially discursive — activities constructed by the behaviour of each participant bouncing behaviour off another — yet quite highly structured by the principles of interaction being employed by the more experienced partner. Thus, for the less experienced person, the activities have the merit of being emotionally supporting in that there is not this drive to achieve a certain, pre-determined thing which the member of staff has in mind. At the same time, however, the activities are in no way purposeless: they are highly purposeful activities, which have the intensely serious aim of helping the person with the learning disability to learn about such matters as relating, the skills and routines of social interaction, attention-giving, concentrating, doing things with another person and so on. In this way, such activities may actually be seen as a form of 'coffee drinking behaviour' — they are so taskless — yet they also give a structure to the staff behaviour and have these highly purposeful intentions.

Again, none of this is in contradiction with other desired attainments such as learning skills, being seen in the community, being involved in leisure activities, all of which are also likely to have a beneficial effect on the way that the person behaves. Indeed, for people who have considerable difficulty communicating and relating, the approaches described above are fundamental and central to these other achievements. They may also have the further beneficial effect of enhancing staff technique in all areas of activity with people with severe and profound learning disabilities and making it more likely that staff may make successful interventions during build-up to episodes of challenging behaviour, due to more effective communications having been thus established.

In the discussion earlier, the word 'home' was used with some deliberation. I am attempting to make a point about residential work in particular, but the implications of it have relevance for all services. In our zeal for developmental work, we must be sensitive to our violations of the individual's sense of personal security, truly being 'at home', being comfortable and feeling secure. Any lack of personal comfort and security is likely in itself to be a factor in the production of challenging behaviours. I will now take this point further to the concept of 'asylum'. Asylum has become an extremely unpopular word, loaded with negative connotations in our work. However, I want to make some more positive observations on the use of the concept, even if the word itself remains unpopular.

A good definition can be seen in *The Shorter Oxford Dictionary:* 'a secure place of refuge or shelter'. We can visualise 'asylum' as a continuum. At one extreme end, there is our most negative view, the big, Victorian place in the countryside where people are kept so that their behaviour is least likely to damage others, or themselves. At the other end of the continuum, there should be a sense of 'asylum' present in the working practices of staff groups and individual members of staff, for all service users who have difficulty with their behaviour and feelings. By this I mean that, whatever other aspirations are present in the staff working attitudes, there is also a tangible acceptance of and respect for the way that the person is, at this moment in time.

The concept and practices of 'Gentle Teaching' (McGee *et al.* 1987) have this 'posture' as central to the advocated working practices. I believe their work has been influential in promoting this working posture, to a greater extent even than in achieving a general adoption of 'Gentle Teaching' as a frequently seen approach for people with learning disabilities. It is also surely essential that in order to make progress with feelings and behaviour, the person is receiving positive valuing signals as a basis for everything else which will happen. It is essential too, that some kind of space (emotional, physical space even) is available to the person to feel and behave the way that she or he is at this moment in time: 'the more I am simply willing to be myself... and the more I am willing to understand and accept the realities in myself and the other person, the more change seems to be stirred up' (Rogers 1961 p. 89).

Sometimes it seems that we have unfortunately lost all concepts of asylum in our desire to move away from the more negative connotations of it. Correspondingly, there has been an unmerited expectation that the provision of an 'ordinary life', the move away from institutions, will of itself have a significant impact on people's challenging behaviours (Felce and Emerson 1996). The point here is not that there is anything wrong with concepts of 'ordinary life' — far from it. Rather, that in our provision of ordinary life for people with challenging behaviours, we should not overlook the need for a sense of 'asylum' within whatever is provided.

It may be seen that the discussion has come full circle here, back again to matters of emotional well-being and self-esteem. That is so in a sense, but this helps to emphasise the connectedness between issues of ordinary life, service provision, giving regard to matters such as the service user's emotions, communication ability, ability to have relationships, and asking people with learning disabilities to adopt better behaviour. Which in turn leads to my ideal of 'Helping the Person Learn How To Behave'.

# Helping the person learn how to behave

The reader will see in Figure 8.4 that many of the topics shown have been discussed already and that this diagram now serves as something of a summary. Further circles could be added to this diagram for your own purposes.

None of the circle categories have been discussed in the detail which would include advice and examples on specific working practices. That is not the purpose of this chapter, which is more concerned with setting out a framework for staff attitudes towards people with challenging behaviours, indeed all service users. In my experience, the hardest thing confronting a team of staff is the work that is necessary for developing joint, mutual working attitudes and beliefs. The more effective teams achieve this, at least in part. For this reason, and for those of space, the chapter has concentrated on theories about working attitudes.

Of the circles in Figure 8.4 which have not had their subject matter mentioned, a significant one is centre at the top left. This one is concerned with discipline and the exterior controls we may attempt to put on a person's behaviour. Doing our best to control a person's behaviour is indeed a part of our duty of care when working with that person. However, it is healthier and more effective for us to view that aspect of working with the person as simply part of the overall approach to helping the person, as set out in the diagram. In setting out the diagram in this way, there is an intention particularly to assist the attitudes of the staff and services whose approach is 'control' and 'good behaviour' at all costs, with some dominating and potentially devaluing practices going with that approach. It is particularly important that staff in schools working with the very young pupils see their job not as 'controlling the child's behaviour' at all costs, but rather as 'helping the child to learn how to behave'.

There is no pretence here that this formulation of a working environment is easy. It can indeed be complicated to give proper regard to all these aspects of helping the person. I do think it is realistic, however. I think it is also a reality to regard concepts of socialisation as part of what we are trying to achieve, but to remember to adopt a highly positive view of what constitutes socialisation.

Most of us in any particular society share a sort of 'mainstream behaviour' style. This is one which most of us agree upon, it is the one which enables us to be in a room together peacefully and in an organised way, to confer, discuss, share, respect each other's freedoms and social privileges. We all individually have many other styles of behaviour besides this one, but most of us have the ability to adopt this mainstream style in most appropriate circumstances. We have all arrived at knowledge and ability

**Figure 8.4** A complex of factors which need to be in place to help the person learn how to behave

with this style of behaviour by a process of being socialised into it, and having its obvious usefulness reinforced to us over and over again.

Presumably everyone desires very much that all people with learning disabilities learn to have knowledge of this 'mainstream behaviour' style of behaving. It may be that it is where their general behaviours, mainly or in part, are a departure from it that we may term what they do to be 'challenging'. Not all of them will achieve this style of behaving and we must remember to celebrate what they are and value them as they are. However, I would also suggest that we look closely and thoughtfully at the 'Helping the Person Learn to Behave' diagram. I would strongly suggest that for all of us, there has been more to the process of socialisation which caused us to arrive at a facility with this mainstream behaviour style than merely being controlled and disciplined, conforming, having our negative behaviours eradicated. Arrival at this happy stage of ability is also to do with the acquisition of at least some part of other human facilities such as understanding, insight, reason, some emotional contentment brought about by a degree of relationship and emotional expression being available, communication abilities which enable us to take notice of the way that other people behave, together with some notion of asylum for the darker, inner parts of all of our individual natures. Even those of us who have been successfully socialised are also nonetheless likely at times to kick over the traces of our socialisation and to behave in ways which are unacceptable to others.

# Conclusion

This chapter has been about 'practical theorising' around issues which I consider to be centrally significant. Hopefully however, the reader will also have derived some practicalities from what is set out. The intention is that these practicalities take the form of thoughts and advice about attitudes and other things which we may carry around in our heads, but which have a direct impact on what we do moment by moment. Here is a bullet-list summary of such thoughts which may have a direct, positive effect on daily work.

- Challenging behaviour is normal for all of us.
- People with learning disabilities may have challenging behaviour for reasons which we can, at least to some degree, understand.
- There are many factors contributing to challenging behaviour for an individual.
- Given their personal and environmental factors, it is almost legitimate for some people with learning disabilities to be challenging.
- Working with people's challenging behaviour is a normal aspect of our work.
- Don't simply focus on the visible behaviours.
- Issues such as relationship, communication, emotions, self-esteem, and a sense of security need to be addressed particularly.
- Be careful that our orientation to task activities does not give continuing devaluing messages to a person.
- Try to use positive styles for getting service users involved in tasks.
- Make sure you also purposefully do nothing in particular with service users ('coffee drinking behaviour').
- Do everything to develop and further a person's ability to communicate.
- Try, for each individual, to have a sense of 'asylum' in your working practices, alongside all of your other expectations.
- Help the person 'Learn How to Behave'.
- Work with your colleagues towards mutually shared and held beliefs and attitudes.
- 'Helping the Person Learn How to Behave' is also a way of thinking about positive socialisation.

I would like to thank all of the practitioners with whom I have shared thoughts and discussion in recent years and particularly the staff of Harperbury Hospital School, 1981–90. They have all contributed to this chapter.

# Part Three:
# Learning

# Chapter 9

# Accounting for Learning and Failure to Learn in People with Profound and Multiple Learning Disabilities

*Mark Barber and Juliet Goldbart*

This chapter contains an attempt to explore different approaches to cognition and learning, with the aim of seeing how they might help us understand thinking and learning, or failure to learn, in people with profound and multiple learning disabilities.

Specifically the question addressed in this chapter can be summarised as follows: 'why do some people with PMLD seem to reach a plateau in the adaptability of their interactive skills from which they appear unable to progress?' The background theory to all of this could take up many textbooks, and a satisfactory account is probably beyond our abilities, certainly beyond our remit for this chapter. So, we will limit the background to the level essential to understanding the applications and refer the enthusiastic reader to other sources.

We will start by briefly exploring what is meant by *cognition and learning*. Cognition deals with the ways in which we gain information about the world around us, the conversion of this information into forms of knowledge our brains can deal with, the organisation of this knowledge and its use in directing and informing our behaviour. *Learning* involves relatively permanent changes in behaviour which come about as a result of experience.

A comparison of these terms suggests considerable overlap, the extent of which depends on the model of human behaviour we adopt. A very simple, behaviourist approach would suggest that learning is a relatively automatic process brought about by connections between events, such as reinforcement of certain behaviours (as in operant conditioning) or the linking of events in predictable relationships (as in classical conditioning). An alternative account would argue that learning is one of the outcomes of cognitive processes; a product of gaining, transforming and incorporating new information. In other words, cognitive psychologists are interested in such areas as attention, perception, pattern recognition, learning, memory, concept formation, thinking, language and intelligence.

In this chapter we will consider three accounts of cognition and/or learning and how they can help us to understand and develop the thinking and learning of people with profound and multiple learning disabilities. The first of the three is drawn from learning theory (or behaviourism).The second is a cognitive approach based on developments in thinking from infancy through to adolescence, based on the ideas of Jean Piaget. The third is drawn from a rather more unlikely source; cognitive research on the interaction between adults and complex machinery – Generic Error Modelling System, (Reason 1990).

Whether an infant touches a mobile because previous similar actions have resulted in pleasant consequences or because the sight of the mobile activates a 'reaching response', depends on the vantage point from which the viewer watches events: just as reading three accounts of a football match in three different newspapers often leaves us wondering whether all of the reporters went to the same game! The only confirmation that they did, is that all of the reporters agree which teams were playing and what the eventual outcome was. In the same way, the intellectual processes behind individuals' decisions to act on or intervene in events occurring around them have been explained in a variety of ways. The psychological mechanisms contributing to an action and the manner in which the individual progresses to the point of action, have been viewed from a number of perspectives. At first glance these perspectives may appear to be mutually exclusive. However, in this chapter there will be an attempt to draw common themes together, so that a more accessible overview of cognition and learning can be presented. This will ultimately be used to present a view of the experiences of individuals with PMLD in order to suggest strategies for intervention, teaching or therapy.

# Learning theory

As we have identified, the mechanisms that underpin learning have been described from a number of theoretical perspectives. These can provide the reader with an often daunting choice of principles on which to base their understanding. Learning Theory itself has at least two aspects: Classical Conditioning and Operant (or Instrumental) Conditioning.

We know from researchers such as Hogg *et al.* (1979) that many, though perhaps not all, people with PMLD can learn through classical conditioning. That is, having a drink of warm milk makes a person feel comfortable. S/he shows this by smiling. Through association, the person comes to smile at the bringer of the milk.

Operant conditioning may be illustrated by the increase in the frequency in the occurrence of an action associated with reinforcing consequences. For example, if vocalisation by a person results in attention from others, the frequency of vocalisation is likely to increase. For further reading on this topic see Remington (1996).

Jon, a young man with profound learning disabilities, has learned to drink from a cup independently. The teaching strategy used was based on task analysis and reinforcement. People who know Jon believe that they can infer which drinks he likes by observing his facial expression, posture etc. when he tastes the contents of a cup. To their surprise, however, Jon repeatedly accepts and drinks from cups containing drinks that, judging from his facial expression and other affective, but non-intentional behaviour, he does not like. Jon would not accept empty cups and would stop attempting to drink from a cup once he had drained it. But, when the apparently disliked drink constituted more than one mouthful, Jon would return it to his mouth to finish it off. Seen from the view of a behavioural or operant view, the action (of drinking) does not appear to have a rewarding consequence, unless strong secondary reinforcements within the experience were operating. It is also doubtful whether there was any part of the experience whose presence would encourage an increase in any of the behaviours displayed; the experience of drinking anything but unflavoured milk seemed to be one that he intensely disliked.

Some light may be thrown on these events when they are viewed from a classical

| Label and Approx age | Description |
|---|---|
| Reflexes/ 'First Habits'<br>0–6 weeks | The infant engages mainly in reflex exercises, e.g. sucking, rooting. |
| Primary Circular Reactions<br>6 weeks–4 months | If the infant does something pleasurable with its own body, it can repeat the action. Undifferentiated schemes are used, e.g. inspection, holding, mouthing whatever the object. By the end of this stage, two such schemes can be coordinated. |
| Secondary Circular Reactions<br>4–8 months | If the infant does something external to itself by chance (e.g. rolls a ball away), it learns to repeat the action. Contingency awareness has been acquired, leading to the first stages of Intentionality. |
| Coordination of Secondary Schemes<br>8–12 months | The infant establishes goals prior to initiation of the activity. Intentionality is fully established. There is functional use of objects. |
| Tertiary Circular Reactions<br>12–18 months | The infant shows new means of achieving ends through experimentation. Tools are used. The infant explores container-contents relationships. |
| Beginning of Thought<br>18–24 months | The infant has new means of achieving ends through mental combinations. The infant can predict cause and effect relationships. |

**Table 9.1** The six sub-stages in the sensori-motor period

conditioning perspective, where it may be seen that the sight or touch of a cup may have become a conditioning stimulus associated with the anticipated experience of a pleasant taste of milk. This association would certainly be promoted by the experience of 16 years of having caring people supplying him with the drink that they knew he liked. 'An available cup' to Jon was reliably linked to its regular contents. Perhaps, then, occasional failures in this 'drink from any cup' protocol (e.g. when the contents were orange juice) made the association more resistant to extinction through intermittent reinforcement.

There is a long history of approaches to teaching and learning based on this model (e.g. Farrell *et al.* 1992). But the above example suggests that Learning Theory sometimes provides us with only a rather contradictory explanation of learning, or failure to learn, in people with PMLD. A useful discussion of this area in relation to children with severe learning difficulties can be found in Porter (1986).

# Cognitive developmental theory

Alternatively, the more cognitively based perspectives view individuals' actions as attempts, made on the basis of information gained from previous attempts, to achieve repeated or improved outcomes. Piaget (e.g. Piaget and Inhelder 1956), one of the most significant cognitive developmental theorists, described the period from birth until the age of approximately two years as the 'sensori-motor period'. This was divided into 6 sub-stages in terms of the progressive complexity of the interaction between the infant and its surroundings.

From around the end of the first month of life, the infant is seen as having a small but increasing range of voluntary behaviours, which are performed along with reflexes in association with experiences and sensations monitored both within and nearby the infant. As the infant accumulates experience of events and becomes progressively more able to interact with them, Piaget proposes the gradual emergence of problem solving strategies. The complexity of these strategies increases, incrementally linked to the child's increasing understanding of the nature of the objects and space.

Progression through the six sub-stages in Piaget's account of the sensori-motor period is presented in Table 9.1. Central to this model is the concept of the infant developing schemes. These are richly interconnected, and therefore immensely powerful, stored knowledge structures, responsible for governing largely predictable sequences of events such as daily routines (Wadsworth 1996).

This progressive coordination of self with events is fuelled by the almost obsessive repetition observed in infant play and leads to an accumulation of crucial competences which make possible the conceptual gains that contribute incrementally to infants' ability to understand and control their environments. The repetitive nature of the interactions provides the child with a wealth of experience relating to the encounters, and may be seen as a practice arena for the development of the perceptually driven judgements that support decision making. It can additionally be seen as activity which provides important intellectual resources needed for the recognition of future encounters and the consequences of assumptions and conjecture. At the same time, interactions with skilled others in the child's vicinity who respond to the child's actions, provide a parallel arena in which the child not only affects objects, but, when the child's actions are richly interpreted by the adult, can result in objects that were formerly out of reach being brought to within the child's range.

Control over social consequences however, is generally not as reliable as control over physical consequences; making a mobile move by hitting it is generally more reliable than making an adult appear by making a noise, but it is generally accepted (see e.g. Bates *et al.* 1979) that the cognitive development underpinning activity in these two arenas not only emerges from the same shared intellectual 'software' but that each contributes to the development of the other. Indeed it may be that the intermittent nature of success in the social arena may serve to orient the child to the benefits of perseverance in the physical.

# Contingency responding

One aspect that Classical Conditioning, Operant Conditioning and a Piagetian account all seem to have in common is that repeated interaction or involvement with events promotes more successful involvement in future encounters. The effectiveness of an action on the external environment depends on its execution occurring at the right location and with the correct timing. This enables the action to be integrated into targeted local events so that the individual's intervention in the flow of events will cause the outcomes to be closer to those desired. Those of us who work with people with profound and multiple disability, however, experience daily illustration that many individuals appear not to learn in an orderly or logical progression, based on the accumulation of previous experience. Although individual skills are often learned, they are frequently isolated from the more general contexts or contextual structures in which they are typically acquired. Additionally, the coordination of multiple skill sequences (e.g. successful drinking from a cup) frequently proves too complex an operation for individuals who appear to have successfully acquired relevant single sequence operations (e.g. picking up a cup).

The mechanisms in operation during encounters between profoundly intellectually disabled children and adults and events around them are often obscured by the atypical learning careers they have experienced. As Remington (1996) and others (e.g. Ware and Healey 1994) have observed, learning or the evidence of learning is often obscured because of the extremely limited nature of individuals' behavioural repertoires. In addition to their combination of disabilities, many of these individuals also experience medical conditions (Rainforth 1982), notably epilepsy, requiring medication. Both seizure activity and some anti-epilepsy medication can have adverse cognitive effects. Thus the effects of what may become a complex matrix of disability can cause the severest disruption to the individual's ability to detect or respond to the causes of important events, if indeed the event itself is discriminated.

For individuals who experience this level of multiple disability, opportunities to engage in crucial, experimental and experiential physical play are severely compromised. Many of the major detectable events that occur in these individuals' lives will involve predominantly physical experiences, including being assisted to change positions, or moving between venues and being placed in contact with equipment or people. Thus the very nature of their disability dictates that the majority of these experiences will be received rather than sought. This increasingly requires the individual to assume what can become a 'recipient role' where events occur because of the uncommunicated agenda of the providers of the experience rather than the self-directed activity of the learner. The limitations imposed on possible communicative dialogues are often equally unassailable, a fact which in turn affects the frequency and spontaneity of the interactions that do occur (see for example Ware 1996).

Isolation from controllable events and traceable causes of important outcomes experienced by multiply disabled individuals contributes to what Brinker and Lewis (1982a) described as 'a deprivation from contingencies'. In other words, the person has severely reduced experience of feedback from actions on the environment, particularly his or her own. The effects of this type of isolation were described by Seligman (1975) in his account of 'learned helplessness'. He describes how the onset of depression and withdrawal from the external environment increasingly leads the individual towards orientation to internal experiences and obsessive behaviours. This may help us understand the stereotyped or even self-injurious behaviours of some individuals with PMLD as a consequence of contingency deprivation. In other words, if people cannot experience control over the external world, their actions may become increasingly self-directed. In an attempt to maintain a tolerable level of arousal they may also become stronger and self-injurious rather than just self-stimulatory.

Similarly, some experiments conducted by Skinner (1948) on what is known as 'superstitious learning' illustrate the effects of dislocation from the causes of events. This phenomenon throws some light on the non-technically minded driver, who, on finding that the car will not start, will open and close the bonnet and tap the steering wheel before attempting to restart the engine on the basis that (coincidentally) 'this worked last time!' The repeated experience of being dislocated from traceable causes of events may be seen to lead the learner to search for causes, often mis-associating random co-occurrences with events rather than identifying the true contingent relationship.

Contingent indicators of events' occurrences must also be related to the event so that, additionally, the indicators' non-occurrence also signals the associated events' non-occurrence. For example, if the tape recorder playing music activates only when the switch is touched, the touching of the switch and the tape recorder's activation can be seen to have a contingent relationship. But if the tape recorder activates when the switch is touched and also randomly when the switch is not touched, then the incidence of the two events occurring together may be seen only as a co-occurrence. In the world of people with PMLD events may often occur without the control of that person. For example, the person may have a single switch with which to activate a tape player. But another tape player in the room may be under someone else's control and may go on and off in a completely unpredictable fashion, quite outside our learner's control.

It is the learners' task to monitor and learn to predict contingent events so that their conceptual construction of the relationships in the environment may be formed. It may be seen that many intellectually and multiply disabled people do not have the required level of familiarity with and ability to predict the environment in order to monitor events so that causes and related ingredients may be identified. Given the amount of discernible information that is available to many individuals, it is surprising how much environmental learning does occur.

The importance of play in promoting learning routes that lead to the formation of goal directed strategies has already been mentioned. The repetition associated with typical infants' play in the early months and years may be seen as the foundation on which predictions about environmental constants are built. The coordination between visual and motor activities is also developed during these marathon repetitive games, which lead the infant to combine objects, lose and find them, judge distances, amounts and weights and to manipulate and monitor all of this information for future comparison. This arena of activity, one of the critical building blocks of learning, provides the resource base on which later development is built. All of our views and theoretical models of development assume the presence of this activity at some point along the continuum of learning.

Views of the increasing competence of the individual within the environment all see the importance of discrimination and reaction to the causes of events. Individuals learn in an environment where many stimuli continuously and simultaneously compete for attention, requiring the learner to orient to the correct indicators of events and ignore those aspects which are not significant. Evidence (Rovee-Collier 1987) shows that young children with PMLD and those with severe physical involvement, e.g. cerebral palsy, show marked early deficits in the habituation and discrimination behaviours fundamental to early learning and, hence, early play. Additionally, they often take longer to orient to stimuli than typical learners. In the dynamic flow of events that surround an individual these factors can only add to the disparity of experience associated with PMLD, taking individuals incrementally further from predictable learning models. Thus it may be seen that, in addition to often confused and inadequate incoming information, many individuals with PMLD who have additional motor and sensory disabilities have been unable to experience this climate of self-directed exploratory play in a predictable environment. The question arises then, is it relevant to apply learning theories associated with typical development and learning structures, to individuals whose experience has deviated so fundamentally from the typical structure?

## Example

Hanna, a 15 year old with profound and multiple disabilities, can initiate social contact with a person sitting near her using reaching to touch, extended looking, vocalisation and orientation. She can demonstrate her awareness of contingencies by her use of a single switch linked to a buzzer, with which she can attract adult attention. Additionally, she is responsive to adult attempts to interact with her.

Hanna was assessed using Uzgiris and Hunt's Assessment with Dunst's adaptation (Uzgiris and Hunt 1975; Dunst 1980). She was found to be exhibiting behaviours confirmed at 5 months on Scale 2: Means Ends, with the addition of locomotion. On Scale 6: Object Related Schemes her behaviours were confirmed at 7 months with possible complex behaviours bringing her up to 9 months. However, Hanna did not appear to be progressing beyond the single, simple generalised intention to initiate communication and to respond to the initiation of others.

It was noted that Hanna initiated with equal frequency across many classroom settings, including towards staff in various orientations and that the overall classroom settings did not affect the rate or outcome of her attempts. However, when investigation was made into whether her 'target' was attending her or not, it was noted that the rate of attempts depended on the proximity of the target rather than his or her orientation. In other words she was missing crucial information in her assessment of the environmental information before her. She had learned that her initiation skills were effective when her target was close, but had not learned to discriminate whether her target was attending to her or not despite far higher success rates when her target was already oriented or partially oriented towards her. It seemed that she was not changing her behaviours as a consequence of success in gaining interaction. As she monitored her surroundings and waited for the prime time at which to initiate successfully, she appeared consistently to miss the vital factor that would assure the success of her attempt.

This error, and her apparent inability to detect its presence, suggested the relevance of Bates *et al* (1979) proposition (referred to earlier) that social and physical learning share a common heritage or underlying 'software': The development of social interaction occurs as the result of the child's learning about the effects of its actions on the environment. In order to be successful actions must be coordinated with the flow of elapsing events so that the combination of factors results in a successful outcome. This requires the competent monitoring of ongoing events pertinent to the interaction. Hanna was apparently not yet monitoring the required range of events necessary for the successful outcome of her strategy. Additionally, she apparently was not aware of a need to change strategy to gain interaction .

# The generic error modelling system

Issues of event monitoring and errors of strategy are the subject of our third perspective on human interaction with the environment which will, we believe, provide another plausible explanation of the learning architecture of those experiencing disparate and confused environmental information.

The link between the learning of individuals with PMLD and the operations of a nuclear power station may at first seem tenuous, indeed unlikely. However, analysis of the crisis management of events in industry has illuminated an interactive exchange that has close parallels with the interactive exchanges between any agent and the fluidly changing conditions that characterise our environment. In this chapter we have sought to use a hybrid view of environmental exchanges to give structure to the often confused and frequently obscured learning processes apparent in the profoundly and multiply disabled population. We accept the relevance of other learning theories and do not seek to oppose them. Rather than being an alternative or exclusive approach, the Generic Error Modelling System (Reason 1990) can be used as a complementary view that comments on the function of behaviours. Its application and logic within special education suggests a style of educational intervention that seeks to navigate individuals through encounters, to accentuate the effectiveness of the use of appropriate recovery strategies in environmental exchanges where initial strategies prove ineffective.

This approach provides a structure through which the actions and reactions of individuals involved in social and physical encounters may be traced so that the functions of these behaviours may be placed in an interactive context. The Generic Error Modelling System (GEMS), portrayed in Figure 9.1, below, offers a schematic way of following the interactive progression of an individual's involvement with ongoing events. It is based on a rationale that views the interaction between the individual and the environment as a complex relationship involving mutual modification. The individual's action interrupts and changes a current sequence of events, which in turn changes the situational requirements placed on the individual. This results in the involved person being required to perceive the change and realign strategies and anticipations to meet the new configuration of events. Realignment or recovery comes about through adjustments to notional allocations of the attentional resources that are involved in the monitoring and coordination among three levels of attentional involvement. These three levels of involvement have been described as:

- a skill based level comprising skilled or routinised repertoires of behaviour;
- a rule based level comprising responsive and recovery behaviours;
- a knowledge based level comprising theoretical and strategic problem solving resources.

Each of these domains is limited and shaped by previous learning experiences. The limits involve restrictions in available information, the need for operational speed and the fact that humans seem to prefer to avoid active problem consideration, opting more

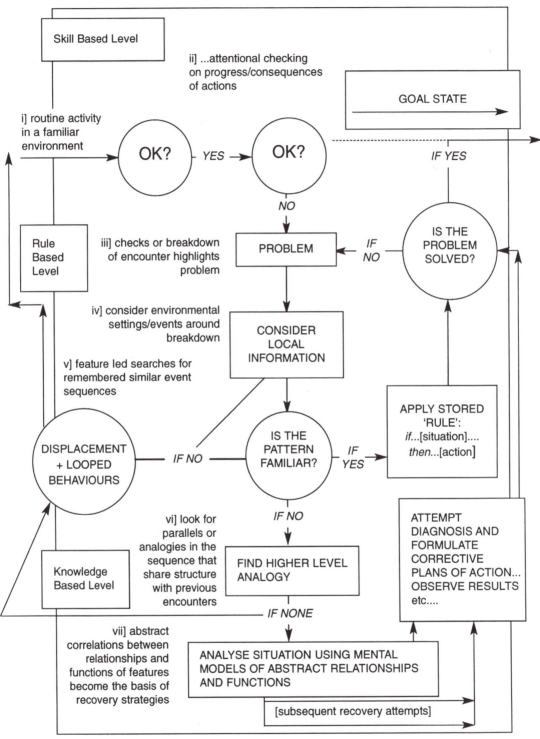

**Figure 9.1** Schematic representation of interactive sequences

frequently for strategies based on familiarity rather than suitability. The approach views the alternation between the three levels of operational activity as being the mechanism that governs the application of attentional and intellectual resources during interaction. It is based on the different approaches to problem solving identified in research in industrial complexes and nuclear power plants (Rasmussen and Jensen 1974; Rasmussen and Lind 1982; Reason 1987). The three levels of attention relate to the styles of problem solving and error tracing that have been observed in these settings.

Rapid and skilled 'good versus bad' judgements are made in relation to perceived event sequences as contextually significant 'signs' are read 'from the face of the instruments', that is from indicators in one's environment. These rapid references are made in the form of attentional checks by the person operating semi-automatically or habitually within the *skill based* level, but give way to *rule based* protocols, (e.g. if condition X and condition Y present themselves then strategy A should be deployed) once the integrated flow of actions and events is disturbed by the occurrence of a mismatch between what is happening and what is thought to be happening. When these recovery rules prove unsuitable to re-establish the harmony, the full attention of powerful (but effortful) problem solving or *knowledge based* systems is employed. All three of these levels of strategy are limited by biases in how the problem is perceived, how the solution is selected, and then how the solution is implemented. More importantly, because of our inherent tendency to act as we have acted before (Reason 1990), much of our decision making is hugely influenced by the breadth and success of previous encounters.

## Example

The approach can be used to help us understand the interactions between individuals with PMLD and their environments. We can gain insight into Hanna's behaviour with clarity and relevance if we use an imaginary [<PAUSE>] button to allow us to insert an explanation at various points in the sequence of events. To make this clearer the descriptions of her behaviour will be put in italics. The explanations will be in normal print.

*We return to Hanna who is initially engaged in habitual (and therefore skill based) activity until she monitors the approach of a staff member whose attention she seeks.* [<PAUSE>]

The staff member's approach activates memories (or schemes) associated with previous similar encounters. Although the schemes that are activated relate to this particular context, Reason (1990) warns that interference may occur, simultaneously, from secondarily activated schemes associated with peripheral events. However, it is from this resource of activated schemes that she must choose her best 'capture the attention of a staff member' scheme.

Reason's GEMS approach now predicts the trying out of a generic 'capture scheme'. Typically, this will repeatedly be amended in the light of its success (or otherwise) as the encounter ensues. However, this adjustment is informed by feature-led searches for relevant schemes that most closely relate to the context. When there is a large number of (intellectually) stored items, the retrieval cues are matched to available strategies by 'similarity matching' (Reason 1990). But, when cues are insufficient or ambiguous, or there are few stored items (i.e. Hanna has low expertise in this area or impoverished knowledge), 'frequency gambling' occurs. This type of response tends to lead the decision towards using the strategy most frequently used in the given context, most recently used or most memorably used. Of course, this is not necessarily the most successful strategy, giving rise to a risk here of 'strong but wrong' strategies being employed, such as driving the route to our place of work rather than, as we had intended, the route to the supermarket. Hanna's most successfully used initiation strategies involve extended looking, smiling and eye pointing, which are only successful at close quarters, once interactions have been established. Nevertheless, because of her motor disabilities, these repertoires represent the dominant portion of her inventory of strategies.

*Hanna intently watches the staff member, who is not monitoring her and therefore fails to notice her behaviours. Hanna waits until the staff member again approaches her and stands close by. Occasionally she will vocalise quietly. However, this too proves ineffectual.* [<PAUSE>]

Although she has chosen a strategy that relates to the close proximity of an adult or target, she has not discriminated that the success of her strategy depends not only on the proximity of the target, but also on its orientation. Within this situation Hanna may be seen to have made a strong (i.e. closely contextually associated) but wrong choice of strategy. Within Reason's (1990) approach, she has made a mistake 'or deficiency or failure in the judgmental and/or inferential process involved in the selection of an objective or in the specification of the means to achieve it' (p.9). Because of the limitations placed on her by the paucity of previous experience (and therefore catalogue of strategies) she has no alternative or adjustment to resort to.

*Hanna resumes monitoring her surroundings and makes several similar attempts. After yet another near miss in gaining a response from a staff member, Hanna shows signs of frustration and the beginnings of distress and then becomes involved in stereotyped hand movements, stopping monitoring her surroundings for a number of minutes.* [<PAUSE>]

It can be seen that she has discriminated the lack of success in her strategy. But, because of both her passive recipient role (Ouvry and Saunders 1996) and the limitations of her experience due to intellectual and motor disabilities, she has little chance to gain more varied experiences in this setting. The repetitive, familiar actions that she resorts to can be seen as having a comforting function, described by Reason (1990) as having the function of dissipating stress . They are described by Seligman (1975) as being ultimately the option of individuals who have been isolated from contingency experience in the external environment. Stereotyped behaviours of this sort may also be seen to be linked to the strong unitary behaviours performed for their own sake during Piaget's 'primary circular reactions' at very early stages of development. Within Reason's approach, in this context, these cyclical behaviours may be viewed as a type of default strategy which can often be seen in undirected or unmotivated pupils in classrooms everywhere.

*A staff member approaches and sits with Hanna. She responds to the staff member's initiation with extended eye-contact and subtle signs of positive effect, encouraging continuation of the interaction with success.* [<PAUSE>]

Although she can maintain or terminate the interaction, her ability to extend the range of the interaction depends on the staff member introducing new topics for shared attention or social interaction. Her socialisation and engagement behaviours have just received confirmation of their success in the engagement of the staff member, but the cause of the adult's approach is not obvious to Hanna, who is likely to either (through superstitious learning) to associate it with her own behaviours or accept it as yet another event in a day full of unexplainable events. In the same way, unless the staff member facilitates an accessible and (to the learner) understandable experience, Hanna will continue to receive social contacts about which she can do little. As Ouvry and Saunders (1996) argue, a series of sensory experiences or a progression of changes in position or venue whose meaning is outside the student's understanding will do little to develop Hanna's ability to extract meaning from situations. Some measure of control is necessary. However, because of her limited physical abilities, she cannot physically engage her environment and because she cannot discriminate the error in her initiation strategies, she cannot optimise her social encounters.

# Intervention

Examining the cause of Hanna's apparent inability to increase her success rate during initiation attempts in terms of errors of planning and execution enables practitioners to identify a new avenue of intervention approaches. The important issue ceases to be a question of Hanna's position on a continuum of cognitive development or communicative skills, but becomes, rather, a more functional investigation into her use of her current repertoire of skilled routines. Teaching through facilitating situations in which her repertoires of skills may be effective may be more relevant to Hanna than educational attempts to add to her repertoires. It can be argued that the current situation exists because she lacks the experience required to endow her current schemes with the flexibility necessary for them to be of use in more complex encounters. In other words, the learning she has acquired has been accumulated in restricted circumstances and Hanna requires greater experience of their application in diverse settings. She is currently in the position where she has to wait until an event occurs whose demands match her skills, rather than being able to adapt her skills to the requirements of the situation.

Clearly, following the logic of this approach, efforts should be directed towards 'fleshing out' Hanna's intellectual resources so that she will be able to interact with her environment more successfully. Typically, however, as Ware and Healey (1994) observe, those who are concerned with promoting 'progress' in the development of individuals with PMLD, measure it in terms of the acquisition of new skills and 'discernible movement towards an objective'. In schools, the importance of promoting demonstrable learning in relation to curriculum and assessment documents has generally been both the aim and predominant ethic of education and therapy since the seventies, even though pupils with PMLD have been 'notoriously poor consumers of (the) curriculum' (Ware and Healey 1994). Reference to the linear sequencing of both curriculum documents and the resulting teaching styles inevitably leads to what they describe as the teaching of selected curricular highlights of socially determined areas of skills that provide (at best) a 'facade of competence'.

Ware and Healey (1994) point out (p.4) that this model of teaching towards increasing mastery over linear sequences of developmentally presented content (aiming towards a notional final goal) is enshrined in many curriculum documents and frameworks of expectation, including the school National Curriculum itself. However, for those individuals who consistently fail to show measurable progress on conventional assessments, a different model of progress is required. It is not that these individuals cannot make progress, but we would argue that the instruments by which progress is measured do not suit the people whose abilities are being measured. (See Chapter 11 for more discussion of progression in an Education context.)

Hanna's inability to acquire more effective interactive skills has been characterised as the product of a low expertise or impoverished domain knowledge brought about by her limited contact with accessible interactive experiences. Her cognitive resources are severely compromised by the simplicity and rigidity of her strategies . She may be seen as being in the centre of a vicious circle where she cannot engage environmental events successfully and cannot acquire new strategies because of the lack of success in her attempts. Her ability to engage events depends on her achieving a threshold of interactive competence that will allow her not only to adjust her schemes but also to perceive the success or failure of her strategies. This threshold of competence appears to be dependent on her discrimination and monitoring of a critical range of environmental events and adjusting her actions to this information.

This resource may be seen to develop through experience and repeated encounters using existing strategies. To attempt to 'progress' through the teaching of new strategies only serves to 'muddy the water' and bring new and introduced complexity into the events. New learning may be assisted to develop through the facilitation of variable but recognisable settings that promote the experience of applying existing strategies in generally predictable arenas. Thus plasticity of skills should be promoted rather than the introduction of novel skills aimed at promoting linear progress along a developmental continuum. Facilitating a breadth of experience should, logically, enable learning structures to evolve through diversity in a similar, if more contrived, manner to that which typically occurs.

## Taking control

A vital element in this view of learning is the issue of the individual's expectation of control over his or her environment. It is generally accepted (see e.g. Brinker and Lewis 1982a; Schweigert 1989; O'Brien et al. 1994; Ware 1996) that it is crucial that the individual develops an expectation of control over his or her environment. The development of microswitches and environmental control mechanisms has brought increasingly affordable and effective equipment that may be placed under the operation of even the most severely physically disabled individuals (e.g. Barber 1990; Brinker and Lewis 1982b; Glenn and O'Brien 1994). However, the related increase in the use of white rooms and sensory areas often misdirects users into a style of usage that promotes further passivity. The 'sensory approach' to providing experiences to individuals with PMLD often simply provides experiences that are, as Ouvry and Saunders (1996) point out, bereft of meaning for the individuals receiving them. They argue that 'Activities using this type of equipment are often carried out in situations which do not provide a meaningful context', continuing that 'the sensory experiences may seem quite random and meaningless to the pupil with PMLD when provided through a subject whose meaning is outside the understanding of the pupil' (p.207).

What must remain central to the use of this equipment is that it is not the level of stimulation that is relevant, but the degree of responsiveness to the user and the context in which it occurs. The systematic and sensitive use of this type of equipment can give individuals the experience of causing dramatic change to the immediate environment as well as augmenting the possibilities of communication and interaction (Rowland 1990; Schweigert and Rowland 1992; Ware 1996).

It has been mentioned earlier that there is an inseparable connection between the learning architecture underpinning responses to social and to non-social events. The use of contingency intervention strategies in the classroom using microswitches can be reflected in social interactions within the exchanges and care routines routinely experienced by individuals with PMLD. All individuals, throughout their lives, experience regular, routine sequences of events, leading these sequences to be easily recognised and predicted. However, because of the recurring nature of these routines, caregivers and workers often become desensitised to the communicative possibilities presented by what can become ritualised events. After all, if they have become practised to the care givers, then the chances are that the care receivers also recognise at least some of the sequences involving themselves.

Rarely conceptualised by staff members as activities rich in teaching possibilities, these daily routines often become seen as barriers to the actual job of teaching. However, by giving the recipient a chance to react to a planned interruption in proceedings, not only is the individual's involvement in the sequence being acknowledged and dignified, but by acknowledging the reaction through using it to restart the sequence, the learner increasingly orients to, monitors and contributes to events in which they find themselves involved. For example, at the end of the day, by causing an unusual pause when the individual is beside the transport vehicle that normally takes the him or her home, or beside the hydrotherapy pool when habitually s/he would be hoisted, time is given for a reaction to the unusual break in a usually predictable sequence. This reaction is acknowledged by staff, who then restart the sequence. (see also Barber 1995; Carpenter and Ashdown 1996; SCAA 1996a).

Similarly, the use of accessible signals and cues often known as 'objects of reference' may be used to indicate the impending start of a sequence of events. Objects that have relevance to the learner (e.g. buoyancy aids/armbands to signal a hydrotherapy session) may be used to cue him or her in to events that are about to happen or to infer preferences (Coupe–O'Kane et al. 1995). Likewise, distinct start and finish sequences can be used to give individuals information about sequences they are about to encounter or make choices about. Routines and signals can be introduced into all regular activities and encounters. It is important that the cues used carry meaning and familiarity to the learner and will promote recognition of the event or of the availability of the imminent event. It is easy to choose items that staff identify with particular events, but often these items do not carry the same signals to the learner, and should be chosen and introduced carefully. The meaningful 'signposting' of events can effectively signal approaching, available, sequences to the learner. The experience of responsive and largely familiar interactive encounters that stay predominantly within the control of the learner is one that we feel to be more in agreement with the condition in which learning evolves in more typical conditions.

# Conclusions

Finally, we (the authors) are currently engaged in research in which we are investigating the adaptive behaviours of a number of students who have PMLD. This work involves designing situations in which students are encouraged or provoked into changing, or deploying new strategies in their attempt to recover their control over a situation when environmental conditions change or possible alternative methods of control are made available. We are seeking to investigate how best to promote more flexible strategies and to highlight the availability of alternate routes to successful outcomes. Any significant results of this research will be disseminated.

As mentioned earlier, it must be stressed that this approach is speculative and, currently, relatively untested. However, it does appear to share important principles with more traditional or mainstream approaches to learning and its logic suggests a style of intervention that is totally in keeping with certain recent intervention styles. The specific examples that we have encountered are the 'Routines, signals and cues' described by Ouvry and Saunders (1996), Ware's work on creating responsive environments (e.g. Ware 1994, 1996), the philosophy underlying Collis and Lacey's (1996) 'Interactive Approaches to Teaching' and finally the use of objects of reference (e.g. McLarty 1997).

The discussion in this chapter has been developed from the original question of 'why do some people with PMLD seem to reach a plateau in the adaptability of their interactive skills from which they appear unable to progress?' Their problem may be likened to that of a novice driver, well able to drive in a straight line, but being completely out of their depth when a gear change or complex manoeuvre is called for. The individuals often have skills allowing them to get purposefully involved in a range of interactions, but once a point is reached in the interaction, events seem to surpass the resources that the individual has at his or her disposal. At this point the interaction collapses, the learner withdraws from the interaction, or becomes distracted by an external event or detail of their own behaviour and in order to continue the interaction, the skilled partner must start the process again.

The view of slips, mistakes and errors proposed by Reason indicates that human interaction is subject to many influences that interfere with efficient interaction with the environment. The failures that occur do so at largely predictable points during the encounters. This suggests that although there is a seemingly limitless variety of possible reasons for unsuccessful interaction with the environment, this is derived from the complexity of the environment rather than the complexity of the psychological mechanisms at work. Within the context of GEMS, individuals move between levels of arousal or attentiveness to make available intellectual resources necessary for recovery, so that actions remain in tune with surrounding events.

Because Knowledge Based activity is characterised by active consideration of the problem configuration, it is profoundly debatable whether, or to what level, individuals with PMLD may be able to alternate among these levels. Skill Based actions are those that require very little consideration or monitoring by the conscious attention; almost certainly the type of activity in which individuals with PMLD are most involved. It is the Rule Based protocols that present the area of most interest in this work as it is this resource that represents 'if situation X and situation Y present themselves, then perform action sequence A'. The efficient use of these protocols depends on flexibility of strategy, so that any recovery or strategy may be adapted during its operation. Practitioners should be involved in intervention approaches that promote this flexibility and adaptability. Intervention, however, must also provide guidance and navigational assistance for learners so that common structures within experiences may be discriminated. At this point, the most effective method of providing 'signposts' is open to discussion. We feel that it is an important discussion that must take place so that more effective support and education may be provided for the individuals in our classrooms and centres.

# Chapter 10

# Teaching and Learning for Children with Profound and Multiple Learning Difficulties

*Claire Marvin*

Vicki and Hakim attend a school for children and young people with profound and multiple learning difficulties (PMLD). Vicki is a fragile six year old with little independent movement. She was born prematurely, spent months in hospital and underwent countless operations. She appears to have suffered massive neurological damage. Her level of awareness is difficult to determine. Hakim, who has very different needs, is in the same class. He is fifteen years old. His profound learning difficulties are compounded by his sensory and physical impairments. He likes familiar routines with familiar people. Usually he is alert and responsive with a ready smile but he protests at changes by increased fitting and signs of distress.

Before 1971 Vicki and Hakim would have been deemed ineducable and, as a result, excluded from the education system in Great Britain. *The Education (Handicapped Children) Act (1970)* transferred the responsibility for children and young people with severe, complex and profound learning difficulties from Health Authorities to Local Education Authorities. Overnight the Junior Training Centres became schools and the instructors became educators. Their jobs changed from being trainers who concentrated on care and the acquisition of functional skills to teachers who were expected to provide broad educational opportunities and experiences in order to nourish the whole child. Very soon the inevitable questions were raised:

- What do children with PMLD need to experience and learn?
- How will they learn and be taught?
- Where will they learn and be taught?

These concerns summarise the fundamental issues related to the education of all children. Managing them is part of a continuous cycle of review and development which presents an ongoing to challenge to those involved. They will form the basis for discussion in this chapter and consideration will be given to each question in turn.

## What do children with PMLD need to experience and learn?

### Starting with a curriculum

Some teachers (myself included) will remember the heady days of the early seventies when the freedom to set own agendas within own classrooms relevant to what teachers deemed to be the individual needs of their pupils was available. Times have moved on and school staff now acknowledge the need for some kind of centrally determined curriculum framework which provides direction for and continuity of learning (Halpin and Lewis 1996). In 1988 a National Curriculum was introduced. It prescribes ten subject areas and progress through them is monitored by means of compulsory national testing. At that time despite the proclamation that this was 'a curriculum for all' (NCC 1989) it was obvious that no thought had been given to children with special educational needs.

Despite initial concerns the legislation and non-statutory guidance of the last decade have encouraged staff teams to review and refresh their thinking on the aims, objectives, policies and priorities in their school. This has informed subsequent discussion and influenced decisions relating to the business of whole-school curriculum planning. Guidance from the School Curriculum Assessment Authority (1996a) on planning a curriculum for pupils with PMLD encourages schools to take account of the following principles:

- planning begins with the pupil's needs, interests, aptitudes and achievements;
- pupils are entitled to a broad and balanced curriculum, including the National Curriculum;
- pupils have access to programmes of study that enable them to progress and demonstrate achievement;
- teachers distinguish clearly between achievement in planning, assessing, teaching, recording and reporting;
- the curriculum provides progression and continuity;
- planning takes account of issues such as communication which permeates the whole curriculum;
- planning is subject-focused, but recognises links between subjects.

(pp. 11-13)

## Curriculum content

Curriculum content must be guided by statutory requirements and the needs of the pupil as defined by the interdisciplinary team of professionals and the pupil's parents. It is important to get it right since the curriculum is 'the medium through which teachers will operate and children will learn' (Carpenter 1997a). It is the main vehicle through which the match of learning experiences to a child's individual needs will be achieved, therefore it should be appropriate yet flexible.

The 1996 *Education Act* (DfE 1996) states that every maintained (special) school shall offer a basic curriculum which includes:

- the National Curriculum;
- provision for sex education for all registered pupils... who are provided with secondary education (para: 352);
- religious education and religious worship (so far as practicable) (para: 342b).

Alongside this, policies may be developed using the cross-curricular elements introduced in *Curriculum Guidance 3: The Whole Curriculum* (NCC 1990). These permeate all activities with children with PMLD. They comprise Key Skills, for example communication and problem solving; cross-curricular Themes, for example health education and transition to adult life within a range of *Dimensions,* for example providing equal opportunities for all pupils.

The National Curriculum was only ever intended to form *part* of the basic curriculum for all pupils and SCAA (1995, 1996a) has recently made it clear that the revised National Curriculum (Dearing 1994) is part of a 'broad statutory framework' within which school communities are encouraged to create and maintain their own curriculum relevant to the very individual needs of their pupils. With this reassuring news one might assume that the curricular content debate raging in the early nineties can now be laid to rest. The time has come for schools to regain control of curriculum development by setting their own agendas. The National Curriculum can no longer be characterised as an overbearing and unwelcome invader pushing aside other important curriculum priorities. Where pupils with PMLD are concerned Ouvry and Saunders (1996) and Carpenter (1997a) remain unconvinced, cautiously reminding us that there is evidence that practitioners continue to strive to achieve a satisfactory synthesis between the various elements that make up the whole curriculum. A full reconciliation of individual needs to curriculum experience remains a source of debate and will do so for some years to come. Halpin and Lewis (1996) following their recent study of curriculum in twelve special schools conclude: 'In various ways the National Curriculum is interpreted as either irrelevant to the special school context or is accepted at the level of rhetoric while making minimal impact on practice' (p. 103).

Motivated by the nature and complexity of their disabilities Figure 10.1 shows a model of the whole curriculum for children with PMLD developed by Ouvry (1991). Enclosed within the eight essential areas of learning identified by HMI (DES 1985) are the developmental curriculum, the additional curriculum and the National Curriculum. The overlap and interrelationship between the differing aspects of the whole curriculum can be seen at a glance along with the possibilities of changing the size of the circles (see modifications in Sebba *et al.* 1995) to provide the 'individual curriculum diet' necessary to 'feed and sustain the whole pupil' as suggested by Ashdown *et al.* (1991). An aim for the future might be to increase the areas of overlap thus demonstrating the possibilities of satisfying the development needs of the child through the programmes of study related to the National Curriculum (see below). This may go some way towards reconciling the tensions which exist regarding claims that schools are reluctantly becoming 'curriculum driven', a process at odds with philosophies and principles (Halpin and Lewis 1996).

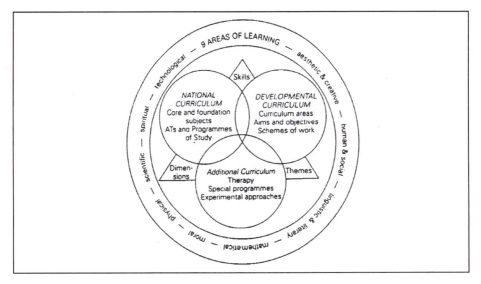

**Figure 10.1** Schematic representation of interactive sequences

Within this framework and in conjunction with an underlying need for total care for some pupils with PMLD the relative roles of education, therapy and care must be clearly defined. Jordan and Powell (1994) pay particular attention to this issue stating that only through a programme in which all three are carefully integrated can all the requirements related to the child's needs be met. Therefore, in order to provide an effective curriculum diet for each pupil it is essential that members of the individual disciplines involved work as a team with a common philosophy and agreed goals to both develop and deliver the whole curriculum.

## Breadth and balance

The SCAA document *Planning the Curriculum for Pupils with Profound and Multiple Learning Difficulties* (1996a) reminds us that in planning to meet the legal requirements for the curriculum and the needs of the child 'schools need to recognise that curricular breadth and balance are an entitlement' (p.8). Brennan (1985) claims that the more personal the special need the more difficult it becomes to provide this. Reports from OFSTED (1993) provide evidence that practitioners in special schools find it difficult to 'offer a satisfactorily broad and balanced curriculum which complies with the National Curriculum requirements'.

One way of conceptualising the challenge is to consider planning for breadth and balance in the widest possible terms. Offering more subjects and subject content to pupils with learning difficulties has enriched what was looking like a lifeless and narrow curriculum but teachers must also offer opportunities to meet needs using different teaching approaches (NCC 1992). The ways in which we encourage pupils to learn must continue to evolve and develop in response to their changing needs. Ouvry (1987) argues that free exploration, trial and error, shaping, modelling and imitation or a combination of such styles will all provide effective routes to learning for pupils with PMLD as will simple problem solving and sometimes passive though attentive watching, listening or experiencing described by Byers (1996).

With recent SCAA publications, encouraging chinks of light have appeared regarding the more prescriptive aspects of the legislation and guidance related to the National Curriculum. A new-found flexibility represents a firmer conviction in teacher judgement and opportunities for wider interpretations of breadth and balance now exist.

For example, the opportunity to 'uncouple' chronological age from Key Stage (Dearing 1994) enables practitioners the flexibility to offer students broader experiences beyond those which measure progress. Most of us like to have the chance to experience activities in which we have little or no prerequisite skills. We participate in the activities 'out of curiosity, to seek novelty or for sheer enjoyment' suggest Sebba *et al.* (1995). Pupils with PMLD have a right to be offered such experiences. We cannot determine the outcome and we may be surprised!

Greater flexibility has also meant that the responsibility for managing balance in the whole curriculum for individual pupils is now firmly located in schools (Stevens 1995). The changing needs of each pupil and of the same pupil over time can now be highlighted at their Annual Review and reflected in the individual curriculum presented to them perhaps over a year or a key stage. For example, a three year old child with PMLD who has recently entered school will experience a very different curriculum content and balance from that of a teenager who is preparing to move on to college. A child just out of hospital following a hip operation will require additional physiotherapy sessions for the immediate future at the expense of other curricular components for some time.

# How will children with PMLD learn and be taught?

## *Individual Education Plans*

For teachers in special education the introduction of formalised Individual Education Plans and accompanying Annual Reviews for all children identified as having special educational needs (*Code of Practice*, DfE 1994) was not new. Many Statements of Special Educational Need legislated for in the Education Act 1981 have referred to the need for such programmes and reviews. Special schools have been using them for some time.

An individual education plan (IEP) is a working document which acts as an interface between the whole-school curriculum and the individual child. It should be an expression of each pupils' explicit longterm learning needs (known as priorities or goals) which are, in turn, translated into a programme containing short-term objectives. Parallel and interrelated strands of the subject-led National Curriculum and the needs-led developmental and additional curricula merge with the IEP which is incorporated into the class planning containing details of how all the priorities for a pupil's learning can be provided for 'both through and alongside the revised National Curriculum orders' (SCAA 1996a).

For every child the success of the IEP in terms of targets achieved depends to a large extent on the quality and impact of the teaching. Children's needs 'cannot be addressed in isolation, divorced from the dynamics of teaching and learning that surrounds the child in his/her classroom situation' (Carpenter 1997a). In order to be effective in relation to IEP targets, members of collaborative multidisciplinary teams need to develop certain key skills which permeate the whole curriculum. In assessing for, planning for, implementing, monitoring and evaluating IEPs the team needs to:

- recognise the importance of context and its relevance;
- set tasks that are enjoyable, realistic and challenging;
- ensure that there is progression;
- provide a variety of learning experiences and environments;
- have high expectations;
- create a positive, interactive working atmosphere;
- provide a consistent approach;
- recognise the efforts and rewards of the pupils;
- organise resources to facilitate learning;
- offer flexibility to be responsive to the needs of the learner at the time;
- accommodate individual learning styles.
  (adapted from Ainscow and Muncey 1989; Collis and Lacey 1996)

## *Teaching approaches*

### Behavioural methods

In an educational climate clamouring for demonstration of instant success the teaching methods developed in special education during the seventies and eighties proved to be attractive to teachers. Based on behavioural theory, precise goals were selected from neatly sequenced developmental checklists that defined the content of the curriculum. Teaching was mechanistic; objectives were broken down into small achievable parts and behaviour was shaped by a teacher within a one-to-one setting.

While undoubtedly teachers have learned a lot from behaviourism, particularly in the context of defining aims and objectives and the importance of precise recording and monitoring, over the years they have become aware of the constraints of this system (see McConkey 1981; Bray *et al.* 1988; Farrell 1991). Certain features have been particularly questioned both concerning the nature of behaviourism and the results of its usage.

For example, this method casts the learner into a rigidly passive role. The pupil is expected to follow the lead. For pupils with PMLD whose communicative intent is often overlooked this cannot be a good idea. The opportunity to seize the moment and to respond to the child's initiations is essential to the development of their social, communicative and cognitive skills (Ware 1996).

However, such a method is still useful in some contexts, for example, where aspects of safety are concerned. Denise must learn not to touch the electric hot plate when she is in the kitchen or roll near to the fire when she is exploring on the floor. In these cases understanding is of secondary importance to her immediate safety.

## Interactive methods

The interest in a social interactionist view of children learning through their own active engagement with adults and their environment has moderated the early influences of behavioural psychology. A more prominent place is given to the processes of learning — developing understanding and problem solving — as opposed to the *products*. Objectives are open-ended and the curriculum is viewed as a whole rather than as a number of fragmented parts. This interactive approach encompasses all of the features necessary for effective teaching and learning stated above. In addition, essential and interdependent characteristics involve encouraging the child to be active, which means:

- taking control;
- developing communicative intent and sociability;
- developing thinking skills (for pupils with PMLD this is represented in simple problem solving).

(adapted from Collis and Lacey 1996)

Good practice exemplifying interactive approaches used with children with PMLD exists throughout the country and is described in the literature (for example Smith 1991; Nind and Hewett 1994; Caldwell 1996; Collis and Lacey 1996; Ware 1996).

## Which method?

Behavioural and interactive approaches stand in contrast to one another. The complexity of the everchanging balance of curriculum content for pupils with PMLD requires a variety of teaching approaches. Put simply 'how one chooses to teach depends on what one wants to achieve' (Black and Harlen 1990). No one methodology can meet all the needs of our pupils nor should meet their needs. Research indicates that teachers who employ a mixture of methods seem to achieve the best results (Smith 1991). The challenge facing staff in special schools is to try to reconcile the two within the whole curriculum for pupils with PMLD, capitalising upon their strengths while avoiding their weaknesses.

## *The interface with the National Curriculum*

The National Curriculum Programmes of Study (PoS), which define the knowledge, understanding and skills to be taught for each subject at each Key Stage, describe processes as well as products. Words such as 'explore', 'experience', 'problem solving' and 'groupwork' are frequently used thus encouraging the active participation of all pupils and emphasising the social nature of the learning process. Despite the difficulties in achieving a satisfactory synthesis discussed previously, the PoS appear to offer an initial framework to which additional and personalised learning experiences can be added which, in turn, correlate with three of the planning phases suggested by SCAA (1995, 1996a) and exemplified in *Planning the Curriculum for Pupils with Special Educational Needs* (Byers and Rose 1996):

- longterm planning – statutory PoS
- medium-term planning – extended PoS
- short-term planning – personalised PoS.

In seeking to relate the separate components of the curriculum indicated in Ouvry's plan (see Figure 10.1 previously) and utilise the strengths of the teaching approaches described above, many special schools have planned integrated schemes of work or cross-curricular approaches based on single subject or multifocused topics. From within these areas of study, the importance of which is acknowledged by OFSTED (1995), pupils pursue highly individualised objectives in meaningful and sociable contexts with the opportunity to progress at their own rate.

The subjects of the National Curriculum can be seen as vehicles through which pupils with PMLD experience and extend their early learning skills (a strategy supported by SCAA (1996a) and described and exemplified in detail elsewhere, for example Byers 1990; NCC 1992; Lacey and Lomas 1993; Sebba *et al.* 1995). But in time some pupils may progress towards attaining subject-specific concepts, skills, knowledge and understanding. Opportunities for recognising this should not be overlooked in planning nor in teacher observations. As mentioned previously the move towards a broad and balanced curriculum for students with PMLD has been long overdue; an over-emphasis on early skills may be at the expense of enjoyment and recognition of the attainment of more subject-specific skills. For example, after regular trips out in the local neighbourhood, Jade was able to post a letter appropriately (with assistance) and hand the correct symbol to the shop assistant in order to buy bread and/ or milk. Thus she has moved a little further towards grasping the *geographical* concept that 'the world extends beyond home and school.'

## The collaborative multidisciplinary team.

In a recent survey carried out for the RNIB (1992) 27 people were found to be involved in the care, therapy and education of one child with PMLD. It is unlikely that all professional networks will be so large but, nevertheless, quite a few people will have important roles in supporting the whole family throughout the child's school years. The school team *regularly* includes a speech and language therapist, a physiotherapist, a school nurse, a classroom assistant, a lunchtime assistant, a home/school escort and a teacher.

It has been argued throughout this chapter that in order for children and young people with PMLD to be offered the best possible environment for learning, a unified view of the curriculum and a holistic view of the child is essential. Teamwork across the professional disciplines and a commitment to involving parents and, wherever possible, the child, is an effective way of ensuring that the pupils' learning opportunities are maximised (SCAA 1996a). While the importance of a collaborative approach is acknowledged as important in whole-school curriculum planning and developing integrated schemes of work drawn up across Key Stages or year groups, it is most desirable when assessing, planning for, implementing and reviewing the needs of *individual* children.

Teachers need to know pupils extremely well to be able to set relevant targets. Working closely with parents and other professionals is of vital importance. Everyone brings knowledge, expertise and differing perspectives to the group resulting in a combination of ideas being greater than the sum of the parts (Lacey and Lomas 1993). Yet it is acknowledged that there are many difficulties in achieving effective collaboration. Shared priorities achieved through negotiation, regular meetings and effective communication are all equally important. Interdisciplinary teams take time to evolve and need considerable support to flourish but in the education of children with PMLD they are considered essential if effective provision is to be maintained.

Initial assessment and the Annual Review procedure will provide an opportunity for parents and staff to consider the priorities for each student. For example, for Scott the team may suggest the following:

*Nurse:*

- massage to improve circulation and stimulate healing.

*Physiotherapist:*

- daily exercises to avoid contractures and deformities;
- regular hydrotherapy to improve circulation ;
- positioning to achieve midline;
- supported sitting experiences.

*Specialist teacher of the hearing impaired:*

- strong visual cues to enable early understanding of the world around him.

*Speech and language therapist:*

- regular routines including objects of reference;
- a desensitisation programme before eating.

Teachers often act as key workers in devising an individual programme which incorporates as many of these priorities as possible and includes work on prerequisites to learning. When this happens negotiation, as mentioned previously, is a very useful tool. Some objectives may have to wait for a while, perhaps until more fundamental ones are established, a process described as 'jostling' and 'queuing' by members of the therapy team at the Wolfsen Centre in London (Collis and Lacey 1996). There can be many opportunities for working on the above objectives. For example, Scott can practise achieving midline to watch a candle burn when learning about light or to look at an owl brought into school during a topic on animals.

## *Progress*

It is an aim of the National Curriculum that each child's progress within it can be identified on an individual basis. Pupils with PMLD are severely limited in their ability to demonstrate their achievements and providing evidence of progress is a major cause of difficulty and frustration for their teachers. It is only recently that this problem has been formally recognised by SCAA within the non-statutory guidance document *Assessment, Recording and Accreditation of Achievement for Pupils with Learning Difficulties* (1996b).

Although the above document and other recently published material (SCAA 1996a) have gone some way towards reconceptualising the meaning of progress for children with PMLD, the notion of a hierarchical curriculum described by Wedell (1981) as 'a framework of expectation' still exists. A child's progress is seen in terms of the rate at which they master the sequence — a concept comparable with developmental curricula and their associated checklists. Some pupils' progress has been enabled following the recommendation made in the Dearing Report (1994) that teachers should be allowed to select material from earlier Key Stages but for children with PMLD formal recognition of achievement below Level 1 remains elusive.

In reaffirming our principles related to progress, we must remember that educational progress is relative to more than one set of criteria. Planning for and assessing it by comparison with a general framework of skills and knowledge alone is inadequate (Ware and Healey 1994). For pupils with PMLD, progress does not always equate with climbing a ladder of developmental skills. Ouvry and Saunders (1996) suggest that the possibility of achievement in a vertical dimension should not be overlooked but a broader more lateral concept of progress should be constructed. This might relate to the child's ability to:

- *understand, interact with and control the environment;*
  for example: anticipate what is coming next in a familiar routine, make choices, reach towards an object, show interest in a social activity rather than in inappropriate behaviour
- *develop and extend existing skills;*
  for example: use an existing skill spontaneously, consistently, in an unfamiliar situation, with a new person, more fluently, more confidently
- *retain or 'reactivate' skills;*
  for example: continue to use a skill if regression has occurred or 'remember' a previously established skill after a lapse in use
- *accept reduced support in completing a task;*
  for example: in moving from a wheelchair to a static chair, in operating a switch.

Clearly this is a more far reaching concept of progress, which consigns the checklists of the eighties to the back of the cupboard, provides a fresh challenge to the members of the interdisciplinary team associated with the education of children with PMLD and highlights the importance of their role. Not only are they responsible for enabling learning to take place but also for recognising it and providing evidence that it has happened.

## Enabling progress — an example

A growing body of researchers conclude that infants who experience a more responsive environment make faster social and cognitive progress (Ware 1996). There is no reason to doubt that this is the same for children with PMLD but it has been found that these students receive only very few responses to their attempts to communicate and express choices. For example, Goldbart (1980) and Ware (1987) both found that 50 per cent of interactions in PMLD classes lasted less than a minute. Overall results from recent research carried out by Ware (1996) however, suggest that where educators are trained to recognise their pupils' attempts to communicate and therefore the pupils receive higher levels of response they communicate intentionally more often. This not only highlights the importance of the skills of individual professionals in promoting and recognising attempts to communicate but also of the staff team working together in the classroom alerting each other to the communicative intentions of their pupils.

## Recognising and providing evidence of progress

Assessment of progress is often disappointing when conventional assessment devices are used since they fail to take account of the extremely small changes in a child's performance. It is important that staff increase their sensitivity to their pupils' behaviour and work towards becoming masters of observation. Ware and Healey (1994) conclude that 'progress to some extent is in the eye of the beholder'. For members of interdisciplinary teams much time can be taken up at meetings discussing pupils' progress where perhaps the notion of progress is different for different team members. To aid consistency one idea is to use prompt sheets which give structure to observations by suggesting areas to observe: for example, changes in movement, changes in expression, changes in appearance.

A slightly different idea which may be useful as part of a whole-school policy related to progression and its meaning can be found below. Adapted from Brown (1996), this framework goes some way towards helping teachers make a 'clear distinction between activities experienced by the pupil and learning outcomes actually achieved' as required by SCAA (1996a, p.12). However, it may be argued that all these levels of response can constitute real 'achievements' as well as mere 'experiences' for individual pupils even if they are not truly 'attainments' in terms of the National Curriculum. For some pupils, for example, the acceptance of a shared activity involving proximity to others is significant in itself. In this case, 'experiences' related to the National Curriculum become active achievements, not simply passive events.

## Experience and Achievement

*Encounter*
being present during an experience

*Awareness*
noticing that something is going on

*Response*
showing surprise, dissatisfaction, enjoyment

*Engagement*
directed attention, focused looking and/or listening, showing interest, recognition or recall

*Participation*
sharing, turntaking, anticipation, supported involvement

*Involvement*
active participation, reaching out, joining in, doing, commenting

*Attainment*
gaining, consolidating, practising skill, knowledge, concepts and understanding
(adapted from Brown 1996)

# Where will children with PMLD learn and be taught?

Many children with PMLD experience 'double segregation' (Ouvry 1987), segregated in a special class within a school for children with severe learning difficulties. Increasingly though they are integrated with their peers in classes in the main part of the school. Conway and Baker (1996) suggest that about 50 per cent are educated this way with some schools retaining the flexibility of a resource base where pupils access specialist facilities and a quieter, distraction free environment. Most special schools have outreach or link schools in the neighbourhood which enable some pupils to interact with their mainstream peers for particular sessions. (There has been little evaluative research of this type of integration for children with PMLD.) Others are educated in units within or on the campus of mainstream schools, a model which Farrell (1996) would like to see expanded.

The complex debate regarding the respective virtues of segregated vs. integrated education has recently been joined by another concerning the meaning of the latest buzzword 'inclusion'. The concepts of integration and inclusion have become interwoven, their meanings confused and open to misinterpretation. A plethora of explanations exist in the literature but as Hall (1996) states, the question of definition addressed to ten different individuals is likely to produce as many quite distinct answers. For some it is a matter of human rights, for others a political process about the transfer of power and for others an issue of matching provision to need.

What has emerged is a dissatisfaction with the term 'integration'. It has often been used or interpreted in a narrow sense of placement only, implying a desegregation process and saying nothing about the quality of that integration. It is an end in itself. As a result of such concerns the word 'inclusion' has become popular. It embraces a much deeper philosophical notion of what integration should mean, conveying both placement and certain qualities of that placement. It refers to the opportunity for people with disabilities to participate more fully in all the activities which typify everyday society, implying active involvement and choice. Inclusion is a process summarised by Uditsky (1993, p.88) as 'A set of principles which ensures that the student with a disability is viewed as a valued and needed member of the school community in every respect'.

So what relevance does this discussion have for pupils with PMLD? Firstly, it is important to confirm that, unlike some definitions of inclusive education, the one put forward here does not imply that every child, no matter what their disability, should be educated in a mainstream setting in the same room as their mainstream peers all of the time. But each member of the staff team can play a role in promoting inclusion through the deployment of teaching approaches which strive to foster the entitlement of all children to a broad, balanced and relevant curriculum which is offered alongside their peers where appropriate. Furthermore, inclusion demands that pupils are encouraged to play a greater part in every stage of their learning (however small this may be) which, in turn, places great emphasis on the fostering of the skills which lead to choice making.

If we support these principles it is essential to provide our pupils with the least restrictive environment possible, thus allowing for a series of schemes and provisions from special schools and special units to mainstream classrooms. Numerous concerns regarding the appropriateness of integrating children with PMLD into mainstream schools have been voiced (Lewis 1995; Jenkinson 1997) and small scale research has confirmed the difficulties (Marvin 1994). In the UK, as stated previously, these pupils are usually educated in special classes or, for part or all of the time, with their peers in the main part of the special school.

Arguments for and against integration wherever it takes place are more than adequately covered elsewhere in the literature (for example, Hornby *et al.* 1997; Farrell 1996; Jenkinson 1993). When under scrutiny, the now famous slogan coined by Hegarty *et al.* (1981) deserves consideration: 'Pupils with special needs do not need integration. What they need is education'. Education should begin with the desire to respond to the individual needs of the pupil by providing a flexible and child-centred learning environment. This to a great extent is the responsibility of the collaborative multidisciplinary team who will need continually to monitor and evaluate the provision, not only in terms of the learning environment but also in terms of the quality of teaching.

For example, it is assumed that social integration with their more able peers automatically presents interaction opportunities to children with PMLD. Cooperative group work, greeting sessions, joint creative activities allow them to be part of an age appropriate cohesive group with a richer flow of social interactions than is usual in a special class. Research has shown that teachers view this as one of the most important outcomes of integration (Ouvry 1986) but genuine interaction does not occur spontaneously; rather it must be facilitated through the continued provision of *carefully structured* opportunities planned and implemented by the staff team jointly responsible for the sessions (Lewis 1995). Furthermore Ouvry (1987) reminds us that children with PMLD may need help to make the best use of the opportunities for interaction that exist. This can present a considerable challenge to those adults supporting the child. Sometimes to be able to record that they have been present during a mixed ability group activity takes precedence over the quality of the interactions experienced. As stated previously, within what may be a bustling, noisy environment staff need to be sensitised to the attempts the child is making to communicate and the other children made aware of the difficulties the child with PMLD is experiencing. Consequently, they may need to be reminded to wait patiently and look very carefully for a response.

There appears to be a lack of theoretical evidence in the UK to support integration as educationally and psychologically sound (Conway and Baker 1996). While inclusive education is undoubtedly the way forward it is equally important that we avoid making the assumption that integration is always beneficial. The warm glow derived from seeing children of all abilities in one classroom must be set aside in favour of appropriateness and sound, considered evidence. In the end the quality of the teaching received — the setting of appropriate objectives, the expectations, the planning of activities and classroom organisation are the crucial issues associated with education and not the presence or absence of peers.

# Towards the 21st century

Following the flood of legislation and accompanying anxiety which has characterised the last ten years of special education it appears that we are reaching safer ground. A time for consolidation and steady progress has arrived during which we can reflect on the innovations and experiments of the past, harness their strengths and combine them with current good practice in order to move confidently forward to the next century.

Theory and practice associated with the education of children with PMLD is still young, yet we have come a long way towards developing a system which meets the highly specific needs of our pupils. These are needs which cannot be met without access to the specialised skills and expertise that derive from parents, caregivers and the multidisciplinary team of professionals associated with their education, care and therapy.

New and imaginative patterns of partnership and support must be explored both nationally and locally. These intiatives must be seen in a positive light and used to the best advantage by serving to stimulate debate, the exchange of information and good practice concerning teaching and learning for pupils with profound disabilities. Similarly, improved communication systems and a growing number of publications which describe and exemplify good practice have enabled us to keep abreast of international perspectives.

The quality of provision for children with PMLD as with all education depends on the commitment and ability of the professionals involved to provide learning experiences which are appropriate to the needs of the children in their charge. Practitioners need to take responsibility for making these choices and be prepared to justify them if challenged. Expertise now exists. We should continue to build on this. The diversity of children's need means that no one form of education should ever predominate because no two children are ever the same. Teaching and teaching approaches will always need to be flexible and our pupils are much better served if everyone concerned is encouraged to work collaboratively to meet their diverse needs.

# Chapter 11

# Person Centred Planning

*Helen Sanderson*

## Introduction

There is a slow yet significant shift in the dominant model or paradigm in the field of learning disabilities. There has been a move from the medical model to the developmental model, and now a new paradigm is emerging which focuses on community membership and functional supports to enhance quality of life (Bradley 1994; Kinsella 1993). This shift requires new ways of planning with people who use services. Traditional planning processes have typically focused on what people could not do and set goals to develop competencies in these areas with the ultimate goal of increased independence. Person centred planning is a different approach rooted in the values of the new paradigm. Instead of trying to 'fix' people, through person centred planning the aim is to discover the individual's preferred lifestyle and how this can be achieved.

In this chapter there is a description of the existing developmental paradigm which primarily seeks to help people to become more independent. This is followed by a description of the emerging paradigm upon which person centred planning is based. Person centred planning is then examined, in terms of where it has come from and how it requires new roles for professionals. One style of person centred planning which many people have found particularly useful with people who have profound and multiple disabilities is known as Essential Lifestyle Planning. This is described and illustrated with Alison's story. Previous planning styles that have been used with Alison have focused on increasing her independence. Essential Lifestyle Planning resulted in a different way of understanding who Alison is, and a different approach to what services needed to offer her. The chapter begins (Jones 1995) with a look at this shift in paradigms — from independence to quality of life.

## What's so great about independence? Shifting paradigms in services

### The existing paradigm

The disability field is currently using models that are 30-40 years old. Group homes, sheltered workshops and segregated schools are all ideas whose time has come and gone. They are extensions of the current model called the developmental model that still has independence as the highest and greatest good. Many people with severe disabilities will never live independently. But almost no one is truly independent. Almost everyone to varying degress depends on the support, concern, and resources of those around us as part of our daily lives. (Dufresne and Laux 1994)

In this existing paradigm (often known as the developmental paradigm) the central focus of professionals is to train people to become more independent. This typically involves using assessments to discover what the person can and cannot do, and then providing programmes, therapies or interventions to increase the person's skills. For many years traditional services have focused on teaching people new skills within an approach that has come to be known as the 'readiness' or 'service continuum' model (Taylor 1988; Jones 1995). This approach involves people being taught skills to become 'ready' for a less restrictive environment, for example moving from a sheltered workshop to open employment, so that they become 'more independent'.

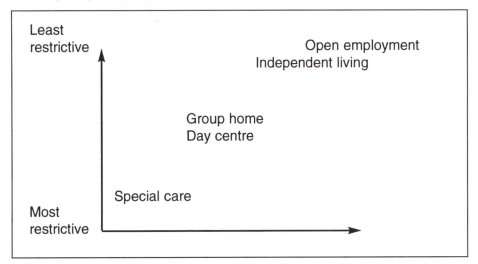

**Figure 11.1** Progress through the readiness model (Jones 1995)

A crucial weakness in this model is that people with the most profound disabilities either progress very slowly or do not seem to move on at all (Seed 1988). This is also compounded by the practice of using artificial settings or simulations to teach new skills hoping that these could be transferred to the real situation or next 'least restrictive environment' (Taylor 1988). Jones (1995) suggests that where a behavioural approach is being used to teach skills it is difficult to ensure continuity of antecedents and consequences from one situation to another as the complex web of norms, values and expectations can only be truly experienced in the natural setting. Questions have also been raised about the ability of adults with severe disability consciously to transfer knowledge to different situations once the critical periods of development in childhood have passed (Kandel *et al.* 1991, cited in Jones, 1995).

In this model people with profound disabilities are never 'ready' to be independent. This risks wasting people's lives as they are never able to move on, and wasting the services' resources. O'Brien (O'Brien and Lyle O'Brien 1991) offers two definitions of independence. The first is the familiar definition where people are trained to be able to meet their own basic needs with minimum assistance. The second definition sees independence as choosing and living one's own lifestyle — regardless of the amount and type of assistance necessary. Independence would therefore not be measured by the number of tasks which people can do without assistance but the quality of life a person can have with whatever support they need. Many disabled people echo this view:

> Real independence is nothing to do with cooking, cleaning and dressing oneself. If you ask me what is my experience of being independent, I would not automatically think about self help skills but of being able to use my imagination to create fantasy, of enjoying music and drama, of relishing sensual pleasures and absorbing the natural life around me. (John Corbett cited in Sanderson *et al.* 1997)

Rather than independence, it is 'interdependence' that services need to focus on. Interdependence more accurately describes the ways in which we depend on each other and the lifestyle we can seek to support for people with profound disabilities. Table 11.1 illustrates the key questions and familiar answers belonging to this existing paradigm.

| | |
|---|---|
| Who is the person of concern? | *The client* |
| What is the typical setting? | *A group home, adult training centre, special school* |
| How are services organised? | *In a continuum of options* |
| What is the model? | *Developmental/behavioural* |
| What are the services? | *Programmes/interventions* |
| How are services planned? | *Individual Programme plan based on professional assessments* |
| Who controls the planning decision? | *An interdisciplinary team* |
| What is the planning context? | *Team consensus* |
| What is given the highest priority? | *Independence/skill development/behaviour management* |
| What is the objective? | *To develop independence and change undesirable behaviours.* |

(adapted from Bradley 1994)

**Table 11.1** Key questions and answers from the existing paradigm

## An emerging paradigm

There is a new, emerging paradigm which focuses on community membership and functional supports to enhance quality of life. This is often referred to as a 'support model' or 'ecological approach' in contrast to the 'readiness' approach described earlier. It is rooted in the values underpinning the five service accomplishments described by O`Brien in 1987 which outline what services should be striving for.

This paradigm challenges us to ask whether the skills that professionals seek to teach have any functional meaning for the person in the real world or whether they are skill acquisition for its own sake. Rather than requiring the person to change and adapt, this paradigm requires that services, supports and environments change instead, and focus on supporting people to develop relationships within the local community and to direct their own lives.

Where services are embracing this new paradigm, learning and education are refocused. Instead of asking 'what skills do we need to teach next and how can we do this?' the question is 'what would it take to support this person to be part of their local community?' This requires a shift from the prevalence of sensory stimulation to an ecological approach which directly supports children and adults to live as members of their community. This does not mean that the senses are ignored, instead they are used in the context of activities which support people with profound multiple disabilities to become more involved in the sort of life which we take for granted (Jones 1993).

| Valued Experiences (for people with learning difficulties) | Community Challenge (the aims we are working to achieve) | Service Accomplishments (what the service should aim to achieve) |
| --- | --- | --- |
| Sharing ordinary places activities | Include all people and | Community presence |
| Making choices creatively resolving conflicts | Protect integrity by promoting choice | Protecting rights and |
| Developing abilities and sharing personal gifts | Develop all available resources wisely competence | Recognising interests and gifts; improving |
| Being respected and having a valued social role | Offer valued roles to everyone by confronting limiting beliefs and their historical consequences | Promoting valued roles |
| Growing in relationships | Promote interdependence among people | Community participation |

(O'Brien and Lyle O'Brien 1991)

**Table 11.2** Values underpinning services for people with learning disabilities

This new focus is often achieved through partial participation (Baumgart *et al.* 1982, cited in Jones 1995). Partial participation requires that people are enabled to participate in appropriate activities in ordinary environments through individualised adaptations. These adaptations compensate for missing skills through support or environmental changes.

Within this new, emerging paradigm adult services look radically different. Innovative supported employment schemes use training in systematic instruction to make real work a reality for people, including people with profound disabilities (Jones 1994). Supported living services enable people to live in their own homes (Fitton 1994; Kinsella 1993). Community support workers or 'bridge builders' enable people to connect with their local community and move into the mainstream of life (Sanderson *et al.* 1997). Day services focus on enabling people to enjoy the range of ordinary leisure pursuits, or ordinary college courses on an individual basis. Examples of this for people with profound disabilities include the Kidderminster Day Service project, Leisure Link in Stockport and Study Link in Liverpool (Sanderson 1995). Outside of services, Circles of Support demonstrate how members of the community can come together to help people (including those with the most profound disabilities) to make changes in their lives. This is being made a reality for people, including people with profound disability, by Circles Network in Bristol (Sanderson 1996; Wertheimer 1995).

| | |
|---|---|
| Who is the person of concern? | *The citizen* |
| What is the typical setting? | *A person's home, workplace or local school* |
| How are services organised? | *Through a unique array of supports tailored to the individual* |
| What is the model? | *Individual support* |
| What are the services? | *Supports* |
| How are services planned? | *Through a person centred plan* |
| Who controls the planning decision? | *The individual or those family or friends closest to the person* |
| What is the planning context? | *A circle of support or person centred team* |
| What is given the highest priority? | *Self-determination and relationships* |
| What is the objective? | *To support the person to have the lifestyle that they choose in their local community* |

(adapted from Bradley 1994)

**Table 11.3** Key questions and answers from the emerging paradigm

In this paradigm people are supported to live full lives in the community by adapting environments and providing individual support rather than requiring that people become more skilled to be 'ready' or more 'independent'. Table 11.3 shows that the same key questions used in Table 11.1 will elicit quite different answers when applied to this paradigm.

To begin to develop these individual supports (based on the lifestyle that a person wants) requires a different way of planning known as person centred planning.

# Person centred planning

Person centred planning is the collective term for a number of planning styles which share the values of this new paradigm. Each of the different styles of planning is used to answer two fundamental questions:

- Who are you and who are we in your life?
- What can we do together to achieve a better life for you now and in the future?

This involves a process of learning about a person; who they are, what has happened to them, what is important to them, what they like and dislike, and what they want from life. This takes place over a period of time. It usually begins with an initial planning meeting, which is just the first step (Sanderson *et al.* 1997).

## The roots of person centred planning

The development of person centred planning has been stimulated by dissatisfaction with existing traditional ways of doing individual programme plans with people. Person centred planning has one of its roots in individual planning. In the 1970s and into the 1980s, many people working in services for people with learning disabilities developed individual planning systems. To begin with, these were essentially plans for rehabilitation and training of the individual. They were the schedule which services imposed on people to help them learn new skills, stop doing things other people did not like and generally become ready for acceptance in the world. Goals were defined by professionals and recorded in terms of what the person needed to do, for example: 'Mary will complete a six piece inset puzzle correctly without any prompting' (Peck and Hong 1988). Individual planning has typically been used to set goals that focus on increasing the person's skills and fitting them into existing services.

As systems of planning developed there was a shift of language — more attention being paid to people's 'strengths' as well as their 'needs', and a much greater concern that the person should be present and should be helped to participate. Individual planning also tended to focus on ensuring harmony between all the professionals involved in the meeting. The emphasis was on the process of multidisciplinary meetings rather than making things happen for the person.

The development of Shared Action Planning (Brechin and Swain 1987) is one example of a direct response to this dissatisfaction with individual planning in the UK. This approach places increased emphasis on self advocacy, with a greater role being played by the person and their family. Assessment is seen as an ongoing process of discussion and observation rather than measuring people against set criteria.

Early practitioners of Shared Action Planning and other styles of person centred planning all had experience of well-developed individual planning systems, which were supposed to be helping people, but these 'service-centred' planning systems were locking people into a service world.

Person centred planning developed with a foundation of values based on the Five Accomplishments (O'Brien 1987), the Social Model of Disability and the Inclusion Movement. It is a set of processes that challenges services to work actively towards building inclusive communities as well as seeking valued experiences for people with disabilities and achieving service accomplishments.

## A changing role for professionals

Information gained from technical assessments of the person can be helpful, but only in the context of a knowledgeable account of a person's history and desired future. Subordinating professional-technical information to personal knowledge turns the typical agency decision making process on its head. (O'Brien and Lovett 1992 p.1)

There are two extremes that people sometimes adopt when thinking about what people with learning disabilities want and need. The first extreme, common in traditional assessment, is that professionals and other people know everything there is to know about the person's needs. The second extreme is that people themselves know everything there is to know about their own needs. Each of us has areas of our life that we are unaware of and that other people can shed useful light upon. A shared style is required where professionals move from being the 'experts on the person' to being 'experts in the process of problem solving with others'. Smale and Tuson (1993) describe this as the 'exchange model' of assessment and planning and recommend it as good practice for care managers and other professionals.

This reflects a significant shift in power, from the professionals having 'power over' the person to sharing power or having 'power with' the person. Here

| The Questioning Model | The Exchange Model |
|---|---|
| Assumes the professional: | Assumes that people: |
| • is expert in people, their problems and needs; | • are expert in themselves; |
| • exercises knowledge and skill to form 'their' assessment, identify people's needs; | Assumes that the professional: |
| • identifies resources required; | • has expertise in the *process* of problem solving with others; |
| • takes responsibility for making an accurate assessment of need and taking appropriate action. | • understands and shares perceptions of problems and their management; |
| | • gets agreement about who will do what to support whom; |
| | • takes responsibility for arriving at the optimum resolution of problems within the constraints of available resources and the willingness of participants to contribute. |

(Smale and Tulson 1993)

**Figure 11.4** The questioning and exchange models. The assumptions compared

professionals, however interdisciplinary, are no longer in charge of collecting and holding information and making decisions about the person's life. In person centred planning the individual and the people who care about the person take the lead in deciding what is important to the person, which community opportunities should be taken or created and what the future could look like. It is not just the person him or herself that we seek to share power with, but family, friends and other people from the community who the person has invited to become involved.

These represent two of the most important challenges in person centred planning: how can we keep the person at the centre of the planning process and support them to participate as much as possible, and how can we encourage and include family, friends and non-service people? Where services seek to become more interdisciplinary in the ways that they work, these two issues need to be kept in the foreground. If this does not happen good interdisciplinary collaboration will remain part of the existing paradigm of 'independence' rather than working within the new paradigm of 'quality of life'.

Often it is family members who know the person best. They have knowledge of her or his history and who she or he really is. They will care about the person in a way that is different from everyone else and (if they are involved) they will probably be involved for the rest of their lives. This kind of knowledge and commitment can mean that family members see the situation differently from the individual him or herself and the others who support them. They might have concerns about safety that have to be acknowledged and addressed. Sharing power with families means seeking the active involvement of the person's family and friends. This ensures that the person is planning his or her future with people who care about her or him rather than simply with people who have a professional opinion about them.

Professionals therefore become people who can provide a limited range of services rather than people who are expected to find all the solutions and put them into practice. In person centred planning clinical or professional staff move from being the owners of the process, centre-stage, to being backstage technicians, the people who know what is technically possible and how to make it happen. This changing in the role of professional is one of the key differences between traditional planning and person centred planning. This and other differences are summarised in Table 11.5.

| Moving from... | towards... |
|---|---|
| planning which focuses on what which<br>people can and cannot do – trying to 'fix' people or wait until they for<br>are 'ready' | planning and problem solving<br><br>seeks to discover the person's desired lifestyle and preferences<br><br>the future |
| professionals being in charge | sharing power with individuals, their friends and family. Working to keep the person at the centre of the planning process and participating as much as possible |
| people being surrounded only by professionals and paid staff | people having friends and strengthening community connections |
| fitting people into existing service options | creating individual and unique support arrangements |

(adapted from Sanderson *et al.* 1997)

**Table 11.5** Moving towards person centred planning

| What we think Derek is communicating to us... | | | |
| --- | --- | --- | --- |
| Whe/Time of Day/Place | When Derek Does This... | We Think it Means | And We Should... |
| When out in the pub/restaurant | Derek pushes the table away *or* slides down the seat | Derek wants to leave | Support Derek to leave. Help him to get up by moving the chair back and guide him to the door |
| When out walking | Derek sits down | Derek doesn't want to walk any more | Encourage Derek to stand up in his own time by holding your hands out, supporting Derek to stand up and going to a bench to rest |
| When out walking | Derek takes your arm, pulls at your clothing | Derek feels a little unsure/unsteady | Offer support to Derek by offering your arm. Derek may link arms |
| Any time of day | Derek picks up a cup/bottle/glass and puts it into his mouth | Dereks wants a drink | Give Derek a drink |
| Anytime of the day if sitting close to Derek | Pushes you away with hands/feet, pulls your hair | Derek feels that you are sitting too close to him | Give Derek more space and move away |

| What we are trying to communicate to Derek... | | |
| --- | --- | --- |
| We Want to Let Derek Know | To Do This We... | And Then Support Derek to... |
| It's time to go out | Show Derek his boots | Put his boots on walk to the door |
| It's time to go out for a walk | Guide Derek past the car to the gate | Walk at his own pace |
| It's time to go out in the car | Show Derek the car keys or rattle the car keys | Walk to the car |
| It's time to go the pub | Show Derek his pint pot glass | Support Derek to go to the pub |
| It's time to go to the shop to buy chocolate | Show Derek a chocolate wrapper | Support Derek to go to the shop and buy chocolate |

**Table 11.6** Examples from Derek's communication section of his Essential Lifestyle Plan

Person centred planning invites us to learn about people in different ways. It involves a different way to develop this into a shared agenda for action, different ways of having meetings, using different planning styles and essentially making things happen. One of these different planning styles is known as Essential Lifestyle Planning and it is being increasingly used with people with profound disabilities.

# Essential Lifestyle Planning

Essential Lifestyle Planning was developed by Smull and Burke-Harrison (1991) as a way of discovering what is important to people in their day-to-day lives. This information is recorded in a clear, simple but powerful way in the person's Essential Lifestyle Plan. 'Our quality of life everyday is determined by the presence or absence of things that are important to us — our choices, our rituals', (Smull cited in Sanderson 1997).

## Developing an Essential Lifestyle Plan

The plan is developed by spending time with the person and talking with other people who know and care about him or her. To do this, the facilitator needs to be able to elicit stories and listen, both to what is said on the surface and what this suggests is important to the person. This means that closed, yes/no questions are avoided and instead people are asked to describe stories of times they have spent with the person, what they think the person's ideal day is, what the person's life is like from morning to evening, what support and assistance the person needs. The answers to these questions enable the facilitator to hear how well these people know the person and get a sense of what is important to the person, not just about their routines but our 'best guess' about how the person may want to live more generally. In developing a plan with someone who does not use words to communicate, the facilitator begins by discovering how people think the person is communicating, and recording this in the communication section of the plan.

After the facilitator has spent time with the individual and talked to the other key people, what he or she has learned about the person's relationships, the things they do, places they go and the rhythm and pace of their life is put under five basic headings (see below). Each plan begins with a list of who contributed to it. Wherever possible and appropriate the plan is presented in the most accessible way for the person, for example, using photographs, drawings, pictures, video or audiotape.

## Basic headings in Essential Lifestyle Planning

### What others say about the person

This is where all the positive attributes of the person are listed. Words such as, 'warm', 'fun to be with', 'caring' or 'makes me laugh' are appropriate. Clinical descriptions that describe what people can do, for example or 'can eat with adapted spoon' are not used.

### Who and what is important to the person

Who and what is important to the person is prioritised into three sections:

*Essentials:*
The most important things that people must have present or absent in their lives for a reasonable quality of life. Positive/must haves are essential for the person's life to be tolerable and pleasant. Negative/must not haves make life so unpleasant and intolerable that their presence will make people unhappy, or cause them to withdraw or become challenging. These requests are usually modest, but essential to the person's well-being. Most of them are stable over time.

*Important:*
These are important to the person, but not as critical as Essentials. If a person is denied something that is an Important, then life would still be tolerable but perhaps only for a certain length of time. When people have a number of the things that are important to them ignored, then this will severely compromise their quality of life.

*Enjoys/prefers:*
These are things that the person enjoys or likes to have present or absent in his/her life.

Services sometimes use different headings to reflect the same things. They were originally described as Non-negotiables, Strong preferences and Highly desirables.

These sections *only* reflect what is important to the person, not what other people value. Things that are important to the other key people in the person's life are reflected in the 'What others need to know or do' section.

## What others need to know or do to successfully support the person

This section includes the person's important routines and what support is needed. It does not include things that the person can do for themselves.

## Communication section

Where the person does not use words to talk, this section is used. It describes how the person communicates with you, and how you communicate with the person. Extracts from Derek's communication section can be seen in Table 11.6.

## Unresolved issues

Where there are issues that people have very different views on, or where there is not enough information, these are recorded as Unresolved issues to be discussed at the meeting.

# *The Essential Lifestyle Planning meeting*

When the plan has been drafted, it is then discussed with the person him or herself wherever possible or with the person most likely to reflect the views of the person. That person should check whether it is right and that it can be shared with other people. An Essential Lifestyle Planning meeting generally has five steps:

1. Review and agree the plan.
2. For each item on the plan, ask whether it is happening in the way that the plan describes.
3. Celebrate/acknowledge the things that are happening and brainstorm what needs to change to make the rest of the plan occur.
4. Agree which ideas are worth pursuing and decide who will do what by when.
5. Agree how people will know when the plan is no longer working and needs changing.

Essential Lifestyle Planning is being used in many ways. It can be used to design a service for someone leaving an institution, for young people in transition from school to other services, for older people and, as in the example of Alison's situation, to record her desired lifestyle and recruit people to help her to achieve it.

**People who know and care say alison:**
- always greets you with a lovely smile
- is a great communicator
- has infectious laughter
- is loyal to her friends
- is good company – can cheer everyone else up
- is assertive
- is straightforward and honest
- has a lively personality – likes to be where it is all happening.

**Alison's Essentials**
- she must continue to live in her own home, by herself
- she must continue to spend time with her family and all those who are close to her:
  she spends time with her parents at least once a week;
  sees her nephew Stephen once a week, and sister Sharon once a fortnight;
  spends time with particular staff members at the day centre, with whom she has built up long-term close relationships (Pat, Chris, Hilda) every weekday.
- she must have conversations, and is often unhappy if two or more people are with her:
  she likes your undivided attention.
- she mustn't be ignored, or made to feel that other people in the room are paying more attention to each other than they are to her:
- she must be *involved* in what's going on around her: in cooking and food preparation (even if it's only being in the kitchen and watching); in daily tasks in her home (keep her informed about what you're doing...);
- she must go out for a walk at least once every day – she can't stand being stuck in (in bad weather, she can still go out for a drive in her van).
- a calm atmosphere – she can pick up on tension and senses when other people have just had an argument.
- her bath every morning – she likes a 10 minute soak on weekdays/15 minutes at the weekend, without being fussed (she doesn't like showers).
- driving out in her van every day.

- **the sorts of other people she prefers to be with are:**
  bubbly, lively, energetic people, who involve her in what's going on; quiet people as well; people who are patient with her and take her out; she doesn't like loud, overbearing people.

- **Alison enjoys/prefers...**
- comfortable, easy-to-wear clothes (eg. track suit trousers);
- likes to be taken to her own seat on the bus (on the right hand side behind the driver);
- likes gentle touch and affection:
  appreciates a light touch on her shoulder or hand when she greets you;
  likes sometimes to sit holding hands with particular people she is close to.
- likes massage with sesame oil and lavender. She enjoys having her shoulders, chest, ribs and stomach massaged at weekends, after her bath. She has a hand and foot massage at least once a week.

**What we need to know and do, in order to support Alison successfully**
- take her to the front door, so that she can see for herself if it's too rainy or windy to go out.
- if she is stressed or agitated, she calms down more easily if left on her own for a while.
- support her friendships with people who are not paid staff, e.g. Luna, friends from the day centre.
- respect and support her daily routines:
  morning routine
  Alison is woken about 7.00 (weekdays), then lies in for half an hour, with the radio on (Radio 2) and the curtains drawn back to let in air. Get up 7.20am cup of tea in bedroom.
  Bath (with her left side covered in water) – she doesn't like to be rushed.
  Alison is supported to get dressed, her left arm and leg need to go first.
  She then has her hair blow-dried (if her hair has not been washed, it should be damped at the bath, then brushed, otherwise it gets frizzy).

  Alison's actual plan also lists her evening routine and other significant routines, a communication section, and describes what people need to do to keep her healthy and safe (health, food and medical issues).

**Table 11.7** Extracts from Alison's Essential Lifestyle Plan

# Alison's story

Alison is a 35 year old woman who has a lively sense of humour and communicates well with those around her, although she cannot use words to speak. She enjoys an active lifestyle, and likes to be fully involved in whatever is going on. Up until about a year ago, she had lived all her life with her mother and father and, until they left home, her four brothers and sisters.

Alison's parents had been becoming increasingly concerned over the years about what would happen to her when they were no longer able to care for her themselves. Alison needs support with all aspects of her life; she cannot eat, wash, dress, or attend to any of her daily needs without support. She uses a wheelchair to get around, and her home is extensively adapted, with a through – floor lift, track hoists etc. to meet her needs. None of the options her parents had considered for her future support seemed appropriate; they had looked at a number of residential establishments, most of which were a distance away from the area of Manchester where they had always lived, and none of which seemed able to offer the very high standard of physical care to which Alison was accustomed.

In 1994, Alison's parents joined up with a small group of other families, who all had adult children with learning disabilities living at home. Together, they formed their own organisation, 'Ordinary Lifestyles', in order to plan for their sons' and daughters' futures. The aim was that the organisation would eventually employ its own staff, who should support people in their own homes, and that the whole service would continue to be run and managed by the families themselves. At around the same time that Ordinary Lifestyles was developing, Alison's parents took the step of moving out of the house they had shared with their daughter for the last 22 years. They moved into a house just around the corner, convinced that the family home, with its familiar surroundings, was where she wished to stay.

## *Developing Alison's Essential Lifestyle Plan*

Before Alison's staff were recruited, Essential Lifestyle Planning was used in order to find out and record all the information that Alison's future staff team would need. The Ordinary Lifestyles Development worker, Kathy Davies, spent time individually with seven people who knew Alison very well; her parents, three members of staff from the Day Centre, her Care Manager, and one of the agency staff who had become very close to her over a short period of time. Alison's sister was involved in the process at the final planning meeting, but could not take part in an interview, through illness. The emphasis was upon getting each of the individuals who knew Alison to give their understanding of what Alison's own wishes and feelings were, in the hope that this would reflect what was important to Alison as far as possible. It is recognised that as Alison cannot tell us directly, this represents the group's 'best guess' at what is important to her and how she wants to be supported.

The questions Kathy asked were based around four different areas:

* What would a 'good' day be like for Alison?
* What would a 'worst' day be like for Alison?
* What do you think makes her happy?
* What do you think makes her sad?
* What do we need to know and do to support Alison?

## Alison's Essential Lifestyle Plan

A lot of detail was included in Alison's Essential Lifestyle Plan, about the sort of people Alison likes, the ways in which she likes people to speak to her, and the way in which she likes to involved in group conversations which are going on around her. A wealth of information was included on her physical support needs and daily routines. For example, a whole section covered eating and drinking, and what people need to know if they assist her to eat and drink.

Another whole section was devoted to communication; it listed the different ways in which Alison talks to people, and what we think she is trying to say. For example, when Alison looks at the glass cabinet in her living room, it means she wants something to eat; when there is a guest present and she looks at the armchair, it means 'please take a seat'.

Alison's mother initially had some doubts about the usefulness of Essential Lifestyle Planning, given that Alison had had many assessments and reports done on her over the years, none of which had seemed to lead to any real changes. However, it was clear that the Essential Lifestyle Plan looked at different sorts of information from that traditionally presented in other documents; i.e. it was not a list of the things Alison can and cannot do, nor a simple description of 'likes and dislikes'. Two documents produced by the Local Authority at around the same time as the Essential Lifestyle Plan provided, amongst other things, detailed information on Alison's particular skills/lack of skills, and summarised her support needs in terms of the amount of support required (24 hour care in her own home), and the safeguards required for her health and safety (medical and financial record – keeping etc.) The Local Authority Community Care Plan confirmed Alison's need for an ongoing high level of care, set out her weekly timetable, and stipulated the basic goals which Social Services would expect to be met by any agency providing her with care. Clearly however, the Community Care Plan did not aim to provide the same sort of detail about what sort of lifestyle Alison wants, or the specific support that she needs, as the Essential Lifestyle Plan does.

Alison's mother gradually came to see that the Essential Lifestyle Plan was a useful tool, especially when it was used in the recruitment process for the staff team.

## Alison's Essential Lifestyle Planning meeting

When the plan had been drafted as a result of the conversations with those who know and care about Alison, her meeting was arranged. One evening the people who had taken part in the interviews were invited to a meeting at Alison's home.

The meeting was facilitated by reviewing each section of the plan, discussing unresolved issues and then setting goals. One general comment from the group was, 'Yes, this is Alison!'

The meeting provided an opportunity to get clarification on one particularly controversial issue in Alison's life. It had often been suggested, during the negotiations with the Local Authority about Alison's services, that a second person should move into her house. Clearly, there were cost implications involved, although some of the people who had argued for a second person had done so by pointing to Alison's need for company etc. as well as to the financial concerns. Everyone at the meeting agreed that Alison was the sort of person who needed her own space and liked the complete, undivided attention of the staff supporting her. People were sure that if she could have her own say, she would not want another person moving into her home, although everyone accepted that this could change in the future. The first statement in the Essential section of the Plan, was therefore written simply as: 'Must continue to live in her own home, by herself'.

Since the meeting, the Essential Lifestyle plan has been used in recruiting Alison's staff. Shortlisted candidates were given a copy of her plan and asked questions about how they would support Alison to achieve the lifestyle described in the plan. The plan has also been used to direct the team's activities on a day-to-day basis and as part of the process of setting personal objectives with individual team members. Alison's team, the development worker and her family are exploring ways for the plan to be a 'living plan' in contrast to the other assessments and plans completed on Alison that made little if any difference to her life.

The contribution of Kathy Davies and Lillian and Alison Doyle

# Conclusion

In this chapter it has been seen how some services are embracing a new paradigm which replaces the preoccupation with independence. It moves towards individual support and community inclusion in order to improve the quality of individuals' lives. Person centred planning can contribute to this. It is essential that person centred planning is not misinterpreted as a new way to do individual planning, as just a new set of paperwork. Person centred planning reflects a new paradigm which involves another way of thinking, seeing people, imagining possibilities with people, re-evaluating our roles within people's lives and the way organisations work.

Chapter 12

# Managing the Learning Environment

*Richard Byers*

## Introduction

Learning, even learning which appears to be primarily internal, happens in a context and very few of us are lucky enough to be able to do our learning under conditions which could be said to be ideal. This may be especially true for people with profound and multiple learning difficulties. These learners may need to find, or be supported in finding, ways around various obstacles, such as sensory, perceptual or motor impairments, before learning can begin to take place. This chapter is aimed at readers who are on the teaching side of the teacher–learner relationship, whether you are a qualified practitioner working in a specifically educational institution or a committed member of the multi-disciplinary team supporting clients with profound and multiple learning difficulties in continuing to learn in the community. The purpose of this chapter is to support you in your task of creating and maintaining conditions under which effective learning is likely to take place. Part of this discussion will concern ways in which those conditions can be modified in order to support and facilitate learning for people who may be experiencing particular difficulties in this area of their lives.

There is a significant body of literature on the organisation of teaching and learning for people with profound and multiple learning difficulties in specialist environments. Evans and Ware (1987) and Sebba (1988), for example, describe approaches which are predicated upon the notion that pupils and students with profound and multiple learning difficulties are most likely to be taught in groupings separated from their age peers and, in all probability, in separate and specially adapted physical spaces with separate and specially trained staff support. These models of 'special care' provision are becoming less common. Pupils with profound and multiple learning difficulties are increasingly being included in teaching groups with their age peers, whether this happens within the segregated provision of a special school for pupils with severe and profound and multiple learning difficulties or, in an arguably more developed but radical model of inclusion, in a neighbourhood mainstream school (Sebba and Sachdev 1997; DfEE 1997).

Adult learners with profound and multiple learning difficulties are also now more likely to gain access to their local mainstream college of further or higher education for courses of continuing education. At the same time, the parallel notions of lifelong learning and community participation (FEU/Mencap, no date given) mean that staff working with adults with profound and multiple learning difficulties find themselves charged with the responsibility of ensuring that teaching and learning continue to take place throughout life and outside the narrow confines of designated educational

146

institutions. While this chapter cannot hope to provide specific answers to all the practical challenges, it does set out to stimulate discussion about some of the considerations which impinge upon the creation of appropriate learning conditions for people with profound and multiple learning difficulties wherever and whenever they may need to be provided.

# Relationships and routines

Considering the nature of the relationships between staff and learners may be seen as the first priority in establishing a positive climate for learning. Sebba *et al.* (1993) discuss a series of models for relationships between teachers and learners. They acknowledge, for example, that some approaches to teaching are founded upon the notion that expertise and control should reside with the teacher. It is the teacher, in this model, who identifies deficits or learning needs within the learner; who then decides what is to be taught and how that teaching will be accomplished; who sets objectives and establishes criteria by which the learner's success or failure may be judged; and who assesses the learner's readiness to move on to further study. The learner's role, in this relationship, tends to be passive. The image is of a powerless learner who is directed through a learning process which is prescribed by staff at all stages.

At the opposite end of the spectrum is a model where practitioners hand over the reins of control to learners. There is an assumption, in this approach, that learners themselves know what they need to learn and that, if a stimulating enough environment is provided, learners will discover for themselves the skills, the knowledge and the understanding to which their curiosity will inexorably lead them. It is the role of the teacher, in this model, to be present in the learning event as a guide, a facilitator, or a provider of requested support, but power resides with the learner.

Other models conceptualise teaching and learning as a form of dialogue – a dynamic relationship in which both parties take opportunities to choose, to direct, to initiate and, by turns, to observe, to listen and to make discoveries. In these models, (Nind and Hewett 1994; McGee *et al.* 1987; Collis and Lacey 1996), teachers and learners negotiate content, goals and pedagogy. Power is shared. As partners in the teaching and learning relationship, both parties are seen as having active contributions to make; both parties are seen as having the need and the capacity to teach and to learn.

This is not the easy route. Creating a meaningful dialogue between teacher and learner so that genuine negotiation can take place is skilled and difficult work. Under the most advantageous circumstances, it requires meticulous preparation and planning and an advanced level of self-awareness on the part of both teacher and learner. To approach the task of teaching learners who experience profound and multiple difficulties in this spirit is therefore a significant challenge. However, there are reasons why this may be a challenge worth accepting.

By becoming used to operating in a position of power over another person, it is all too easy to begin to lose sight of their rights. Practitioners who routinely take full control over the teaching and learning process, albeit in the 'best interests' of their students, may find themselves, without intention but inevitably, slipping into the kinds of rituals, habits and degrading practices which characterised much institutional care and occupational training for people with profound and multiple learning difficulties until relatively recently (Furneaux 1969). The result is not only poor practice, but also a situation in which the learner ends up at the bottom of the hierarchy and comes to be defined and limited by powerlessness. By the same token, practitioners who work constantly in a supporting role, offering, again with the best of intentions, help, care and guidance where these commodities seem to be required, may begin to lose sight of their responsibility to enable the learner to achieve maximum self-determination. Over-helping or the unquestioned provision of routine support may engender in clients a state of learned helplessness. Under these conditions, deepening dependency rather than independence is the true outcome.

By contrast, the levels of empathy and respect which will enable teachers to confer dignity upon learners and promote choice and autonomy in even the most intimate of personal care routines will be enhanced by dialogue and negotiation. Undertaking a process of dialogue and negotiation, which, of course, may not be conventionally verbal for many learners, will involve practitioners in careful consideration of the balance between rules, authority, help and support. It will also entail a review and re-evaluation of the use and application of routines, rituals, timetables and schedules.

It is often said that pupils and students with learning difficulties benefit from consistent approaches and the opportunity to revisit key learning opportunities. However, the imperative to provide consistency should not become an excuse for endless repetition, tedious patterns or fixed habits of behaviour. These are the features of a lazy and unimaginative approach to education. Ware (1994) suggests that at least part of the value of developing consistent approaches lies in also providing, in balance, variety and the challenge of new stimuli. We might almost suggest that the purpose of a consistent approach is to move learners towards a point of recognition and anticipation precisely so that deliberate interruptions and changes in daily patterns and routines can be introduced. New experiences will create new learning challenges and should be seen as an entitlement for all learners in promoting development and a sense of progress. This balance between the security and confidence which can be engendered through familiar experiences and the deeper levels of self-esteem which are promoted in learners through successful encounters with unfamiliar and testing situations can help to ensure that teaching and learning have a changing sense of pace (OFSTED 1995) as well as a focused sense of purpose.

Achieving these ideals of well-paced and purposeful learning will entail sophisticated approaches to the management of staff. Ouvry (1987), Sebba (1988) and Ware (1994) describe approaches to room management, zoning and the allocation of key worker roles. Lacey and Lomas (1993) and Coles (1994) suggest that collaborative and multidisciplinary approaches to the work of the staff team will be most appropriate in avoiding unproductive fixed hierarchies while ensuring maximum access to the expertise of all team members.

# The sensory environment

Practitioners working with people with profound and multiple learning difficulties will, inevitably, find themselves working in a range of different environments. You will therefore need to gain skills in adapting, and adapting your teaching approaches to take advantage of, for example:

- multi-purpose rooms which were not designed for teaching and learning at all;
- traditional teaching areas, including classrooms, seminar rooms, gymnasia, swimming pools, halls and workshops, which were not designed with pupils and students with profound and multiple learning difficulties in mind;

- if you are lucky, some specialist facilities, including purpose-built sensory environments.

Specially designed sensory environments have come to occupy a significant role in the education of pupils and students with profound and multiple learning difficulties. Building on the work of pioneers in the field such as the proponents of Snoezelen in the Netherlands, the designers of soft play environments in the UK and the sensory approaches of Longhorn (1988), many schools and specialist colleges now have at their disposal some form of resource drawn from the range of white rooms, dark rooms, hydrotherapy pools, aromatherapy and massage facilities, or light and sound installations. As these resources become more technologically sophisticated, they become more expensive and, often, more daunting for staff to use creatively and flexibly. This section will explore the functions of such environments and the possibility of giving learners access to similarly stimulating experiences without the benefit of specialist resources.

Proponents of the use of sensory environments claim that they have a multiplicity of functions. They may, for example, be used for relaxation, simply giving clients an opportunity to unwind amid gently meditative sights, sounds and smells. This relaxation may be seen as being in itself therapeutic, or the therapeutic value of the experience may be enhanced by the input of music therapists, aromatherapists, occupational therapists or physiotherapists. The latter professionals may seek to use the stimuli provided by sensory environments as a means of promoting movement, mobility, or the purposeful use of switches, for example, as part of a planned therapeutic programme.

The sensory environment may also be purposefully used by educationalists. Just as staff in mainstream classrooms use blackboards, books and audio-visual aids in order to support and enhance their teaching, so staff working with pupils and students who have profound and multiple learning difficulties must begin to view the wealth of equipment often provided within light and dark rooms as part of the resource base which will support them in the parallel tasks of teaching and assessment. The contention here is that an enhanced sensory environment should not be seen as an end in itself but rather as one approach among many to the challenge of providing an education for people with profound and multiple learning difficulties (Ouvry and Saunders 1996). However sophisticated the electronics may become, there will always be a requirement for teachers to make intelligent, reflective, critical use of such facilities and to avoid the routine use of sensory environments simply as forms of entertainment or occupation. Of course, there will be moments in any teaching day when the option of a period of simple relaxation or leisure time becomes appropriate. Used unthinkingly, however, expensive and sophisticated sensory environments become little more than high-tech versions of the repetitive jigsaw puzzle, raffia weaving, mobile gazing, time filling regimes which used to characterise institutions for people with learning difficulties many years ago.

If they are put to an appropriate purpose, sensory environments can be very productive. It is possible, for example, to use a sensory approach to:

- assess a learner's perceptual skills in becoming aware of, directing attention towards, tracking or focusing upon a sight, sound, vibration or smell;
- facilitate the development of functional learning strategies, such as observation, anticipation, prediction and the use of memory;
- support learning in a variety of modes – auditory, visual, verbal, concrete, olfactory, tactile or kinaesthetic;

- encourage purposeful exploratory and investigative behaviour by creating significant and stimulating links between actions and effects;
- promote behaviours with communicative potential through the intentional use of a variety of switches;
- develop skills in positioning and mobility by stimulating learners to trigger or maintain preferred sensory outcomes.

Of course, a sensory approach can also be fun and it can also be used to compensate for specific impairments. Thus a learner who has very limited physical movement can be enabled to generate dramatically amplified visual or tactile events through the use of electronics; a learner with a visual impairment can be given access to a world where aural and olfactory stimulation is enhanced; a learner with a profound hearing loss can begin to be taught the communicative significance of sights and visual events.

# Adapting existing environments

These effects do not, however, depend entirely upon the provision of purpose-built environments. Wherever staff work with people with profound and multiple learning difficulties, there is a need to consider the sensory impact of the learning environment. Rooms which are routinely noisy or visually cluttered are unlikely to help learners with profound and multiple learning difficulties to make orderly use of sensory input. Staff may find the permanent presence of the radio reassuring; for learners the constantly shifting background sound may constitute a serious distraction. Similarly, a room filled with hanging toys, mobiles, flashing lights and reflective surfaces may seem appropriately busy to staff who wish to create a lively atmosphere, but may simply lead to confusion for learners with any degree of visual impairment. This is not to say that sensory stimulation is a bad thing. There will be many occasions when the introduction of carefully selected sights, sounds, textures and smells will be a crucial factor in the learning process. But these sensory events need to be used with thought, to a specific purpose, if they are to be educative rather than indiscriminate in their effect.

In this way, staff working in very ordinary environments can enhance their sensory potential. The use of simple techniques (thick carpet, wall hangings, cloth suspended as a false ceiling, padded screens as sound baffles) to reduce reverberation in certain areas of a room can help learners with hearing impairments to focus on the sounds you do want them to hear. Although radio mike and loop systems, used with headphones or hearing aids, are available for learners with significant hearing losses, becoming aware of and eliminating unwanted background noise (humming fans, whirring heaters, clattering from the kitchen, loud chatter from other staff members, traffic noise) can help these learners, and others who simply experience difficulties in attending, to focus on intentional sound. The volume, tone and timbre of 'live' intentional sound (including speech) can be controlled, enhanced and amplified electronically to great effect. Further, it is worth spending some money on good quality sound reproduction equipment (to play music or sound effects or to record and play back speech and vocalisation) with adequate amplification for the size of room. Visitors to teaching spaces and sensory environments may often be surprised to see expensive light wheels, fibre optics, bubble tubes and projectors being supported by sound from an inadequate and distorting cassette tape recorder. It may not be possible, or, indeed, necessary, to aim for professional sound quality but is is useful to take informed advice on the purchase of equipment designed for the domestic market and to take appropriate care of tapes, microphones and discs in order to preserve their clarity.

Again, it is not necessary to remain satisfied with standard institutional strip lighting nor to devote huge proportions of available funding to sophisticated light sources in order to create an environment that is visually stimulating and useful. Lighting for various purposes is easily available on the domestic market, and carefully chosen and situated background lighting, flood lighting and directional spot lighting can enhance a teaching space greatly. Reasonably priced items of equipment offering particular lighting effects can also be purchased individually or in collections from commercial catalogues and set up as permanent fixtures or be taken from room to room to provide particular forms of enhancement. Light, or its absence, can be used to mark out different spaces within a room or to emphasise certain areas, objects or activities. Coloured bulbs can be installed in wall or ceiling lights, and torches, slide projectors and overhead projectors can all be used, in conjunction with blinds, curtains or tented areas, to generate interesting visual effects in an ordinary room. Overhead projectors are also very useful for throwing magnified silhouettes of objects on to screens and white-painted wall spaces. These sorts of strategies will be of particular benefit to learners with visual impairments, but they can also be used to help other learners to use their visual faculties most effectively.

In the same sort of way, the imaginative teacher will exploit scent and texture as a means of identifying people in the room (so that learners with dual sensory impairment can recognise the approach of the person who consistently wears patchouli oil or the proximity of she-who-wears-many-bangles) and as a way of marking different areas of the learning territory. Changes in the texture of the floor (from carpet to sisal matting to vinyl, for example) or tactile markers fixed at learner height around the walls (an acrylic strip leading into the shower and toilet area; carpet tiles marking the walls in the story corner; tactile tracks of different textures set into the walls of corridors to indicate routes around large buildings) can all reinforce, at little expense, the possibility of independent mobility for learners experiencing sensory impairments.

Finally, it is important to take account of temperature and humidity in teaching areas. Light and sound rooms often seem to be located in small confined spaces, with opaque materials covering the windows. Without adequate ventilation and air conditioning these spaces can become dangerously hot and stuffy. Although many learners with physical disabilities require warm ambient temperatures in order to compensate for their restricted mobility, they should not be expected to tolerate overheating or stale air. Indeed, these conditions may have adverse effects on health and should not be tolerated for any learner. It is also worth noting that many of the specific sensory effects described in this section may be unsuitable for use with certain pupils who, for example, may react strongly to flashing lights, loud sounds, unexpected touches, unusual smells or the use of certain massage oils. The use of sensory phenomena should always be carefully researched, taking account of specialist knowledge where this is appropriate, and particular learners should be carefully and individually assessed for their reactions to and tolerance of gross sensory input.

# Using resources and facilities in the community

Special schools may be equipped with spaces which have been created deliberately, or adapted specifically, to meet the needs of learners with profound and multiple learning difficulties. At college or in the phase of further and continuing education, staff may, in practice, do their work in less than ideal circumstances, for example in standard teaching spaces in demountable buildings and in unmodified seminar rooms. As we have seen, these rooms can, to some extent, be permanently adapted on a realistic budget to enable them to mimic the costly relevance of some specialist environments and meet the needs of learners with profound and multiple learning difficulties. Staff in schools and colleges have also found it useful to create temporary simulations of interesting environments, turning the hall into a funfair for the day or setting up a factory floor environment in the classroom for a week of 'work experience', for the benefit of those learners for whom certain site visits are extremely problematic. While some useful adaptations to teaching spaces are possible and desirable (see above) it may also be appropriate to seek out other learning environments in the community and to find ways of using these non-specialist contexts to best advantage.

This may not simply be a matter of necessity being the mother of invention. O'Brien's (1987) philosophy about learners' entitlements to lead, as far as possible, an ordinary life, gaining access to community resources, would mean that the library, the shops, the swimming pool, the pub and the park should be considered as appropriate environments in which practitioners who work with people with profound and multiple learning difficulties can continue to provide new experiences and to promote new learning. These environments will have the distinct advantage of providing age-appropriate contexts for learning for older students and adults with profound and multiple learning difficulties and they will also offer the added potential for community participation and social interaction. Practitioners will be faced with the challenge, however, of ensuring that these environments are safe, accessible and cognitively meaningful for students with profound and multiple learning difficulties. It may not be possible physically to adapt the pub in order to produce an improved sensory environment for a learner with visual and/or hearing impairments, but expertise in creating environments which are responsive and contingency-sensitive is transportable. Ware (1996) clearly articulates the notion that it is people, rather than rooms or items of equipment, who constitute the most important resource base. The intervention of skilled practitioners can transform an unpromising physical environment into an exciting and stimulating learning zone.

# Resources, aids and equipment

Pupils and students with profound and multiple learning difficulties tend increasingly to accumulate extensive sets of large and cumbersome items of equipment. This range of resources may include a variety of seating systems for a variety of purposes (travelling in a car or minibus, being mobile around buildings or for short journeys outside, sitting comfortably upright for work at a table); other equipment designed to achieve a range of therapeutic positions and outcomes (standing vertically, side-lying, walking with support, prone stretching, vibro-massage, extension and relaxation) as well as the hoists and aids essential for moving learners from one position into another. Even in the best equipped of schools, the storage of this ever increasing range of equipment is a problematic issue (Lacey 1991). For those working in the community or in inclusive settings, this problem may become a serious health and safety challenge. Stacking standing frames across doorways and lining corridors with wheelchairs may provide a convenient short-term solution to storage difficulties but these strategies will also create potentially life-threatening obstacles in the event of a fire or medical emergency.

There is no doubt, however, that the provision of furniture and equipment for people with profound and multiple learning difficulties is an expanding and improving area of endeavour. For many pupils and students with profound and multiple learning difficulties, this makes it even more important to match the appropriate item of equipment to the planned activity. Ouvry (1987) suggests that 'positioning is a major consideration in all situations' and emphasises that 'a frequent change of position is vital for physical well-being and comfort'. She suggests that the time taken up by such regular repositioning should be valued, in its own right, as part of the teaching and learning experience and made as interactive as possible for learners. To argue that such time provides access to the content of curriculum subjects can be tokenistic; to attempt to reduce such time by hurrying through positioning and transitional procedures is demeaning for learners and potentially dangerous. As SCAA (1996a) proposes, these processes 'should be recognised positively and incorporated into planning rather than being regarded as an interruption'. Learners themselves should be prepared for and involved in processes of transition, in order to take full advantage of all opportunities for communication and interaction (Byers 1994a). In this way, it is possible to minimise the sense of disruption and fragmentation that learners may experience through being re-positioned or moved from one activity to another and maximise the extent to which they can become self-determining participants.

Ouvry (1987) also stresses the need to match the heights of tables and work tops to the faces and hands of learners in chairs, lyers and standers. We might add that imaginative teachers will regard other items of equipment as non-fixed and place these in positions which are also accessible to learners. Sinks, hobs and cookers can all be fixed to operate at a variety of heights and there is no rule which requires computer monitors to be placed horizontally on standard trolleys. Information and communications technology can and should be adapted to the needs of users (Banes and Coles 1995) and, provided that heavy, electronically energised equipment is managed safely, there is no reason why learners should not access their switches, keyboards and display units from low chairs, from the floor or at a range of heights and angles. The ideal to work towards here is that of giving learners self-motivated access to the equipment and resources they will need within an activity, just as would be expected in the mainstream of education (Smith and Laslett 1993).

As well as considering the positioning of learners, it is, of course, also important to respond to other aspects of their physical comfort and well-being. Pupils and students who are hungry or thirsty; tired or suffering from the unpleasant side effects of drug regimes; unwell or in pain will not be well-motivated or effective learners. Pupils and students with profound and multiple learning difficulties may be unable to communicate their discomfort in conventional ways and experienced staff will remain on the alert for the subtlest signs of distress. It may not always be possible to remove the causes of such distress completely, but attempts at least to moderate them should be seen as part of the task of managing the learning environment. (See Hutchinson in this volume for further discussion of these issues.)

# Learner groupings

Whether they are in an essentially segregated special environment, experiencing part time integration, or working in a fully inclusive environment, people with profound and multiple learning difficulties will benefit from the experience of being grouped in a variety of ways. In the past, it was considered obvious that the smallest possible teaching group, and ultimately a one-to-one teaching situation, would be ideal. As practitioners have come to appreciate the social dimension of learning, this is no longer necessarily considered to be the case and educationalists tend to argue that learners need to experience a balanced range of groupings. There will still be some situations where a one-to-one session in a quiet and private room will be most appropriate – for example, it could be argued that clients have the right to expect that their privacy will be ensured along with their dignity within certain therapeutic relationships, such as that with their physiotherapist. At other times, interactions across a small group of learners, for example in a session focusing on communication skills, will be essential to the purpose and content of the lesson. On occasion, for example, when the achievements of certain individual learners are to be publicly acknowledged and celebrated, the widest possible gathering of peers and professionals together will be appropriate.

Where learners are threatened by the additional challenge of working in a group (UNESCO 1993), it may be possible to develop a sense of a hierarchy of preparatory experiences designed to build the sorts of skills which are required of learners in group situations. For example, learners who are extremely isolated and withdrawn from social contact may first learn simply to tolerate the distant presence and then the proximity of members of staff working near their personal space on separate tasks. It may then become possible for certain trusted members of staff to begin to involve such a learner in the beginnings of an interactive relationship (Nind and Hewett 1994; Hewett in this volume). These emerging interactions with members of staff can be seen as early forms of experience of working in groups. Subsequently, this level of trust and tolerance may be extended to encompass work with a member of staff while a peer sits nearby or, in a further development, working with a member of staff alongside a small group of peers engaged in another activity. Later still, the previously isolated learner may accept working in a pair with another learner under the constant direction of a volunteer supporter. This intensity of instruction may be faded until paired work or peer coaching from another learner under supervision is achieved.

Moving on from this experience, it may become possible to encourage inclusive groups of three or four peers, with staff support and guidance, to engage in carefully constructed activities (Rose 1991). It may never be possible for a learner who is threatened by the social dimensions of group activity to learn to function as a fully contributing member of a self-managing, collaborative, problem solving group. This is not an excuse, however, for denying pupils and students the entitlement to a range of experiences which will include opportunities to participate in small or large group activities which are quiet and passive, active and boisterous, focused and business-like, light-hearted and enjoyable. Learning to function in a variety of social situations will help to promote learners' personal and social development (Byers and Rose 1996) and to achieve increased levels of participation in their lives beyond education.

# Conclusion

This chapter set out to support practitioners who work with pupils and students with profound and multiple learning difficulties in:

- creating the conditions in which learning is likely to flourish;
- facilitating and supporting the learning process;
- managing transitions from activity to activity;
- maintaining learning;

and in promoting the five major service accomplishments: community presence, choice, competence, respect and participation (identified by O'Brien 1987). The role of pupils and students themselves as partners in the teaching and learning process has been emphasised throughout a chapter in which the interactive nature of learner groupings has been briefly discussed; the importance of making resources and equipment accessible and available to self-determining learners has been proposed; and the significance of taking account of learner responses in creating and adapting environments has been highlighted. The theme running through all of these considerations, however, is the importance of the dialogue between teacher and learner (Byers 1996). If the learning environment, in all its complexity, is to provide a context for progress, achievement and development which is at once focused, purposeful, stimulating and challenging, yet relaxed, secure and, as often as possible, positively enjoyable, then the views and responses of learners must be constantly taken into account. Opening up forms of communication which enable pupils and students to contribute to the processes of monitoring, evaluation and review will make the task of managing the learning environment at once more meaningful and more effective.

# Chapter 13

# Technology for Living and Learning

*Jennifer Taylor*

## Introduction

As we become aware of the possibilities of new technology, more computers are being bought by schools and services for use by people with profound disabilities. Advances are coming from the dissemination of good practice, inventive use of new equipment, and informed software development, rather than from research findings. Information and innovations, until recently, have been shared amongst networks of enthusiasts in the field. The published material that is now becoming available is mostly concerned with the contribution that technology can make to educational programmes, and the ways in which it can be used to enhance and develop communication; see, for example, *Learning Through Interaction* by Bozic and Murdoch (1995). In this chapter the potential for using technology in a wider context with adults as well as children will be explored.

There will also be a brief review of some relevant literature and a look at some of the areas in which people described as having profound disabilities might benefit from technology, with some specific illustrations. This will be followed by discussion of the implications for families and services, and the factors to consider when looking to provide new equipment for an individual or group of people.

This chapter will focus on the use of computers and associated equipment controlled by switches. All the children and adults referred to in this chapter have been described as having profound and multiple learning difficulties and have been subject to education and services thought to be appropriate for people described in this way.

## Technology

Research into the use of technology in the past twenty five years has shown that there are many ways in which it can enhance opportunities for learning and interaction.

### Constructive activities

One of the challenges for staff and carers is to find constructive, independent activities which engage and motivate people. Kiernan (1974) considered this in relation to children's play, having found that children with profound disabilities were less likely to engage with regular toys than their non-disabled peers. He suggested two possible explanations for this: the first, that they are not able to acquire the necessary skills through imitation, and consequently require a structured behavioural approach in learning these skills; and the second, that reinforcers that maintain play in other children might not be effective for children with profound learning difficulties.

These two hypotheses were investigated by Murphy *et al.* (1986) in two successive studies carried out in 1983. In the first study half the children had behavioural programmes in which they were taught to play with normal toys. The 'play' went up during the teaching stage, but following this phase, there was no difference between the children who had instruction and those who had none.

The second study used toys that could give some optional extra form of sensory reinforcement — a panda that played music when its tummy was pressed, a car that had a seat that would vibrate when it was touched, and a wooden train with a flashing light when it was pushed or pulled. The children were observed playing with these toys both with and without the extra reinforcers. They found that when the reinforcers were used, not only did the children make contact with the toys more often and showed 'active manipulation' but they also showed a reduction in behaviour such as rocking and finger sucking.

An early piece of sensory equipment based on this principle is the Pethna System developed by Woods and Parry (1981). This is an automated system which uses these extra reinforcers and enables a variety of sensory reinforcers to be linked with different tasks. The student input or in-box can be any form of switch from a simple touch pad to a complex task such as a jigsaw which completes a circuit when the last piece is put in. This is connected to an 'out-box' which can be any combination of a vibrating cushion, a light show, any recorded sound, a puff of air.

## Demonstrating intentionality

Glenn and Cunningham (1984a; 1984b), Glenn *et al.* (1996) and Glenn (1987) carried out several studies using automated equipment with babies and children with profound disabilities. They found that the children were clearly demonstrating discrimination and preference. In a discussion of this work they stress the importance of active learning through physical interaction with the environment. Children without physical disabilities learn that consistent actions on objects around them produce consistent results (contingency learning). A child with physical disabilities may have far fewer opportunities to interact with and explore the environment in consistent ways. This may result in additional cognitive difficulties as well as a lack of motivation. Research carried out over the last twenty five years has demonstrated that new-born babies are far more competent in their interactions with the environment than was previously believed. Glenn hopes that automated equipment will help profoundly disabled people demonstrate similar abilities, and will certainly help with their difficulties in producing consistent responses.

## Establishing switching

Although it is often difficult to find activities for people with profound and multiple difficulties, switching is usually easy to establish, given a range of equipment and some experience on the part of the practitioner. In an unpublished study by Taylor (1990), a BBC computer, touchscreen, range of switches and software were taken into a class for nine non-ambulant, non-verbal, secondary-aged students. These were the most severely disabled teenagers in the borough, three others were in residential facilities. The students had had no access to computers for at least three years.

A reward survey was conducted with the whole group using computer sound and graphics, an emergency siren and flashing light, a battery operated fan and a vibrating cushion. For each student some time was spent finding the movement — either voluntary or involuntary — and switch combination which he or she would find easiest to control. Where an involuntary or chance movement activated the switch, students often shaped the response themselves, beginning to pause and move in an increasingly deliberate manner. Where a voluntary action was required the student was physically prompted, with the prompts being faded as fast as possible. The switches chosen were the simplest and most robust that were available. This included a simple lever switch, a wobble switch, micromike and a touchscreen. By the end of the morning everyone had shown a marked increase in switch pressing except one student who had just had a severe fit. Most of the students showed increased alertness, vocalisation and engagement. Staff, who confessed themselves initially sceptical, were surprised and delighted by the results.

## Enhancing interactions

Hogg and Seba describe the work of Lovett with a group of profoundly disabled children who lived in a large institution. He made a battery powered car which was worked with an ultrasonic switch. The children had a wonderful time in the car showing 'contingent responding and an increase in smiling and vocalising'. But probably the most important outcome was the effect on the interaction between them and their carers. Staff gained a new awareness of each child as an individual, and re-evaluated their estimation of his or her abilities.

The study of Glenn *et al.* (1996) of children with multiple disabilities in a multi-sensory environment also demonstrated that these children had developed clear individual preferences and showed enjoyment. As in Lovett's study, their parents expressed interest at their own child's preferences and gained new insights into their child's abilities.

# Communication

Most people have seen Stephen Hawking on television and are aware that computers can give people a voice. Many parents and carers have hoped that a computer or an electronic aid would provide the solution for a person who does not use conventional means of communication. However, 'Communicating' in a conventional word-based sense via a computer is much more difficult than talking or gesturing. You have to know how to do it as well as what you want to say. In addition to this, the skills and time needed to converse in this way by all the people involved tend to mitigate against its use by all but the most able users.

'Low-tech' methods such as photo books and symbols are often more effective for people with no speech. Computer software and new ways of producing instant photographs can help as it is now quick and easy to give people their own sets of pictures or symbols to use in a range of contexts.

Computers also give opportunities for communicating in other ways. Nicola is a young woman who spends her days in the special care unit of her local day centre. She spends most of her time watching what other people are doing and very little actively participating. She does not appear to have much use of her hands. Since the rest of her large family moved on to their own homes it has been painfully clear how limited her activities are. A friend has made her a 'talking photo album' using a still video camera and ordinary office software. Pictures have been taken of her home, family and special things that she keeps in her room. These have been put together on the computer with spoken captions. The 'pages' can be turned by pressing the space bar on the family computer. As in the studies cited above, Nicola astonished her mother by learning to find and press the space bar after being prompted a couple of times. She also showed that she was able to click the mouse button, but did not find this so comfortable. After some rapid presses of the space bar, she settled to looking at the pictures and was clearly more interested in those of people and the dog, Henry. Again, it was fascinating to see what interested her the most.

During this first session a number of visitors came in and Nicola continued to operate the computer. When her father came in, she looked at him and then at the computer several times and the rate of 'page turning' shot up — a 'look at this' signal. Someone else entered the room and her hands went into her lap — no amount of encouragement or prompting could get her to continue until that person had left. In a single session Nicola had found something that interested her, and that she could do independently. She had also shown that she wanted to share her interest with some people and had a fairly sophisticated method of choosing who to communicate with.

Now for a cautionary tale (with a good ending) which shows how important it is to think carefully about introducing technology and what the implications might be both for staff and clients. Chris was fifteen when he was resettled to a bungalow in the community from a long-stay hospital. Although he was very stiff and curled up he spent much of the time visually scanning his surroundings — probably due to slight deafness. He had reliable 'yes' and 'no' expressions in response to 'do you want...?' questions and his gorgeous smile ensured that he had plenty of positive social interaction but it was felt that he was not really motivated to communicate.

Staff started by taping a green 'yes' and red 'no' onto his tray. After demonstrating over a fortnight that he could use these he stopped and went back to facial expressions. People were simply making communicating more difficult for him and putting an unnatural barrier in the way. There was an uncomfortable period while Chris demonstrated that he could hold out longer than the adults around him before the system was abandoned.

The next suggestion was to have a switch attached to a buzzer so that he could call for attention in class. This only lasted a couple of days before it was taken away. He used it all the time and the teacher said she got no peace. When she started to ignore it, she said that he did it to make the rest of the class laugh. Chris was certainly using the equipment to communicate, but in ways that had not been foreseen.

The next attempt was made by a young and enthusiastic nursing assistant who devised a game for Chris on a computer that they had been given at home. She worked on the principle that Chris was getting all his basic needs met but what he wanted to do was to control people around him. The program displayed a grid with four symbols. These were highlighted in turn. When the switch was pressed the highlighted symbol was displayed below the grid. The symbols chosen were those representing *dance*, *tickle, sing* and *sleep*. This became a favourite game played by as many people as possible with Chris directing the pantomime from the computer. He was now well on his way to using a switch to access the computer and using symbols to communicate.

# Facilitated communication

Facilitated communication is one of the more controversial techniques that non-verbal people are using and has many supporters as well as critics, but it is certainly being used by an increasing number of therapists and parents in this country as well as in other parts of the world.

Facilitated communication is a technique used to help some persons with limited or no speech to communicate by typing or pointing. A facilitator provides both physical and emotional support. The physical support functions as an accommodation for neuromotor problems that may interfere with independent pointing which, over time, is usually faded. Some users eventually communicate without any physical contact with their facilitator (University of Maine, U.A.P. 1995).

Although many people use simple alphabets written on paper, others have found a computer keyboard and the resultant hard copy useful.

Darren is a ten year old who has challenged all the people that have come into contact with him. He spends much of his time screaming and injures himself, his clothes and his environment. He started to use facilitated communication on his home computer with his mother and now uses it at school too. For some time it seemed to be a fairly useful 'trick' which interested Darren but did little to affect the rest of his life. The breakthrough came one Saturday when he threw a major tantrum in the local shopping centre. On arrival back home his mother took him to the computer and asked him what the matter was — he typed 'teddies, teddies, teddies...' and she remembered that she had promised him a comic about teddies. They went straight back out and bought it. Darren has begun to realise that he can communicate in quieter and more subtle ways and his mother feels that with persistence they will be able to establish effective communication.

# Creating personalised resources

New technology has made the business of producing photographs much cheaper and easier. The local supermarket will often deliver conventional glossy prints within a couple of hours, but video technology makes this even cheaper and quicker. Excellent work has been done to make personal history books for people. The books can be used to introduce them to new staff or friends and to ensure that staff and carers in different parts of their lives know about favourite foods and can talk about significant people and events. By using still or regular video photography, pictures can be instantly seen on a television screen. People can see what was done last week, this morning or a couple of seconds ago and this can be a particularly useful focus for discussion. Using newer computers, pictures can be quickly transferred and printed out to take to school or centre, or to bring home in the evening showing what has been done during the day.

In similar ways, sounds can be captured on tape or on computer. Many people show interest and some recognition of their voices when they are played back, and want to hear them again.

# Demonstrating hidden potential

Detheridge (1990) tells a story of small Andrew who learned to press a big switch to say 'Give me a kiss'. Over time he learned to lift his face after pressing the switch waiting for the kiss. One day he pressed the switch twice by accident and his teacher was astonished to find him with his cheek raised for the second kiss. Andrew, a pupil with very high support needs, was showing that he had a concept of 'two' and even one-to-one correspondence! As in the earlier story of Nicola, technology was allowing Andrew to demonstrate hitherto unsuspected abilities.

# Control

There is now a huge range of ordinary electrical equipment, from remote controlled cars to infra-red movement detectors, as well as purpose built specialised devices that can give people more control over their environment. Shamina has enjoyed using battery operated toys at school since she was small; her favourite used to be a dog that played a drum when she pressed a switch. When she was older, the toys were replaced by a fan and tape recorder. Now that she is about to move into her own home with two other young people the staff are thinking about ways in which she can control some of the electrical equipment in her own room. They have borrowed a system which will allow Shamina to turn the lights off and on. This could be extended to drawing the curtains, switching on the TV and so on. They have also discovered that she enjoys playing with the video controls which have big buttons — something that was forbidden in her parents' house as it annoyed the others. They are also trying out a range of regular radio, TV and video equipment together with remote control devices that she might learn to use.

# Shared focus and inclusion

One of the most important things in working with people with high support needs is to discover activities in which they can participate alongside everyone else, and to find areas of interest and topics for discussion which extend beyond their immediate environment.

Many art programs are relatively simple to use and only require the addition of a touchscreen for many people to be able to make good use of them. This means that a person can paint by dragging a finger across the screen rather than using a mouse. John learned to use an art program at his day centre. He can 'paint' pictures by using a special touchscreen, which fits over the monitor. During the past year he has learned to change colours and has recently copied a member of staff in an attempt to load the program himself. He sits quietly watching other centre-users for long periods and if the computer is turned off will pull a member of staff to it, showing that he wants it turned on. His parents, seeing the satisfaction that he gained from this activity, decided to buy a computer themselves. This involved endless consultations with John's younger brother as well as the people next door and, following the purchase, numerous visits to John's brother's house as well as through the fence to the neighbours. John has been a silent but central part in this process and is now a welcome visitor when he goes to watch the children next door playing computer games. His brother is also happier to have him over now that he knows that they have interests in common.

Christian is a floppy child who needs constant reminders to hold up his head. He too watches what other people do on a computer and can use a switch to build pictures on a screen but seems to quickly tire of these 'appropriate' activities. He seems to come to life when he sees ordinary computer games — the louder and more violent the better. He has been fostered by a family with a good computer and lots of games. His new foster brother is happy to spend (some) time with him and set the games up so that Christian can hit the space bar to 'fire' while he controls the movement. Christian's motivation, in his new home situation, is tremendous. He is making attempts to move independently and is becoming increasingly vocal.

The multimedia explosion has great potential, too. There are thousands of new CD ROMs, similar to regular music CDs but containing computer pictures and movies as well as sounds. These take the form of games, illustrated novels, information about cookery, art galleries, rock bands, health education, space and so on. Although many of the discs are information sources or expanded books the developers of these discs have tended to come from a film, TV or graphic background. There is often spoken dialogue and instructions to support the text and there are helpful graphics too. There is a wealth of material here aimed directly at adults but not dependent upon reading ability and made deliberately attractive and accessible. Even random exploration of some of these discs with a touch screen leads to exciting journeys through sound and pictures. For some people it may show the sorts of colours, sounds and changes that they enjoy, others with unfathomed abilities may be broadening their horizons in new ways.

## Making an individual contribution

No one knows how much Alison hears, she moves very little by herself but she certainly looks around at things. She goes to her local primary school for two days a week. Her class was doing a cross-curricular project on 'Homes' and were bringing in information about their own houses. The school was happy to lend the family their still video camera for a weekend. Her brother and sister joined in the project and moved Alison around the house following her line of gaze. Anything that seemed to be of particular interest to Alison was photographed. They looked at the pictures straight away on the television at home and Alison was more than usually animated, laughing and looking backwards and forwards from the television to the children. The camera, with the pictures, was taken back to school and when all the others were talking about their homes, she showed her pictures too. The photographs were then turned into pictures which could be used on the school computer by some of the older pupils in the school. These were put together to make Alison's own book about 'My Home'.

## Service provision

Having decided that computers are 'good for' people with disabilities, some people have been hugely tempted to see them as teaching machines or assessment tools. Many of the activities that people are subjected to in day centres or at college are early learning tasks such as shape and colour matching and picture building. Even where the teddies and clowns have been removed, the overwhelming impression is that of infant school provision. Messages are sent to staff, the public, to family members and to clients themselves by the resources that they are given and people may be put at risk by further devaluing them in a more than ever public context. There is a tremendous challenge to find creative ways by which people can access regular equipment and to develop the use of good, commonly available resources.

It is important that the new technology is used in a way which fits within the service's overall aims. This might be community participation, improving communication, individual skills development — or perhaps, in a domestic context, freedom and control over one's own space and time. Time spent discussing these issues and defining roles in relation to developments, rather than simply giving one person new responsibilities, is particularly useful at this stage. There is also a need to meet to share experiences, as family, staff and clients develop new skills, and to incorporate developments as interest and enthusiasm grows. Creativity and commitment to the regular use of technology is more important than specialist skills, although each member of staff will make their own particular contribution.

An increasing number of people in adult services are using computers in creative ways (although it is still not very common) and more and more families do have their own equipment. Friends in the community that are experienced and interested home or work computer users are particularly useful sources of support, as well as students, volunteers and family members. Involving a variety of people has added benefits of new connections and friendships too, but within a coherent context of shared interests.

Getting good equipment is crucial. Speed of access and the quality of sound and pictures are particularly important for people with more severe difficulties. Any budget should incorporate the purchase of enough equipment and software to ensure that the computer can be used in flexible ways and this may need to include appropriate furniture or trolleys. Cast-off equipment is unlikely to have the power or resources that you need and is likely to create more problems than it solves.

Learning to use a computer is like learning to drive. There are some basic things to learn, but the most important thing is time to fiddle and practise and to have someone who can give on the spot or telephone support at the time of need. In a pilot project, run by the National Council for Educational Technology, eight colleges running courses for students with special needs were given multimedia computers with still video facilities. The most successful users were those who had found an arbitrary niche for the computer from the outset – such as making more attractive notices and typing memos. These people turned the machine on regularly and used it throughout the day. In this way they became confident and positive about the machinery and started to broaden their activities. Staff have got to feel interested and enthusiastic if they are to become successful facilitators for other people. The initial skills needed are those that you would expect of a family going out to buy a computer to help them write letters to the bank manager and play the latest games.

College courses can sometimes be useful, but most tend to focus rather narrowly on office software rather than home and leisure or specialised applications, and can create frustration and demoralisation. However, there may be courses, such as desk top publishing, which teach the use of equipment such as scanners and cameras and picture manipulation. Short courses run by agencies specialising in disability as well as computer exhibitions raise awareness of the possibilities and help to build constructive networks, but only indirectly increase participants' computer skills.

# Technology for individuals

As has been illustrated above there are many ways in which technology can be used to the benefit of individuals in both direct and indirect ways. Indirect ways would include the design and making of materials — for example symbol charts for communication or photographs to facilitate the sharing of information.

There are many activities that can be done on an occasional basis such as:

- using CD ROMs with touchscreens — interactive video at your fingertips!
- as an interesting and age-appropriate topic to communicate about, with opportunities for shared attention, saying 'no' and expressing surprise and enjoyment;
- switch or space bar operated picture albums with or without sound;
- switch operated battery equipment for fun and independence;
- participation in computer games with other people;
- touchscreen art and music programs;
- using the computer as a reward or time out.

Some activities, however, need a greater and regular commitment of time and access, and if appropriately developed may eventually lead to the need for a personal system. These include:

- development of switching skills;
- aided communication;
- environmental control.

After an initial period of settling down with the equipment there are a number of factors to consider in relation to any particular person.

- Aims for the activity should be clear and shared, so that all interested parties have ownership of the ideas. Ideally it should become part of a personal plan. It is not unusual for people to be bombarded with instructions once they have demonstrated an interest or competence; 'keep your head up, look at this, come on, what a clever fellow, press here, do it like this, don't let your other hand flop like that, try this way now, good boy....' This can quickly deter early users. Clear, shared aims should ensure that the right sort of help is given by everybody.
- Long term goals should be discussed. It is important to ensure that there is a possibility of progression, especially when talking about building individual skills. This may mean a commitment in terms of equipment, advocacy, staff continuity and time, as well as the exploration of new resources.
- Optimal seating positions can be a source of disagreement and debate. There may have to be some compromise to allow someone to see the monitor as well as reaching a switch or a touchscreen. This needs the cooperation of physio and occupational therapists at the start of any programme. Again shared aims and constructive discussion can minimise problems of this sort.
- The most appropriate form of access needs to be investigated. Initially, try the space bar if a person can be positioned so that their hand rests on the keyboard; a touch screen for people who can reach out and touch what they are looking at; and a lever switch for almost everyone with some movement in an elbow, foot, head or knee, before looking for more sophisticated devices. Again the expertise of therapists is vital in terms of positioning for maximum mobility and building of useful new skills.
- Find out what the person enjoys in terms of sound, music, colour, photos, but make sure that he or she experiences a range of resources to help develop informed preferences.
- Create social and communicative opportunities. Although independence, and the ability to entertain oneself, is an important goal it sometimes becomes too easy to leave someone alone with a computer for long periods. Computers can be a good

focus in a group setting, a speech therapy group for example, or simply a chance for two friends to sit together and share the experience. It might be possible to involve someone if a volunteer or staff member is working on the computer.

- Share information with people outside the service (or maybe vice versa). Families and carers need to see the possibilities of what their son or daughter is doing – as in John's story, it might help build relationships.

The new computers give a wealth of opportunities for adult activities. They can help to capture events and share them with other people; there are many information sources which do not depend on reading; they can help people develop new skills; many people can find new self-directed independent activities but most important they provide a valued and appropriate context in which people with high support needs of all ages can work and relax.

# Glossary

Hardware — computer equipment.

Software — the programs that are used on a computer.

Touchscreen — a frame or membrane which fits over the screen, detecting the point at which the screen is touched.

Lever switch — a small, oblong, robust switch which gives a satifying click when pressed. Often mounted with velcro on a wheelchair tray, arm or head rest.

Wobble switch — a flexible switch that is activated when it is knocked, can be used by people with small but well controlled movements, such as finger curling, or those with large powerful sweeps. Generally difficult to use with the same degree of purposefulness as a lever switch.

Micromike — a switch made out of a microphone which is activated when the user makes a noise. Detects volume but not particular speech sounds so, when effective,may encourage shouting.

Newer computers — PCs, Apple Macintosh, Amiga and others capable of reproducing good quality sound and graphics, probably with CD ROM drives.

Infra-red movement detectors — the sort of technology used in burglar alarms, activated by breaking or creating invisible beams of infra-red light.

Symbol charts — a chart made up of symbols (for example Rebus, Picture Communication Symbols, Bliss) that a person can finger or eye point to for the purposes of communication.

CD ROMs — small discs similar to audio compact discs on which computer information and programs are stored.

Aided communication — communication helped by equipment, photographs, symbols or another person.

New technology — computers, fax, video, remote control devices and so on.

# Part Four:

# Community

# Chapter 14

# Supporting Families

*Loretto Lambe*

## Caring at home

Families caring for someone with profound and multiple learning disabilities (PMLD) are probably less concerned over issues of definitions and categories than many professionals. For them the technical problems of assessment rightly raised by Fryers (1984) have less meaning than the challenges they face on a day-to-day basis. These typically involve a total commitment to the wellbeing of their relative. Significantly, the American Association on Mental Retardation (AAMR), which for many years has grappled with issues of the definition of 'mental retardation', has suggested an approach to classification which converges with family carers' perceptions of their role. The AAMR now refers to the need for 'pervasive support' for people with what we are, here, referring to as 'profound and multiple learning disabilities' (see the Introduction for a fuller discussion). This approach emphasises not only the extent of needs, but also the input that will be required for the person with PMLD to develop to full potential. On the one hand, this will entail professional work by educators and day service staff, on the other, what is offered by family carers. In helping families to sustain such support, it is essential that we address the issue of how their needs can best to be met. A failure to do so may at worst lead to a breakdown in family support and at best result in a significantly poorer quality of life for the whole family.

## Nature of care tasks

The number and range of daily care activities that have to be undertaken by families is daunting. These include basic tasks such as assistance at mealtimes, toileting, bathing, dressing, undressing, and undertaking therapeutic exercises. For many, more specialised interventions — tube-feeding, administration of medication, including rectal diazepam — are daily necessities. It must be borne in mind that all these are undertaken in conjunction with the equally important requirement to meet both the social and emotional needs of the person with profound and multiple disabilities.

Surveys of family carers by Hogg and Lambe (1988) and Lambe and Hogg (1995a) considered the self-help abilities of the daughters and sons of respondents and found that the majority of both children and adults were entirely dependent upon someone else to carry out the main basic care tasks, a critical example of 'pervasive care'. Although there was a range of abilities reported, few if any could independently eat, drink, wash, or dress. Where the level of skills was higher, no one person was independent in more than two or three areas. Adults were generally in advance of children, though the patterns of abilities reported in both groups were similar in that the distribution of items was always heavily skewed to total or a very high levels of support.

While family carers may experience great stress in meeting these needs in the home, this may be increased by the failure of service providers themselves to give sufficient support to meeting those same needs. Some services are denied to families if the person is either tube-fed or requires rectal diazepam to control seizures unless there is a medically qualified person on duty to undertake these tasks. Such denial may involve refusal to admit to a respite service, or being left behind in a day centre when less vulnerable peers access the community. It is difficult for parents to accept these decisions bearing in mind their own lack of training for what are in fact easily learnt procedures, and which they themselves carry out daily. The answer is not to insist that there must always be a qualified nurse on duty, which may not be feasible, but that there should be a member of staff properly trained in whatever care procedures are required. What is needed is a flexible approach to how services are delivered and by whom. Nursery nurses in schools and social care officers in day, residential and respite services can be and have been trained in these procedures. Their respective employers and trades unions should take this on board as a matter of urgency. Once trained, there should be some recognition of this in their salary structure.

Where these difficulties persist in the UK there is a need for campaigning to bring about change in this area of care, and examples may be given of a group of parents working in the PAMIS Special Interest Group in Glasgow who are campaigning with the support of the Epilepsy Association of Scotland (EAS) to bring about change with respect to the administration of rectal diazepam. Similarly, the voluntary epilepsy organisation, Enlighten, based in Edinburgh, is working with local health, social work and education departments, to have at least one person in each special school, day centre, and respite care facility trained in this procedure. In due course a national policy with respect to both the administration of rectal diazepam and tube-feeding needs to be put in place.

It should be added that the consequent time demands on the family are considerable. Hogg and Lambe (1988) report families as spending an average of seven and a half hours per day in basic care tasks, leaving aside meeting the social and emotional needs of their relative. Against such a background, to refer to these parents as 'informal carers' is frankly insulting. Todd and Shearn (1995) in their study *Struggles with Time* concentrated specifically on this much-ignored issue.

> Without exception, all parents in the study reported that 'time' was a major preoccupation and that being a parent of an adult with learning difficulties continued to involve juggling temporal resources to the dictates of 'clock time'... They had to confront daily issues of how time was to be used, how it was to be divided and according to what rules (p.13).

When suggesting ways of helping and supporting parents, the time factor and the time commitment must be considered as priorities, otherwise the advice offered will not be effective.

## The needs of carers in their own right

Parents and other family carers need to recognise their own individual needs over and above their role as a carer. PAMIS (Profound and Multiple Impairment Service) workshops on stress management for family carers have emphasised this requirement, leading two participants to comment: 'In future I will think more about "me" (the person) and the "me" that does things', and: 'the session highlighted how you can "lose" yourself and think only in terms of "you" the carer (not the person)'.

The issue of gender here is crucial. Hogg and Lambe (1988) reported that 72 per cent of mothers were full-time carers, of these only 5 per cent were in full-time and 16 per cent in part-time employment. Todd and Shearn (1995) noted 'The tendency for the parental identity to disrupt any other line of activity for mothers in particular was acutely problematic and acted as a significant barrier that prevented them from seeking full-time employment' (p.19). The mothers in this study felt strongly that once a potential employer knew that they were a parent of a person with disabilities this immediately disqualified them from being considered as a serious candidate for work.

## Siblings and their brothers and sisters with PMLD

Several organisations have recognised that sisters and brothers also require support. Nevertheless, some parents report that as far as they are aware their own 'other' children do not adversely suffer from having a brother or sister with disabilities. Certainly in terms of their concept of themselves, a recent study suggested that there are no special difficulties in the psychological adjustment of adolescent siblings of children with profound learning disabilities (Auletta and DeRosa 1991). Contact-a-Family (CAF), however, identified a number of common issues that do concern siblings, including: limited time and attention from parents; worries about bringing friends home; restrictions on family activities; guilt – for being angry with the brother or sister with disabilities; embarrassment in public; worry, fear about the future. Examples of how parents have responded to these are given in CAF's Factsheet *Siblings and Special Needs* (1996) and in NCH's Action for Children leaflet, *Hello, Sister! Hello, Brother!* Tozer (1996) emphasises the need for parents to make time for all their children, to have time together as a family and also special time for the siblings, while Carpenter (1997b) writes about positive experiences from a family perspective, the siblings' observations here being particularly telling. *The Children Act* 1989 too, refers to meeting the needs of siblings of children with disabilities as part of the overall package of services for the child with disabilities. How this is interpreted and implemented at local level needs to be monitored. Siblings and parents find being able to explain exactly the nature and aetiology empowering, and factsheets from many of the specialist self-help groups on specific syndromes and conditions can be of assistance here. Terms such as 'profound disability', 'developmental disability', 'brain damage' are often much harder concepts with which to deal.

# Needs of caring families

Families of people with PMLD are not an homogeneous group. They, like every other family, have their own specific requirements, their dreams and expectations of life, as do their daughters and sons with disabilities. However, they do have a number of needs in common. These are expressed in Mittler (1995) in which the views of families from both the developed and developing world are represented. Some concerns are specific to the age of the offspring with disability and they change as the person grows older while others remain throughout life. There are general requirements and very specific requirements. The first group includes: the right for their daughter or son to be recognised as a citizen, a person first; access to a range of services appropriate to their daughter's or son's individual requirements; and rights to full education, health and social services alongside their peers without disabilities. The second group is very specific. This includes: information on a range of issues relevant to the well-being of the person with disabilities and the family as a unit; information on whatever equipment, new technology or therapy is available, that will enable their daughter or son to reach full potential; and practical help and advice on a variety of both instrumental and emotional support issues, which should be available as and when needed.

## Ethnic minorities and their special needs

Service providers and professionals working in the field of disability are increasingly aware of the special difficulties faced by people from ethnic minorities. Many will endeavour to ensure that services are sensitive to the beliefs and values of all service users. Nevertheless, much still remains to be done. Families from ethnic minorities with a child with disabilities report that they often feel isolated and stigmatised both within and outside their own cultural groups. Sham (1996), for example, stresses the need for professionals working with Chinese families to be aware of their belief that there is a 'cure' for all ailments, and their non-acceptance of the idea of permanent impairment. Ignorance of such views on the part of service providers, coupled with the inability of many people from ethnic communities to understand material written in English, can result in such families being unable to access services or even being aware of their very existence. Families from Indian, Pakistani and Bangladeshi communities suffer similar isolation. The answer is not simply to translate written information into the various languages, nor is it satisfactory merely to use an interpreter to translate verbatim the spoken word. Interpretation and translation must be undertaken by persons who not only speak the language, but most importantly, understand the subject of profound disability. Shah, in this volume, discusses these issues in greater detail.

## Instrumental support

Ask any family what services or type of support they require and high on the list will be flexible respite provision; a smooth transition from school to adult provision; reliable day services — pre-school, school or adult — depending on the age of their daughter or son; and access to a range of leisure services. This type of instrumental, practical support is crucial and must be in place if the family is to be enabled to continue caring for the person in the home. While some of this provision is a statutory right, the quality and range of such services varies enormously depending on where the family lives.

### Pre-school support

The issue of disclosure regarding the disability remains one of the most important experiences in the lives of all families with a child with disability. With specific reference to children born with multiple disabilities, Hogg and Lambe (1988) reported that 43 per cent of parents both of adults and children reported that disclosure was 'supportive and sympathetic'. In the case of parents who judged disclosure to be 'callous and unsympathetic' there was little difference between the parents of adults and those of children though an average of 15 years had elapsed. This unsatisfactory situation has been confirmed almost 10 years later in a recent survey (Mencap 1997).

Here it is noted that a positive approach to disclosure was fairly rare, with many families being given the news 'in a wholly unsympathetic, negative, or even dismissive manner' (p.8). In only 36 per cent of cases was the person who gave the diagnosis described as supportive, a figure even lower than that of Hogg and Lambe's survey. This is a disturbing finding given that the ability range of infants in the Mencap 1997 study was much greater than in the earlier survey.

For some families ongoing emotional support will be called for, ideally through some form of counselling. Of those for whom this would have been relevant, 43 per cent of children's parents received such support in contrast to parents of adults where the figure was only 17 per cent (Hogg and Lambe 1988). The picture was even bleaker in the Mencap 1997 study, which reported just 7 per cent of families receiving support. Crucial to the period after disclosure is information assisting the parent to come to terms with the nature of their child's condition and the development of services that are responsive to the child's and family's needs.

Early intervention programmes are seen by many families as a priority. Parents should be given as much information as possible on what is available so that they can make an informed choice as to what is best for their own child. Whatever model of intervention is decided upon, it should fit in with the lifestyles of the whole family and should not place any additional demands on the parents, who may already be coping with the stress of coming to terms with their child's disabilities.

Examples of good pre-school family support do exist even though they may be very patchy. Of particular importance is the need for consistent input without having to deal with a procession of professionals, all well meaning in their own right. To this end, Limbrick (1993), has developed a model of family support, '100 Hours', in which a specially trained key worker brings together information from a wide range of disciplines to ensure that a focused programme is developed by a single worker in the family home. This service has proved of enormous help to families (White 1994).

## Respite care

Although the need for regular respite care is recognised by service providers and should be identified at the assessment stage and written into care plans it is still often an 'unmet need'. Respite provision throughout the UK is very varied and although there are many models of excellence, the lack of appropriate and adequate respite provision in a number of areas adds to families' stress. Families want regular, flexible respite services, for both children and adults, delivered in small community settings or their own home. The voluntary sector has been campaigning for some time to ensure that families receive such services as a statutory right. Mencap supported a *Short-term Breaks (Respite Care) Bill* prior to the last election which regrettably did not reach the statute books. Campaigning on this issue will continue and everyone concerned with people with PMLD and their families should become part of this lobby.

## Accessing information

Carers require a variety of different types of information. On the one hand the vast array of pamphlets dealing with practical issues can be of help, if written in accessible form, though Sturmey's (1993) analysis of leaflets for parents and care staff indicated how uninteresting and inaccessible such material often is. However, information tailored to the individual will always be required, possibly offered on a face-to-face basis by a well-informed individual. Note, too, should be taken of recent advances in information provision. Williams (1997) poses the question *Internet: a useful communication tool for parents?* and clearly demonstrates how useful he, as a parent, finds this resource. Such information can, of course, assist with personal problems, the solution of which may be helped by increased knowledge.

## Emotional support

Families caring for a person with profound disabilities require a great deal of emotional support. This is very often provided by the immediate family circle, although many families report that their 'in-laws' often do not understand or accept the disability. Meeting with other families in similar circumstances, through parent organisations and special interest groups, is highly rated by families. Here their need for emotional support and total understanding of their concerns are met. The local branches of the large voluntary organisations such as Mencap, ENABLE, Scope, Capability, RNIB, Sense, etc. run a range of services at local level and also provide information for families. As they are all concerned with learning disability or cerebral palsy in general, families caring for a person with profound and multiple learning disabilities often feel that their specific needs are not met by such groups. However, some of these organisations have either a project or section devoted to the needs of people with profound and multiple disabilities to which I will return.

Other voluntary organisations are more focused on specific conditions and syndromes that give rise to PMLD, such as Ann Worthington's In Touch Trust and the voluntary agency Contact-a-Family. Both these organisations are considerable sources of support and help for families. In Touch Trust publishes a quarterly newsletter that is an invaluable source for both parents and professionals as well as two publications; *Glossary of Syndromes Associated with Learning Difficulty* and *Useful Addresses for Special Needs* (Worthington 1993 and 1996). Contact-a-Family's publication, *CAF Directory* (CAF 1991) is also a very useful publication. I am not suggesting that parents should purchase this directory, although the information contained in it is highly relevant to families with a child with a specific condition or rare syndrome. Parents should be able to access the directory through local voluntary agencies, libraries, schools, day services. All such establishments and agencies providing services for people with learning disabilities, as well as General Practitioners' surgeries, should have copies of these publications both as a resource for parents and for their own staff. Both publications are updated regularly.

## Getting older and the key transitions

There are many key transition times in the lives of families caring for a person with profound and multiple disabilities when they require very specific help. The move from child to adult services is often traumatic. Both educational and medical services during childhood years, although not without their many problems, are viewed as infinitely better than adult provision. Adult services are not mandatory, and there is no absolute right to a five-day-a-week adult day service. The uncertainty of what lies ahead puts considerable stress on the carers, while the Future Needs Assessment prior to school leaving and the Community Care Assessment conducted by an appointed care manager involve very complex processes. Many people with disabilities and/or their carers require help and support to ensure that needs are met.

There is a role here for the voluntary sector to intervene and offer independent advice to families. Books such as McKay and Patrick's (1995) *The Care Maze* explain very clearly how community care law works in Scotland, and is relevant to family carers and professionals alike. This book, written for the Scottish context, guides the reader, defining the legal framework, looking at good practice and suggesting solutions where problems have arisen. Similar publications are needed for the rest of the UK; Ashton and Ward's (1992) *Mental Handicap and the Law* dealing only with legislation and learning disability up to 1992, and not covering the *Children Act*, the Carers Act and the new anti-discriminatory legislation.

## Day services

Day service provision for people with PMLD should offer a key input with respect to education, therapy and leisure. From the family perspective it offers two sources of crucial support. First, it can assist the individual's personal development, sometimes reducing the care needs in the home itself. Second, it offers the family a break from active care, and can make the difference between continued ability to care in the home and pressure to seek residential provision elsewhere (Lambe and Hogg 1995b).

## Future planning

Though their life expectancy remains much lower than for the general population, people with PMLD are living longer. Parents who were told that their daughter or son had only the most limited life expectation find themselves caring late into their lives. As family carers age, so the task of coping at home can become increasingly difficult. The idea of a transition by their relative with PMLD from living in the family home to a community group house or supported living arrangement, however, may be one they just cannot face. Even if the family is ready for such a break, no appropriate accommodation may be available locally. As both the person with disabilities and their carers age, they each require flexible services that adapt to their changing needs. Wider issues also need to be dealt with related to future financial and legal provision. The voluntary sector has responded in a variety of ways to this situation. MENCAP, PAMIS and ENABLE (the Scottish Society for the Mentally Handicapped) have all developed workshop programmes for carers to review their own needs and future against a background of expert information.

# Specialist initiatives

Statutory authorities will continue to provide or commission the principal services for both children and adults with PMLD. However, it is equally essential that specialist initiatives are developed by the voluntary sector in such a way that families themselves receive direct support to continue their caring role. In the following section some examples of model provision that have been developed in recent years are reviewed.

## Specific models of support

Mencap's Profound Intellectual and Multiple Disability (PIMD) Section, based in Manchester has developed the following workshop training packages for parents and carers: *Planning for the Future; Rights and Entitlements*; *Communication and Feeding*; and *Dental Care and Diet*. The packs are used by Mencap divisional staff to organise workshops locally. They are also available for purchase by other professionals or parent groups who may use them to run training initiatives for parents. The Mencap PIMD Section's National Officer works with Mencap personnel throughout the country on issues related to PMLD. Other Mencap services relevant to families caring for a person with profound disabilities are the Family Adviser Service and the National Information Service. These services support families and provide information on all aspects of learning disability. Family Advisers are being appointed to work with Mencap Local Societies and any families that require support or advice. Mencap services operate in England, Wales and Northern Ireland. In Scotland, ENABLE has, in collaboration with Mencap, also established a Family Adviser Service.

The Royal National Institution for the Blind (RNIB) has a service on multiple disability, the Information and Practice Service on Multiple Disability. This publishes a monthly newsletter, *Focus*, aimed at staff working with people with visual and learning disabilities. Although it is produced for staff, the information is equally beneficial to parents and carers. A series of useful and informative Factsheets on different aspects of learning disability and vision is also produced.

## Parents as partners model

The organisation PAMIS is concerned with people with profound and multiple disabilities, and their parents and carers. The principal aim of the organisation is 'to provide up-to-date information and training on care, education and social provision for people with PMLD and their families'. PAMIS runs a number of projects and initiatives in Scotland, many of which are in association with ENABLE. Parents are very much involved in the planning and development of the work. They choose the topics on which they want training, when this takes place and the way in which the training is delivered. For each subject covered — at present there are some fourteen topics in the programme — an extensive three-day workshop is held. The course tutors chosen are experts in the respective subjects and wherever possible are professionals working locally. Evaluation shows that both the general and specific aims of the programme have been met. Working together with other parents in similar situations has led to supportive networks being established. Professionals have equally benefited from working with families in this very close and structured way. Their appreciation of the needs of families and people with PMLD has increased and this has significantly improved working relationships. These relationships have continued and the parents and professionals are now actively working together in PAMIS Special Interest Groups (SIGs) to bring about effective change.

The issues tackled by PAMIS SIGs are wide ranging and include campaigning for improved design of supermarket trolleys for people with multiple disabilities, lobbying for appropriate changing facilities in public toilets, and appropriate provision in play and leisure facilities. More longterm goals being worked on are: the extension of the training of staff in specific procedures, such as administration of rectal diazepam and tube-feeding, to include respite and day service staff; intellectual access to the arts; and inclusion of families in the planning process for community care services. Considerable progress has been made in a relatively short time on these and other issues. For the families involved the fact that their direct action has brought about change is very empowering. The work of PAMIS, particularly the *Caring at Home* programme, is being implemented in Northern Ireland by Dr Chris Conliffe of the Institute of Counselling and Personal Development, Belfast.

## Future direction

Greater community presence, increased integration in educational and other settings, the disability rights and anti-discrimination movements, have all led to people with profound disabilities being seen as taking their rightful place in society. However, to return to the point made at the outset of this chapter; people with PMLD require high quality pervasive support from both the statutory and voluntary services to ensure such a presence becomes a reality. So too, do their parents and carers. Parents also require recognition by professionals that they are key people in the lives of their daughters and sons with PMLD. They really are the experts, and this should be acknowledged. Only then will we have true partnerships between parents and professionals.

Note: Addresses of all organisations referred to in this chapter are available from the author.

# Chapter 15

# Advocacy and Empowerment: What Does it Mean for Pupils and People with PMLD?

*Christina Tilstone and Celine Barry*

## Introduction

The first people with disabilities to engage in self-advocacy were those with good social and communication skills. In the late 1960s people with physical disabilities who were living in residential and group homes began to question the dependent model of care which they were receiving (Miller and Gwynne 1974); the lack of physical access to buildings (Walter 1971; Jay 1974); and the infringement of their rights (Oliver 1990, 1996).

In Britain in the late 1970s people with learning difficulties began to group together, encouraged by the pioneering work of the Campaign for Mentally Handicapped People (CMH), to talk about their experiences and to raise the issues for which they were later to crusade. Their *voices* joined those in other countries, where formal conferences were taking place at which participants debated their lack of choices and independence. Valuable and comprehensive accounts of the development of this innovative *People First* movement were given by Hersov (1996) and Whittaker (1996).

A small band of professionals joined those with learning difficulties in order to help them to become more effectively empowered (Shearer 1973; Williams and Shoultz 1982; MENCAP 1982, 1983; Cooper and Hersov 1986; Clare 1990; Whittaker *et al.* 1991; McConkey 1994). They were the *advocates* for people with learning difficulties and not only acted on their behalf but represented their interest and views. These campaigners have challenged the providers of the full range of services and charged them with the task of creating opportunities for people with learning disabilities to live acceptable lifestyles and to form normal and intimate relationships. Such opportunities include preparing them to become self advocates and to speak for themselves.

There are now over 500 self-advocacy groups world-wide, and in 1991 the international movement *Self Advocates Becoming Empowered* (SABE) was formed. Its mission statement emphasises that it will work to improve the quality of life of those with disabilities by:

- teaching individuals with developmental disabilities to speak out for their beliefs;
- enabling them to learn about their rights and corresponding responsibilities as citizens;
- helping them to learn how to make the choices and the decisions that affect their lives;

- providing them with the skills to obtain accessible transport;
- closing institutions;
- ending segregation through the use of sheltered workshops;
- promoting inclusive practices in schools;
- allowing them to make choices in friendships, relationships and the expression of sexuality.

The ability to meet such challenges, however, relies on an individual's ability to take control of his or her life, to set and to achieve individual goals, and to make selections (Ramcharan *et al.* 1997). People with PMLD can only rise to such challenges if self-advocacy is a meaningful goal and the prerequisite skills are clearly identified.

# The elements of self-advocacy

The SABE mission statement suggests that the following are prerequisites to self-advocacy:

- the effective use of some form of communication;
- the ability to access information;
- practice in choice and decision making;
- exposure to a range of relationships in order to gain experience in making choices;
- sessions in sex education.

In order that self-advocacy for people with PMLD becomes a meaningful goal, it is necessary to take each of the above elements and to identify the necessary pre-requisite skills. As other chapters of this book consider some of these elements (see Bradley, H. and Downs) we intend to concentrate on the remainder. The two examples of practice, which take place in different settings, illustrate approaches to self-advocacy through combinations of these factors.

It is inevitable that in learning to become autonomous, people with PMLD will have to rely on professionals, their parents and their peers to interpret their wishes and needs in the early stages. Not only is there a danger that, by representing others, the advocate becomes the guardian who protects the person with PMLD from the world, and the world from that person (Garner and Sandow 1995), but also that the advocate imposes his or her views and standards and consequently does not make informed judgements based on objective data collection.

## *Access to information*

How do people with PMLD initially gain access to information? Firstly, they must recognise that they are individuals in their own right, and are different from anyone else (i.e. they *learn about themselves* within their immediate environment). Secondly, they have the capacity to teach others about their needs and wants, their distinctive personalities, and their achievements in order that professionals and parents can become better advocates for them. Both processes rely on collecting evidence, have their roots in the Records of Achievement movement, and build on the success of raising expectations.

In schools, evidence is automatically collected in various ways and presented in a variety of forms: for assessment; for IEPs (Individual Education Plans); for annual reviews; and for Records of Achievements. In adult settings information is collected in a similar way for Individual Programme Plans; for Lifestyle Planning; and for Mapping. Sanderson (1995 and in this volume) advocates *Essential Lifestyle Planning* as a positive approach to assessment as, instead of measures which highlight deficits, there is a shift in emphasis to person-centred planning based on the abilities and aspirations, however limited, of the person with PMLD. Fitton (1994), a parent of a young person with PMLD, collected evidence in a similar way, but for a very different reason. Her concern was to act as an advocate for her daughter and she describes in detail how she compiled a *Care Book*.

> I found I had to tell many different people about Kathy, in all kinds of situations. She could not speak for herself, so she could not say how she felt at different times, how she liked to spend her time, what made her happy and comfortable. She could not explain where her pain and discomfort was. It was not always easy to tell from her cries and unhappy sounds whether she was really distressed, or bored and annoyed because things were not happening as she wished. She did not understand that some things she did, such as grabbing at interesting objects, pulling at strings or cloths, or pushing things aside could cause problems and even catastrophes. (p.1)

The book contains basic information on, and photographs of, her daughter. By constantly checking on Kathy's responses, and recording her new skills and awareness as well as updating information on basic medical routines, she tried to ensure that it really *spoke* for her daughter. The book enabled others to interpret Kathy's needs more accurately and more effectively and, consequently, to measure her requirements against her rights. People became more powerful in fighting for her and professionals gained strength from working together. By implication, Fitton suggests that collective skills and strengths were discovered which had not been recognised before and she stresses how much everyone learned from the shared experience: 'We saw that Kathy was able to teach us and others many truths about ourselves' (p.186).

Fitton's ideas have been developed further by the National Association of Bereavement Services which has produced a workbook chronicling a person's life history, *My Story: a Celebration of my Life* (NABS 1996). It is particularly useful for people with PMLD as it allows a *life picture* of an individual to be built up. Family, friends and professionals can contribute pictures, drawings or photographs, but it is essential that the end product is the personal property of the person with a learning disability. Although originally designed as a tool to address communication problems at particular times of stress, the book can provide professionals in new environments with a picture of each person's social and environmental history. Consequently, valuable information is instantly available and integration into a new situation is made easier. The creation of 'Life Quilts', described by Grove and Park (1996a), is another way in which a person's life history can be represented in a form that has meaning for the person with PMLD.

## The first steps in involving people with PMLD in meaningful consultations

This approach to the collection of information is evident in an example of practice in a borough with an official policy on the provision and quality of an open and accessible consultation service. All service users are regarded as consumers who have a right to information, to voice their opinions on the services they receive, and to express their needs and wants (Watkins 1996). Two main interrelated channels of communication were established within the borough, the purpose of which was to share ideas about, and make decisions on, the services available: a *Joint Service Planning Team* and *Consultation Open Days*. Both are still active at the time of writing.

The Joint Service Planning Team (JSPT) is made up of professionals from health, housing and social services, Mencap, local voluntary organisations, a disability consortium and the community health council, which meets regularly to consider policy and practice. In order to obtain the views of consumers, regular formal Consultation Open Days have been established which allow service users and carers to meet the professionals responsible for all the services. The results of these discussions are presented to the JSPT, who have a duty to consider them in detail. In 1995, concern was expressed that service users with severe communication difficulties were not participating in the consultation process and consequently did not have a voice in shaping and evaluating the services on offer. A report from one of the Open Days stated that 'People with profound disabilities and communication difficulties were not listened to and that this limited their ability to make choices' (Watkins 1996, p.46). The information was fed back to the JSPT which set up a sub-group (Focus Group) to look specifically at the issues and implications of involving people with PMLD in meaningful consultations.

The Focus Group included staff from a Local Authority day-centre for people with learning difficulties who were keen to enable those with PMLD to become self-advocates. The staff decided that their first task in helping their clients to enter into a consultative process lay in obtaining more detailed information on the ways in which each individual was communicating. Although all members of staff knew a great deal about each one, there was no agreed format for recording communicative competence. Working in consultation with the speech and language therapists the staff devised what McEwen and Millar (1977) have described in another context as a *Communication Passport*. The Passport, or *Communication Profile* (as it was called by the staff), not only conveyed vital information about each person's style of interaction (including verbal and non-verbal communication) but, equally importantly, provided a common format from which to work. There are similarities between the *Communication Profile*, Fitton's *Care Book* and the NABS *Workbook* and it is interesting that, for very different reasons, professionals and parents are producing similar documents.

In order to complete the profile, it is necessary to observe the client over a period of time, and it is essential that all professionals, parents and carers are involved. M's *Profile* was completed in conjunction with her mother, and the following extract, written from M's viewpoint, gives a clear indication of the manner and way in which she communicates: 'If you offer me one thing I will indicate I want it usually by making my own particular sign for "please" (two hands held together in front of my chest as if praying.)'

Although the project is in its early stages, feedback from the professionals involved has been encouraging. They report that having such Profiles ensures a more consistent response by all members of the interdisciplinary team to individual communication strategies, and consequently communication is encouraged at all times. Members of the team are confident that the use of *Communication Profiles* has led to a clearer recognition and acknowledgement of the communicative ability of each client, and although progress is inevitably slow, it is a positive step towards his or her involvement in the consultative process. The Joint Service Planning Team has requested the trialling of the Communication Profile in other adult settings, and it is hoped that such a move will be a positive step towards the involvement of service users with PMLD in the planning and evaluation of the services offered.

## *Practice in choice and decision making*

Helping children and adults with PMLD to make choices is an essential part of teaching programmes in any setting. In schools, as Hinchcliffe (1994) reminds us, there is no reference to self-advocacy in the National Curriculum programmes of study, but many of the Orders include, 'explore', 'investigate', 'find out about', which, as Byers (1994b) strongly emphasises, means that pupils must be active in the learning process. Choice making is the right of every individual but it requires acceptance by each member of the multidisciplinary team that choices made by a person with PMLD are as valid as the choices we ourselves would make in similar circumstances. The task is not an easy one when society (even in the present climate) regards teachers as knowing best and, in general, staff are less willing to expose pupils to risk. The fear may be that the children and the young people themselves may fail, or that an unwelcome choice can lead to administrative and managerial problems. If a person with PMLD gives a clear indication that he does not want to go horse riding and wishes to be included in another activity which has been planned for a specific number of participants, how does the institution cope with the choice? Is he regarded as someone who, because he usually likes going horse riding, 'will enjoy it once he gets there' and is considered to be having a 'difficult day,' or will his choice be valued and acted upon?

A number of sources suggest possible hierarchical structures for choice and decision making. Cooper and Hersov (1986) give details of a range of graded opportunities for making choices at various levels and Griffiths (1994) provides a list of specific questions which need to be answered in order to avoid infringing rights, or ignoring interests and preferences. The list includes examples (of which we are all aware, but often fail to take into account) such as 'Are young people always consulted over being touched, lifted or moved?' The answer in theory is 'yes', but are these procedures always evident in practice in *all* situations?

The following questions are typical of those which the staff of a local authority day centre asked themselves in completing the *Communication Profile* on each client.

- How does the person express preferences?
- What sort of effort is needed in order to make a choice?
- Under what conditions was the preference made?
- How long did the person take to make up his or her mind?
- Were all staff comfortable with the decision?
- What are the immediate consequence of the decision making?
- How does the decision inform the activity schedule/curriculum?

The answers should enable the team to consider the barriers to choice making and to celebrate the achievements of people with PMLD. It is over 25 years since children with severe learning difficulties were accepted into the education system but the continuous and pervasive underestimation of their abilities by professionals and parents is still apparent and is constantly referred to in the literature (see Mittler 1996; Corbett 1996). Staff need to reconsider their own priorities if students with PMLD are to also become 'empowered agents of social change' (Mittler 1996). Souza, a young person with Down's Syndrome, makes the point that schooling is not just about academic education; it is also about finding one's place in society and about the development of a civic identity (Souza, with Ramcharan, 1997).

## *Exposure to a range of relationships*

If people with PMLD are to choose their own friends and to develop diverse relationships, it is necessary for them to have access to a wide range of social situations. All too often children and adults live in the restricted world of immediate family, carers, teachers and peers. People with learning difficulties who can voice their feelings often describe their loneliness, their unhappiness, and the limited opportunities they have to make relationships (Sander 1996; Rathnow 1996). And yet they are infinitely more fortunate in their ability to respond in whatever ways society finds acceptable. There is, however, a tension. In order to make sense of the world it is important that, in the early stages of their development, children and young people with PMLD are not exposed to a multiplicity of stimuli and that they learn about their world through routines, repetition and contact with *familiar* adults.

# A whole school approach to the development of self-advocacy

Members of staff of a London school for pupils with severe and complex learning difficulties were aware of the importance of repetition and routines in their quest to find a starting point for work on self-advocacy with their pupils with PMLD. After a long period of discussion the interdisciplinary team adopted Kiernan's (1991) view that 'Enhancing communication skills provides the foundation on which the individual can build to exert his or her self-advocacy' (p.183).

Their approach was also influenced by the involvement of a member of staff in the research programme *Safeguards, Strategies and Approaches Relating to the Sexuality of Children, Adolescents and Adults with Profound and Multiple Impairments* (Downs and Craft 1997a and b), and they all agreed that the enhancement of communication skills was an essential prerequisite for any meaningful sex education programme for students with profound and multiple learning difficulties. Communicating choices and preferences in a range of contexts, including experiencing and choosing who to build relationships with, is an essential element of sex education.

A small scale research study was undertaken with a group of pupils aged 14–19 years all of whom had high support needs and were heavily dependent on staff/carers. A total of thirty two communication sessions of forty five minutes each were devised, all of which were based around regular routines and were conducive to a *responsive environment* (see Ware 1996). Each session strove to:

- establish a familiar process involving
    - systematic planning
    - the use of routines
    - recording and evaluating the work undertaken;
- create opportunities for students to want to communicate;
- generate an environment in which any communication was considered to be meaningful (Brinker and Lewis 1982a; Goldbart 1994);
- enable staff to compile a portfolio of the communication strategies used by the students.

The work was heavily influenced by the view that communication would be encouraged if the expectations of each student's ability to interact were high. Working collaboratively on the development of the communication skills of pupils with PMLD was also considered to be of crucial importance for the interdisciplinary team, as team work would be enhanced through the shared responsibility for the improvement of practice.

Teaching strategies, grounded in the work of Goldbart (1994), Holdgrafer and Dunst (1986), Brinker and Lewis (1982a), Hinchcliffe (1994), and Nind and Hewett (1994) were devised by the team. All strategies attempted to enhance the *quality* of interaction that took place between students and staff (Barry 1996), and in each session all movements and vocalisation were regarded as intentions to communicate. Within an environment which was structured to increase the sociability of the students, staff assumed a facilitating role and often waited for responses before intervening. The interdisciplinary team considered that the opportunities for each student to experience contingency were directly related to the responsiveness of the staff to students' behaviours. Nind and Hewett's work (1994) on mother/child interaction was incorporated into every session.

## The experiences of the interdisciplinary team

The process of working together on an agreed prerequisite skill for self-advocacy was, for the staff, as important as the development of the skills in the pupils themselves. Members of the team brought to the task their own professional responses to the recognition of diversity and individuality, and their own views on the limitations and abilities of their pupils. The planning and collaborative work in each session helped to raise expectations and to value the contributions offered. The following comments from four members of the team were typical:

> As a result of building a rapport with students through the session, we have been able to respond to the students' every attempt to communicate.

> We all learned to value, acknowledge and reaffirm the contribution of the students, no matter how small.

> We learned a lot more about what students wanted individually. The students used their bodies and whole selves to communicate. We learned to observe them very closely.

> Students learn more and develop self-esteem when their communications are repeatedly responded to.

The intervention strategies devised by the team required each member to work more closely with the students than more traditional methods of teaching. Staff were required to observe closely, to wait for and interpret responses, and to reciprocate consistently. They were asked if they felt that these strategies contributed in any way to the development of self-advocacy. Feedback was positive:

> Definitely yes, yes, yes... they learned they could express a preference and see it acknowledged and responded to... they had some control.

> They had an assurance that their choice would be accepted and acted upon.

Individuals referred to the quality of interaction which developed through the work:

> 'A greater bond is evident between students and staff.'

... the emphasis was on establishing a real relationship with the student so as to become sensitised to the way they expressed their choices.

Relationship building, like everything else for those with PMLD, needs to be tackled in a structured and systematic way. Not only is it necessary to consider the development and maintenance of relationships, but members of the team also need to examine how they can help pupils to develop *new* and *different* forms of relationships. Such facilitation is not easy as it requires staff to examine their own values and to reject the traditional role of the authority figure in favour of one based on acceptance, participation and the enjoyment of each other's company (Tilstone 1991; Tyne 1994). The interdisciplinary staff of this special school have risen to the challenge.

# Conclusion

Both examples of practice have involved members of interdisciplinary teams. Staff were not specifically trained in collaborative work, but their enthusiasm for the tasks, and their agreement on the principles which guided them, reduced some of the potential barriers to *working together*. The professional teams recognised the need to take a lead in fighting for the voices of their pupils and young people to be heard, but realised that in the past they had only paid lip-service to pupil/client involvement. In their struggle to encourage self-advocacy their activities in both settings had forced them to consider their own belief systems critically. The concept of self-advocacy and empowerment for people with PMLD presented a major challenge when people with different experiences, backgrounds and expertise were required to find common starting points in order to enable those whom they support to make judgements (and possibly accusations) about the education and the services that they offer and uphold. It was obvious that the work undertaken challenged establishment thinking on the potential abilities of those with PMLD and on the skills they have already acquired.

The strength of the collaborative work in the two examples lay in the process of the work undertaken over a period of time. Single in-service days on self-advocacy would not have fostered the growth and development of the teams themselves. The shared ownership of the activities; the constant adjusting and readjusting to the responses of their clients and pupils; the discussions and debates; the need for reflection are all aspects which enabled the teams to place their roles within the broader context of educational purpose.

The road to self-advocacy will be a long one for many pupils and people with PMLD, but professionals have a duty to place them on the road and to give them the tools to make their voices heard. As the examples in this chapter show, they have much to tell us.

# Chapter 16

# Community Integration and Ordinary Lifestyles

*Roy McConkey*

'To dream, the impossible dream.' So sings Don Quixote in the musical, 'Man from La Mancha' as he rides forth to tilt at yet more windmills. Somehow the words seemed appropriate when I came to pen this chapter.

It is an impossibility to give people with profound and multiple disabilities an ordinary lifestyle. By definition their very survival depends on extra-ordinary help and support, as this volume details. So what then does an ordinary lifestyle mean for these people and their families?

We are presented with two complementary challenges. First, can we provide the extra help and assistance within the parameters of an 'ordinary lifestyle' rather than through specialist services? For example, can the young person live in a normal house instead of residing in a 'nursing home'? An 'ordinary life' has become the dominant philosophy in recent years for many people with learning disabilities but this consensus often does not extend to people with the most severe disabilities. For them, special schools, special care units and specialist residential centres seem essential.

The second challenge is even more daunting. Can our society broaden its perception of 'ordinary' so that the needs of exceptional people can be accommodated more readily? Take for example our housing stock. Fully accessible houses for wheelchair users means ramps and lifts rather than stairs; wider doorways and user-friendly showers, baths and toilets. All of these are just as convenient for non-disabled persons, and even more so for the 'not-yet-disabled', i.e. the majority of the population who will become disabled through ageing. Similar arguments apply to creating user-friendly public transport and community buildings.

## Specialist services and cost-effectiveness

Cost-effectiveness is usually given as the rationale for maintaining selective services in both of the above instances. Specialist services will have lower unit-costs through congregating people with similar needs and, likewise, costly adaptations should be targeted only to those people who have need of them. This logic appears difficult to fault but there are at least three grounds for questioning it.

First, people with profound and multiple handicaps are not a homogeneous group. Rather, their needs are likely to be very individual and idiosyncratic. In grouping people, the danger is that staffing levels and resources are geared towards the most dependent person. Those individuals with lesser needs nonetheless incur the same high cost, hence there is a consequent loss of efficiency in costings.

Second, the benefits which the money buys also need to be borne in mind. A service can be cost-effective while offering little benefit to the consumer or, more likely, a small increase in costs can bring disproportionate gain in benefits. This lesson is increasingly well documented in residential service models for people with moderate to severe learning disabilities (Felce 1994).

Third, the wider social and environmental changes need to be entered into the equation. To return to the example of housing; fifty years ago, our public housing stock had mostly outside toilets and no bathrooms. Why the change? A combination of increases in people's expectations alongside growth in overall standards of living meant that 'old' approaches were no longer acceptable. Likewise today, we have increased advocacy from a rights perspective coupled with an overall raising of standards in personal and social services as witnessed in the shift from institutional to community-based care.

Hence the striving for an ordinary lifestyle for people with profound and multiple disabilities is both an honourable and a valid endeavour even if we fail to make the dream become fully real. At least we will have challenged the presumptions that too often sustain existing practices. But for this to have any chance of success it demands collaborative working among professionals, families and communities.

In this chapter I shall try to identify some of the landmarks in the quest; discuss likely conditions for the expedition's success and forewarn of some pitfalls often encountered.

# Landmarks in the quest for ordinary lifestyles

At the outset we must admit that an ordinary lifestyle is as mythical a concept as normal people. In modern Western society, the parameters of 'normality' and 'ordinary' have widened considerably. Individual freedom of choice and expression is tolerated with fewer limitations than were found even a generation past. Hence at a minimum we must think in terms of lifestyles rather than a common lifestyle.

But that said, there are certain significant features which are common to the lifestyles of most adult persons in Britain and elsewhere. For instance, the listing will include some or all of the following (Ager 1990):

- We live in a place we call 'our home'.
- We usually share our home with other people to whom we are related.
- We rely on some form of income to meet our needs; commonly earned through work.
- We have a network of relatives, friends and acquaintances with whom we socialise.
- We use community resources and facilities; such as shops, health centres and cinemas.
- We travel by car or public transport at least once a week.

Within each of these domains variations abound, hence the heterogeneity of lifestyles found, and tolerated, in our culture. But even a simple listing such as this reveals starkly the exceptional lifestyle often led by people with disabilities within our society ... no home they can call their own ... living with others they have not chosen ... having little or no disposable income ... impoverished networks of friends ... and few opportunities to use community facilities or to travel outside their residence.

But lifestyles are dynamic processes which evolve rather than are manufactured for us. Moving house to another town or city is testimony to that. What then are the landmarks in evolving a lifestyle for oneself within a community? Experience suggests three significant steps which apply to everyone but that are especially relevant when creating a community lifestyle for people with disabilities.

## Community presence

The first step is for people to be visible within neighbourhoods and at community events. Admittedly hermits and ascetics deliberately chose a radically different lifestyle by opting out of communities; a positive choice still made by some people today. However, other people have this option forced on them through threats and intimidation (real or imagined) or by their incapacities. But most people in all cultures around the world avail themselves of community resources and value social contacts with others.

Where do people with profound and multiple handicaps fit in the above scenarios? Some may make a positive choice for isolation although can we be sure that this choice is fully informed and based on the personal experience of being part of communities? I think not. Rather, we can safely assume that the bulk fall within the second category of having isolation forced upon them.

Indeed, this starts from birth. Parents in various cultures speak of the sense of shame they feel in having a child with a disability and their fear of jaundiced reactions from others (Mittler 1994). Moreover the daily chores of feeding, toileting and dressing a multiply handicapped infant leave parents with little time for outings and socialising. Even a shopping trip without the child can provide a welcome respite for mothers!

The cycle of hospital and clinic appointments and/or home visits by specialist workers further separates the family from its neighbours and local communities. What time is left for mothers to join mother and toddler groups, to take their turn on the rota at playgroups or merely to visit friends in their homes? Circumstances too readily conspire to isolate the child and family from meeting their peers.

As the child grows older, isolation is further reinforced through attendance at special schools located some distance from the child's home and with special transport provided. Because of the time and effort involved in getting wheelchair users and others in and out of cars and buses, not to say public buildings, the 'best' of special schools and centres will be equipped with all the necessary facilities such as swimming pools, sensory rooms, 'cafes' and even 'shops'! By their teens, a style for life has been set for these young people and their families in which contexts may change — the special school gives way to the special unit in the adult day centre — but the culture of apartheid remains. And all this has been done for the best possible reasons, or so it seemed at the time. In retrospect, we can identify four flaws.

First, attention is focused on the children's special needs with little attention paid to their ordinary needs, for instance of having peer playmates, going on outings and joining in community events.

Second, families are not supported at home, for example an extra pair of hands to help with the daily chores would leave more time for family socialising and outings (Tennant 1994).

Third, community attitudes remain unchallenged and local facilities remain inaccessible because we have chosen segregation rather than integration. A change of emphasis and endeavour can enable these children to attend local playgroups, go swimming at the leisure centre and join in community events such as concerts and religious celebrations.

Fourth and arguably most crucially, our interventions often fail to take account of longer-term consequences. If we want to create a community-based lifestyle for people with profound and multiple disabilities we must start from childhood as we do with all other children and our decision making must balance present needs and future outcomes. As one parent told me, 'I want my child to go to the local school so that she gets to know people in our town who will support her when I am no longer able to do so'.

Professionals, in particular, urgently need to review their practice in the light of these comments as families will look to them for inspiration, guidance and support. But the goal for each worker is simply stated: to maximise the community presence of people with profound and multiple disabilities.

## Choice and opportunities

The second step in evolving a community lifestyle is even more challenging: giving people a range of opportunities and experiences so that they may begin to make choices for themselves. Fortunately we have the experiences of others to inform and inspire us. For example, here's a listing of examples workshop participants gave of community involvement within Scottish communities (McConkey 1994):

* eating out: restaurants will liquidise food if asked. a phone call in advance can help to confirm this
* pubs: people with disabilities seem to react better when there is lots going on, e.g. music nights
* swimming: many pools have lifting equipment
* shopping: especially to local shops so that the shopkeepers can get to know the people
* bowling: special equipment can be requested to help people to bowl
* cinemas and concerts: more venues are wheelchair accessible with toilet facilities.
* football matches: wheelchair areas are provided
* fishing: fish farms provide all the equipment and facilities
* visits: museums, butterfly farms, leisure parks
* clubs: PHAB clubs aim to integrate young people with physical handicaps and their non-handicapped age peers. Holiday and day trips are also organised in addition to weekly club nights

A number of recent publications provide many other ideas (Denziloe 1994; Hogg and Cavet 1994; FEU/Mencap 1994). However, a number of common difficulties are also commonly reported:

* the lack of community facilities in rural areas;
* problems of arranging suitable transport;
* difficulty in gaining access to some public buildings which can mean two able-bodied people accompanying a person in a wheelchair;
* people with profound disabilities can be resistant to change and unwilling to try new experiences;
* self-abusive behaviours, hyperactivity and loud vocalising are hard to manage in public settings;
* finding activities that are appropriate to the person's age but which are meaningful to them.

Undoubtedly people with profound disabilities can join in community life but it requires special efforts and determination from their carers. Enthusiasts for community participation report being demoralised by the attitudes of colleagues in centres or residences who felt it was a waste of time and effort! Teams of professional workers need to agree common objectives.

The difficulties noted above must be addressed proactively. For example, undertaking an audit of community resources; lobbying for improved access; budgeting or fund-raising for improved transport; and writing policies and procedures for staff accompanying people with disruptive behaviours. Once again, collaborative working not only shares the workload but it ensures more consistent approaches across services and communities.

Needless to say, the preferences of people with disabilities will increasingly dictate their pattern of community activities. Such choices will be informed by past experiences and expressions of likes and dislikes. Indeed various researchers have reported heightened animation and communication in people with profound disabilities who experience increased participation in community activities (Conneally *et al.* 1992).

## Circles of friends

The third critical feature of community living is developing a circle of friends and acquaintances. Vanier (1991) describes community as a place of belonging, a place where people are earthed and find their identity. This is no less true for people with multiple disabilities except that through tradition and practice their belonging and identity is to the community of the handicapped. Perhaps such communities give a much needed sense of security but at a price! Christopher Nolan, the Irish author, writes thus in his autobiography (1987):

> Pupils in the Central Remedial Clinic School were always nestled in a caring collective society ... Oftentimes they watched the international rugby squad doing their pre-match runs and passes. But that was the world of the able-bodied; poor Joseph was only a looker-on. More and more he longed to rub shoulders with the young able-bodied people but keeping in mind his difficulties, he feared for his chances.

His book recounts his search for an identity.

> And so the battle was staged between a crippled sane boy and a hostile, sane, secretly savage though sometimes merciful world. Can I climb man-made mountains ... can I climb socially constructed barriers? .... What can a crippled, speechless boy do ... my handicap curtails my collective conscience, obliterates my voice, beckons ridicule of my smile and damns my chances of being accepted as normal.

Enabling people with profound disabilities to form acquaintances and relationships with other people outside the disability community is a frighteningly new endeavour for professional staff. Lurking within all of us are the same fears of rejection and ridicule of which Nolan wrote that threaten our carefully cultivated feelings of self-worth derived from our work with the 'disabled'.

Certainly some of the fears are justified judging by the experiences reported in the media. Neighbourhood protests have led to the relocation of residences; people have been denied access to zoos on the grounds that they would disturb the animals; and groups have been refused service in restaurants because of disruption to other diners.

Of course these negative incidents need to be balanced against the many more success stories of community acceptance and changed attitudes. Successful strategies include (McConkey 1994):

- the example of care staff when they are with the person in community settings, in particular talking to them, offering choices and and consulting with them about preferences;
- introducing the person by name to local shopkeepers and suchlike so that over time a relationship gets built up;
- carers taking time to explain the particular needs of each individual and how they can be overcome, for instance how to cope with impaired hearing;
- carers bringing the person to their home to meet family members, especially children;
- social events such as dances or in pubs when people can meet together in a relaxed atmosphere;
- leisure schemes, play schemes and working as volunteers on special holidays have all proved useful in engaging teenagers with peers who were profoundly disabled;
- videos of people with profound disabilities in activities with non-disabled peers; these can be shown prior to actual meetings taking place;
- young people on work experience or students on placement influencing the attitudes of their families and peers.

Out of such acquaintances, friendships may develop, especially when given some judicious nurturing from professional staff; such as invitations to join in special events or celebrations, a request for help on a one-to-one basis, and providing people from the locality with feedback about their contribution to the people's lives.

Special befriending and advocacy schemes are another route for relationship building but their success is equally dependent on leaders having intimate knowledge of local communities; being adept at enlisting the help of community leaders and activists; and at gaining entry into existing groups. Sadly most staff in disability services lack training and experience in community work; an argument perhaps for service agencies to review both their recruiting policies and definitions of relevant experience, as well as the provision of new training opportunities for staff in community work and relationship building.

People's quality of life is invariably enriched by having circles of friends. The issue now is how to make this a reality for people who apparently have little to offer in return — the very fear that Christopher Nolan expresses but which his experiences showed was unjustified. After all, relationships are not built around competencies but on shared feelings, emotions and interests.

# Conditions for success

The foregoing analysis suggests that an ordinary lifestyle for people with profound disabilities can become more of a reality than heretofore. But achieving this entails not only new ways of working but also a changed perception about the fundamental role and function of services.

In this section, I want to focus on three essential qualities which need to typify services which aspire to integrate these people into local communities: communication, collaboration and creativity. Arguably, these same qualities should underpin all our services for people with profound and multiple disabilities but my argument is that these features are often underplayed and undervalued because the expected service outcomes lack a strong community focus.

## Communication

By definition, nearly all people with profound and multiple disabilities cannot communicate verbally. This presents a formidable hurdle to building relationships, especially as one of the most common problems reported by members of the public in their dealings with people who have a 'mental handicap' is 'not knowing what to say to them or how to react' (McConkey 1994).

As reported in this volume, much therapeutic and research effort has gone into remediating or aiding the person's communications. These have revolved around alternative communication systems such as Makaton, and, latterly, the use of communication aids. Both approaches have one immense drawback; they are not easily shared or readily understood by people outside the specialist setting where they were created.

Two solutions to this dilemma are worthy of fuller investigation. First, all the people who commonly interact with the person should be trained in the communication systems used. Hence professional advisers must make strenuous efforts to reach and teach the circle of friends in each person's network, or provide means whereby significant others in the person's life (such as parents and teachers) can do this. For this strategy to be successful the methods of communication being proposed should be as user-friendly as possible and focus on 'core messages' which can cover common interactions. Sad to say, some popular systems fail on both counts and they even actively discourage their widespread usage except through formal training sessions.

A second strategy adopts a different philosophy, namely, having able communicators adapt their communications to better match those of the individuals who have limited competence. An analogy is the adaptations we intuitively make when addressing foreign language speakers with limited knowledge of English; for instance, increased use of gestures, simple words, repetition, rephrasing and checks on the recipient's understanding.

However, recent research which my colleagues and I have undertaken suggests that able-bodied communicators have difficulty in adapting their communications, even to people whom they know well (McConkey et al. 1996). In particular, they can be unaware of their own style of communication and its limitations. For instance, carers working in residences and day centres with adult persons, used three times as many verbal communication acts as non-verbal acts, even though they thought they were using both equally. Moreover, this imbalance persisted in communications with partners who were predominantly non-verbal communicators.

A related problem is their limited capacity to adopt more suitable means of communication. Often, the carers had little insight into the useful adaptations they could make but even when they were able to state these in advance of interacting with a familiar client, objective data from video-recordings provided little evidence of an altered strategy, even though they rated themselves as having changed! We had to resort to video-playback or detailed feedback from a sympathetic 'tutor' before changed behaviours were established.

In sum, many challenges remain in enhancing communication between able communicators and those with profound disabilities but of this we can be sure, the solution lies outside the therapy clinic and must involve each person's natural interactors.

## Collaboration

This point leads neatly on to the second ingredient of success for community integration, namely collaborative working. This volume is testimony to the need for this to be the hallmark of professional practice but I want to make a plea for this to be extended to embrace families and communities. However, as hinted earlier, neither our service systems nor existing training courses for professional workers are designed to produce this outcome. Indeed they remain wedded to an increasingly outmoded 'treatment' philosophy that often mitigates against collaboration and cooperation.

Radical alternatives are being tried with promising signs of success (Schwartz 1992). Among the features they have in common are:

- *Key-worker:* Each family and client is allocated from the 'team' one worker who establishes a personal relationship with them and who listens, guides and advises on the range of difficulties they encounter.
- *Home and community based:* The key-worker visits the home regularly and has an intimate knowledge of the local community, and devotes time to building links with formal and informal services.
- *Circle of friends:* The key-worker aims to link families with one another, and into existing networks. The recruitment and support of befrienders or advocates from among other parents or interested members of the community is a key task.

To date, such schemes have developed outside of, and parallel to existing health, educational and social services; an inevitable consequence of the clash of cultures inherent in both models. But can we afford to sustain both styles of services and even if we could, is this a healthy state of affairs?

Such debates have rarely begun in affluent countries but experience among the world's poorer nations suggests that effective community-based services can be offered through a non-professional workforce and at a fraction of specialist service costs (McConkey and O'Toole 1997; Bradley, A. in this volume). In times of financial stringency and the search for cost-benefits, the pressure will be on professionally-led services to adapt their systems and prepare their personnel for new styles of collaborative working beyond the specialist setting.

## Creativity

The third component of success is arguably the most important. In the past decades the field of disability has been blessed by visionaries and inventors; people who were able and willing to dream of things which never were. Too often we impute to such individuals personal qualities which are unique to them. While in part this may be true, the dimension of creativity which I want to stress is the culture within which individuals live and work, and characteristics of this culture if it is to promote and nurture creative responses from them.

First and foremost we have to examine the culture of disability services, although the wider social and political culture may also have a significant influence.

Organisational culture is a topical issue but rather understudied in the field of disability (Peters 1994). At the risk of stereotyping, disability agencies — whether in the statutory, voluntary or private sector — have found it extremely difficult to shake off their 'care culture'. Indeed recent legislation and statutory procedures may have reinforced this role. The main features of a 'care culture' are summarised below and contrasted with the facets of what might be termed an 'opportunities culture'.

| CARE CULTURE | OPPORTUNITIES CULTURE |
|---|---|
| • Dependence | • Independence |
| • Protection | • Self-determination |
| • Safety | • Risk |
| • Low expectations | • Aspirations |
| • Socially isolated | • Community integration |

The epitome of the care culture arguably is nursing homes for the elderly although hospitals and prisons also provide exemplars. An opportunities culture has fewer social analogues but examples can be increasingly found in education, business development and leisure, such as activity holidays. Just think what it would mean if our respite care services for people with profound and multiple handicaps were modelled on activity holidays rather than hospital wards!

Christopher Nolan describes being on holiday with his family in the West of Ireland and swimming in the 'billowing Atlantic waves': 'They floated him with them as they moved out to sea; he glowed with pleasure as he skimmed along for he felt totally relaxed and safe in their hands and through their efforts he sampled the joys of the able-bodied.'

How readily do services provide their users with opportunities to sample the 'joys of the able-bodied'? The excuse so often given of lack of staff is only a partial answer because it is likely to produce more of the same! Rather, we need to reconceptualise the culture of our services.

Organisational gurus posit three dimensions for culture change — leadership, dismantling structures and empowering front-line workers.

## Leadership

Visionary leadership is more likely to come from individuals than committees, which probably identifies one of the root causes for a lack of entrepreneurial initiatives in disability services! Nonetheless, we all know charismatic leaders who have questioned existing practice, expressed a vision of new possibilities and motivated others to make it a reality. How do we attract such souls to services and nurture them within systems?

## Decentralising

Bob Woodward's maxim that 'all good work is done in defiance of management' rings strangely true in disability services! Hierarchical structures are renowned for stifling initiative and discouraging risk-taking. A favoured solution is to break the structures down into small units of management with flatter structures of accountability and to maximise the autonomy of the unit leader in the key areas of budgeting and staffing. But what then happens to the career structures around which our service systems are built?

## Empowerment

The third attribute of creative cultures is the philosophy of making every member of staff a leader. This entails devolved decision making by front-line staff with concomitant trust and support from managers. I suspect that in most services we are a long way off achieving this goal, not least because the most common front-line workers remain 'care assistants' who are paid miserly wages and anyway, doesn't their job title speak volumes! But the biggest stumbling block to change is likely to be the existing pay differentials among professionals in health and social services.

Institutional cultures face one of two choices; extinction or evolution. The former is by far the more common outcome; old systems wither while newly seeded ones blossom. These tend to be smaller, with more focused objectives and flexible staffing but they may or may not embody the features of an 'opportunities culture' noted earlier. Nor can we assume that these new models of service are wholly good. Two emerging problems are coordination across a diversity of providers and the provision of a guaranteed lifelong service which is invariably required by people with profound and multiple disabilities. In both instances purchasers or commissioners of services must shoulder these responsibilities.

# What not to do!

In this chapter, my argument has been that, with extraordinary efforts, people with profound and multiple disabilities can join communities and experience something approaching ordinary lifestyles. But to demonstrate the radicalness of the change needed in thinking, I end by listing elements of practice which will ensure that exactly the opposite occurs!

If you want to ensure that people with profound and multiple handicaps do *not* integrate with their local community and do *not* have an ordinary lifestyle, then you should:

- build special centres for them and equip them with the latest therapeutic devices and leisure facilities;
- employ only trained therapists and educators who work full-time in the centre;
- focus on individual therapeutic programmes to remediate their deficits;
- install sophisticated communication systems, preferably based around computer technology;
- provide preschool clinics and playgroups within the specialist facility;
- provide out-of-home residential care – either short-term or longterm – in specially equipped accommodation with trained nurses on hand;
- strive to make your service known as a centre of excellence which by implication makes any other service inferior;
- develop a distinctive therapeutic brand label, or labels to describe your work; music therapy, conductive education and sensory-integration are all popular ones!

As Mark Twain wryly put it, half the results of good intentions are evil! Undoing some of the unintended evils of the past decades will hopefully feature in the new millennium. The process will not be speedy nor, I suspect will it ever be fully accomplished – because we are grappling with an awful paradox, enabling extraordinary people to live ordinary lives. Some would call that tilting at windmills; others, dreaming impossible dreams! I leave you to decide your response.

Chapter 17

# Addressing Equality in the Provision of Services to Black People with PMLD

*Robina Shah*

## Introduction

Services and support for people with profound learning disabilities from minority ethnic communities are often open to challenge and debate. This is prompted almost always by the lack of appropriate services and a lack of understanding about their cultural needs.

In this chapter there will be a discussion of why it is important to develop a coherent understanding of the needs of black children and adults with profound multiple learning disabilities (PMLD) and their families in order to provide appropriate and accessible services to them. Reference will be made to various research studies to discuss the practical implications for those working with black people with PMLD and their families. The significance of meeting the cultural and religious make-up of the family and people with PMLD will also be discussed in relation to the importance of collaboration in effecting change and therefore providing good quality services.

Access to services and support for black children and adults with profound multiple learning disabilities may depend, first and foremost, on the support and involvement of their carers in the service system. Many studies have shown that the needs of carers are numerous and range from education on health, diet and care, to support with caring. Importantly, just as is the case for some white carers, black carers appear to be unsupported and isolated. This is often exacerbated by communication difficulties and the lack of sensitive and appropriate services. Service provision continues to remain ethnocentric, that is, geared to meeting the needs of the white majority (Butt and Mirza 1996).

One measure of the quality of services and their appropriateness to black people with PMLD is how they are perceived and understood by their carers. This in turn is influenced by how services perceive and understand the complex needs of black people with PMLD and their families. Traditionally, a fundamental aspect of developing this understanding has been centred on responding primarily to the cultural needs of the carers while hoping that this has a direct impact on the social and personal care of black people with PMLD.

There are few specific studies which discuss the needs of black people with PMLD and their families directly, thus the research discussed in this chapter will address disability generally, and, where appropriate, related to people with PMLD. However, these studies have proved to be invaluable in providing information about the variety of experiences of black carers in the social care system and the impact that this inevitably has on those they are caring for.

# Disclosure practice — how parents are told about their child's disability

There is strong evidence to suggest that the quality of life for those people with multiple disabilities is affected by the lack of support provided for their parents and families at the time of disclosure. This is an area currently receiving much attention as service providers within health and social care services are seeking to improve their communication and behavioural skills. From her research findings Shah (1992, 1997) argues that Asian parents cannot adequately care for their child with disabilities because the information about the diagnosis of their child's impairment may be unclear and follow up support is limited. If this is the situation for most families then how can they be expected to access appropriate services? Further, if they continue to lack knowledge and understanding about the diagnosis of their child how can they respond appropriately to their child's subsequent personal care needs?

Few responsibilities demand more of the doctor than that of disclosing a diagnosis of a child's impairment to parents. It calls for sensitivity, honesty and willingness to be available and to be vulnerable. Carried out in the right manner it can facilitate the parent's adjustment to the situation by relief of uncertainty, in itself therapeutic, and by clarification of what must be faced. It can plant seeds of genuine optimism that life is still worth living and that, however bad the news, there may be some hope. Shah's study on disclosure practice (1997) suggests that there is an urgent need to provide adequate and appropriate support services. Pre and post intervention needs to be culturally appropriate and sensitive to the dynamics of the family as a whole unit. For example, Asian parents felt their support needs were neglected. They felt that because their language needs were not addressed the amount and accuracy of information they received was limited.

Communication is a very powerful tool as it opens doors to services and to support. Speaking a common language is important. However, even when professionals and parents share the same language base, misinformation and misunderstanding may sometimes still occur. If parents do not speak English this will affect how the disclosure is made as well as how parents and their families receive it. Detailed research that does not address ethnicity specifically, supports the experiences of Asian parents. For example, in 1992 the Spastics Society conducted research into parents' experience of the assessment and statementing process under the 1981 *Education Act* (The Spastics Society 1992). Although not the object of the research, a large proportion of the parents quite spontaneously needed to talk about how they were informed about their child's diagnosis.

Findings from other studies investigating this area such as Cunningham *et al.* (1984) found that between 40 per cent to 80 per cent of the parents interviewed expressed dissatisfaction with how they were told. In a complementary study Sloper and Turner (1993) found that out of detailed questioning of 107 parents of disabled children, over half were dissatisfied with the experience of the disclosure of the disability. It is interesting that the Asian parents who participated in this project identified similar experiences to the studies mentioned above, and all of these experiences seem to have emerged in three distinctive areas:

- The manner of the person giving the diagnosis; for example, unsympathetic, cold, insensitive, expressed in a language too difficult or vague to understand.
- Problems with information; for example, lack of information and guidance about the diagnosis and what could be done. Highly negative and often misleading, contradictory and inaccurate information or being denied information.
- Organisational aspects; delay and difficulty in getting access to help, lack of privacy, and a lack of coordination between services.

Despite the fact that around 1.5 million people from Asian communities live in the UK, we know very little about the needs of, and service responses to Asian parents who have a child with a disability. A number of studies have shown that the support needs of Asian carers are high, that they experience high level of material deprivation in terms of inadequate housing, high levels of unemployment and poverty. (Azmi *et al.* 1996, Shah 1995). These studies have also found that Asian families report very few family members available to provide informal support and Asian carers reported higher levels of stress and associated mental health problems.

It is at this initial stage of disclosure that black carers will experience their first taste of outside intervention into a very private and personal situation. The manner in which this intervention is done and requested is varied. For example, if the family do not fully understand the extent of their child's disability this may delay them in accessing or requesting appropriate services. Furthermore, the personal care needs of their child may initially fall upon the mother as the primary carer. However, there may be religious and cultural issues once the child enters puberty and adulthood. Toileting and bathing in particular can be very stressful for the mother if she has a son with PMLD. In some religions such as Islam it is inappropriate for a woman to see her son naked after puberty because of issues around modesty. Similarly, a father who had assisted with the personal care needs of his daughter when she was very young may refrain from carrying out specific personal care tasks when she is older. This can be a very difficult time for parents who often then turn to other children in the family to assist with the care of their brother or sister.

In order to understand the needs of black people with PMLD and their families, it is helpful at this stage to discuss the issues about the experience of disability and attitudes towards disability; then, in the wider context, to address the impact this may have on the way in which services are provided to people with PMLD and their families.

# The experience of disability

During the last decade, attention has been drawn to the fact that the dual dimension of race and disability often makes the experiences of black disabled people and their carers different from those of the indigenous population (Begum 1992). Evidence suggests that individual and institutional racism manifests itself in many aspects of the lives of black disabled people and their carers. Sometimes it is part and parcel of the everyday experiences of black non-disabled people, but at other times it is specific to the experience of disability and the factors associated with this. For example, in talking about sickle cell anaemia, Roberts (1991) explains: 'One of the most serious social issues that is affecting 'sicklers' at present is that because sicklers usually have no outward signs of painful crisis they are often considered to be stereotypes and labelled as malingerers and drug abusers' (p.3).

Begum (1992) notes that 'racism and discrimination or harassment was a very real part of the lives of the people she interviewed'. The reality of this is poignantly highlighted in the responses of the disabled people interviewed: 'I sometimes wish I wasn't Asian so I didn't look the odd one out'. About half of the research sample reported that they had experienced racial harassment. This ranged from verbal abuse (experienced by 50 per cent of disabled people and 20 per cent of carers) to personal physical violence (14 per cent of the disabled people said they had experienced physical personal violence as had 7 per cent of carers). She quotes one respondent:

> Whilst sitting in a restaurant a white man walked in and screamed at me 'You blackie buy me breakfast'. I got scared and now I cannot go out because fear grips me and I keep feeling that something like this will happen again. (disabled person in Begum 1992)

> My child doesn't want to go to school anymore because she is frightened by the way children swear at her and attack her. (carer in Begum 1992, p.65)

Institutional racism has been cited as one of the barriers restricting opportunities and access to much needed resources. Baxter *et al.* (1990) challenge myths such as Britain's black and ethnic minority population is young, fit, transitory, and therefore not in need of community support services; or black communities have extensive family networks, they prefer to care for their own. Their research shows that black families with disabled relatives are in as great, if not greater need of support from outside their immediate families as are white families.

From her study looking at attitudes and stereotypes in terms of service provision to Asian families with a disabled child, Shah (1986) writes:

> There is a consensus of thought among social workers that short term care is something quite abhorrent and unacceptable to the Asian community since it suggests that parents are incapable and incompetent to look after their own. This feeling of anti short term care was expressed by some of the parents interviewed, but this should not be taken to be representative of other Asian families. Such a negative response to short term care and fostering seems to reflect the lack of understanding Asian parents have about this particular service. Almost all of the parents in this study did not know what short term fostering involved. (p.2)

The fact that major surveys of the experience of disability persist in hardly mentioning the experience of black disabled people should not deter us from appreciating the messages that emerge from existing work. Racism, sexism and disablism intermingle to amplify the need for supportive social care. However these same factors sometimes mean that black disabled people and their carers get a less than adequate service.

# Attitudes towards disability

It is frequently argued that black communities and in particular Asian communities view disability differently from the white community. A survey on the employment experiences of Asian disabled people notes that:

It has to be said that some of the related problems did seem to originate from within Asian communities themselves. Disability is sometimes seen as a 'curse' and this can cause the disabled person, particularly if a woman, to stay hidden away, or even worse to be hidden away. (Confederation of Indian Organisations (CIO)1986)

Such attitudes towards disability have been identified as one of the main factors which have deterred people from taking up services. For example, a report by the Greater London Association for Disabled People (GLAD 1987) of a study of disability among black people in three London boroughs points out that 'the general view in the social services departments was that the Asian communities regarded disability as a stigma and believed that a disabled person should be cared for within the whole family' (GLAD 1987, p.4).

Shah specifically addresses the issue of attitudes in the Asian community. She notes that many social workers 'have various expectations of how Asian parents view their mentally/physically disabled child'. These include stereotypes such as Asian parents:

- reject their child immediately on finding out it has a disability/disabilities;
- encounter feelings of resentment by other members of their family;
- feel stigmatised by the family;
- see the birth of a disabled child as a punishment for sins or a test from God;
- promote feelings of inadequacy especially for the mother;
- express embarrassment;
- fail to see the necessity to prepare for the welfare of their child i.e. God will protect him/her;
- the Asian male is the dominant figure of the household and all communications should be made through him.

Shah (1986) argues that what this list completely dismisses is feelings of profound guilt, confusion and disbelief. But what parent, regardless of race, would not, she asks, have those very feelings? Such feelings are usually short-lived and parents begin to accept the situation and look for ways to help their child. Begum (1992) notes that, despite the fact that negative attitudes towards disability are evident within the Asian community, these have to be put into perspective. She found that many of the ideas expressed were similar to those that prevail in the indigenous population: a lack of information and knowledge about disability which leads people to formulate their ideas, opinions and expectations on the basis of myths and superstition.

In many situations religious and cultural beliefs had become entwined and confused. For example, the notion that Muslims believe that disability is some form of punishment is likely to be based on cultural rather than religious grounds, because in Islam disability is not seen as a punishment but rather as a gift from God. As in any other community there was considerable diversity in the attitudes and ideas which prevailed, some being more positive than others.

Clearly, the whole area of attitudes towards disability is complex. On the one hand, there is a body of literature pointing to a suggestion that disability is perceived in very negative terms, especially within the Asian community. On the other hand, researchers are warning against the danger of stereotyping, without really looking for explanations or understanding some of the factors influencing people's thinking. However, it is clear that perhaps the only firm conclusion that can be drawn from the literature is that extreme caution needs to be exercised when trying to interpret the evidence. Whilst the difficulties associated with negative attitudes need to be acknowledged and responded to, great care also needs to be taken to ensure that the whole debate does not fall into the trap of blaming the 'victim' (Begum 1992).

It is important that service providers do not evade their responsibility by using negative attitudes towards disability and 'over protective families' as an excuse for the low take up of services and for ensuring an appropriate service which meets the specific needs of black people with PMLD and their carers. Some studies suggest that for black people living in Britain disability has been given a low priority, because the process of living in Britain has meant there are a lot of other competing demands. For example, Perkins points out that:

It is only in the last twenty years that the indigenous population has come to accept that disabled people need access, equal opportunity and encouragement if they are to lead an active and purposeful life. It is not surprising then that disability does not yet have a high priority within the Afro-Caribbean community, most of whose time has been spent in tackling other priority areas such as housing. (GLAD 1987)

# Knowledge and use of services

A significant finding by the studies which have focused on black disabled people is the lack of knowledge about social and health services and their use. This is a theme constantly repeated in an examination of incidence, prevalence and characteristics of social care needs of black people. The following examples from research describe the situation for black disabled people who do not specifically have PMLD. However, these experiences offer a useful insight into the importance of assessing the amount of knowledge carers have about services and the relevance of this to the personal care of black people with PMLD. A study by the Asian Disability Advisory Project Team (ADAPT) found that many of the Asian families interviewed had no knowledge of the services available (ADAPT 1993).

Echoing this point, other studies have shown that those who care for black disabled people also know very little of services available and consequently they are under-used. Cocking and Athwal (1990) note that 'There was a considerable lack of knowledge about local services for people with learning difficulties', (p.12). For example, 23 people were incontinent yet only six of their families knew about the incontinence laundry scheme. Language barriers and lack of accessible information have been identified as the biggest obstacles faced by black disabled people and their carers in gaining knowledge about services. A conference report on Asians and disabilities points out that:

Asian people's experiences of disabilities are essentially different from other people with disabilities because of language difficulties and institutional racism. There appears to be a severe lack of accessible information regarding available services, such as employment, education, training, recreation, grants and allowances for disabled people. (CIO 1987, p.7)

The issue is discussed in other studies; for example, Begum (1992) found that access to information in an appropriate form was one of the main factors preventing black disabled people and carers from taking up services in the London Borough of Waltham Forest. Cocking and Athwal (1990) noted that many of the Asian parents of children with learning difficulties in their sample had little contact with schoolteachers or day centre staff. They conclude, 'While the same is true to some extent of the UK European families in the sample, the problem was exacerbated for the Asian families by language difficulties' (Cocking and Athwal 1990, p.12).

Communication and access to information is a problem not restricted to those who do not speak English, but presents difficulties for other black people too. Perkins (1987) found that many of the Afro-Caribbean disabled people could not understand the complex jargon of the claims procedure unless someone with patience and understanding explained it to them. He notes:

> People should be told not only what services are available but also the extent of the powers of social services departments, because some of the questions they were asked during assessment for services were perceived as unnecessary and too personal. (GLAD 1987, p.12)

Evidence that social service departments have begun to translate material as well as provide interpreters is a sign of progress, but this should take place in the context of ensuring that communication is improved with all black communities.

## Insensitive or inappropriate services

Beyond lack of information and communication barriers, it also is likely that many of the services currently available tend to be insensitive or inappropriate to the specific needs of black people. An often cited barrier to providing a service which is not only sensitive and appropriate but specific to each individual's needs is a lack of knowledge amongst care providers of what those needs are and the commitment to change. Badat and Whall-Roberts (1994) found that professionals (including social workers, health visitors and general practitioners) who came into contact with deaf people from black communities were often unaware of the cultural and religious implications of their advice.

GLAD (1987) similarly found that though statutory providers had some knowledge of the kinds of needs amongst Asian disabled people, they were not aware of their specific needs. This they noted was evident in the low uptake of services. The lack of ethnic record keeping and monitoring further accentuated the problem and appeared to contribute to statutory bodies being unable to plan provision adequately. For example, one black physically disabled man had already spent 12 years in a residential home where he was the only black user and a substantial distance away from his family. He had managed to negotiate (with some difficulty) the provision of food appropriate to his needs, but his overriding requirement was to live near his family with 14 hours of support. The user did not seem to think his care package had been reviewed since the implementation of care management, but he was somewhat sceptical about what care management could offer him, as he was not aware of any independent living services in the area where his family lived.

These studies suggest that social care services need to collaborate more effectively in the context of assessment, evaluation and meeting the cultural and religious needs of black people with disabilities and their families. To do this it is important to identify the barriers to providing access to services and the consequential outcomes regarding their value in meeting the needs of black people with PMLD appropriately.

# Identifying the barriers

Even if black carers know about services, there is evidence to show that these are often rejected because what is on offer is inappropriate, inadequate and not flexible enough to meet individual needs. Cocking and Athwal (1990) found that services were often rejected because they were inappropriate:

> Mr and Mrs Rashid, in their sixties and caring for their adult daughter who was seriously ill, had turned down respite care in the past because they were told it was only available in blocks of one or two weeks. They wanted occasional nights so that they could attend weddings and funerals. (p.12)

Cocking and Athwal argue that services need to be more flexible, and to be offered not just once but several times in accordance with changes in people's needs over time. They further noted that although all but two people with learning difficulties were at school, nursery or attending social services day care, there was often very little contact between carers and service providers. They suggest that while the same is true to some extent of the UK and European families in the sample, the problem was exacerbated for the Asian families by language difficulties. For instance:

> Mr and Mrs Mishra never attended reviews at their daughter's day centre. In fact they had never visited there, and their only contact was by phone. Mr Mishra's command of English was not good; consequently he did not understand everything that was said. The family would have liked regular reports on Sushma's progress, or to have some assistance via an interpreter, in understanding reviews. (Cocking and Athwal 1990, p.12).

They conclude that providing an interpreter who would be available to make home visits with day centre staff, and be present at review days, could have easily rectified this.

Baxter (1989) notes that the lack of flexibility on the part of service providers meant that black carers and those that they cared for were not given the necessary assistance which would have made their work easier and helped their relatives to develop independence. She quotes one respondent:

> It tore me apart to see my mother struggle up the stairs, because due to her religious convictions she refused to use the commode (as a Muslim you are supposed to wash yourself after using the toilet). I applied to the Social Security for a chair lift and I was told because she was over 60 she did not qualify for it. They could not understand the importance of her religion. Baxter 1989)

Gunaratnum (1990) argues that services need to be both imaginative and flexible in order to meet the specific needs of black carers. Such an approach can improve services to all, not just to black carers. In a study of Asian carers she found that 'Asian carers' as a group do not exist. The experiences of the carers differed according to who they were and where they lived. The needs of Bengali carers in Tower Hamlets, for example, were different from the needs of Punjabi carers in Derby. In support of this she found that all the carers in Tower Hamlets lived in council housing and most of them did not read or write. In such a situation translated information made little difference to those who could not read and did not have access to friends or families who could. This left many Asian carers in the study feeling that they, rather than the services, were the problem. As one carer said 'If only I knew how to read and write, I would know where to go, what to do and whom I should see. I wouldn't have all these problems'. Gunaratnum argues that illiteracy is obviously an issue that can affect all carers, yet little progress appears to have been made in exploring different ways of information giving. At its most basic, lack of appropriate information is disenfranchising carers from their right to services. Another carer said, 'These days you have to fight for your rights, but I don't know what my rights are'.

The ethos of flexibility and creativeness is an area where services can collaborate to become more effective in providing individual care packages that are meaningful to the carers and the cared for. It is clear that a number of families need information disseminated in a form other than the written word, for example by making video and audiocassettes, in addition to translating leaflets (Cocking and Athwal 1990).

A recent study by Walker and Ahmad (1994) concludes that the statutory services are ill equipped to meet the needs of black disabled people and their carers. Though community care opens up possibilities, these can only be realised if it is recognised how problematic the stereotypical expectation is, the extent of the pressures on black carers and the limitation of the black voluntary sector.

In summary, evidence suggests that service provision continues to be ethnocentric, geared to meeting the needs of the white majority. Until service providers collaborate to recognise the importance of services to cater for all needs, black carers will continue to be marginalised and remain invisible. This in turn will influence the provision of social care and personal care to black people with disabilities in general and black people with PMLD in particular.

# Conclusion

While the notion of the extended family raises the possibility of a range of carers, evidence shows that, just as in the white community, carers in the black community are unsupported and isolated. However, the lack of knowledge with regard to services both for carers and those cared for, and the particular barriers to access and delivery have meant that for black carers the burden of caring is higher than for the white carers. The higher levels of poverty and bad housing and a service provision geared to meeting only the needs of the white majority have exacerbated this.

From much of the research presented here there are strong messages about how the research evidence may be used to bring about change both in the provision of social care, and in the lives of black service users with disabilities.

A constant theme in this review, when considering the needs of black children and adults with PMLD and their families or indeed people with all types of disability, is that the values brought to considering the problems which black communities and black carers face will impact on how their needs are defined as well as how to respond to them and those they care for.

Social care providers who have attempted to develop and provide appropriate services have also been shown to make value judgements as to what the needs are and how they should be met. Decisions to set up interpreting and translation services or to treat all disabled people the same are some examples.

Taking account of discrimination does not mean the creation of a situation where all actions are explained (and excused) because of the different values various people or groups may have. Nevertheless, any examination of what is a good service (or a bad service) must include an exploration of the judgements social care providers have made in deciding whether a particular problem faced by black people with PMLD is a need, and that this is the way they intend to respond to it.

The evidence reviewed also suggests that those agencies who respond by saying 'we treat everyone the same' have either not considered the needs of black communities or have taken a decision to ignore them. Furthermore, the *Children Act 1989* and the *NHS and Community Care Act 1990* place a responsibility on social care providers to identify the needs of particular population groups and individuals in order to plan the delivery of services as well as to tailor services to particular individuals.

Evidence from this review often draws on research completed before the implementation of either Act. However, it does act as a signpost. Agencies that do not make a specific effort to analyse the needs of black communities are not making any serious effort to respond to the needs of these communities. As the process of assessment becomes more formalised (both by developments in practice as well as through the requirements of the *Children Act 1989* and the *NHS and Community Care Act 1990*) its importance appears to have grown. One can safely conclude that at present the assessment process — the information recorded and given to black people with PMLD and their families, how information is collected, and the decisions that result — must be shown not to be making judgements based on stereotypical views of black family life.

However, if social care is to contribute to black people with PMLD living full and active lives, assessment will have to do more: it will have to demonstrate how it is leading to allocation of appropriate services to black people with PMLD. Any inspection would then have to consider how well this has been achieved. Lack of information has been seen as an explanation for the failure to consider whether black people with PMLD have specific social care needs as well as the failure to provide appropriate services. Importantly, the discussion shows that information has been and is a problem for black communities also. The failure to use some services is associated with a lack of information about their availability and how to access them. This may have led in some circumstances to black people only coming to the attention of social care agencies when the situation requires significant intervention. However, response to the information needs of social care agencies and black communities appears to be limited. The results from the 1991 Census should be used wisely, the fact that the information is there is not enough. How the results can be used effectively is a far better use of the information presented.

In similar fashion, translated material is made available with little consideration of the role of information in providing appropriate services and often excludes some black communities (particularly the Afro-Caribbean community). If better communication with black communities plays a part in providing better services, then social care agencies must exploit the information resources available to them with this in mind, and must also make information available with this intention.

As social care agencies begin to be increasingly required to provide a purposeful service, their ability to identify the outcomes of their interventions is drawing attention. In this chapter there has been a suggestion that in many instances it is still not possible to achieve what is probably the first stage of this process: identifying who is getting which service. The non-availability of ethnicity based information for black people with PMLD is an area worth exploring and developing collaboratively and across the spectrum of social care services.

# Chapter 18

# Leisure and the Arts

*Judith Cavet and Penny Lacey*

## Why leisure?

'The use of leisure time indicates better than anything else the richness or impoverishment of their lives' (Edgerton 1987, cited in MacLean 1990, p.169). Although written about the lives of American people with learning disability thirty years ago, this statement continues to have relevance to people with PMLD in the UK today. Leisure time use is increasingly recognised as an important determinant of quality of life. Studies seeking to evaluate the quality of life of people with learning disability now routinely include a quantification of leisure activities (e.g. Hughes *et al.* 1996).

A reading of the literature about leisure for the UK population as a whole reveals some of the reasons for this developing acknowledgement. An active leisure life style leads to a sense of wellbeing. It is associated with good physical health, especially if it includes exercise. Less expectedly, it is also linked with good mental health. This may be due to beneficial effects for the immune system created by positive mood (Iso-Hola 1997). Leisure also offers opportunities for building social contacts and friendships, and these are important in providing social support. Kelly (1997), in a study of retired people, suggests their main motivations for leisure were firstly 'the challenge of action' and secondly 'the expression of community' (p.178). There is some evidence, however, that these potential gains in social contacts and feelings of competence are not fully available to people with PMLD.

The barriers to full leisure participation which affect all disabled people have been well documented by Barnes (1991). These include attitudinal and physical barriers, plus those associated with relative poverty. In addition, there is a good deal of evidence that people with PMLD are particularly disadvantaged, as regards leisure activities even as compared with other people with learning disability. This is a well established trend which is supported by recent research. A national inspection of recreation and leisure in day services for people with learning disabilities found that those with physical and sensory disabilities seldom enjoyed the same opportunities as other service users, and that wheelchair users were similarly disadvantaged (Social Services Inspectorate 1994). Moreover, when Rapley and Beyer (1996) examined the leisure of some people with learning disability who lived in ordinary housing, they found those with higher levels of dependency had a less active social and recreational life outside their homes than other service users. Also and significantly, the data from this study underline the importance of people's social lives for their quality of life.

However, the picture is by no means without hope. Knowledge, expertise and even a supportive legislative framework are developing. Practitioners have documented a variety of ways of offering stimulation and pleasure (Hogg and Cavet 1995; Denziloe 1994). We do not propose to repeat this information here, save to highlight again the importance of care-givers' morale if the many potential activities are to be made accessible. This latter point has implications for service providers and for purchasers because underpaid and badly resourced staff are unlikely to work energetically to promote the participation of people with PMLD. The main thrust of this chapter is to identify some current themes and issues relevant to interdisciplinary working, before going on to explore how one aspect of leisure, the arts, can be made available to people with PMLD.

# Defining leisure for people with PMLD

Leisure is an elusive concept. The same activities may be performed as a means of earning a living, or simply for the pleasure and enjoyment generated. As Haworth (1997) points out: 'One person's work is another person's leisure' (p.1). Recent definitions of leisure tend to include some or all of the following:

- free time, after paid work and other life sustaining activities have been accomplished;
- a variety of interests and activities;
- freedom, choice and relaxation.

In our view the key characteristic of a leisure activity is that it is intrinsically rewarding.

Denziloe (1994) suggests that leisure is an artificial creation, associated with the rise of industrialisation. She compares it adversely with 'play' which she describes as an 'innate need', one which she attributes to both adults and children. Nevertheless, many activities which we associate with leisure have a long history and a very varied cultural pedigree. Music, dancing, story telling and the celebration of festivals have been aspects of the social life of cultures throughout history. Today's leisure activities continue to be major manifestations of current culture, and participation in them is an important part of full membership of society. Leisure pursuits should not be regarded as an optional extra.

There is some ambiguity about what constitutes the leisure time of adults with PMLD. Once they move on from the education system, they are ascribed the low status attached to unemployment, and there is a lack of clarity about what should be the focus of their day. In recent years traditional day services for adults have shifted in their rationale, from preparation for employment (in fact, low paid contract work) to education and leisure. Thus leisure activities are now a common form of occupation in day services. The SSI (1994) expressed some concern about the rather aimless nature of many of these activities. Their view was that these should be used in a more purposeful way, referring to 'the potential use of recreation and leisure *as a working tool*' (our italics) and 'recreational activities as a means of promoting social development and growth' (p.25).

This desire to promote development is understandable in the search for meaningful activity. Training for leisure skills has a role to play – as does training via leisure activities. Dattilo (1991) notes the variety of skills relevant to leisure which staff should encourage: choice and decision making skills; social interaction skills;

awareness of potential leisure activities; skills in leisure participation. But it is also important not to forget that the real point of leisure is pleasure and fun. It is useful in this context to note Wehman and Schleien's list (1980) of characteristics of leisure of people with severe disability:

- fun and enjoyment;
- constructive and purposeful behaviour;
- participation (even if only partial);
- self-initiated behaviour and choice.

# An interdisciplinary approach to leisure

The provision of a broad range of leisure opportunities for people with PMLD requires contributions from a wide variety of people, both professional and non-professional. Our assumption is that these contributions will be coordinated by one or more persons, who may be a primary care-giver, key worker, teacher, care manager or leisure service organiser. The role of the coordinator is to ensure the leisure environment is suited to the needs of the person with PMLD. Drawing on the work of Beresford and Trevillion (1995), Loxley (1997) suggests in a discussion of collaborative practice between professionals that the service user should be 'at the centre of a web of communication, empowered to exercise independence' and choice with a needs-led response' (p.75). While this approach is essentially drawn from social work practice with adults, its value base is worth reiterating as a general reminder of the essential basis for the rather informal collaborative arrangements that are likely to be associated with leisure activities. In fact, the amount of information sharing and organisation involved in leisure provision should not be underestimated. This is especially the case for people with complex health needs.

Information from informal carers about physical care, user preferences and means of communication is an essential starting point. Positive expectations are also an integral aspect of promoting leisure participation. Ensuring that all those involved have the necessary information can prove demanding in leisure settings which must combine careful coordination with a casual ambience. For one model of good practice in this regard, see Fitton *et al.* (1995) who give a detailed account of how two young women with profound and multiple disability gained a home together. Care books for each resident gave early priority to outlining to staff their preferred activities, supplemented by photographs showing the young women enjoying a variety of pastimes.

Risk taking is an inherent part of leisure activity, and an interdisciplinary approach to risk assessment is important if a realistic evaluation is to be made. This may include seeking advice from doctors, nurses or paramedics on occasions. For example, epilepsy may need careful consideration in relation to swimming; and it is necessary to recognise the possibility of atlantoaxial instability in the case of vigorous exercise for a minority of people with Down Syndrome (Collacot 1987; Cope and Olson 1987). The emphasis, of course, should be on enabling participation through a constructive approach, not the denial of potential dangers or, at the opposite extreme, the limitation of opportunities. Volunteers are often utilised to help provide a leisure activity. Attention must be paid to their setting, training, supervision and support.

Lack of material resources can prove a very real barrier to leisure participation and overcoming this problem requires an interdisciplinary approach. Knowledge of legal rights and possible sources of financial support are becoming increasingly important in this context. *The Chronically Sick and Disabled Person's Act (CSDPA), 1970*, offers some legislative backing for leisure activity. Moreover, a recent court decision, *R. v Islington LBC ex parte Rixon (1996)*, reported in *The Times* on 17 April, also gave some support to the view that local authorities should provide more than occasional daytime activities for adults with PMLD. However, it is also true that the recent decision of the House of Lords, *R. v Gloucestershire County Council, ex parte Barry (1997)*, allows local authorities to take resources into account when allocating services under the CSDPA. In these circumstances leisure seems unlikely to receive a high priority.

Obviously, ensuring service users claim their full welfare benefits is important, and this is one way of helping to pay for outings and holidays. However, further guidance is needed on how far these monies can be employed to fund social excursions. A recent letter in the social work press (Clowes 1997) has drawn attention to the haphazard nature of present arrangements. The letter's author asks whether it is acceptable to use Disability Living Allowance to pay for staff travel and accommodation when they accompany a service user on holiday. Similar questions about who pays for what on other leisure outings also arise.

# Using community resources

The shift to using community settings for leisure is, of course, part of a longterm and well established trend away from institutional care, towards community care (in its most positive sense). The acquisition of leisure skills by people with PMLD is probably best accomplished in natural settings. Care-givers, both formal and informal, need to know what local and national resources and opportunities are available so that they can think creatively and imaginatively about how to extend the choice of leisure pursuits available. Guides about access to leisure facilities are becoming increasingly available (e.g. Lake District National Park Authority 1996), this impetus stemming both from those with an interest in disabled people's access and from those with commercial concerns. Voluntary organisations nationally and locally have extensive information to impart, one example being the Holiday Care Service (tel: 01293 774535) which is a central source of holiday and travel information for disabled people.

There are many implications for staff selection, training and supervision which stem from the movement to using community resources. Residential staff need to be able to develop links with the local community, and have sufficient flexibility in funding arrangements so that spontaneous outings are possible. When planning leisure activities, they should consider which pursuits and locations are most likely to facilitate the development of social relationships (Amado 1993). This is because it is deficits in social relationships, rather that in the use of community resources themselves that affect people with severe learning disability (see, for example, Hughes *et al.* 1996).

Care-givers promoting leisure activities for people with profound and multiple disability need to consider how best to consult and work with staff and volunteers whose expertise is relevant to leisure provision rather than to disability. This includes a very varied group of people, from those with specialist sports qualifications to the local priest, vicar, rabbi and other spiritual leaders. Exchanges of information can provide useful preparation, and those coordinating leisure opportunities for a person with PMLD may find themselves acting as negotiators, ambassadors, spokespeople and models of appropriate behaviour. *The Disability Discrimination Act (1995)*, despite its well recognised shortcomings, lends useful support to those utilising community facilities in the sense that some obvious discrimination is now illegal. However, access alone is only a start, and a really enjoyable and relaxing experience rests on deeper levels of acceptance and valuing.

# Promoting enjoyment and choice

Dattilo (1991) states 'If practitioners are to provide opportunities for participants with severe disabilities to demonstrate leisure preferences, it is critical that they develop strategies to recognise the exhibition of preference by people unable to indicate choices through conventional means' (p.175). This includes the sharing of information about the non-verbal ways each service user demonstrates pleasure and distress. It also encompasses the development of more specialist means of communication. One example which is particularly relevant to a leisure context is the use of objects of reference. These can be developed from leisure-related materials (Rowland 1996;Turnell and Carter 1994). Information technology can also be utilised to promote participation in leisure activities and social interaction (Detheridge 1997).

These sorts of approaches help to reduce the degree of care-giver subjectivity present in assessments of service users' preferences. There are several potential pitfalls in this area. One of these relates to the danger that a Eurocentric approach will be adopted by staff working with service users from minority ethnic groups. Fallacious assumptions are sometimes made by white staff about what is a valued leisure activity, rather than their ascertaining what service users from ethnic minority groups and their families feel is appropriate (Baxter *et al.* 1990). The enriching potential of the cultures of minority ethnic and religious groups has been well demonstrated by Wood (1996) in her discussion of how a Jewish perspective might be made available to Jewish service users with PMLD. This type of approach is equally relevant to other minority ethnic and religious groups.

One further way in which leisure choices may be restricted relates to the debate about how far only age-appropriate activities should be offered. While this issue has been hotly contested already and does not relate only to leisure, it is particularly important in this area where choice and enjoyment are paramount. Nind and Hewett (1996) have put forward a useful summary of the arguments against age-appropriateness, distinguishing between the Scandinavian and North American models of normalisation. They note that keeping all experiences age-appropriate can result in a deprivation of personal power. This has to be set against a demonstration by Porter *et al.* (1996) of how two teenagers with rather limited leisure repertoires were encouraged to develop towards more age-appropriate behaviours. The key point here is that both sets of authors sought to maximise choice, although from different philosophical standpoints. Smith (1996) points out that there is little research evidence supporting the contention that public respect is determined by participation in age-appropriate activities, and states that service users themselves seem to give priority to better social lives plus more freedom and choice.

Another tension which relates to the promotion of enjoyment arises from the question of how care-givers can establish a service user's knowledge of the widest possible range of activities. When introduced to a new leisure pastime some service users may reject the pursuit, out of anxiety and fear of new experiences. The dilemma which confronts the leisure provider is how long to persist in offering the novel activity which is apparently being rejected. A balance has to be struck based on a judgement as to whether the service user is making an informed choice.

Also relevant to the expansion of leisure choices available to people with PMLD is the recent development of special environments. The use of multi-sensory environments is now firmly entrenched, although an independent and detailed evaluation of their manufacturers' claims has yet to be carried out. Bozic (1997) has demonstrated that any evaluation would have to take into account local aims and uses, since his study demonstrated that school staff differ in their approaches, between what he calls 'a child-led repertoire and a developmental repertoire' (p.54). In the child-led situation, the emphasis was on leisure and relaxation, while the developmental repertoire focused upon stimulation and activity. Other special environments which have become popular with care-givers are sensory gardens (e.g. Brill 1997; Gillyon and Lambert 1997), which combine a multi-sensory approach with an environment with broad appeal. There also appears to be leisure potential in the development of virtual rooms, judging from the following description:

> ... a student skis down the virtual ski slope, using a joy stick to circumnavigate the ski gates, with the PC placed in the centre of the visualisation room, which last week was mocked up to look like Ben Nevis. The student working at a computer is surrounded by models of mountains, whilst the computer speakers ring out cowbells and people cheering the skiers on. At the same time, the wind machine churning out an icy blast, is switched on and the light machine interprets the delicate balance of the sun refracting off snowy slopes. (Brown *et al.* 1997, p. 16)

Complex access issues are involved in the application of this type of technology, but its educational and leisure aspects appear to present exciting potential for some people with PMLD.

# The Arts

There is a strong feeling amongst those who promote them that the Arts are powerful subjects both to study and engage in. The Arts develop the senses and aesthetic sensitivity, but each artform educates a different sense and develops a different aesthetic vocabulary. They provide stimulation, challenge, pleasure and fulfilment and involve the whole variety of human experience. This includes the intellectual, the intuitive, the physical, the emotional and the spiritual (SCAA and Department of Heritage 1997, p.4).

The second part of this chapter is given to the Arts, as one very important aspect of leisure. Arts opportunities for people with PMLD are, like all leisure activities, dependent upon the enthusiasm, training and imagination of the staff who work with them. Some clients are involved in a variety of different activities and others are virtually starved of all exposure to the Arts. Many are subjected to the ubiquitous radio or enormous visual clutter in the name of music and art, neither of which actually give a satisfactory experience. Most opportunities to paint, mould clay, make music or dance are highly controlled by staff, leaving little chance for people with PMLD to make choices and decisions. Moreover, many adults with PMLD are denied finger painting or percussion playing as these are felt to be inappropriate activities for their age. All these aspects of the Arts will be covered in this section, as will reference to Arts Therapies, Arts Education and Community Arts.

## The Arts and people with PMLD

There are four widely acknowledged claims for the arts in meeting special needs: enabling individual achievement; self expression and communication; social development; and promotion of self confidence and self-esteem (Cahill 1992). All these are desirable aims for people with PMLD, and very good reasons for offering art opportunities despite potential difficulties with participating both physically and intellectually.

Work in the arts takes both time and effort (Peter 1997). People with PMLD, in particular, need to be given time to respond. It is tempting to hurry onto the next experience before the reaction to the previous one has been registered, especially in the school years where the arts are part of pupils' curriculum entitlement, along with many other subjects. In the adult years when arts activities are regarded more as leisure, the sense of urgency may be less but still staff who are waiting for a reaction can see this as time wasting. It is also easy for the contributions of people with PMLD to be tokenistic or the involvement is envisaged only as social interaction, while someone else carries out the actual painting or making music. There is a danger, in these circumstances, that social interaction is also minimal. Purposeful engagement requires considerable thought (Peter 1997) and a fund of practical ideas for activities (see Mount 1995; Baxter *et al.* 1994; and Robson 1997).

It is easy to give people with PMLD bland arts experiences, convinced that arts are less demanding than other activities and can be experienced in a merely passive way. Promoting the active involvement of individuals is challenging. However, if staff build in simple choices and hone their observational skills to interpret these choices, they can begin the process of giving some element of control to people with PMLD. Peter (1997) suggests that individuals who have a way of indicating 'yes' and 'no' can potentially become choreographers, designers, directors or composers, in charge of decisions about their artistic creations. Staff who facilitate this process have to be what Peter (1997) describes as 'one step behind', so that they give just the right amount of support when it is needed. She does not, however, dismiss a more passive role, suggesting that even if active participation is limited, people with PMLD can be sensitive to atmosphere and dramatic tension in a group drama session. They can share in the peaks of excitement and calm (Peter 1997).

At the school stage, devising a suitable arts curriculum for the most profoundly disabled youngsters can be a challenge to their teachers, especially in terms of encouraging progression to the next stage. It is easy to envisage this development only in hierarchical terms but pupils with PMLD may well be able to show progress in that they can do the same thing, only better or more independently or with more understanding (Peter 1997), or even perhaps with slightly different materials. For example, music making may remain at an exploratory stage but a young child could use traditional school instruments, whereas a young adult could use electronic instruments. In this case, progression is through resources. (Progression is discussed in more detail in Chapter 10).

This example of progression is one way of addressing the need to find age-appropriate activities for teenagers and adults with PMLD. So many accessible songs, art techniques and dances are aimed at young children and are less suitable for adults. It is very difficult to find published repetitive songs or dances which offer the support of routine to people who have limited understanding of the world around them. Many staff resort to making up their own, fitting new, more adult ideas to well-known folk or pop songs. However, it must not be forgotten that even the most sophisticated artists use very simple techniques, for example paint splattering or finger painting.

As with many aspects of working with people with PMLD, the challenge of the age-appropriateness of arts activities is more complex than simply banning cartoon characters and children's songs for adults with PMLD. In the so-called 'normal' adult world, when a new cartoon film is released, many adults get as much enjoyment from it as their children, as indeed they do from singing nursery rhymes and repetitive songs. Simple childlike songs can be heard all around us, for example the football terraces are full of 'one nil, one nil, one nil, one nil etc.' to the tune of '*Amazing Grace*'. So age-appropriateness is more than denying what appears to be childlike. What, perhaps, is more important, is respecting and valuing likes and dislikes, alongside a constant effort to broaden ideas and experiences.

## Working with artists

Many staff feel that they cannot offer sufficiently imaginative art experiences as they have neither the training nor the interest. However, there are many ways in which arts activities can be made available, some of which demand resources for fees and materials but others which are free or supported by charities. Going to concerts, galleries and theatre performances can become regular occurrences in most parts of the country and partly in response to the *Disability Discrimination Act 1995*, more and more theatres, galleries and other arts venues are making their premises wheelchair accessible and disability friendly. It is important to encourage people with PMLD to sample new opportunities and for staff not to become set and limited in their expectations.

Another way to become involved with the arts is through workshops with artists. These are available for both children and adults and can become learning experiences for staff as well, as artists can not only provide new experiences for people with PMLD but can also pass on fresh attitudes, ideas and skills. In addition, it can be valuable for staff to see how people react to someone who has different expectations of them (Sharp and Dust 1997).

Artists working with people with PMLD need considerable active support from staff if they are to be successful (Farell and Mann 1994). There needs to be careful preparation, common understandings, agreed aims and time given for evaluation. At its best it can give all the benefits of working collaboratively. It is suggested that sustained contact with a few individuals is likely to have greater impact than trying to spread the expertise more thinly across many (Sharp and Dust 1997). Hopefully, though, staff can learn much from the intensive sessions which can be transferred to their own work with other clients.

There are a number of art groups who are specifically involved with people with PMLD. The Interplay Theatre Company is an example of a group who have attempted to meet the needs of people with PMLD, through the development of multi-sensory environments for small intimate groups. Palmer (1997) writes of '*Fairground Attractions*' which is a mixture of theatrical and sensory experiences. Clients are taken through the hall of mirrors, try the one-armed bandits, tests of strength and candy floss, meeting a variety of characters through a minimal narrative. Their other shows have been '*The Library of Life*' which was mainly a tactile experience and '*Family Matters*' an exploration of 'story'.

Other examples of Arts activities, groups or published material which embrace people with PMLD include *Sonic Arts* (Gee 1997); *Sound Therapy* (Ellis 1996); *SOUNDABOUT* (Brown 1997); '*Odyssey Now*' (Grove and Park 1996b); *Community*

*Arts* (Webster 1997); *Fundamental Activities* (Baxter *et al.* 1994). Useful addresses are at the end of the chapter.

## Arts therapy

Arts therapy is a movement within which professional artists have specific interest in people with learning disabilities, including those with PMLD. Most branches of the Arts have developed therapy aimed at improving the quality of life of its clients. These are still relatively young professions, developing a variety of different ways of approaching therapeutic relationships. Many of those who write about arts therapies stress the importance of the relationship which develops between the therapist and the client and how this is used to help the client to communicate, build confidence and self-esteem and generally come to a greater understanding of social interaction between people. Although all are committed to their arts, the intention is rarely to teach art skills. The artform is used as a vehicle for the therapy.

Baker (1997) suggests, for example, that music therapy offers a safe, secure place for release of feelings and is particularly useful for those who find verbal communication difficult. The relationship between the therapist and the client is at the centre and there is no attempt made to teach clients to sing or play musical instruments. Voices and accessible instruments are used to explore sounds and create a musical language which belongs to the clients. Therapists use musical improvisation to support the relationship between them and their clients, helping them to develop a sense of self awareness and communicative interactions. Baker (1997) cites some benefits of music therapy for people with PMLD as increased eye contact, eye gaze, tracking of objects and people, motivation, concentration and posture. However, she also reminds the reader that music therapy is more than just developing skills, it is about facilitating and accepting different forms of self-expression and non-verbal communication in a relationship between people.

As with other therapies, music therapists are actively taking their place in collaborative multidisciplinary teams (Heal and Wigram 1993). They strive to develop new models for understanding clinical practice, which involves cross-fertilisation of ideas from a variety of different disciplines. Over recent years, much interest has been shown in both the nature and process of music therapy, but as yet it is a far from explored field (Robbins 1993). There is great diversity but Robbins sees this as not only inevitable but as a strength as the therapy develops. He suggests that, throughout history, people have created music for self expression, for socio-political and religious rituals, for artistic and cultural experience and now, in music therapy, to influence an individual's condition or state. He is extremely eloquent about the variety and power of music, seeing it as deeply interrelated with human beings, adding that, 'The inborn ability in human beings to appreciate and respond to music usually remains unimpaired by handicap, injury or illness, and is not dependent on music training' (Baker 1997 p.6).

Ritchie (1993) presents two music therapy case studies of adults with PMLD who also display challenging behaviour. She paints a very distressing picture of life in hospital wards for these two people and then describes how she feels music therapy has helped to change them. These are not miracle stories but, in both cases, she attributes the ability of both clients to begin to form relationships with others to valuing their actions and non-verbal communications through interpreting them verbally and musically. She asks herself, 'What is special about music therapy?' Her answer is a combination of clinical improvisation (both musical improvisation and therapy improvisation), the therapist him or herself and the building of a relationship between the therapist and the client. This relationship is all-important, transcending words and intellectualisation (Ritchie 1993, p. 101).

The case study approach to evaluating music therapy has been much criticised as lacking sufficient rigour to be considered as useful research. Hooper (1993) attempts to answer this criticism with a study of an adult with multiple disabilities, where he compares the social interactions achieved within music therapy sessions with those in occupational therapy sessions. His results show that there were twice as many interactions in music therapy as in occupational therapy, thus concluding that music did have an impact on the client's behaviour. He attributes some of this impact to the use of the client's stereotypic behaviour in playing musical instruments, thus enabling the diversion of these sterotypies into alternative and worthwhile experiences.

# Conclusions

The second part of this chapter has been concerned with the Arts, relating them primarily to the leisure theme of the first part, although both Education and Therapy have also featured. Life for people with PMLD can become filled with the mundane or the utilitarian, and long periods of complete passivity. They can be continuously trained for some future which never comes. Active participation in leisure and arts activities not only can give purpose to life but can also provide enjoyable ways in which to develop both skills and understanding of the world. Struggling to perform the tasks of daily living could be conceived as legitimate work for many people with PMLD, while leisure and arts provide much needed relief from this as well as the opportunity to explore feelings and emotions and to enjoy the company of other people sharing pleasurable activities. Staff and carers can also feel a sense of purpose as they help to provide leisure and arts activities for their clients.

Most leisure activities can be experienced by people with PMLD alongside the rest of the community thus promoting integration. However, some pastimes need specialist facilities, such as multisensory rooms, hydrotherapy pools or adapted games (such as the *Meldreth Manor Games*). Sometimes these specialist facilities can also be offered to the general public, successfully achieving what might be called 'reverse integration'. Coventry Sports Centre for the Disabled has accomplished this very effectively, through the invitation to the public to use facilities which were developed for disabled people. Disabled and non-disabled people play sport alongside each other, sharing their interests and supporting each other's endeavours. The ultimate aim of either approach must be the provision of environments which expand the experiences and opportunities available to all.

# Addresses

Arts and Disability, Arts Council of Great Britain, 14 Great Peter Street, London, SW1P 3NQ

Association of Swimming Therapy, 4 Oak Street, Shrewsbury, Shropshire, SY3 7RH

British Society for Music Therapy, Guildhall School of Music and Drama, Barbican, London, EC2Y 8DT

Cerebral Palsy Sport, 11 Churchill Park, Colwick, Nottingham NG4 2HF ( for video of Meldreth Manor School adapted games)

Disability Arts Magazine, 10 Woad Lane, Great Coates, Grimsby, DN37 9NH

Disabled Living Foundation Advisory Service, 380-384 Harrow Road, London, W9 2HU

Hands On Training, 62 Cobden Street, Wollaston, Stourbridge, West Midlands, DY8 3RT (training in aromatherapy for people with learning disabilities)

Interplay Theatre Company, Armley Ridge Road, Leeds, LS12 3LE

Kaleidoscope Theatre Company, 19 Mellish Road, Walsall, West Midlands WS4 2DQ (company of actors with learning disabilities)

Live Music Now, 4 Lower Belgrave Street, London, SW1W 0LJ (music performances for those who are too disabled to get to concerts)

Mailout, Kirklees Media Centre, 7 Northumberland Street, Huddersfield, HD1 1RL (information on Community Arts)

Orcadia Creative Learning Centre, 3 Windsor Place, Portobello, Edinburgh EH15 2A (arts courses and activities for people with learning disabilities)

Playtrac, Horizon Trust, Harperbury, Harper Lane, Shenley, Nr Radlett, Herts, WD7 7HQ

Riding for the Disabled Association, Avenue A, National Agricultural Centre, Kenilworth, Warwicks., CV8 2IY

RNIB Holidays and Leisure Services, RNIB, 224 Great Portland Street, London, W1N 6AA

SHARE Music, 15 Daremore Drive, Belfast, BT9 5JQ (residential music and theatre courses for people with disabilities)

Sonic Arts, Francis House, Francis Street, London, SW1P 1DE, Tel 01438 359344

SOUNDABOUT, 12 Alfred Terraces, Chipping Norton, Oxon, OX7 5HB

Soundbeam Project, 10 Cornwallis Crescent, Bristol, BS8 4PL

Special Music, 50 Collington Street, Beeston, Nottingham, NG9 1FJ

The Drake Research Project, 3 Ure Lodge, Ure Bank Terrace, Ripon, North Yorks., HG4 1JG (research and production of musical materials for people with learning disabilities)

The Voluntary Arts Network, PO BOX 200, Cardiff, CF5 1YH

UK Sports Association for the Physically and Mentally Handicapped, 30 Phillip Lane, Tottenham, London, N15 4JB

# Chapter 19

# Community Based Rehabilitation in Developing Countries

*Alice Bradley*

## Introduction

Community based rehabilitation is a concept which has been analysed, debated and refashioned countless times over recent years. Like *Care in the Community* in the UK, it has given rise to greater controversy than almost any other issue about disability in developing countries. So, what are the contentions, and how is community based rehabilitation relevant to the central theme of this book, collaborative multidisciplinary work with people with profound and multiple learning disabilities?

## The origins of community based rehabilitation

Caring for disabled people in the community is nothing new in developing countries, as several writers point out (Kisanji 1995; Miles 1993); it has been going on for generations. But it was not until the 1970s that community based rehabilitation (CBR) became a recognised term. The World Health Organisation (WHO), drawing on the community based model of Primary Health Care (PHC), sought to extend provision for people with disabilities to meet increasing demand. Most services at that time were based on the institutional model prevalent in industrialised nations and had several shortcomings. Fewer than 2 per cent of people with disabilities benefited, and most provision was in cities, inaccessible to the vast majority who lived in rural areas. Families struggling with poverty were unable to pay the fees required by many services. It was clear that other solutions had to be found. As O'Toole (1993) explains, 'There was a need for new patterns of service with fewer experts, less advanced forms of training and simplified methods of rehabilitation' (p.201).

Institutionalised models of rehabilitation were increasingly becoming discredited globally. To continue to separate people with disabilities from their own communities was clearly unacceptable and a flagrant infringement of basic human rights. Disabled people themselves, and their families, were beginning to question the paternalistic, authoritarian approach which prevailed in traditional services.

In instigating community based rehabilitation, WHO sought to disseminate basic rehabilitation knowledge and techniques to families and communities with no access to conventional rehabilitation services. Communities would be involved in the design, implementation and evaluation of rehabilitation strategies. To encourage the spread of community based rehabilitation, WHO produced a manual, *Training the Disabled in the Community*, which presented simple rehabilitation techniques and covered all disabilities. The emphasis was predominantly medical and on functional skills such as might normally be taught by occupational therapists or physiotherapists.

The large scale transfer of rehabilitation techniques envisaged by WHO was to be accomplished through the use of local supervisors selected by the community. They would train families, or disabled people, using the appropriate parts of the manual. Specialist rehabilitation professionals would train the local supervisors for their role, and would monitor their work. Governments were expected to be active partners, and commit themselves to the promotion of CBR, using available resources to support programmes initiated at community level. Community resources would complement government resources and communities would, as a result, become partners in the rehabilitation process. Partnership was an essential component of CBR from the outset. People from different backgrounds and different sectors would have to work together if the approach was to be effective.

The WHO manual was piloted in several countries, outcomes reviewed and the CBR concept officially accepted by WHO in 1982. CBR was well and truly launched and attracted a great deal of international interest. It was subsequently endorsed by all of the major international organisations. By 1984, 40,000 copies of the WHO manual had been produced and translated into twenty languages (O'Toole 1993).

# CBR in action

CBR in some form now operates in most developing countries. One of its greatest strengths lies in its flexibility, and this is evident in the myriad approaches adopted. Some projects draw heavily upon the WHO model, and others have followed their own path. Whatever the approach, collaborative multidisciplinary teamwork is essential. A few examples illustrate the diversity which exists.

The CBR project in Negros Occidental in the Philippines, which began in 1981, is based upon the WHO model. Local supervisors are residents of their respective communities and the project is supported externally by a non-government organisation (NGO). Community awareness is a fundamental aspect of the programme, and is demonstrated by the way in which disabled people are regarded as integral members of local life. The project has a strong multidisciplinary element both at community level and through its referral network, with links at district, provincial and national level. This is essential for sustainability (Valdez 1991).

By contrast, the CBR project in Janakpuri, an outlying area of Delhi, owes its origins to a woman who had never heard of community based rehabilitation, let alone the WHO model. Started in 1990 in response to the needs of one child with polio, the project now serves over 200 people, children and adults of all ages and with all types of disability. Families of children with PMLD are given loans to start businesses in their homes, which means that they can keep their children with them rather than put them into institutional care or leave them with relatives. CBR workers are drawn from various sectors of the community, include the mothers and some disabled people, and work together closely. The project has minimal financial and administrative help from a local non-government organisation and a strong network of medical, rehabilitation, vocational and educational support (Saxena 1993).

Some CBR projects are government initiated, such as those started by the Ministry of Health in Kenya and integrated into primary health care (PHC), as was first envisaged by WHO. District CBR teams are multidisciplinary, drawn from various ministries and NGOs (Lagerwall 1992). Others begin as outreach programmes from centre based rehabilitation services, such as one in Tamil Nadu, in India, which started as a disability awareness programme in the community and evolved into CBR. The CBR team uses volunteers from the community and includes parents and disabled people (Spastics Society of Tamil Nadu, 1995–96).

Sometimes projects owe their origin to disabled people's organisations, to families or to parents' groups, with or without help from outside agencies. The Zanzibar Association of the Disabled (an organisation *of* rather than *for* disabled people) runs a CBR project, with support from an international NGO. The intention in starting the project was to convince both the community and the government that CBR is the best way of rehabilitating disabled people, especially those from rural areas. The project has grown considerably since it began in 1988 and includes education, employment, housing and transportation, as well as parents' workshops and playgroups for disabled children. Establishing partnership with parents was difficult in the early stages. Several families had hoped for curative facilities or material help and saw little benefit in CBR. The government had low expectations of the programme and it took time to convince them of its value. Now, however, there is strong family involvement and the project leaders are instrumental in influencing government policy and raising community awareness (Khalfan 1992).

The Nairobi Family Support Service (NFSS) was started by families in 1981, and is today used as a model by the Kenyan government. The project is managed by a local committee of parents, community leaders, disabled people and professionals. Over 200 children are catered for in various parts of Nairobi, several with profound and multiple learning disabilities. Activities include playgroups, home visits, vocational training, workshops for families and the production of equipment (Asindua 1995).

It will be clear from these examples, a few selected from many, that there are differences in the way in which the CBR concept is interpreted and implemented in different situations. It will also be obvious that CBR without teamwork is impossible. If programmes are to meet individual needs and improve life for all disabled people, collaboration and flexibility are crucial. WHO had always intended their CBR model to be flexible, but just how flexible is not clear, and this is one of the issues which has caused greatest conflict. What can and cannot justifiably be called 'community based rehabilitation'? As often happens, the arguments became polarised. Purists declared that only programmes which were home based could rightly be called CBR, while those at the other end of the spectrum simply re-named practically everything CBR, even programmes which were quite clearly institutional. In many ways, this debate resembles that associated with *Care in the Community*.

One thing that emerged from experience was that CBR is much more than just a rehabilitation programme. You cannot 'do' CBR as you can 'do' therapy, assessments or exercises. The CBR concept embodies philosophy, ideology and strategies for effecting change. The goal is to work towards social justice and equity for disabled people and their families. If CBR is effective, it should change communities, bring people together, increase understanding about disability and result in improved quality of life for people with disabilities. Like *Care in the Community* in the UK, community based rehabilitation should be a process of empowerment for disabled people and their families.

Werner (1993) reminds us that both primary health care and CBR have emphasised empowerment and community participation, but that, in practice, planning and implementation has been top-down. He asserts,

> Participation was too often reduced to compliance, which in terms of self determination was counter-productive. Obedient compliance to the designs of those in positions of authority and control only perpetuates the low social status and powerlessness of underprivileged groups (p.vii).

He contests the idea of 'involvement' for disabled people and families, saying that this is not enough. 'Only when programs for disabled people are led and controlled by disabled people (and/or their families) are they likely to help disabled persons gain self determination and a respected, equal position in society (p.viii).

In the 20 years that have elapsed since WHO first mooted the idea of community based rehabilitation, the concept has developed considerably, shaped by the experiences of individuals, communities and governments across the world, and by the criticisms levelled at the WHO model. There has been increasing resistance to top-down pre-packaged solutions in which communities are expected merely to cooperate with what has been planned for them, rather than initiate and control what happens. In many parts of the developing world, disabled people themselves, and to a lesser extent, the families of disabled children, have reacted strongly to having their lives managed for them. Like their counterparts in industrialised nations, they are demanding more control over what is happening. Disabled people's organisations in several countries are beginning to influence the design and implementation of CBR programmes (Miles 1996).

But what of people with PMLD? While many of them may be able to advocate for themselves in some situations, it is unlikely that they will be able to do so on a large scale. So how does CBR serve their interests?

# CBR and people with PMLD

It is difficult to obtain an overall picture of CBR coverage for people with PMLD. One reason for this is the generic nature of CBR. Since it is a strategy for people with all types of disability, it tends to be non-categorical in approach. Some projects are designed to provide for people with a specific disability, but many more are for everyone, regardless of the type of disability. While people may keep records for their own information, few generic projects formally record the different disabilities of their participants. This is commendable ethically and philosophically, but it does make it more difficult to find out just how many projects cater for children and adults with PMLD, and to ascertain whether people with PMLD are sharing in the benefits of community based initiatives. Another reason for the shortage of information is that the term 'profound and multiple learning disabilities' is relatively unknown in developing countries. Children and adults with PMLD are often referred to as 'mentally retarded' or 'spastic'. Thus, when questioned about whether a project provides for people with multiple disabilities, many project workers will be unclear about what is meant.

There are several ways in which CBR projects provide for people with PMLD and their families. These include:

- direct work with the disabled child or adult, either in the home or in a community based centre;

- work with the family, such as livelihood loans, grants or home based employment, usually for mothers;
- parent-to-parent programmes, where a more experienced parent will support other families with disabled children;
- providing low cost aids and adaptations, such as seating, buggies or wheelchairs;
- referring the child or adult on to more specialised services and meeting financial costs;
- parent support groups;
- integrated play or activity schemes where able bodied siblings participate;
- family based activities, such as outings or social events.

The Janakpuri project in Delhi, referred to earlier, does not work directly with the children, but the loans and the employment given to mothers benefit the whole family. This means that it is less likely that parents will seek institutional placements for their children. The Nairobi Family Support Service, also mentioned earlier, caters for all children, including those with PMLD, through playgroups, home visits, the provision of equipment and parent support groups.

Parents themselves are often instrumental in developing services. Florence Chitiyo, a mother of a disabled child, writes about a neighbourhood centre run by parents. The centre, she tells us 'offers a range of activities — stimulation for children, relief care for exhausted mothers and a mothers' group for income generating activities' (p.3). Profits are divided between mothers and the centre. She says, 'Both the support offered by the centre and the income we make helps us. Many of us have children who are too handicapped ever to find a school place' (Chitiyo 1996, p.3).

In the KASAMAKA community based projects in the Philippines, all of which cater for children and adults with PMLD, the CBR workers are mothers of disabled children. The Portage style programme organisers decided to use mothers as home visitors because volunteer workers kept dropping out. These same mothers now manage the programme. As well as home teaching, they organise community workshops and have an advocacy role. They have established strong links with schools, hospitals and rehabilitation centres. Disabled people and families have become empowered through active participation in planning, implementation and decision making. Opportunities to come together in groups provide support and solidarity, and help parents and disabled people work together with professionals to effect change (McGlade and Aquino 1995). How many projects in industrialised countries have achieved the same degree of collaboration?

In Mexico the families of children with physical, intellectual and multiple disabilities have established mutual support groups, rehabilitation facilities and a school for children unable to gain admission to state schools. They are pressurising the government for better services. The programme was started by a social worker, but elected family members are gradually assuming control. Some of the teachers are severely disabled and are good role models for disabled children (Werner 1993).

There are similar stories from other countries. Empowerment is vital for the families of people with PMLD if things are to change. 'Parent empowerment is a tool in the fight against stigmatisation and low social status felt among parents of disabled' (NAMH 1996). Empowerment happens in a variety of ways and professionals have an important role as facilitators, as they have in every country across the world.

A CBR programme, run by the Christian Foundation for the Deaf and Blind in the Philippines, originally catered only for people with sensory impairments, but now works with multiply disabled children and their families. As well as direct work with the children, they also supply custom-made mobility aids such as buggies and wheelchairs, which means that many children are able for the first time to be taken out. Poor families are given grants to help them care for their children, or livelihood loans which will enable them to start small businesses at home. Professionals train and support community workers. Parents and children now have much more of a visible presence in the community, an essential prerequisite for community inclusion (Campos 1992).

Most project participants find great strength and solidarity in group activities, and parent-professional boundaries often disappear when people share common goals. But different expectations can mean that relationships between families and CBR workers, whether professionals or non-professionals, do not always go smoothly. Some parents are hoping only for a residential placement for the disabled person. Convincing them that community based intervention is a better option is a difficult task. Lagerwall (1992) tells of a return visit to a family with a twelve year old daughter with severe cerebral palsy, whose family had intended to leave her to the CBR team or an institution, and remarks, 'Although it was disturbing to find the girl lying on the sack on the ground with a severe scoliosis, she was now clean and well dressed which had not been the case at previous visits' (p.3). Most parents, however, struggle to keep their children at home, whatever their circumstances.

Shared vision is essential in CBR, and vision develops as a result of exposure to other people's ideas and aspirations. This is another reason why partnerships are vital: partnerships which include families, disabled people, professionals and front line workers, all working towards a common goal.

# Partnership through collaborative multidisciplinary practice

Multidisciplinary collaboration is one of the goals of CBR. Projects which are urban based are much more likely to have easy access to professionals than those in more remote rural areas. But even in urban projects professionals are few in number compared to the need. CBR was designed specifically to deal with the shortage of services and of specialists. But it was also intended as a means of de-mystifying professionalism; sharing rehabilitation techniques and practice with 'non-professionals'. It is a move towards power sharing, so that disabled people and their families will no longer be at the bottom of the hierarchy.

Professionals may not be the best people to implement CBR. They may have the technical expertise, but do not necessarily have the community skills, the organisational skills or the management experience required. They are unlikely to understand community needs and community development as well as the people who actually belong to the community. At the same time, CBR workers who are not professionals need access to the technical skills if they are to be able to understand the effects of different disabilities. Collaborative multidisciplinary practice in CBR is much broader than that normally experienced in more traditional services. It includes disabled people, families, CBR workers who are likely to be drawn from various sectors, professionals from various disciplines, community leaders and government officials, amongst others.

Projects employ professionals in a variety of ways, according to need and the nature of the project. Most professionals have to assume a number of different roles:

- that of front line workers; visiting homes and running sessions in centres;

- advisers, helping to steer the programme in the right direction; giving advice on problems in their own field of expertise;
- consultants, visiting from time to time, receiving referrals, dealing with children or adults with particular types of disabilities or problems;
- members of management bodies, helping to run or monitor the project;
- supervisors, supporting and advising front line workers;
- trainers;
- counsellors, working with families;
- a link between community groups and national organisations, particularly government bodies;
- disseminators of ideas and information.

CBR is primarily about power sharing, and not everyone finds this easy. Community members are accustomed to deferring to professionals, while professionals have their status to consider. As Miles (1996) says, 'The transition from omniscient professional to facilitator in the community requires an enormous shift in thinking and, too often, institutional attitudes are carried over' (p.501). Different disciplines have their own professional boundaries and few professionals are trained in collaboration. But once the initial hurdles are overcome and everyone adjusts to the new roles, CBR is fertile ground for collaborative multidisciplinary practice.

There are many advantages. Collaborative multidisciplinary work makes available a larger pool of ideas and expertise. Professionals have access to resources the community might not have. They are also part of larger networks and of the infrastructures which exist in a country. Projects which use a team approach are much more likely to be sustained than those which rely on one leader, however strong or charismatic that person might be. Professionals are surprised how much there is to learn when they begin to listen to disabled people and families. A group of Malaysian teachers, doctors and social workers found that the most successful feature of a three week course on CBR was an ad hoc session where a group of parents from a CBR project came to talk about their own experiences. Participants and visitors worked in small groups and the session continued long after the official closing time. The professionals, all experienced in the field of disability, said that they had learned more from that session than from any other training they had done (Bradley 1993).

Collaborative multidisciplinary training facilitates working partnerships, especially when it also involves disabled people and families. Training through video courses, designed and produced locally, has proved particularly useful. Trainers collaborate in the production of the materials, are trained in their use and then take the training back to the people in their project. The package acts as a catalyst, giving guidelines and ideas, and providing a basis for discussion and planning (McConkey 1993). One example from India, designed for those working with children with PMLD, is based on a play project. Components include drama, painting, locally made toys and equipment, movement activities, basic positioning and handling, simple aids and adaptations. The children filmed were in a residential situation, but the programmes were also designed for families in home settings as well as CBR workers. The purpose was to show how many different things children with PMLD can achieve if given the right kind of support and encouragement, rather than being left lying all day doing nothing (Bradley 1994).

Interactive training is particularly suitable for people who have to work as part of a multidisciplinary team in a CBR project. It provides opportunities for discussion, exchange of ideas, learning from others and problem solving. If a programme is to reflect the needs and wishes of a community there is little point in training people in pre-packaged, standardised approaches. In fact, CBR needs not just to be multidisciplinary, but multisectoral. Unless CBR is integrated as part of community development, and has links with all relevant government and non-government organisations, the chances of sustainability are low. Collaboration at all levels means that there is more chance of capitalising on lessons learned both locally and nationally.

# Evaluation, interdisciplinary practice and CBR

In some places CBR seems to have been ground breaking: empowering parents, raising public awareness, bringing people closer together and steering government policy. In others, projects started with great hope and enthusiasm have died away leaving no tangible sign of change. The most successful projects are built on collaboration. McGlade and Aquino (1995) write: 'The value of CBR may be rooted as much in the relationship between CBR workers and family members, as in the actual practical interventions carried out' (p.187). So what constitutes success in CBR, particularly with regard to collaborative multidisciplinary practice and people with PMLD? To date we have little evidence to draw upon, but we can at least begin to ask the right questions.

- To what extent are people with PMLD being served by CBR projects in different countries?
- What kinds of interventions are most effective as perceived by the different people involved? Is there agreement?
- What kinds of support do non-professional practitioners need from professionals (Brar 1992)?
- Which factors are instrumental in making multidisciplinary teams effective?
- Which combination of services suit families and people with PMLD?
- What part do families and communities play in the project?
- How are parent-to-parent supports utilised?
- How does the project build on pre-existing community support systems?
- How can technical expertise about PMLD best be disseminated?

Evaluations are influenced by the role and perspective of the person or persons in control. There is little sense in promoting a collaborative multidisciplinary strategy such as CBR and then adopting a traditional, one-dimensional approach to evaluation. And yet this is what often happens. Projects are evaluated by outsiders who understand little about the community in which the project is located. Rural projects are evaluated by professionals from the urban elite, whose lifestyles are at the other end of the spectrum. Programme workers have vested interests. Consumers feel constrained and give the answers they think workers want to hear. Projects are evaluated separately by outsiders and insiders with contradictory results. There are also problems finding evaluation measures which will allow comparison across projects and across countries. By definition each project should reflect the needs, aspirations and demands of individual communities. What is appropriate in one situation may be entirely unworkable in another. CBR projects are not easily replicated or compared. And most evaluations deal with methodology and outcomes, rather than process, which is a fundamental element of CBR (Thomas and Thomas 1995).

Participatory evaluation is the approach that seems most suited to CBR, based as it is on partnership, collaboration and equality. However, many of those who are central to the CBR process are too busy getting on with the job, and are reluctant to spend time on monitoring and evaluation, especially if they feel it has little value. So, how do you convince front line workers that evaluation is important and within their capabilities? Thomas and Thomas (1995) tell of a phased strategy designed to change CBR workers' attitudes to evaluation. They used a proactive, phased approach to convince workers that evaluation was in their own interests, and not just that of the NGO supporting the programme. By means of newsletters, discussions, workshops and joint action, they showed that monitoring and evaluation could lead to better and more cost effective services and that evaluation was not as difficult as workers thought.

Evaluation, if done properly, will enable us to capitalise on the knowledge and expertise accumulated by CBR projects across the world. It will help us compare strategies and uncover some of the factors which facilitate effective teamwork, while still maintaining the diversity necessary in CBR. Most fundamentally, it will deepen our understanding of how families and professionals can complement one another's expertise. CBR is a two way learning process: families learn more about disability and rehabilitation techniques; practitioners learn about the real lives of disabled people (Brar 1992). Participatory evaluation will facilitate ownership, a prerequisite for sustainability.

Dissemination of information is equally vital. Brar (1992) highlights the weaknesses in dissemination, asserting that we must find a range of methods of making information accessible to those who need it. In Indonesia, she tells us, this was done by means of traditional research reports, slide shows, question and answer formats, case histories and network mapping. Thomas (1997) pinpoints a reluctance of CBR projects to share information with one another. Because of this, valuable lessons have been lost and people have had to reinvent the wheel. 'There is a need for donor organisations to recognise the importance of pooling resources, developing strategies for collaboration and coordination, avoiding duplication of efforts and aiming for optimal resource utilisation.' (p.31). Miles (1989) reminds us that there is a fund of rehabilitation knowledge and skills dispersed in the community, acquired from people's own experiences.

# Concluding comments

There are parallels to be drawn between CBR in the developing world and community based initiatives in industrialised countries, notably *Care in the Community* in the UK. At the root of all such initiatives is the empowerment of disabled people and their families, and a shift from top-down development to true collaboration between families and professionals. For children and young people with PMLD, the role of the family is crucial. Parents must be at the forefront of development and not just followers. Even in the best informed communities, in both industrialised and developing countries, there is little spontaneous effort to improve the lives of disabled people. Where communities have changed, this has seldom been due to altruism. The origins of education and integrated services for disabled children in industrialised nations are usually to be found in parental effort. In developing countries, it is unrealistic to expect that all parents will play a leading role, since the sheer act of daily survival is challenge enough for many. But there are those who can, and who are already doing so. There are similarities, albeit different in degree, with their counterparts in more affluent societies.

The Parent Mobilisation Resource Group (PMRG), working under the umbrella of Inclusion International (formerly the International League of Societies for People with Mental Handicap), has parent representatives from several African countries, Jamaica and Norway, and is a good example of partnership across nations. Through high profile activities and parent empowerment seminars, the group aims to share experiences, exert political pressure and work towards full inclusion for all persons with intellectual disability (NAMH 1996).

The most effective community based initiatives recognise that the person with PMLD is part of a larger network, comprising both the immediate and extended family. Improving the circumstances of the family can often be the best way of improving the quality of life for the person with PMLD. The livelihood loans to parents, discussed earlier in the chapter, make a difference to the life situation of the disabled child or young person. Similarly, in an industrialised country, providing child care which allows a mother to work alters the circumstances of both child and family. In both, there is respite and support for the mother, a recognition of her individuality and needs and an improvement in economic status.

There are similarities too, in the way in which the best community based services worldwide have evolved to match local circumstances. There is no such thing as a typical community, nor a blueprint for service provision. One of the strengths of community based provision lies in its flexibility; an ability to take on the nature and shape required to suit the needs of those it serves and to capitalise on available resources.

Partnership has an increasingly important part to play, although it is not always easy, especially where professional boundaries and lines of demarcation between professionals and non-professionals are clearly marked. Specialist expertise within institutional settings can be made available to community groups through joint ventures. Communities can influence professionals, drawing upon their own experiences of real life situations. Governments can play a coordinating role, as some already do, facilitating and supporting partnerships between government and non-government organisations, communities, families and disabled people.

Disabled people's organisations have been a powerful voice for change within and across nations. But so far most have neglected the rights and needs of those who are more severely disabled. If empowerment and equality for all is the goal, it makes no sense to be selective about which types of disability will and will not be represented.

In both CBR and *Care in the Community*, the relationship between education and other sectors providing services is still much too tenuous. Stronger links are essential if multidisciplinary collaboration is to become a reality. In CBR, emphasis is largely on health, with little on education. Children are referred to school from CBR projects, but these are generally children with less severe disabilities. In developing countries it is unlikely that many children with PMLD will be in mainstream schools in the short, or even medium term, but this must be the ultimate goal. In the meantime, there are imaginative ways of integrating children with PMLD and able bodied children, such as play schemes and family activities. Integrated activities should be a planned component of all CBR projects.

Even those professionals who are committed to multidisciplinary collaboration struggle with both the concept and its practice. Many professionals remain role bound. Shared training at qualifying level is rare. Experience suggests that it may be more common at post qualifying level in developing countries than in industrialised, possibly because professional organisations are stronger in the latter, and numbers greater. Yet, if community based services are to succeed, we need to move far away from the style of professionalism we have grown up with. Professionalism may be the biggest obstacle to multidisciplinary collaboration at community level.

Like *Care in the Community*, CBR has not yet proved its true worth, and is not without its critics. Momm and Konig (1990), from their experiences of reviewing projects in several countries, cast doubts on its sustainability without outside support. But, at least for the present, it is the best hope for many people with PMLD and their families. The challenge is to strive for sustainability, to increase the number of people with PMLD who benefit, and to strengthen the impact. It is not an antidote to the inequalities experienced by large numbers of people with PMLD and their families, but it is a genuine attempt to even out some of them. It is a learning experience with potential for change, and there is still a long way to go.

Fundamentally, provision in the community for people with profound and multiple disabilities depends on a vision of a more equitable society, locally, nationally and internationally. Vision is shaped and altered by exposure to other people's ideas and aspirations. Monitoring and evaluating our services enables us to draw upon experience, deepen our understanding and share achievements. Together, internationally, we have much to learn from one another.

# References

AAMR (1992) *Mental Retardation: Definition, Classification, and Systems of Support*, 9th edn. Washington DC: American Association on Mental Retardation.

Adair, J. (1987) *Effective Teambuilding*. London: Pan Books.

Ager, A. (1990) *Life Experiences Checklist*. Windsor: NFER–Nelson.

Ainscow, M. and Muncey, J. (1989) *Meeting Individual Needs*. London: David Fulton.

Aitken, S. and Buultjens, M. (1992) *Vision for Doing. Assessing Functional Vision of Learners who are Multiply Disabled*. Edinburgh: Moray House Publications.

Amado, A. (1993) 'Steps for Supporting Community Connections', in Amado, A. (ed.) *Friendships and Community Connections between People with and without Developmental Disabilities*. Baltimore: Paul Brookes.

Arnett, A. (1989) *Dealing with Violence*. Privately published coursebook, Hertfordshire Social Services Training Department, New Barnfield, Hatfield, Hertfordshire.

Arscott, K. (1997) 'Assessing the competence of people with learning disabilities to make decisions about treatment', *Tizard Learning Disability Review* **2** (2), 17–28.

Ashdown, R., Carpenter, B. and Bovair, K. (1991) 'The curriculum challenge', in Ashdown, R., Carpenter, B. and Bovair, K. (eds) *The Curriculum Challenge*. London: Falmer Press.

Ashton, G. (1994) 'Medical Treatment', *SLD Experience* **8**, Spring 1-2.

Ashton, G. and Ward, A. (1992) *Mental Handicap and the Law*. London: Sweet and Maxwell.

Asian Disability Advisory Project Team (1993) *Asian and Disabled. A Study into the Needs of People with Disbilities in the Bradford Area*. York: Barnardos Keighly Project and the Spastics Society.

Asindua, S. (1995) 'Comparing urban and rural CBR', *CBR News,* **19**, Jan.–April, 6–7

Auletta, R. and DeRosa, A. (1991) 'Self–concepts of adolescent siblings of children with mental retardation', *Perceptual Motor Skills* **73**, 211–4.

Azmi, S., Emerson, E., Caine, A. and Hatton, C. (1996) *Improving Services for Asian People with Learning Disabilities. The views of users and carers*. Manchester: Hester Adrian Research Centre, University of Manchester.

Badat, H. and Wahll–Roberts, D. (1994) *Bridging the Gap*. London: RNID.

Baker, J. (1997) 'Music therapy for clients with profound and multiple learning difficulties', *PMLD Link* **27**, 6–8.

Baker, R. (1993) 'Medical Needs in a Service for People with Learning Difficulties', in Brigden, P. and Todd, M. (eds) *Concepts in Community Care for People with a Learning Difficulty*. Hampshire: Macmillan Press.

Banes, D. and Coles, C. (1995) *IT for All – developing an IT curriculum for pupils with severe or profound and multiple learning difficulties*. London: David Fulton Publishers.

Barber, M. (1990) 'Identifying and meeting the needs of students with PMLD using micro–technology', Paper presented to International Special Educational Needs Congress, Cardiff, July–August.

Barber, M. (1995) 'Contingency awareness: Putting research into the classroom', in Coupe–O'Kane, J. and Smith, B. (eds) *Taking Control: Enabling People with Learning Difficulties*. London: David Fulton Publishers.

Barnes, C. (1991) *Disabled People in Britain and Discrimination*. London: Hurst.

Barraga, N. (1986) 'Sensory Perceptual Development', in Scholl, G. *Foundations of Education for Blind and Visually Handicapped Children and Youth*. New York: American Foundation for the Blind.

Barry, C. (1996) 'Self–advocacy and students with PMLD: What does it mean in practice?' Unpublished MEd dissertation. Birmingham: School of Education, The University of Birmingham.

Bartley, S. (1980) *Introduction to Perception*. New York: Harper and Row Publishers.

Bates, E., Benigni, L., Bretherton, I., Camaioni, L. and Volterra V. (1979) *The Emergence of Symbols: Cognition and Communication in Infancy*. New York: Academic Press.

Baxter, C., Poonia, K., Ward, L. and Nadirshaw, Z. (1990) *Double Discrimination. Issues and Services for People with Learning Difficulties from Black and Ethnic Minority Communities*. London: King's Fund Centre.

Baxter, C.K. (1989) *Cancer Support and Ethnic Minority and Migrant Work Communities*. Cancerlink.

Baxter, K., Knight, S., McCullough, L., McLeod, B., Reynolds, W. and Tilley, J. (1994) *Fundamental Activities*, available from PO Box 149, Nottingham NG3 5PU.

Bayley, M. (1997) *What Price Friendship? Encouraging the Relationships of People with Learning Difficulties*. Minehead, Somerset: Hexagon Publishing.

Beattie, A. (1994) 'Healthy alliances or dangerous liaisons? The challenge of working together in health promotion', in Leathard, A. (ed.) *Going Inter-professional: Working Together for Health and Welfare*. London: Routledge.

Bedko, J. M., Perry, A. and Bryson, S. (1996) 'Multiple Method Validation Study of Facilitated Communication: II: Individual Differences and Subgroup Results', *Journal of Autism and Developmental Disorder,* **26**, February.

Bee, H. (1995) *The Developing Child*, 7th edn. New York: Harper and Row.

Begum, N. (1992) *Something to be Proud of: the lives of Asian Disabled People and Carers in Waltham Forest*. London: Race Relations Unit and Disability Unit, London Borough of Waltham Forest.

Beresford, P. and Trevillion, S. (1995), *Developing Skills for Community Care: a Collaborative Approach*. Aldershot: Arena.

Best, A. (1992) *Teaching Children with Visual Impairments*. Milton Keynes: Open University Press.

Best, A. (1997) 'Management issues in multiple disability', in Mason, H. and McCall, S. (eds) *Visual Impairment: Access to Education for Children and Young People*. London: David Fulton Publishers.

Black, P. and Harlen, W. (1990) 'How to teach learning', *Education Guardian,* 24 April.

Bloom, L. (1973) *One Word at a Time. The Use of Single Word Utterances before Speech*. The Hague: Mouton.

Bobath Centre for Children with Cerebral Palsy (1996) *Explanatory Literature*. Bradbury House, 250 East End Road, London N2 8AU

Bower, T. (1977) *The Perceptual World of the Child*. London: Fontana.

Bower, T. (1979) 'Origins of meaning in perceptual development, in Pick, A. (ed.) *Perception and its Development: A Tribute to Eleanor J. Gibson*. New York: John Wiley.

Bozic, N. (1997) 'Constructing the room: multi–sensory rooms in educational contexts', *European Journal of Special Needs Education,* **12** (1) 54–70.

Bozic, N. and Murdoch, H. (eds) (1995) *Learning Through Interaction*. London: David Fulton Publishers.

Bradley, A. (1993) 'Evaluation of Community Based Education Course', Unpublished Report to Ministry of Education, Malaysia.

Bradley, A. (1994) Better Chances – Better Lives. Video course for Children with Multiple Disability, Leonard Cheshire Foundation International, London.

Bradley, H. (1991) *Assessing Communication Together: A Systematic Approach to Assessing and Developing Early Communication Skills in Children and Adults with Multisensory Impairments*. Cardiff: APLD Publications.

Bradley, H. (1994) 'Communication for Living: assessment and intervention strategies based around using everyday activities and routines', Module 2: *Unit 3,Interdisciplinary Work with People with Profound and Multiple Learning Disabilities*. Birmingham: School of Education, The University of Birmingham.

Bradley, H. (1994) *Encouraging and developing early communication skills in adults with multiple disabilities.* Focus Factsheet. London: RNIB Publications.

Bradley, H. and Norris, D. (1993) 'The Development of Communication'. Unpublished paper.

Bradley, H. *Assessing Challenges Together,* (in preparation)

Bradley, P. and Darbyshire, P. (1993) 'Helping with Multiple Handicap', in Shanley, E. and Starrs, T. (eds) *Learning Disabilities: A Handbook of Care,* 2nd edn. Edinburgh: Churchill Livingstone.

Bradley, V. (1994) 'Evolution of a new service paradigm', in Bradley, V., Ashbaugh, A. and Blaney, B. (eds) *Creating Individual Supports for People with Developmental Disabilities – A Mandate for Change at Many Levels.* Baltimore: Paul H. Brookes.

Brainwave Charity (undated) *Explanatory Literature.* The Brainwave Centre, Huntworth Gate, Bridgwater, Somerset TA6 6LQ

Brar, B. (1992) 'Research and evaluation in community based rehabilitation – some views derived from UNICEF experience', *ActionAid Disability News* 3 (2) 35–41.

Bray, A., MacArthur, J. and Ballard, K. (1988) 'Education for pupils with profound disabilities: issues of policy, curriculum, teaching methods and evaluation', *European Journal of Special Needs Education,* 3 (4) 207–24.

Brechin, A. and Swain, J. (1987) *Changing Relationships – Shared Action Planning with People with a Mental Handicap.* London: Harper and Row.

Brennan, W. (1985) *Curriculum for Special Needs.* Milton Keynes: Open University Press.

Brill, S. (1997) 'Josephine's sensory garden', *Information Exchange,* 49, March, 22–23.

Brinker, R. and Lewis, M. (1982a) 'Discovering the competent handicapped infant: a process approach to assessment and intervention', *Topics in Early Childhood Special Education,* 2 (2), 1–16.

Brinker, R. P. and Lewis, M. (1982b) 'Making the world work with microcomputers: a learning prosthesis for handicapped infants', *Exceptional Children,* 49, 163–70.

British Epilepsy Association (undated) *Towards a New Understanding: The Modern Management of Epilepsy.* Leeds: BEA.

British Institute for Brain Injured Children (undated) *Explanatory Literature.* Knowle Hall, Bridgwater, Somerset TA7 8PJ.

Brown, A. (1997) 'An exciting new approach to music making', *PMLD Link* 27, 20.

Brown, D., Stewart, D. and Mallett, A. (1997) 'Virtual rooms', *The SLD Experience* 17, Spring, 15–16.

Brown, E. (1996) *Religious Education for All.* London: David Fulton Publishers.

Brown, F. and Lehr, D. (1989) *Persons with Profound Disabilities: Issues and Practice.* Baltimore: Paul H. Brookes.

Brown, H. (1982) 'Grown–up Children: an Exploration of Parents' Experience of their Mentally Handicapped Sons and Daughters in Adulthood, with Regard to Sexual Issues'. Unpublished Dissertation, Chelsea College, University of London.

Burchess, I. (1990) *Interaction Profile Designed by the Intensive Support Team.* Woodfield House, Bewdley Rd, Kidderminster, Worcs.

Burford, B. (1986) 'Communication through movement', in Shanley, E. (ed.) *Mental Handicap – A Handbook of Care.* Edinburgh: Churchill Livingstone.

Burford, B. (1989) 'Action cycles: rhythmic actions for engagement with children and young adults with profound mental handicap', *European Journal of Special Needs Education* 3, 189–206.

Butt, J. and Mirza, K. (1996) *Social Care and Black Communities: A review of recent research studies.* London: HMSO.

Buultjens, M. (1997) 'Functional vision assessment and development in children and young people with multiple disabilities and visual impairment', in Mason, H. and McCall, S. (eds) *Visual Impairment: Access to Education for Children and Young People.* London: David Fulton Publishers.

Byers, R. (1990) 'Topics: From myth to objectives', *British Journal of Special Education* 17 (3), 109–12.

Byers, R. (1994a) 'Providing opportunities for effective learning', in Rose, R., Fergusson A., Coles, C., Byers, R. and Banes D. (eds) *Implementing the Whole Curriculum for Pupils with Learning Difficulties.* London: David Fulton Publishers.

Byers, R. (1994b) 'Teaching as a dialogue: teaching approaches and learning styles in schools for pupils with learning difficulties', in Coupe, J., O'Kane, B. and Smith, B. (eds) *Taking Control: Enabling People with Learning Difficulties*. London: David Fulton Publishers.

Byers, R. (1996) 'Classroom processes', in Carpenter, B., Ashdown R. and Bovair, K. (eds) *Enabling Access*. London: David Fulton Publishers.

Byers, R. and Rose, R. (1996) *Planning the Curriculum for Pupils with Special Educational Needs*. London: David Fulton Publishers.

Cahill, M. (1992) 'The arts and special educational needs', *Arts Education* December, 12–16.

Caldwell, P. (1996) *Getting in Touch: Ways of Working with People with Severe Learning Disabilities and Extensive Support Needs*. Brighton: Pavilion Publishing/Joseph Rowntree Foundation.

Campbell, T. (1994) 'Equipped for Independence or Self-Determination?' *British Journal of Occuptional Therapy*, March **57** (3).

Campaign for Mentally Handicapped People (1972) *Our Life*. London: CMH.

Campos, M. (1992) Personal Interview.

Carpenter B (1997b) 'The interface between the curriculum and the Code', *British Journal of Special Education,* **24**, (1),18–20.

Carpenter, B. (ed.) (1997b) *Families in Context: Emerging trends in family support and early intervention*. London: David Fulton Publishers.

Carpenter, B. and Ashdown, R. (1996) 'Enabling access', in Carpenter, B., Ashdown, R. and Bovair, K. (eds) *Enabling Access: Effective Teaching and Learning for Pupils with Learning Difficulties*. London: David Fulton Publishers.

Carson, D. (1992) 'Legality of responding to the sexuality of a client with profound learning disabilities'. *Mental Handicap*, **20**, (2), 85–87.

*Children Act* 1989. London: HMSO.

Chitiyo, F. (1996) Letter to *CBR News,* **22**, Jan.–April, 3.

Churchill, J., Craft, A., Holding, A. and Horrocks, C. (eds) (1996) *It Could Never Happen Here! The Prevention and Treatment of Sexual Abuse of Adults with Learning Disabilities in Residential Settings*. Chesterfield and Nottingham: Association for Residential Care/National Association for the Protection from Sexual Abuse of Adults and Children with Learning Disabilities.

Clare, M. (1990) *Developing Self–Advocacy Skills with People with Disabilities and Learning Difficulties*. London: Further Education Unit.

Clarke, M. (1990) 'Epilepsy: Identification and management', in Hogg, J. Sebba, J. and Lambe, L. *Profound Retardation and Multiple Impairment: Volume 3 Medical and Physical Care and Management*. London: Chapman and Hall.

Clegg, J. A., Standen, P. J. and Cromby, J. (1991) 'Interactions Between Adults with Profound Intellectual Disability and Staff', *Australia and New Zealand Journal of Developmental Disabilities.* **17**, 377–89.

Clough, P. and Lindsay, G. (1991) *Integration and the Support Services: Changing Roles in Special Education*. Windsor: NFER/Nelson.

Clowes, M. J. (1997) 'Guidance needed on social excursion funds', *Community Care,* 3–9 April, 12.

Cocking, I. and Athwal, S. (1990) 'A special case for treatment', *Social Work Today,* **21** (2), 12–13.

Cole, O. (1986) 'Medical Screening of Adults at Social Education Centres: Whose responsibility?' *Mental Handicap* **14**, June 54–6.

Coles, C. (1994) 'A multidisciplinary approach to the whole curriculum', in Rose, R., Fergusson, A., Coles, C., Byers, R. and Banes, D. (eds) *Implementing the Whole Curriculum for Pupils with Learning Difficulties*. London: David Fulton Publishers.

Collacott, R. A. (1987) 'Atlantoaxial instability in Down's Syndrome', *British Medical Journal* **18**, April, 988–9.

Collis, M. and Lacey, P. (1996) *Interactive Approaches to Teaching – a Framework for INSET.* London: David Fulton Publishers.

Confederation of Indian Organisations (1986) *Asians and Disabilities*. London: CIO.

Confederation of Indian Organisations (1987) *Double Bind: to be disabled and Asian.* London: CIO.

Coninx, F. and Moore, J. (1997) 'The Multiply Handicapped Deaf Child', in McCraken, W. and Laoide–Kemp, S. (eds) *Audiology in Education.* London: Whurr Publishers.

Conneally, S., Boyle, G. and Smith, F. (1992) 'An evaluation of the use of small group homes for adults with a severe and profound mental handicap', *Mental Handicap Research* **5**, 146–168.

Contact a Family (1991) *The CAF Directory of Specific Conditions and Rare Syndromes in Children with their Family Support Networks,* London: Contact a Family.

Contact a Family (1996) *Siblings and Special Needs Factsheet,* London: Contact a Family.

Conway, P. and Baker, P. (1996) 'Integration and education: theory and practice', in Coupe O'Kane, J. and Goldbart, J. (eds) *Whose Choice?* London: David Fulton Publishers.

Cooper, D. and Hersov, J. (1986) *We Can Change the Future* (A staff training resource on self–advocacy for people with learning difficulties). London: NBHS/SKILL.

Cope, R. and Olson, S. (1987) 'Abnormalities of the Cervical Spine in Down's Syndrome: Diagrams, Risks and Review of the Literature, with Particular Reference to the Special Olympics', *Southern Medical Journal* **80**,1, 33–6.

Corbett, J. (1996) *Bad–Mouthing: The Language of Special Needs.* London: Falmer Press.

Coton, E. and Kinsman, R. (1983) *Conductive Education and Adult Hemiplegia.* Edinburgh: Churchill Livingstone.

Coupe, J. and Goldbart, J. (1988) *Communication Before Speech.* London: Croom Helm.

Coupe, J., Barton, L., Barber, M., Collins, L., Levy, D. and Murphy, D. (1985) *Affective Communication Assessment.* Manchester:MEC. Available from Melland School, Holmcroft Road, Gorton, Manchester M19 7NG

Coupe–O'Kane, J., Porter, J. and Taylor, A. (1994) 'Meaningful content and contexts for learning', in Coupe–O'Kane, J. and Smith, B. (eds) *Taking Control: Enabling People with Learning Difficulties,* London: David Fulton Publishers.

Cox, Y. (1993) 'Tailor made for the job', *Nursing Times* **89** (22), 66.

Craft, A. (1987) *Mental Handicap and Sexuality: Issues and Perspectives.* Tunbridge Wells: Costello.

Craft, A. and Craft, M. (1979) *Handicapped Married Couples.* London: Routledge.

Cragg, R. and Garvey, K. (1991) *What's on – A comprehensive menu of ordinary living activities for adults.* Available from 302 Station Road, Kings Heath, Birmingham Bl4 7TZ

Cunningham, C., Morgan, P. and McGucken, R. B. (1984) 'Down's Syndrome: Is dissatisfaction with disclosure of diagnosis inevitable?' *Developmental Medicine and Child Neurology* **26**, 33–9.

Dattilo, J. (1991) 'Recreation and leisure', in Meyer, H., Peck, A. and Brown L. (eds) *Critical Issues in the Lives of People with Severe Disabilities.* Baltimore: Paul H. Brookes.

Davie, R. (1993) 'Implementing Warnock's multi–professional approach', in Visser, J. and Upton, G. (eds) *Special Education in Britain After Warnock.* London: David Fulton Publishers.

Dearing, Sir R. (1994) *The National Curriculum and its Assessment.* London: SCAA.

Denziloe, J. (1994) *Fun and Games. Practical Leisure Ideas for People with Profound Disabilities.* Oxford: Butterworth Heinemann.

Department for Education (1994) *Code of Practice on the Identification and Assessment of Special Educational Needs.* London: DfE.

Department for Education (1996) *Education Act.* London: HMSO.

Department for Education and Employment (1997) *Excellence for All Children – meeting special educational needs.* London: HMSO.

Department of Education and Science (1970) *Education (Handicapped Children) Act.* London: HMSO.

Department of Education and Science (1978) *Special Educational Needs (The Warnock Report).* London: HMSO.

Department of Education and Science (1981) *Education Act.* London: HMSO.

Department of Education and Science (1985) *Curriculum Matters. The Curriculum from 5–16.* London: HMSO.

Department of Education and Science (1988) *Education Reform Act.* London: HMSO

Department of Health (1970) *Chronically Sick and Disabled Persons' Act.* London: HMSO.

Department of Health (1992) *The Health of the Nation: A strategy for health in England.* London: HMSO.

Department of Health and Social Services (1995) *Disability Discrimination Act.* London: HMSO.

Department of Health (undated) *Learning Disability: Meeting Needs through Targeting Skills.* London: Department of Health.

Detheridge, T. (ed.) (1990) *Resources for Severe Learning Difficulties.* Coventry: National Council for Educational Technology.

Detheridge, T. (1997) 'Bridging the communication gap (for pupils with profound and multiple learning difficulties)', *British Journal of Special Education,* **24**, (1), 21–5.

Dorrell, S. (1996) *Primary Care: The Future.* London: NHS Executive.

Downs, C. and Craft, A. (1996a) 'Sexuality and people with profound and multiple impairment: A positive approach', in Coupe O'Kane, J. and Goldbart, J. (eds) *Whose Choice? Contentious issues for those working with people with learning difficulties.* London: David Fulton Publishers.

Downs, C. and Craft, A. (1996b) 'Sexuality and Profound and Multiple Impairment', *Tizard Learning Disability Review,* **1** (4) 17–22.

Downs, C. and Craft, A. (1997a) *Safeguards in Systems: A Handbook. Strategies for Devising Guidelines Relating to the Sexuality of Children and Adults with Profound and Multiple Impairments.* Brighton: Pavilion Publishing.

Downs, C. and Craft, A. (1997b) *Sex in Context: A Personal and Social Development Programme for Children and Adults with Profound and Multiple Impairments; Strategies for Devising a Programme and Recommendations for Teaching and Learning.* Brighton: Pavilion Publishing

Dufresne, D., and Laux B. (1994) 'From Facilities to Supports – The Changing Organisation', in Bradley, V., Ashbaugh, J., and Blaney, B. (eds) *Creating Individual Supports for People with Developmental Disabilities – A Mandate for Change at Many Levels.* Baltimore: Paul H. Brookes.

Dunst, C. J. (1980) *A Clinical and Educational Manual for use with the Uzgiris and Hunt Scales of Infant Psychological Development,* Baltimore: University Park Press.

*Education Act* 1981. London: HMSO.

Ellis, A. and Beattie, G. (1986) *The Psychology of Language and Communication.* London: Weidenfeld and Nicolson.

Ellis, P. (1996) *Sound Therapy: The Music of Sound.* Bristol: The Soundbeam Project.

Emerson, E., Barrett, S. and Cummings, R. (undated) *Using Analogue Assessments.* Canterbury: University of Kent at Canterbury.

English Nursing Board for Nursing, Health Visiting and Midwifery (1985) *Caring for People with Mental Handicap, a Learning Package for Nurses.* London: ENB.

Ephraim, G. (1986) *A Brief Introduction to Augmented Mothering. Playtrac Pamphlet.* London: Save the Children.

Erin, J. (1996) 'Functional Vision Assessment and Instruction of Children and Youths with Multiple Disability', in Corn, A. and Koenig, A. (eds) *Foundations of Low Vision: Clinical and Functional Perspectives.* New York: AFB.

Essex, C. (1991) 'Screening for People with Mental Handicap', *British Medical Journal,* 302, 239.

Evans, P. and Theiss–Tait, K. (1986) 'Massage: An alternative starting point', *Talking Sense* **32,** (1).

Evans, P. and Ware, J. (1987) *Special Care Provision – The Education of Children with Profound and Multiple Learning Difficulties.* Windsor: NFER–Nelson.

Fairbairn, G. (1996) *Sex Matters.* Keynote speech at conference held in Belfast, March 1995. Brighton: Pavilion Publishing.

Farrell, I. and Mann, K. (1994) *Music Unlimited: The Performer's Guide to New Audiences.* Reading: Harwood Academic Publishers.

Farrell, P. (1991) 'Behavioural teaching: a fact of life?' *British Journal of Special Education,* **19** (4), 145–8.

Farrell, P. (1996) 'Discussion: integration – where do we go from here?', in Coupe O'Kane, J. and Goldbart, J. (eds) *Whose Choice?* London: David Fulton Publishers.

Farrell, P., McBrien, J. and Foxen, T. (1992) *EDY: Teaching People with Severe Learning Difficulties,* 2nd edn. Manchester: Manchester University Press.

FEU/MENCAP (1994) *Learning for Life.* London: FEU/MENCAP.

Felce, D. and Emerson, R. (1996) 'Realities and Challenges', *Journal of Applied Research in Intellectual Disabilities,* **9**, 284–8.

Felce, D. (1994) 'Costs, quality and staffing in services for people with severe learning disabilities', *Journal of Mental Health,* **3**, 495–506.

Firth, H. and Rapley, M. (1990) *From Acquaintance to Friendship: Issues for People with Learning Disabilities.* Kidderminster: BIMH Publications.

Fitton, P. (1994) *Listen to Me: Communicating the Needs of People with Profound Intellectual and Multiple Disabilities.* London: Jessica Kingsley.

Fitton, P., O'Brian, C. and Willson, J. (1995) *Home at Last.* London: Jessica Kingsley.

Fletcher, B. C. and Payne, R. L. (1982) 'Levels of reported stressors and strains amongst school teachers: some UK data', *Educational Review* **34**, (3).

French, S. (1993) 'What's so great about independence?', in Swain, J., Finkelstein, V., French, S. and Oliver, M. *Disabling Barriers – Enabling Environments.* London: Sage Publications/The Open University.

Fryers, T. (1984) *The Epidemiology of Severe Intellectual Impairment: The Dynamics of Prevalence.* London: Academic Press.

Fulford, G. E. and Brown J. K. (1976)' Position as a Cause of Deformity in Children with Cerebral Palsy', *Developmental Medicine and Child Neurology* **18**, 305–14.

Fulton, J. (1994) 'Journey', in Keith, L. (ed.) *Mustn't Grumble.* London: The Women's Press.

Furneaux, B. (1969) *The Special Child.* Harmondsworth: Penguin Books.

Further Education Unit/Mencap (1994) *Learning for Life: A pack to support learning opportunities for adults who have profound intellectual and multiple physical disabilities.* London: FEU/Mencap.

Ganesh, S., Potter, J. and Fraser, W. (1994) 'An Audit of Physical Health Needs of Adults with Profound Learning Disability in a Hospital Population', *Mental Handicap Research,* **7** (3) 228–36.

Gardner, A., and Smyly, S.R. (1997) 'How do we stop 'doing' and start listening: responding to the emotional needs of people with learning disabilities', *British Journal of Learning Disabilities* **25**, 26–30.

Garner, P. and Sandow, S. (1995) 'Dilemmas for advocacy and self–advocacy', in Garner, P. and Sandow, S. (eds) *Advocacy, Self–advocacy and Special Needs.* London: David Fulton Publishers.

Gee, S. (1997) 'Connected by music', *The Times Educational Supplement* 29 August.

Gibson, R. (1983) 'The Education of Feeling', in Gibson, R. (ed.) *The Education of Feeling.* Cambridge: Cambridge University Institute of Education/Cambridge University Press.

Gillyon, M. and Lambert, T. (1997) 'Realm of the Services (a colourful and innovative project to develop and stimulate the services of clients with disabilities)', *Nursing Times,* 7 May, 32–5.

Glenn, S. M. and Cunningham, C. C. (1984a) 'Selective auditory preferences and the use of automated equipment by severely, profoundly and multiply handicapped children'. *Journal of Mental Deficiency Research* **28**, 281–96.

Glenn, S. M. and Cunningham C. C. (1984b) 'Special care – but active learning', *Special Education: Forward Trends* **11**, 33–6.

Glenn, S. (1987) Activities to encourage children's development within the early sensori–motor period, in Smith, B. (ed.) *Interactive Approaches to Teaching Children with Severe Learning Difficulties.* Birmingham: Westhill College.

Glenn, S. and O'Brien, Y. (1994) 'Microcomputers: do they have a part to play in the education of children with PMLDs?', in Ware, J. (ed.) *Educating Children with Profound and Multiple Learning Difficulties.* London: David Fulton Publishers.

Glenn, S., Cunningham, C. and Shorrock, A. (1995) 'Social interaction in multisensory environments', in Bozic, N. and Murdoch, H. (eds) *Learning Through Interaction.* London: David Fulton Publishers.

Goldbart, J. (1980) Play Context and Language in the Special Classroom. Seminar Paper. Manchester: Hester Adrian Research Centre.

Goldbart, J. (1994) 'Pre–intentional communication: opening the communication curriculum to students with profound and multiple learning difficulties', in Ware, J. (ed.) *Educating Children with Profound and Multiple Learning Difficulties.* London: David Fulton Publishers.

Goldbart, J. (1995) 'Communication' *Module 1 Unit 5 of Interdisciplinary Work with People with Profound and Multiple Learning Disabilties*. Birmingham: School of Education, University of Birmingham.

Goldbart, J. and Rigby, J. (1989) 'Observational assessment of early interactions. Establishing relationships with people with PMLD'. Paper presented to the University of Manchester Department of Child and Adolescent Psychiatry Regional Study Day, 10 April.

Goldsmith, E., Golding, R. M., Garstang, R. A. and MacRae, A. W. (1992) 'A Technique to Measure Windswept Deformity', *Physiotherapy* **78** (4), 235–42.

Goldsmith, J. and Goldsmith, L. (1996a) Sym*metrical Body Support: A Carers' Guide to the Management of Posture*. Ledbury: The Helping Hand Company.

Goldsmith, J. and Goldsmith, L. (1996b) *Symmetrical Body Support: A Therapists' Guide to Prescription*. Ledbury: The Helping Hand Company.

Greater London Association for Disabled People (1987) *Disability and Ethnic Minority Communities: a Study in Three London Boroughs*. London: GLAD.

Greenhalgh, P. (1994) *Emotional Growth and Learning*. London: Routledge.

Griffiths, M. (1994) *Transition to Adulthood: The Role of Education for Young People with Severe Learning Difficulties*. London: David Fulton.

Grove, N. and Park, K. (1993) 'A declaration of intent: The dangers of "functional" communication', *PMLD Link* **17**, 8–11.

Grove, N. and Park, K. (1996) 'Life Quilts' for people with severe and profound learning difficulties: a venture into the unknown'. *PMLD Link* **24**. Spring.

Grove, N. and Park, K. (1996b) *Odyssey Now*. London: Jessica Kingsley.

Grove, N., Porter, J. and Bunning, K. (in preparation) Validating the Meaning of Communication by People with Severe and Profound Learning Disabilities.

Gunaratnum, Y. (1990) 'Asian Carers', *Carelink* **11** (6).

Hall, J. (1996) 'Integration, inclusion – what does it all mean?' in Coupe O'Kane, J. and Goldbart, J. (eds) *Whose Choice?* London: David Fulton Publishers.

Halle, J. W. (1987) 'Teaching language in the natural environment: An analysis of spontaneity', *Journal of the Association for People with Severe Handicaps*. **12**, 79–86.

Hallett, R., Hare, N. and Miller, A. D. (1987) 'Description and Evaluation of an Assessment Form'. *Physiotherapy*. **73** (5), 220–5.

Halliday, P. (1990) 'The Management of Continence', in Hogg, J., Sebba, J. and Lambe, L. *Profound Retardation and Multiple Impairment: Volume 3 Medical and Physical Care and Management*. London: Chapman and Hall.

Halpin, D. and Lewis, A. (1996) 'The impact of the National Curriculum on twelve special schools in England', *European Journal of Special Needs Education* **11** (1), 95–105.

Hanby, G., Atkinson, M. and Howard, J. (1997) *Controversial Issues in Special Education*. London: David Fulton Publishers.

Hanko, G. (1995) *Special Needs in Ordinary Classrooms: from staff support to staff development*. 3rd edn. London: David Fulton Publishers.

Harris, J. and Hewett, D. (1996) *Positive Approaches to Challenging Behaviours*. Kidderminster: BILD First Draft Publications.

Hart, E. and Bond, M. (1995) *Action Research for Health and Social Care*. Milton Keynes: Open University Press.

Hart, S. (1991) 'The collaborative dimension: Risks and rewards of collaboration', in McLaughlin, C. and Rouse, M. (eds) *Supporting Schools*. London: David Fulton

Hastings, C., Bixby, P. and Chaudhry–Lawton, R. (1987) *Superteams: A Blueprint for Success*. London: Fontana.

Haworth, J.T. (1997) *Work, Leisure and Wellbeing*. London: Routledge.

Heal, M. and Wigram, T. (1993) Introduction, in Heal, M. and Wigram,T. (eds) *Music Therapy in Health and Education*. London: Jessica Kingsley.

Hegarty, S., Pocklington, K. and Lucas, D. (1982) *Integration in Action: Case Studies of the Integration of Pupils with Special Needs*. Slough: NFER/NELSON.

Hegarty, S. (1993) 'Reviewing the literature on integration'. *European Journal of Special Needs Education* **8** (3), 194–200.

Hegarty, J. R. and Gale, E. (1996) 'Touch as a Therapeutic Medium for People with Challenging Behaviours', *British Journal of Learning Disabilities* **24** 26–32.

Hersov, J. (1996) 'The rise of self–advocacy in Britain', in Dybwad, G. and Bersanti, H. Jr. (eds) *Self–advocacy by People with Disabilities*. Cambridge MA: Brookline Books.

Hewett, D. (1995) 'Challenging Behaviour'. *Module 2 Unit 4, 'Interdisciplinary Work with People with Profound and Multiple Learning Difficulties*. Birmingham: School of Education, University of Birmingham.

Hinchcliffe, V. (1994) 'A special need, self advocacy curriculum and the needs of children with severe learning difficulties', in Sandow, S. (ed.) *Whose Special Needs?* London: Paul Chapman.

HMI (1991) *Interdisciplinary Support for Young Children with SEN*. London: DES.

Hogg, J. and Cavet, J. (eds) (1995) *Making Leisure Provision for People with Profound Learning and Multiple Disabilities*. London: Chapman and Hall.

Hogg, J. and Lambe, L. (1988) *Sons and Daughters with Profound Retardation and Multiple Handicaps Attending Schools and Social Education Centres: Final Report*. London: Mencap.

Hogg, J., Reeves, D., Mudford, O. and Roberts, J. (1995) 'The Development of Observational Techniques to Assess Behaviour States and Affective Behaviour in Adults with Profound and Multiple Intellectual Disabilities'. Unpublished Paper. White Top Research Centre: University of Dundee

Hogg, J., Remington, R. E. and Foxen, T. H. (1979) 'Classical conditioning of profoundly retarded, multiply handicapped children', *Developmental Medicine and Child Neurology* **21** 779–86.

Hogg, J. and Sebba, J. (1986) *Profound Retardation and Multiple Impariment*. Vol. 2 Education and Therapy. London: Groom Helm.

Holdgrafer, G. and Dunst, C. J. (1986) 'Communicative competence: from research to practice', in *Topics in Early Childhood, Special Education*. **6** (3) Texas USA: PRO–ED.

Holman, A. (1997) 'In the absence of legislation, follow the best interests guidelines', *Community Living* **10**, (3), 2.

Holmes, A. and Parrish, A. (1996) 'Health of the Nation for People with Learning Disabilities', *British Journal of Nursing* **5**, (19) 1184–88.

Home Office, Department of Health, Department of Education and Science, Welsh Office (1992) *Working Together under the Children Act 1989*. London: HMSO.

Hooper, J. (1993) 'Developing interaction through shared musical experiences: a strategy to enhance and validate the descriptive approach', in Heal, M. and Wigram, T. (eds) *Music Therapy in Health and Education*. London: Jessica Kingsley.

Hornby, G. (1994) *Counselling in Child Disability, Skills for Working with Parents*. London: Chapman and Hall

Hughes, A., McAuslane, L. and Schur, H. (1996) 'Comparing quality of life for people with learning disabilities and people who are unemployed or retired', *British Journal of Learning Disabilities* **24** (3), 99–103

Iso-Hola, S. E. (1997) 'A psychological analysis of leisure and health', in Haworth, J. T. *Work, Leisure and Wellbeing*. London: Routledge.

Jan, J. E., Espezel, H. and Appleton, R. E. (1994) 'The treatment of sleep disorders with melatonin', *Developmental Medicine and Child Neurology* **36**, 97–107.

Jay, P. (1974) *Coping with Disablement*. London: Consumers Association.

Jeffery, H. and Hoggs, M. (1995) 'How to Get Good Healthcare', in Brown, H. and Benson, S. (eds) *A Practical Guide to Working with People with Learning Disabilities* 2nd edn. London: Hawke Publications.

Jenkinson, J. C. (1993) 'Integration of students with severe and multiple learning difficulties', *European Journal of Special Education* **8** (3), 320–35.

Jenkinson, J. C. (1997) *Mainstream or Special? Educating Students with Disabilties*. London: Routledge.

Jones, C. (1994) 'Innovative practice. Employment for People with Multiple Disability', in French, S. (ed.) *On Equal Terms*. Oxford: Butterworth-Heinemann.

Jones, D. (1995) 'Learning disabilities: an alternative frame of reference', *British Journal of Occupational Therapy* **58**, (10), 423–6.

Jones, L. (1989) *The Kidderminster Curriculum for children and adults with profound, multiple learning difficulties.* Birmingham: School of Psychology, University of Birmingham.

Jones, L. (1993) 'Working with students who have profound and multiple learning difficulties', in Harris, J. (ed.) *Innovations in Educating Children with Severe Learning Difficulties.* Chorley, Lancashire: The Brothers of Charity.

Jones, P. and Cregan, A. (1986) *Sign and Symbol Communication for Mentally Handicapped People.* London: Croom Helm.

Jordan, R. and Powell, S. (1994) 'Whose curriculum? Critical notes on integration and entitlement', *European Journal of Special Needs Education* **9**, (1), 27–39.

Kay, B., Rose, S. and Turnbull, J. (1995) *Learning Disability Nursing Project: Resource Package.* London: Department of Health.

Kay, B., Rose, S. and Turnbull, J. (1996) *Continuing the Commitment: The Report of the Learning Disability Nursing Project.* London: Department of Health.

Keilhofner, G. (1995) A Model of Human Occupation. Theory and Application, 2nd edn. Baltimore: Williams and Wilkins.

Kelly, J. R. (1997) 'Activity and ageing: Challenge in retirement', in Haworth, J. T. *Work, Leisure and Wellbeing.* London: Routledge.

Khalfan, K. H. (1992) 'CBR in Zanzibar', *CBR News* 12 Sept.

Kiernan, C. (1974) 'Behaviour Modification', in Clarke, A. M. and Clarke, A. D. B. (eds) *Readings from Mental Deficiency; the Changing Outlook.* London: Methuen.

Kiernan, C. (1991) 'Research: progress and prospects', in Segal, S. and Varma, V. (eds) *Prospects for People with Learning Difficulties.* London: David Fulton Publishers.

Kiernan, C. and Reid, B.(1987) *The Preverbal Communication Schedule.* Windsor: NFER–Nelson.

Kiernan, C., Reid, B. and Goldbart, J. (1986) *Foundations of Communication and Language (FOCAL) Core Manual.* An impact inset pack in association with the British Institute of Mental Handicap (unpublished).

Kings Fund Project Paper (1981) *Number 30, Bringing Mentally Handicapped Children Out of Hospital.* London: Kings Fund.

Kinsella, P. (1993) *Supported Living – A New Paradigm?* Manchester: National Development Team.

Kisanji, J. (1995) 'Attitudes and Beliefs about Disability in Tanzania', in O'Toole, B. and McConkey, R. (eds) *Innovations in Developing Countries for People with Disabilities.* Chorley, Lancashire: Lisieux Hall Publications.

Kitson, D. and Supple, C. (1997) *Equipped to Cope.* Chesterfield and Nottingham: Association for Residential Care/National Association for the Protection from Sexual Abuse of Adults and Children with Learning Disabilities

Kitt, L., Flynn, M. and Rimmer, M. (1997) *Advocating for Health: Personal Health Records.* Harlow Publications (in Press).

Kotagel, S., Gibbons, V. P. and Stith, J. A. (1994) 'Sleep abnormalities in patients with severe cerebral palsy', *Developmental Medicine and Child Neurology* **36**, 304–11.

Kyriacou, C. and Sutcliffe, J. (1978) 'Teacher stress: prevalence, sources and symptoms', *Journal of Educational Psychology* **48**, 159–67.

Lacey, P. (1991) 'Managing the classroom environment' in Tilstone, T. (ed.) Teaching Pupils with Severe Learning Difficulties – Practical Approaches. London: David Fulton Publishers.

Lacey, P. (1995) 'In the front line: special educational needs co–ordinators and liaison', *Support for Learning* **10**, (2), 57–62.

Lacey, P. (1996) 'The Inner Life of Children with Profound and Multiple Learning Disabilities', in Varma, V. (ed.) *The Inner Life of Children with Special Needs.* London: Whurr Publishers.

Lacey, P. (1997) 'Multidisciplinary Teamwork: Practice and Training'. Unpublished PhD thesis, School of Education, University of Birmingham.

Lacey, P. and Lomas, J. (1993) *Support Services and the Curriculum: A Practical Guide to Collaboration.* London: David Fulton Publishers.

Lagerwall, T. (1992) *Review of Community Based Rehabilitation Services run by the Ministry of Health in Kenya.* Vallingby, Sweden: The Swedish Handicap Institute.

Lake District National Park Authority (1996) *Countryside Access for People with Limited Mobility.* Kendal, Cumbria: Lake District National Park Authority.

Lambe, L. and Hogg, J. (1995a) *Children who have Profound and Multiple Learning Disabilities in Tayside Region.* Dundee: White Top Research Unit, University of Dundee.

Lambe, L. and Hogg, J. (1995b) *Their Face to the Wind: Service developments for older people with learning disabilities in Grampian Region.* Glasgow: ENABLE.

Langley, B. (1986) 'Psycho–educational assessment of visually impaired students with additional handicaps', in Ellis, D. (ed.) *Sensory Impairments in Mentally Handicapped People.* Beckenham: Croom Helm.

Latchford, G. (1989) 'Towards an Understanding of Profound Mental Handicap'. Unpublished PhD Thesis. Edinburgh: University of Edinburgh.

Leathard, A. (ed.) (1994) *Going Interprofessional: Working Together for Health and Welfare.* London: Routledge.

Lehr, D. and Noonan, M. (1989) 'Issues in the Education of Students with Complex Health Needs', in Brown, F. and Lehr, F. D. *Persons with Profound Difficulties: Issues and Practices.* Maryland: Paul H. Brookes.

Leifer, D. (1996) 'Take Time to Explain Nursing', *Standard,* **11** (2) 14.

Lewis, A. (1995) *Children's Understanding of Disability.* London: Routledge.

Light, J., Collier, B. and Parnes, P. (1985) 'Communicative interaction between young non–speaking physically disabled children and their primary caregivers: Part 1 – Discourse Patterns', *Augmentative and Alternative Communication* **1**, 74–83.

Limbrick, P. (1993) *First Families, First work: Annual report of One Hundred Hours Service.* West Yorkshire: 100 Hours.

Liswood, I. (1990) *Serving Them Right: Innovation and Powerful Customer Retention Strategies.* New York: Harper and Row.

Longhorn, F. (1988) *A Sensory Curriculum for Very Special People.* London: Souvenir Press.

Loxley, A. (1997) *Collaboration in Health and Welfare.* London: Jessica Kingsley.

MacLean, E. (1990) 'Things to do – people to see ... Leisure, young people with mental handicaps and the community', *Mental Handicap* **18** (4), 169–171.

MacRae, D. (1997) 'Health Care for Women with Learning Disabilities', *Nursing Times* **93**, (15), 58–9.

Male, D. (1996) 'Who goes to SLD Schools?' *Journal of Applied Research in Intellectual Disabilities* **9**, (4), 307–23.

Mansell, J. (1994) 'Challenging Behaviour: The Prospect for Change', *British Journal of Learning Disabilities*, **22**, (1), 2–5.

Marvin, C. (1994) 'Pupils with Profound and Multiple Learning Difficulties and the Changing Face of Integration – an Evaluation of a Mainstream Integration Project'. Unpublished M Ed dissertation. Birmingham: School of Education, University of Birmingham.

Matthews, D. (1996) *The OK Health Check: For assessing and planning the healthcare needs of people with learning disabilities.* Preston: Fairfield Publications.

Maychell, K. and Bradley, J. (1991) *Preparing for Partnership: Multi-agency Support for Special Needs.* Slough: NFER.

Mayston, M. J. (1992) 'Movement disorders in Children', *Medicine and Sports Science* **36** 1–6 Basel: Karger.

McConkey, R. (1981) 'Education without understanding?' *Special Education: Forward Trends* **8** (3), 8–10.

McConkey, R. (1993) *Training for All: Developing Video-based Training Packages for Parent and Community Education.* Paris: UNESCO.

McConkey, R. (1994) *Innovations in Educating Communities about Disabilities.* Chorley, Lancashire: Lisieux Hall Publications.

McConkey, R. and O'Toole, B. (1997) 'Improving the quality of life of people with disabilities in least affluent countries: Insights from Guyana, South America', in Schalock, R. L. and Keith, K. (eds) *Cross-cultural perspectives on Quality of Life.* Washington: American Association on Mental Retardation.

McConkey, R., Morris, I. and Purcell, M. (1996) 'Enhancing communication with adult persons who have an intellectual disability'. Paper presented at the International Conference of IASSID, Helsinki.

McCraken. W. (1994) 'Deaf children with complex needs: a piece in the puzzle'. *Journal of British Association of Teachers of the Deaf.* **18**, (2), 54–60.

McCurtin, A. (1997) *The Manual of Paediatric Feed Practice*, Bicester: Winslow Press.

McEwen, G. and Millar, S. (1997) 'Passports to communication', *CALL Information Sheet No.5*. Edinburgh: The University of Edinburgh.

McGee, J. J., Menaloscino, M. D., Hobbs, D. C. and Menousek, P. E. (1987) *Gentle Teaching – a non–aversive approach to helping persons with mental retardation.* New York: Human Sciences Press.

McGlade, B. and Aquino, R. (1995) 'Mothers of Disabled Children as CBR Workers', in O'Toole, B. and McConkey, R. (eds) *Innovations in Developing Countries for People with Disabilities.* Chorley, Lancashire: Lisieux Hall Publications.

McGrath, M. (1991) *Multidisciplinary Teamwork – Community Mental Handicap Teams.* Aldershot: Avebury.

McInnes, J. M. and Treffrey, J. (1982) *Deaf–Blind Infants and Children.* Milton Keynes: Open University Press.

McKay, C. and Patrick, H. (1995) *The Care Maze: The Law and your Rights to Community Care in Scotland.* Glasgow and Edinburgh: ENABLE and the Scottish Association for Mental Health.

McLarty, M. (1997) 'Putting objects of reference in context', *European Journal of Special Needs Education.* **12**, (1), 12–20.

McLean, J. and Snyder–McLean, L. (1978) *A Transactional Approach to Early Language Training.* Columbus OH: Charles E. Merrill.

McLean, J. and Snyder–McLean, L. (1987) 'Form and function of communicative behaviour among persons with severe developmental disabilities', *Australia and New Zealand Journal of Developmental Disabilities* **13**, 83–98.

Medical Defence Union (1996) *Problems in General Practice: Consent to treatment.* Manchester and London: MDU.

Meehan, S., Moore, G. and Barr, O. (1995) 'Specialist Services for People with Learning Disabilities' *Nursing Times.*, **91**, (13), 33–5.

MENCAP (1997) *Left in the Dark: A report on the challenges facing the UK families of children with learning disabilities*, London: Mencap.

MENCAP London Division Participation Forum (1982) *Speaking for Ourselves.* London: Mencap.

MENCAP London Division Participation Forum (1983) *Have we a Future?* London: Mencap.

Miles, M. (1989) 'Information–Based Rehabilitation for Third World Disability', *Social Science and Medicine* **28** (3), 207–10.

Miles, M. (1993) 'Service development by information, not ideology', in Finkenflugel, H. (ed.) *The Handicapped Community,* Amsterdam: VU University Press.

Miles, S. (1996) 'Engaging with the Disability Rights Movement: the experience of community based rehabilitation in southern Africa', *Disability and Society*, **11**, (4), 501–17.

Miller, C. (1996) 'Relationships between teachers and speech and language therapists', *Child Language Teaching and Therapy.* **12**, (1), 29–38.

Miller, E. J. and Gwynne, E. R. (1974) *A Life Apart: a Pilot Study of Residential Institutions for the Physically Handicapped and the Young Chronically Sick.* London: Tavistock Publications.

Mittler, H. (1994) *Parents Speak Out: International Perspectives on Parents' Experiences of Disability.* Boston: Brookline Press.

Mittler, H. (1995) *Families Speak Out: International Perspectives on Families' Experiences of Disability.* Cambridge MA: Brookline.

Mittler, P. (1996) 'Preparing for self-advocacy,' in Carpenter, B., Ashdown, R. and Bovair, K. *Enabling Access: Effective Teaching and Learning for Pupils with Learning Difficulties.* London: David Fulton Publishers.

Momm, W. and Konig, A. (1990) *From Community Based Rehabilitation to Community Integration Programmes.* Geneva: International Labour Organisation.

Morgan, C. and Murgatroyd, S. (1994) *Total Management Quality in the Public Sector.* Buckingham: Open University Press.

Mount, H. (1995) 'Art, drama and music', in Hogg, J. and Cavet, J. (eds) *Making Leisure Provision for People with Profound Learning and Multiple Disabilities.* London: Chapman and Hall.

MOVE International ((Europe) (undated) *Standing Room Only/Making Strides* (Video). Robertsbridge: Rifton.

MOVE International (Europe) (undated) *Explanatory Literature.* Wolverhampton: University of Wolverhampton.

Mulcahy, C. M., Pountney, T. E., Nelham, R. L., Green, E. M. and Billington,G. D. (1988) 'Adaptive Seating for the Motor Handicapped – Problems, a Solution, Assessment and Prescription', *Physiotherapy*, **74**, (7), 531–6.

Murdoch, H. (1994) '"He can hear when he wants to!" assessment of hearing function for people with learning difficulties'. *British Journal of Learning Disabilities*, **22**, 85–9.

Murphy, G., Carr, J. and Callias, M. (1986) 'Increasing simple toy play in profoundly mentally handicapped children', *Journal of Autism and Developmental Disorder*, **16**, 45–58.

Nafstad, A. (1989) *Space for Interaction: An Attempt to Understand how Congenital Deafblindness Affects Psychological Development.* Dronninglund, Denmark: Nordic Staff Training Centre for Deafblind Services.

NAMH (1996) *A Society for All.* Norwegian Assocation for Mentally Handicappped.

National Association of Bereavement Services (1996) *My Story: a Celebration of my Life.* London: NABS.

*National Health Service and Community Care Act 1990.* London: HMSO.

NCC (1989) *Curriculum Guidance 2. A Curriculum for All.* York: NCC.

NCC (1990) *Curriculum Guidance 3. The Whole Curriculum.* York: NCC.

NCC (1992) *Curriculum Guidance 9. The National Curriculum and Pupils with Severe Learning Difficulties.* York: NCC.

NCH (undated) *Hello, Sister! Hello, Brother!, Leaflet.* London: NCH Action for Children.

Neville, M. (1996) 'Around in a Circle', *Community Care*, February/March, 4–5.

Nind, M. and Hewett, D. (1994) *Access to Communication: Developing the basics of communication with people with severe learning difficulties through Intensive Interaction.* London: David Fulton Publishers.

Nind, M. and Hewett, D. (1996) 'When Age–appropriateness isn't Appropriate' in Coupe O'Kane, J. and Goldbart, J. (eds) *Whose Choice? Contentious issues for those working with people with learning difficulties.* London: David Fulton Publishers.

Nolan, C. (1987) *Under the Eye of the Clock.* London: Pan Books.

Novaco, R. W. (1997) Preface in Stenfort Kroese, B., Dagnan, D. and Loumidis, K. *Cognitive-Behaviour Therapy for People with Learning Disabilities.* London: Routledge.

Nutrition Committee, Canadian Paediatric Society (1994) 'Undernutrition in children with neurodevelopmental disability', *Canadian Medical Association Journal* **151**, (6), 753–9.

Nunkoosing, K. and John, M. (1997) 'Friendships, relationships and the management of rejection and loneliness by people with learning disabilities', *Journal of Learning Disabilities for Nursing, Health and Social Care.* **1**, (1), 10–18.

O'Brien, J. (1987) 'A guide to personal futures planning', in Bellamy, G. and Willcox, B. (eds) *A Comprehensive Guide to the Activities Catalogue: an Alternative Curriculum for Youth and Adults with Severe Disabilities.* Baltimore: Paul H. Brookes.

O'Brien, J. and Lovett, H. (1992) *Finding a Way Toward Everyday Lives. The Contribution of Person Centred Planning.* New York: Centre on Human Policy, Syacruse University.

O'Brien, J. and Lyle O'Brien, C. (1991) *Framework for Accomplishment: Manual for a Workshop for People Developing Better Services.* Georgia: Responsive System Associates.

O'Brien, Y., Glenn, S. and Cunningham, C. (1994) 'Contingency awareness in infants and young children with severe and profound learning difficulties', *International Journal of Disability, Development and Education* **41**, 231–4.

O'Hagan, K. (1993) *Emotional and Psychological Abuse of Children*. Milton Keynes: Open University Press.

O'Toole, B. (1993) 'Community Based Rehabilitation', in Mittler, P., Brouillette, R. and Harris, D. (eds) *World Yearbook of Education 1993*. London: Kogan Page.

Oakes, P. (1997) 'Sexual and Personal Relationships' in Gates, B. (ed.) *Learning Disabilities,* 3rd edn. Edinburgh/London: Churchill Livingstone.

Ockelford, A. (1994) *Objects of reference. Promoting communication skills and concept development with visually impaired children who have other disabilities*. London: RNIB Publications.

OFSTED (Office for Standards in Education) (1993) *Special Needs and the National Curriculum*. London: HMSO.

OFSTED (Office for Standards in Education) (1995) *The OFSTED Handbook – guidance on the inspection of special schools*. London: HMSO.

Okawa, M., Takahashi, K. and Sasaki, H. (1986) 'Disturbance in circadian rhythms in severely brain damaged patients correlated with CT findings', *Journal of Neurology*, **233**, 274–82.

Oliver, M. (1990) *The Politics of Disablement*. Basingstoke: Macmillan.

Oliver, M. (1996) *Understanding Disability from Theory to Practice*. Basingstoke: Macmillan.

Orelove, F. and Sobsey, D. (1991) *Educating Children with Multiple Disabilities: A Transdisciplinary Approach*. Baltimore: Paul H. Brookes.

Oswin, M. (1978) *Children Living in Long–Stay Hospitals, Spastics International Medical Publications, Research Monograph 5*. London: Heinemann.

Ouvry, C. (1986) 'Integrating pupils with profound and multiple handicaps', *Mental Handicap*, **14**, (4), 157–60

Ouvry, C. (1991) 'Access for Pupils with Profound and Multiple Learning Difficulties', in Ashdown, R., Carpenter, B. and Borain, K. (eds) *The Curriculum Challenge*. London: David Fulton Publishers.

Ouvry, C. (1987) *Educating Pupils with Profound Handicaps*. Kidderminster: BIMH Publications.

Ouvry, C. and Saunders, S. (1996) 'Pupils with profound and multiple learning difficulties', in Carpenter, B., Ashdown, R. and Bovair, K. (eds) *Enabling Access: Effective Teaching and Learning for Pupils with Learning Difficulties*. London: David Fulton Publishers.

Palmer, J. (1997) 'Theatre for young people with PMLD – who benefits?', *PMLD Link* 27, 15–19.

Park, K (1995) 'Using objects of reference: A review of the literature', *European Journal of Special Needs Education*, **10**, (1), 40–46.

Partridge, C. J. (1996) 'Physiotherapy approaches to the treatment of neurological conditions – an historical perspective', in Edwards, S. *Neurological Physiotherapy, A Problem Solving Approach*. Edinburgh: Churchill Livingstone.

Peck, C. and Hong, C. S. (1988) *Living Skills for Mentally Handicapped People*. London: Croom Helm.

Perkins, N. (1987) 'Disability and Ethnic Minority Communities: a study in three London Boroughs', in *GLAD*. London: Greater London Association for Disabled People.

Perske, R. and Perske, M. (1988) *Circles of Friends: People with Disabilities and Their Friends Enrich the Lives of One Another*. Nashville: Abingdon Press.

Peter, M. (1997) 'The arts for all?' *PMLD Link 27*, 2–6.

Peters, A. (1997) Children's Rehabilitation Manager, The Children's Centre, Kings Mill Hospital, Mansfield Road, Sutton in Ashfield, Notts NG17 4JL Unpublished bid for funding.

Peters, T. (1994) *The Tom Peters Seminar: Crazy times call for crazy organizations*. London: Pan Books.

Piaget, J. (1952) *The Origins of Intelligence in Children*. New York: International Press.

Piaget, J. and Inhelder, B. (1956) *The Child's Conception of Space*. New York: Norton.

Polio, S. (1994) 'Being Sam's Mum', in Keith, L. (ed.) *Mustn't Grumble*. London: The Women's Press.

Pope, P. (1997) 'Management of the physical condition in people with chronic and severe neurological disabilities living in the community', *Physiotherapy*, March, **83**, (3).

Porter, J. (1986) 'Beyond the simple behavioural approach', in Coupe, J. and Porter, J. (eds) *The Education of Children with Severe Learning Difficulties.* London: Croom Helm.

Porter, J., Grove, N. and Park, K. (1996) 'Ages and stages. What is appropriate behaviour?' *Whose Choice? Contentious issues for those working with people with learning difficulties.* London: David Fulton Publishers..

Porter, J., Miller, O. and Pease, L. (1997) *Curriculum Access for Deafblind Children.* Research Report No 1. DfEE.

Poutney, T. E., Mulcahy, C. and Green, E. (1990) 'Early Development of Postural Control', *Physiotherapy* **76**, (12), 799–802.

Quinn, F. and Mathieson, A. (1993) 'Associated Conditions', in Shanley, E. and Starrs, T. (eds) *Learning Disabilities: A Handbook of Care.* 2nd edn. Edinburgh: Churchill Livingstone.

Rainforth, B. (1982) 'Biobehavioural state and orienting: implications for educating profoundly retarded students', *Journal of the Association for the Severely Handicapped* **6**, (4), 33–7.

Rainforth, B., York, J. and MacDonald, C. (1992) *Collaborative Teams for Students with Severe Disabilities.* Baltimore: Paul H. Brookes.

Ramcharan, P., McGrath, M. and Grant, G. (1997) 'Voices and choices: mapping entitlements to friendships and community contacts', in Ramcharan, P., Roberts, G., Grant, G. and Borland, J. (eds) *Empowerment in Everyday Life.* London: Jessica Kingsley.

Rapley, M. and Beyer, S. (1996) 'Daily activity, community participation and quality of life in an ordinary housing network', *Journal of Applied Research in Intellectual Disabilities* **9**, (1) 31–9.

Rasmussen, J. and Jensen, A. (1974) 'Mental procedures in real life tasks: A case study of electronic trouble shooting', *Ergonomics* **17**, 293–307.

Rasmussen, J. and Lind, M. (1982) *A Model of Human Decision Making in Complex Systems and its Use for the Design of System Control Strategies*, Denmark: Riso National Laboratory DK4000.

Rathnow, P. (1996) 'Phil's past and present', in Bessant, P., Rathnow, P., Joustra, R., Spooner, E., Dunkley, A., Sander, D., Jelley, A., Chappell, M. and Priestley, C. *Positive Tales.* Milton Keynes: Living Archives Press.

Reason, J. (1987) 'A framework for classifying errors', in Rasmussen, J., Duncan, K. and Leplat, J. (eds) *New Technology and Human Error.* Chichester: Wiley.

Reason, J. (1990) *Human Error.* Cambridge: Cambridge University Press.

Rebecca Goodman Centre (1987) *Communication Curriculum for Deaf–Blind Students.* Available from Whitefield School and Centre, McDonald Road, Walthamstow, London, E17

Reichle, J. and Sigafloos, J. (1991) 'Establishing an initial repertoire of requesting', in Reichle, J., York, J. and Sigafloos, J. (eds) *Implementing Augmentative and Alternative Communication.* Baltimore: Paul H. Brookes.

Remington, R. E. (1996) 'Assessing the occurrence of learning in children with profound intellectual disability: A conditioning approach', *International Journal of Disability, Development and Education*, **43** (2), 101–18.

Rikhye, C. Gothelf, C. and Appell, M. (1989) A classroom environmental checklist for students with dual sensory impairments'. *Teaching Exceptional Children*, **22**, (1), 44–6.

Ritchie, F. (1993) 'Opening doors: the effects of music therapy with people who have severe learning difficulties and display challenging behaviour', in Heal, M. and Wigram, T. (eds) *Music Therapy in Health and Education.* London: Jessica Kingsley.

RNIB (1992) *Curriculum Materials Used with Multihandicapped Visually Impaired Children and Young People.* Report from the Working Party (MHVI) London: RNIB.

Robbins, C. (1993) 'The creative processes are universal', in Heal, M. and Wigram, T. (eds) *Music Therapy in Health and Education.* London: Jessica Kingsley.

Roberts, P. (1991) 'Sickle Cell Anaemia: The Hidden Disability within the Black Community'. Unpublished.

Robson, A. (1997) 'Art activities for people with a visual and learning disability', *PMLD Link* **27**, 17–19.

Rochat, P. (1989) 'Object manipulation and exploration in 2–to–5–month old infants', *Developmental Psychology*, **25**, 871–84.

Rodgers, J. and Russell, O. (1995) 'Healthy Lives: The health needs of people with learning difficulties', in Philpot, T. and Ward, L. (eds) *Values and Visions: Changing ideas in services for people with learning difficulties*. Oxford: Butterworth-Heinemann.

Roffey, S., Tarrant, R. and Majors, K. (1994) *Young Friends*. London: Cassell.

Rogers, C. R. (1961) *On Becoming a Person*. London: Constable.

Roland, C. and Schweigert, P. (1993) 'Analysing the communication environment to increase functional communication', *Journal of Association of Persons with Severe Handicaps* **18**, (3) 161–76.

Rose, R. (1991) 'A jigsaw approach to group work', *British Journal of Special Education* **18**, (2), 54–7.

Rosen, S. (1997) 'Kinesiology and Sensorimotor Function', in Blasch, Wiener and Welsh (eds) *Foundations of Orientation and Mobility*. New York: American Foundation for the Blind.

Rovee–Collier, C. (1987) 'Learning and memory in infancy', in Osofsky, J. (ed.) *Handbook of Infant Development*. New York: Wiley.

Rowland, C. (1990) 'Communication in the Classroom for Children with dual sensory impairments: Studies of teacher and child behaviour'. *AAC* **6**, 262–74.

Rowland, G. (1996) 'Objects of reference: a communication option for people with a severe learning disability', *Journal of APLD* **13**, (4), 16–21.

Ryan, J. and Thomas, F. (1987) *The Politics of Mental Handicap*. London: Free Association Books.

Sander, D. (1996) 'My journey', in Bessant, P., Rathnow, P., Joustra, R., Spooner, E., Dunkley, A., Sander, D., Jelley, A., Chappell, M. and Priestley, C. *Positive Tales*. Milton Keynes: Living Archives Press.

Sanderson, H. (1995) 'Self-advocacy and inclusion: supporting people with profound and multiple disabilities', in Philpot, T. and Ward, L. (eds) *Values and Visions: Changing Ideas in Services for People with Learning Difficulties*. London: Butterworth-Heinemann.

Sanderson, H. (1996) 'Planning Ahead', *Community Care*. **29**, February–March, 6–7.

Sanderson, H., Kennedy, J., Ritchie, P. and Goodwin, G. (1997) *People, Plans and Possibilities – Exploring Person Centred Planning*. Edinburgh: Scottish Human Services Publications.

Saxena, M. (1993) Personal Interview.

SCAA (1995) *Planning the Curriculum at Key Stages 1 and 2*. London: SCAA.

SCAA (1996a) *Planning the Curriculum for Pupils with Profound and Multiple Learning Difficulties*. London: SCAA.

SCAA (1996b) *Assessment, Recording and Accreditation of Achievement for Pupils with Learning Difficulties*. London: SCAA.

SCAA and Department of National Heritage (1997) *The Arts in the Curriculum*. London: SCAA.

Schwartz, D. B. (1992) *Crossing the River: Creating a Conceptual Revolution in Community and Disability*. Cambridge, Mass: Brookline Books.

Schweigert, P. (1989) 'Use of microswitch technology to facilitate social contingency awareness as a basis for early communication skills', *Augmentative and Alternative Communication* **5**, 192–8.

Schweigert, P. and Rowland, C. (1992) 'Early Communication and Microtechnology: Instructional Sequence and case studies of children with severe multiple disabilities', *Augmentative and Alternative Communication* **6**, 262–274.

Scott, L. (1994) *On the Agenda: Sex education for young people with learning difficulties*. London: Image*in*Action, Jackson's Lane Community Centre, Archway Road, London N6 5AA

Scott, L. (1996) *Partnership with Parents in Sex Education. A guide for schools and those working in them*. London: National Children's Bureau.

Scrutton, D. (1984) *Management of the Motor Disorders of Children with Cerebral Palsy*. London: Spastics International Medical Publishers.

Sebba, J. (1988) *The Education of People with Profound and Multiple Handicaps – resource materials for staff training*. Manchester: Manchester University Press.

Sebba, J. and Sachdev, D. (1997) *What Works in Inclusive Education?* Ilford: Barnardos.

Sebba, J., Byers, R. and Rose, R. (1993) *Redefining the Whole Curriculum for Pupils with Learning Difficulties*. London: David Fulton Publishers.

Seed, P. (1988a) *Children with Profound Handicaps: Parents' Views and Integration.* London: Falmer Press.

Seed, P. (1988b) *Day Care at the Cross-roads: an Evaluation of the Local Authority Contribution to Day Care Services for Adults with a Mental Handicap in Scotland.* Tunbridge Wells: Costello.

Seligman, M. (1975) *Helplessness: On Depression, Development and Death.* San Francisco: Freeman.

Selvin, E. (1995) 'Student Nurses' Attitudes Towards People with Learning Disabilities', *British Journal of Nursing* **4**, (3), 761–6.

Selvin, E. and Sines, D. (1996) 'Attitudes of nurses in a general hospital towards people with learning disabilities: influences of contact, and graduate and non graduate status, a comparative study', *Journal of Advanced Nursing,* **24**, 1116–26.

Shah, R. (1986) *Attitudes Stereotypes and Service Porvision.* Manchester: Manchester Council for Community Relations.

Shah, R. (1992) *The Silent Minority: Children with Disabilities in Asian Families.* London: National Childrens Bureau.

Shah, R. (1995) *The Silent Minority – Children with Disabilities in the Asian Community.* London: National Children's Bureau.

Shah, R. (1997) *Disclosure of a Child's Impairment: Sharing the news with Asian Parents.* London: Mental Health Foundation.

Shah, R. (1998) *Sharing the News. A good practice guide and training pack for professionals working with Asian families when they are first told about their child's disability.* London: Mental Health Foundation.

Sham, S. (1996) 'Reaching Chinese children with learning disabilities in Greater Manchester', *British Journal of Learning Disabilities* **24**, 104–9.

Shanley, E. and Starrs, T. (eds) (1993) *Learning Disabilities: A handbook of care.* 2nd edn. Edinburgh: Churchill Livingstone.

Sharp, C. and Dust, K. (1997) *Artists in School.* Slough: NFER.

Shearer, A. (1973) *Listen.* London: Campaign for Mentally Handicapped People/Values into Action Publications.

Siegal Causey, E. and Downing, J. (1987) 'Non symbolic communication development. Theoretical concepts and educational strategies', in Goetz, L., Guess, D. and Stremell-Campbell, K. (eds) *Innovative Program Design for Individuals with Dual Sensory Impairment.* Baltimore: Paul H. Brookes.

Sinason, V. (1992) *Mental Handicap and the Human Condition: New Approaches from the Tavistock.* London: Free Association Books.

Skinner, B. F. (1948) 'Superstition' in the pigeon', *Journal of Experimental Psychology* **38**, 168–72.

Sloper, P. and Turner, S. (1993) 'Determinants of Parental Satisfaction with Disclosure of Disability', *Developmental Medicine and Child Neurology* **35**, 816–25.

Smale, G. and Tuson, G. (1993) *Empowerment, Assessment, Care Management and the Skilled Worker.* London: HMSO.

Smith, B. (1991) 'Introduction and background to interactive approaches', in Smith, B. (ed.) *Interactive Approaches to Teaching the Core Subjects.* Bristol: Lame Duck Publishing.

Smith, B. (1996) 'Discussion: Age–appropriate or Developmentally Appropriate Activities?' in Koupe O'Kane, J. and Goldbart, J. *Whose Choice? Contentious issues for those working with people with learning difficulties.* London: David Fulton Publishers.

Smith, C. J. and Laslett, R. (1993) *Effective Classroom Management – a Teacher's Guide.* London: Routledge.

Smith, J. with Copley, J., Evans, N. and O'Connell, M. (1997) 'Emotional Development and the Relevance of Intimate Relationships', EDSE 31 Unit 4 of *The Developmental Psychology of Childhood and Adolescence.* Birmingham: The University of Birmingham.

Smull, M. and Burke–Harrison, S. (1991) *Supporting People with Severe Reputations in the Community.* Virginia: National Association of State Directors of Developmental Disabilities Services.

Snow, C. E. (1984) 'Parent–Child interaction and the development of communicative abilities', in Schiefelbusch, R. L. and Pickar, J. P. (eds) *The Question of Communicative Competence.* Baltimore: University Park Press.

Sobsey, D. and Wolf–Schein, E. (1991) 'Sensory Impairments', in: Orelove, F. and Sobsey, D. (eds) *Educating Children with Multiple Disabilities. A Transdisciplinary Approach.* Baltimore: Paul H. Brookes.

Social Services Inspectorate (1994) *Opportunities or Knocks, National Inspection of Recreation and Leisure in Day Services for People with Learning Disabilities.* London: Social Services Inspectorate and Department of Health.

Souza, A. with Ramcharan, P. (1997) 'Everything you ever wanted to know about Down's syndrome, but never bothered to ask', in Ramcharan, P., Roberts, G., Grant, G. and Borland, J. *Empowerment in Everyday Life.* London: Jessica Kingsley.

Spastics Society (1992) *A Hard Act to Follow. A Report into parents' experience of the assessment and statementing process under the 1981 Education Act.* London: The Spastics Society.

Spastics Society of Tamil Nadu, India (1996) *Annual Report.*

Stevens, C. (1995) Foreword in: Byers, R. and Rose, R. (eds) *Planning the Curriculum for Pupils with Special Educational Needs.* London: David FultonSmith, B. (1996) 'Discussion: Age–appropriate or Developmentally Appropriate Activities?' in Koupe O'Kane, J. and Goldbart, J. *Whose Choice? Contentious issues for those working with people with learning difficulties.* London: David Fulton Publishers.

Stillman, R. and Battle, C. (1985) *Callier Azuza Scale (H). Scales for the assessment of communicative abilities. Programme in communication disorders.* Dallas, Texas: University of Texas at Dallas, Callier Centre for Communication Disorders.

Sturmey, P. (1993) 'The readability and human interest of information leaflets from major British charities: An intelligible boring replication?', *Mental Handicap Research*, **6**, 174–83.

Taylor, J. (1990) 'Using Switches with Children with Profound Learning Difficulties'. Unpublished paper.

Taylor, S. (1988) 'Caught in the Continuum: a critical analysis of the least restrictive environment', *Journal of the Association for Persons with Severe Handicaps* **13** (1), 41–53.

Tennant, H. (1 994) 'LINK– Home support for people with learning disabilities and their families', in Mittler, P. and Mittler, H. (eds) *Innovations in Family Support for People with Learning Disabilities.* Chorley, Lancashire: Lisieux Hall Publications.

*The Children Act*, 1989 London: HMSO.

Thoman, E. (1981) 'Affective communication as a prelude and context for language learning', in Schiefelbusch, R. and Bricker, D. (eds) *Early Language Acquisition and Intervention.* Baltimore: University Park Press.

Thomas, M. (1997) 'CBR in Developing Countries – The Shifts and Changes in the Last Decade', *Asia Pacific Disability Rehabilitation Journal* **8**, (1), 2.

Thomas, M. and Thomas, M. (1995) 'Evaluation based Planning for Rehabilitation Programmes in India', in O'Toole, B. and McConkey, R. (eds) *Innovations in Developing Countries for People with Disabilities.* Chorley, Lancashire: Lisieux Hall Publications.

Thornton, C. (1996) 'A focus group inquiry into the perceptions of primary health care teams and the provision of health care for adults with a learning disability living in the community', *Journal of Advanced Nursing*, **23**, 1168–1176.

Tilstone, C. (1991) 'Pupils views', in Tilstone C. (ed.) *Teaching Pupils with Severe Learning Difficulties.* London: David Fulton.

Tizard, J. (1960) 'Residential care of Mentally Handicapped Children', *British Medical Journal*, 1041–6.

Tizard, J. (1978) Foreword in Oswin, M. *Children Living in Long-Stay Hospitals. Spastics International Medical Publications, Research Monograph 5*, London: Heinemann.

Tjosvold, D. (1991) *Team Organisation: An Enduring Competitive Advantage.* Chichester: John Wiley.

Todd, T. and Shearn, J. (1995) *Struggles with Time: The careers of parents of adult sons and daughters with learning disabilities.* Cardiff: Welsh Centre for Learning Disabilities.

Tozer, R. (1996) *Brothers, Sisters and Learning Disability: A Guide for Parents.* Kidderminster: BILD.

Turnell, R. and Carter, M. (1994) 'Establishing a repertoire of requesting for a student with severe and multiple disabilities using tangible symbols and naturalistic delay', *Australia and New Zealand Journal of Developmental Disabilities*, **19**, (3), 193–207.

Turner, S. and Moss, S. (1996) 'The Health Needs of Adults with Learning Disabilities and the Health of the Nation Strategy', *Journal of Intellectual Disability Research*, October **40**, (5), 438–50.

Turrill, S. (1992) 'Supported positioning in intensive care', *Paediatric Nursing.* May, 24–7.

Tyne, J. (1994) 'Advocacy not just another subject', in Rose, R., Fergusson, A., Coles, C., Byers, R. and Banes, D. (eds) (1994) *Implementing the Whole Curriculum for Pupils with Learning Difficulties.* London: David Fulton Publishers.

Uditsky, B. (1993) 'From integration to inclusion: the Canadian experience', in Slee, R. (ed.) *Is There a Desk with My Name on It?* London: Falmer Press.

UNESCO (1993) *Special Needs in the Classroom – teacher education resource pack.* Paris: UNESCO.

University of Maine (1995)

University of Syracuse http://soeweb.syr.edu/thefci

Uzgiris, I. and Hunt, J. McV., (1975) *Assessment in Infancy: Ordinal Scales in Psychological Development.* Urbana: Univ. of Illinois Press.

Valdez, J. (1991) Personal Interview.

Vanier, J. (1991) *Community and Growth.* London: Darton, Longman and Todd.

Visser, T. (1988) 'Educational programming for deaf–blind children: Some important topics'. *Deafblind Education*, **2**, 4–7.

Wadsworth, D. (1996) *Piaget's Theroy of Cognitive and Affective Development: Foundations of Constructivism*, 5th edn. New York: Longman.

Walker, R. and Ahmad, W. I. U. (1994) 'Asian and black elders and community care: a survey of care providers', *New Community*, **20**, (4), 636–46.

Walsh, J. (1986) *Let's Make Friends.* London: Souvenir.

Walter, F. (1971) *Four Architectural Studies for the Wheelchair and Ambulant Disabled.* London: Disabled Living Foundation.

Ware, J. (1987) Providing Education for Children with Profound and Multiple Learning Difficulties: A Survey of Resources and an Analysis of Staff–Pupil Interactions in Special Care Units. Unpublished PhD Thesis. University of London Institiute of Education.

Ware, J. (ed.) (1994) *Educating Children with Profound and Multiple Learning Difficulties.* London: David Fulton Publishers.

Ware, J. (1996) *Creating a Responsive Environment for People with Profound and Multiple Learning Difficulties.* London: David Fulton Publishers.

Ware, J. and Healey, I. (1994) 'Conceptualising progress in children with profound and multiple learning difficulties', in: Ware, J. (ed.) *Educating Children with Profound and Multiple Learning Difficulties.* London: David Fulton Publishers.

Warren, D. (1982) 'The Development of Haptic Perception', in Schiff, W. and Foulke, E. (eds) *Tactual Perception.* Cambridge: Cambridge University Press.

Warren, D. (1994) *Blindness and Children: An Individual Differences Approach* Cambridge: Cambridge University Press.

Watkins, J. (1996) *Report from the Joint Services Planning Team, Services for People with Learning Difficulties.* (Internal Publication). London: Haringey Local Authority.

Webster, M. (1997) *Finding Voices, Making Choices: Creativity for Social Change.* Nottingham: Heretics Press.

Wedell, K. (1981) 'Concepts of special educational need', *Education Today*, **31**, 3–9.

Wehman, P. and Schleien, S. (1980) 'Assessment and selection of leisure skills for severely handicapped individuals', *Education and Training of the Mentally Retarded*, **15**, 50–57.

Werner, D. (1993) 'Preface: What should be the goal of Community Based Rehabilitation: to normalize or to liberate?', in Finkenflugel, H. (ed.) *The Handicapped Community.* Amsterdam: VU University Press.

Wertheimer, A. (1995) *Circles of Support: Building Inclusive Communities.* Bristol: Circles Network.

White, S. (1994) *'When the Bough Breaks': An independent survey into families' perceptions of the 100 Hours model of service.* West Yorkshire: 100 Hours.

Whittaker, A. (1996) *'The fight for self–advocacy'*, in Mittler, P. and Sinason, V. (eds) *Changing Policy and Practice for People with Learning Difficulties.* London: Cassells.

Whittaker, A., Gardner, S. and Kershaw, J. (1991) *Service Education by People with Learning Difficulties.* London: Kings Fund.

Whittington, D. (1993) 'The Social Networks of People with Learning Difficulties: Factors Influencing Networks, and a Method of Promoting Network Growth'. Unpublished thesis submitted for MSc, University of Birmingham.

Williams, P. and Shoultz, B. (1982) *We Can Speak For Ourselves.* London: Human Horizon Series.

Williams, S. (1997) 'Internet: a useful communication tool for parents?', *Eye Contact: RNIB Journal,* **18**, 27–8.

Wilson, D. and Haire, A. (1990) 'Health Care screening for people with mental handicap living in the community', *British Medical Journal,* 15 December, 301, 1379–81.

Wilson, D. and Newton, C. (1996) 'Circles of Friends', *Eye Contact* Autumn, 16–18.

Wistow, G. and Hardy, B. (1991) 'Joint management in community care', in *Journal of Management in Medicine* **5**, (4), 40–8.

Withers, P. (1991) 'Assessing the Response of Adults with Profound Learning Difficulties to Various Forms of Stimulations'. Unpublished BPS Diploma in Clinical Psychology. Bolton, Lancashire.

Wolfensberger, W. (1972) *Normalization: The principle of normalization in human services.* Toronto, Canada: National Institute of Mental Retardation.

Wood, J. (1996) 'The Needs of Jewish Service Users in PMLD Settings', *PMLD Link* 26, 4–6.

Woods, P. and Parry, R. (1981) 'Pethna: Tailor–made toys for the severely handicapped', Apex, **9**, 53–6.

World Health Organisation (1946) *Constitution.* New York: World Health Organisation.

World Health Organisation (1986) *The Ottawa Charter for Health Promotion.* Ottawa, Canada: WHO, Canadian Public Health Association, Health and Welfare.

World Health Organisation (WHO) (1992a) *The ICD–10 Classification of Mental and Behavioural Disorders: Clinical Descriptions and Diagnostic Guidelines.* Geneva: WHO.

World Health Organisation (WHO) (1992b) *Training the Disabled in the Community.* Geneva: WHO.

Worthington, A. (1993) *Glossary of Syndromes Associated with Learning Difficulty.* Cheshire: In Touch Trust.

Worthington, A. (1996) *Useful Addresses for Special Needs: 8th edn.* Cheshire: In Touch Trust.

Zarkowska, E. and Clements, J. (1988) *Problem Behaviour in People with Severe Learning Disabilities: A Practical Guide to a Constructional Approach.* London: Croom Helm.

# Index

Note: page numbers in *italics* refer to tables and figures.

This index was compiled by Frank Merrett who is a Registered Indexer of the Society of Indexers.

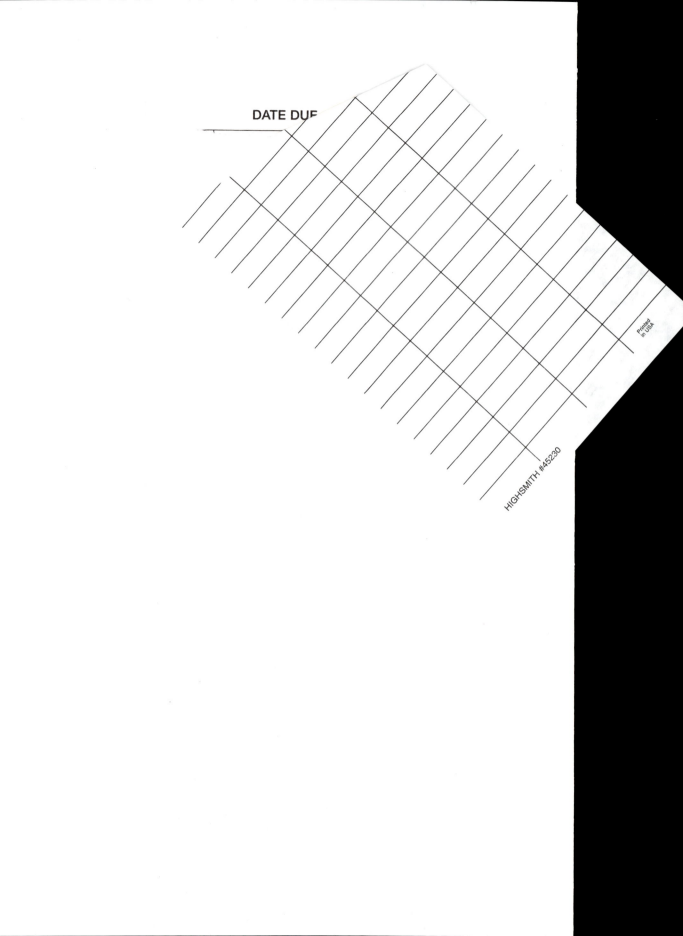

DATE DUE

HIGHSMITH #45230

Printed in USA